EDITED BY ROBERT BLAKE

The English World

HISTORY, CHARACTER AND PEOPLE

TEXTS BY

ROBERT BLAKE · FRANK BARLOW

GEORGE HOLMES · MICHAEL MACLAGAN

HUGH TREVOR-ROPER

HERBERT NICHOLAS · MAX BELOFF

EDWARD NORMAN

QUENTIN BELL · KENNETH MUIR

RICHARD MUIR · SYDNEY CHECKLAND

ASA BRIGGS

With 306 illustrations, 85 in colour,
221 photographs, drawings
and maps

THAMES AND HUDSON

Editor and publisher wish to acknowledge the generous advice given by all the authors on the selection of the illustrations and the wording of the captions; it must be made clear, however, that final responsibility for the picture sections remains entirely with the publisher.

Endpapers: *Rose* wallpaper (1877)
by William Morris
Half-title: a map of England and Wales from *The British Monarchy* (1743) by George Bickham

Designed and produced by Thames and Hudson

Managing Editor: Ian Sutton
Design: Ian Mackenzie-Kerr
Editorial: Mary Worth
Picture Research: Alla Weaver and
Susan Johnson

Filmset in Great Britain by Keyspools Ltd, Golborne, Lancs.
Monochrome origination in Great Britain by DSCI, London
Colour origination in Switzerland by Cliché Lux, Neuchâtel
Text and illustrations printed in the Netherlands by Smeets B.V., Weert
Bound in the Netherlands by Van Rijmenam

Contents

Introduction

◇

The Englishness of England

*

ENGLAND'S coastline has helped to shape both the history of the English nation and the psychology of the English character. The knowledge – unconsciously assimilated since childhood – that there was a wide stretch of water between Englishmen and 'foreigners' encouraged a sense of security that could easily slide into one of superiority. And it was true that her physical isolation made England different. The long centuries during which the land was free from invaders meant that there could be a continuity of tradition impossible on the war-torn Continent. Englishmen have always been conscious of the history that surrounds them, and, from traditional royal and parliamentary ceremonies to Tudor-style villas in the suburbs, have sought at every level to revive and remind themselves of that history.

Some English characteristics upon which both natives and visitors have tended to agree have to do with national psychology: egoism, self-confidence, intolerance of outsiders, ostentatious wealth, independence, social mobility, love of comfort and a strong belief in private property. Others, equally marked, have to do with the physical appearance of English town and country, and are more easily illustrated than described: an urge to wander over the earth and bring back its products to make England a microcosm of the world; a preoccupation with 'home' that has led to the evolution of both the English house – informal, relaxed and domestic – and its landscape setting; a love of games in which (until the rise of spectator sports) competition was less important than enjoyment; and that special feeling for the sea that made Englishmen not only great sailors and explorers but also the inventors of the seaside holiday.

We come back to the cliché that Britain is an island, a fact that has been subtly decisive in so many aspects of her history: in the Reformation, which determined the course of religion in England; in the pattern of trade, which led to the formation of the Empire; in the growth of a navy at the expense of an army, with its repercussions on the political system; . . . even in the well-known 'insularity' of English art and English music. The cultural moat, as we shall see in the final section of the book, has often been wider than the twenty-one miles of water that separate Dover from Calais.

Freshwater Bay at the western end of the Isle of Wight. Beyond the headland in the distance are the Needles, a line of sharp rocks long feared by seamen; in the foreground are the Stag and Arch rocks. The beauty of the English coastline was a Romantic discovery: up to the 18th century people looked on the sea as a natural obstacle threatening danger and discomfort. The Romantic poets saw sublimity in its stillness, its hidden depths, its sudden storms – symbols of the passions of the human soul. With the later 19th century came a more mundane appreciation. Bathing was found to be first healthy and then enjoyable. The seaside holiday became a part of ordinary expectations and the unspoiled coastline a part of the national heritage.(1)

'A moat defensive to a house'

Many of England's most decisive battles have been sea-battles, not necessarily near England's coasts. But the Channel was always the ultimate protection.

The Armada of 1588 – seen here in a detail from a contemporary painting – would have conveyed the Spanish army from the Netherlands to the English coast, but was broken by Elizabeth's ships and by the weather. (2)

England's naval strength reached a peak in the years before the First World War, with the production of capital ships stimulated by rivalry with Germany. *The Channel Squadron*, painted about 1912, combines realism with a certain patriotic aggressiveness. (3)

The epic victory of Trafalgar in 1805 became part of the national mythology almost as soon as it was won. The country in danger . . . a fight against odds . . . outstanding courage . . . brilliant seamanship . . . the death of the hero at the moment of triumph: the story had everything to appeal to the imagination. Turner's painting (*left*) of 1806–8 makes Nelson's death the centre of a titanic struggle. (4)

Dunkirk was no victory, but is remembered almost as if it were (*right*). In 1940 the beleaguered British army was rescued from the beaches by the Royal Navy and by hundreds of small private craft from the ports of Kent and Sussex. (5)

The English and the sea

For English poets and painters the sea has always been rich in present associations and in echoes of the past, from national glory to the opportunities of trade, from Elizabethan exploration to childhood holidays.

Play: a popular Victorian genre scene of 1864, *Weston Sands*, shows the seaside already being used in a modern way. Donkey rides are still part of the scene, but goat-carts disappeared about 1914. The 1930s were probably the boom years for English holiday resorts, when even discomforts were made into virtues. In this advertisement for Skegness, Lincolnshire, 'bracing' is a euphemism for 'cold'. (6, 7)

Work: *The Pool of London*, painted in 1888 by G. V. Cole, before the building of Tower Bridge. The heavier ships unloaded at new specially built docks, but lighter goods such as hay still used the river. (9)

'The Boyhood of Raleigh': Millais's vivid painting reveals more about Victorian attitudes than Elizabethan. What to the 19th-century traveller was a longing for the unknown and the exotic had for Raleigh and his contemporaries been primarily the lure of boundless wealth. (8)

The English diaspora

An itch to travel seems to have affected the English at least from Tudor times onwards. Sometimes this urge was justified as exploration or research; sometimes it was motivated by competition; sometimes it was the result of simple curiosity, love of adventure and desire for exotic experience.

The Grand Tour was part of every 18th-century gentleman's education – to learn languages, to see classical sites and to acquire polish. Charles Cecil Roberts (*above*) was painted in Rome by Pompeo Batoni with the Castel S. Angelo and St Peter's in the background, sculptured fragments at his feet and a plan of the city in his hand. Sir Joseph Banks (*left*) made a grand tour of the whole globe. He travelled with Cook to the South Seas at his own expense (1768–71), bringing back a large collection of native artefacts, natural objects and information. In this painting by Benjamin West he is dressed in a Tahitian cloak and surrounded by the fruits of his journey. (10, 11)

Package tours began in the late 19th century, specifically for wealthy English people who wanted both excitement and comfort. Here (*right*) one of Messrs Cook's early parties returns from Karnak, in Egypt, *c.* 1900. (12)

Lady Hester Stanhope, granddaughter of the elder Pitt, stands in the line of true English eccentrics. The daughter of an earl, she left England in 1810, settled in Lebanon and adopted a semi-Islamic way of life. The sketch is by David Wilkie. (13)

Scott of the Antarctic (*right*) is in some ways the archetypal English hero. A brave man but a poor organizer, he led an expedition to the South Pole in 1912, failed by a few days to beat the Norwegian Amundsen, and perished on the return journey. (14)

Sir Francis Chichester (*above*) sailed round the world single-handed – still a great adventure even in a world where there is almost nothing left to explore. (16)

Marianne North (*left*) made it her life's work to paint the plants and trees of every continent. As fearless as she was indefatigable, she accumulated thousands of pictures now exhibited at Kew Gardens, London. (15)

The man-made countryside

English fondness for gardens was noted by early travellers, but what had began as a self-consciously artificial creation became a free version of nature itself.

Complexity and wit characterized Renaissance gardens, mathematically contrived environments as different as possible from the untamed countryside. This imaginary scene, with its symmetrical pools, fountains and statuary, is from a tapestry of about 1720. (17)

Freedom and nature returned in the 18th century with the landscape gardeners Humphry Repton and 'Capability' Brown. The intention was to give the effect of untouched scenery. In reality, the elements were carefully balanced to create the right impression. As the 'English garden' the resulting style spread throughout Europe. Often, as here at Croome Court, Worcestershire, a formal Palladian house remained from an earlier period, distinct from, yet harmonizing with, the landscape. (19)

The cottage garden continued meanwhile, unaffected by fashion. *Left*: Stanley Spencer's *Cottages at Burghclere* – the topiary bird a solitary piece of display. (18)

Artifice revived: the gardens designed by Edwin Lutyens and Gertrude Jekyll took the simplicity of the cottage garden and gave it something of the artistry of the Renaissance. This is one of the earliest, Deanery Garden, at Sonning. (20)

The Englishman's home

Up to the 17th century, the houses in which ordinary Englishmen lived were broadly similar to those of the rest of Europe. But after that the paths diverge. On the Continent towns were densely built up and most people lived in apartments in large blocks. In England the idea of the single-family house with its own small garden persisted; towns spread outwards, creating that uniquely English phenomenon, the suburb. And here one finds at least three eminently English traits: love of comfort, conservatism in taste, nostalgia for the past.

Stone and timber brought traditional late medieval houses into harmony with their settings (*above*: Ebrington, Gloucestershire, and Colchester, Essex). In the later 17th century, brick came into wider use, and houses began to acquire the domestic comforts that we expect today. The 18th century evolved the terrace, a row of such houses joined together. The Royal Crescent, Bath (*opposite*), is the grandest example of all. By the next century the terrace was universal and had reached the humblest level; and, in the 20th, sweeping gables and half-timbering allowed the city-dweller to return in imagination to the Tudor cottage where his ancestors had been born. (21, 22, 25)

Four styles of living exemplified in four typical London districts (*below*): a mid 19th-century terrace for fairly humble families; more pretentious stucco terraces of the late 19th century; the 'aesthetic' suburb of Bedford Park, a deliberate break with the terrace tradition; and Neo-Tudor houses in a housing estate of the 1930s. (23, 24, 26, 27)

'Fair play all round'

The organized sports that today dominate the leisure thinking of a large part of mankind began in England. How they evolved is a strange but fascinating by-way of national history.

Cricket on the playing-fields of Eton (*above*): organized games, thought to promote team-spirit and to train character, became a feature of the public schools in the mid-19th century. From there they spread to larger and larger groups, until spectators outnumbered players. (28)

The racecourse was the venue for more activities than sport. Aaron Green's *The Derby* (*above*) manages to pack a whole cross-section of English life into the canvas. (30).

The hunt has its origins back in the Middle Ages, when it was an aristocratic privilege confined to a small élite. In the 19th century it still carried overtones of social prestige, as is proved by the number of hunting scenes in country houses. This painting (*left*), *The Meet*, is by Henry and Charles Shayer. (29)

Sport today has grown to national – indeed international – proportions, arousing passionate loyalties and even posing problems of public order. *Right:* Liverpool football fans, 1981. (31)

Dreams of the past

A fantasy Middle Ages haunted the imagination of the 19th century. Fed by literature, art and architecture, it was more than an escape – it was an ideal, moulding the chivalric code of the Victorian gentleman and finding its apotheosis on the battlefields of the First World War.

The romance of Arthur, given its final form by Sir Thomas Malory in the 15th century, enjoyed a potent revival in the 19th. Morris and Tennyson in poetry, Rossetti and Burne-Jones (*above*) in painting tried to re-tell the legends in ways that had relevance to contemporary life, but inevitably they ended by surrendering to the dream-like quality of the narrative. Here Sir Launcelot in a vision is shown the Chapel of the Holy Grail but is told that he will never achieve his quest because of his adultery with Queen Guinevere. (32)

The Gothic Revival began in England and was taken more seriously than in any other country. As far back as the early 18th century Sir John Vanbrugh had built himself a mock castle (*above left*) on the outskirts of London. By the 1840s Gothic was accepted as suitable for the rebuilt Houses of Parliament. Designed by Charles Barry and A. W. N. Pugin, it became the prototype for parliament buildings all over the world. (33, 34)

Nourished by Scott's novels,
historical make-believe had a vogue
among the wealthier classes. Sir
Francis Sykes had himself painted with
his wife, Disraeli's mistress, and
children as a medieval knight on his
way to a tournament. (35)

The investiture of the prince of Wales
was revived in 1969 for Prince Charles
in its original setting of Caernarvon
Castle. *Right*: the image of 'Merrie
England' in a painting of the 1870s
(*top*) and in a Yorkshire village today.
(36, 37, 38)

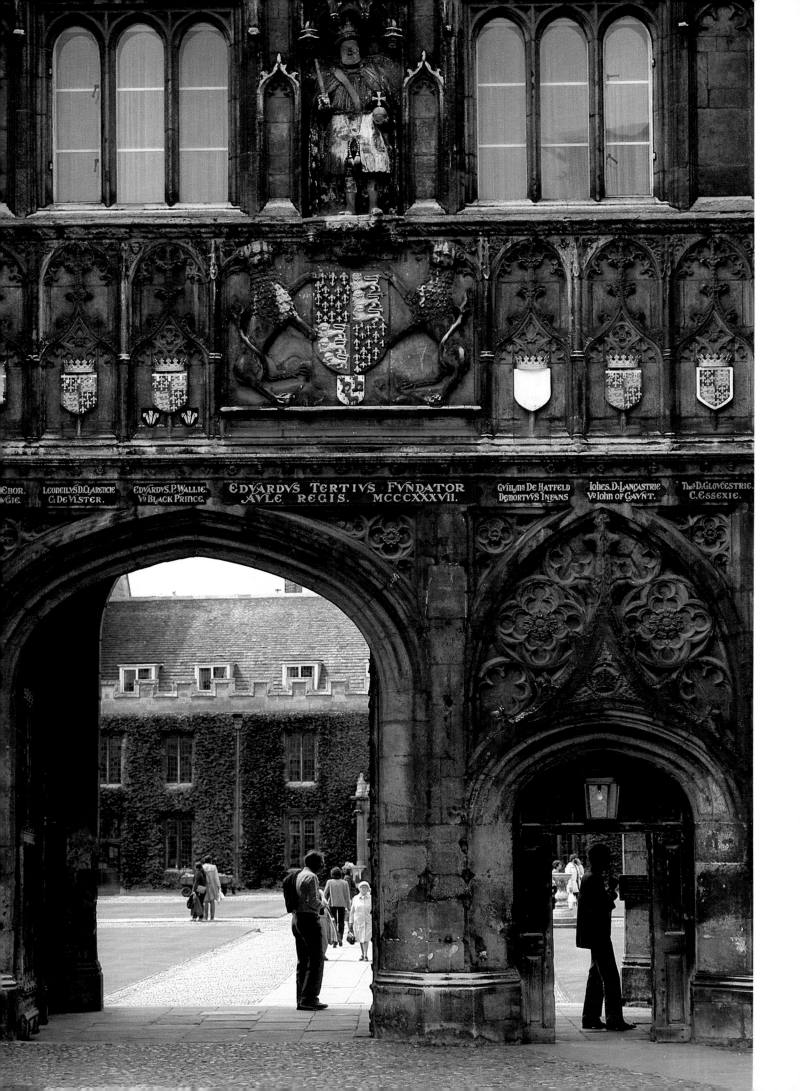

EBOR. | Leoneilvs D. Clarencie. | Edvardvs P. Wallie. | EDVARDVS TERTIVS FVNDATOR | Gviilms De Hatfeld | Iohes. D. Lancastrie | Thos D. Glovcestrie.
VGIE. | C. De Vlster. | Vo Black Prince. | AVLE REGIS. MCCCXXXVII. | Demortvvs Infans | Vo Iohn of Gavnt. | C. Essexie.

Introduction
The Englishness of England
ROBERT BLAKE

'ENGLAND IS A CURIOUS COUNTRY and few foreigners can understand her mind.' These words of Winston Churchill to the pre-war German ambassador, Ribbentrop, were uttered more as a threat than as a statement. They are, however, profoundly true. England is no doubt in one sense a part of Europe, but the differences between the English cultural, political and social heritage and that of any other European country are far greater than the differences within mainland Europe itself, substantial though these are. It was long ago recognized by travellers from abroad that there was something peculiar about England, something which, to a Frenchman for example, required explanation in a way that was not needed when he crossed the frontier to Germany, Italy or Spain. Precisely what needed to be explained was a matter for dispute, and the nature of the explanation was even more controversial. But the consciousness of differences has been there through most of recorded history, and it has been an awareness which has worked both ways. Foreigners who came to England and Englishmen who travelled in Europe noticed the contrast with their native lands.

The two features of English life which from the 15th century onwards struck almost every observer were the country's wealth and its strong sense of individualism. It was fashionable at one time to correlate both with the success of the Reformation and the growth of Protestantism. In fact, there is no such simple connection. England was not the only country of Europe where the Protestant cause won the day, and these aspects of English life were the subject of observation many years before Luther nailed his ninety-five theses to the church door in Wittenburg. Andrea Trevisano, Venetian ambassador to the court of Henry VII, wrote in 1497: 'The riches of England are greater than those of any country in Europe . . . there is no small innkeeper, however poor and humble he may be, who does not serve his table with silver dishes and drinking cups'. No one, he went on, counted as a person of consequence unless he had 'in his house silver plate to the amount of at least £100 sterling, which is equivalent to 500 golden crowns with us'. This wealth was also manifested in English apparel. The English 'from time immemorial wear very fine clothes'. They were also luxurious in their eating habits even in a military campaign: 'When the war is raging most furiously, they will seek for good eating, and all their other comforts, without thinking of what harm might befall them.' Anyone who visited the HQ Mess of a Guards battalion in the Western Desert in 1942 knows what Trevisano meant.

The Venetian also noticed the egotism, self-confidence, pride and boastfulness of the English, and their contempt for foreigners – a contempt which was quite compatible with deep suspiciousness towards their compatriots: 'They do not trust each other to discuss either public or private affairs together, in the confidential manner we do in Italy.' This was part of a pushful individualism; Trevisano also shrewdly observed that in England there was none of the sense of family as an economic unit which was found on the Continent. He deplored as heartless the English custom of boarding out children at the age of seven to nine to be apprentices for the next eight years, or even servants, in other houses and families. He refused to believe the customary explanation that parents did this to ensure that their children learned better manners. On the contrary, he believed that they did so because they themselves would be better served by strangers and would not be obliged to provide as good food as they might feel obliged to give their own children. He noted also that they did not take their children back when their apprenticeship was over, but expected them to make their own way in the world, assisted by their patrons, not their parents.

The system prefigures the English boarding-school tradition. Foreigners have always found it incomprehensible that little boys at the teddy-bear age should be sent away from home for three-quarters of the year, and that little girls, anyway until recent times and in houses which could afford it, scarcely saw their parents but were confined to the ministrations of nurses and nannies. Both traditions made for anxiety, insecurity

The ancient colleges of Oxford and Cambridge are something without parallel in continental universities, and have given their own stamp to English higher education. The Great Gate, Trinity College, Cambridge, overtly recalls its own history. Founded (as the inscription says) as 'King's Hall' by Edward III in 1337, it was refounded under its present name by Henry VIII, whose statue appears above the arch. Through the opening we see Great Court, the largest of any college, surrounded by medieval and later buildings.(39)

and determination of younger sons to acquire a fortune. It also made for what it is fashionable to call 'social mobility' – movements both up and down the class ladder – which, until quite recently, occurred much more frequently in England than in most of Europe.

Trevisano's account is one of the earliest quoted by Alan Macfarlane in his remarkable book, *The Origins of English Individualism* (1978). If Macfarlane's general theme is correct – and it is a departure from received wisdom – England became very different from the rest of Europe much earlier than is usually accepted. There are many later accounts by foreigners who observed and were puzzled by the contrast with European society. A famous case is that of Alexis de Tocqueville, whose great book, *L'Ancien Régime et la révolution*, published in 1850, is not only a history of the origins of the French Revolution but also an analysis of the differences between English and French society. He noted that English agriculture was 'the richest and most perfect in the world'. And he asked: 'Is there any single country in Europe, in which national wealth is greater, private property more extensive, more secure, more varied in character?' He believed that the difference was that whereas the feudal system in Europe produced a 'caste', in England alone 'it returned to aristocracy'. It was, he thought, strange that the peculiarities of the English system had not attracted more attention either from foreigners or the English themselves:

It was far less its Parliament, its liberty ... its jury, which rendered the England of that date so unlike the rest of Europe, than a feature still more peculiar and more powerful. England was the only country in which the system of caste had not merely been changed but destroyed. The nobles and the middle classes (*bourgeoisie*) in England went into business together, entered the same professions, and – what is much more significant – inter-married.

Tom Brown defends a younger boy from being derided by a bully for saying his prayers. The novel 'Tom Brown's Schooldays' embodied the Victorian code of gentlemanly conduct as taught at the newly reformed public schools.

There was, if Dr Macfarlane is correct, another important difference which may have been a cause or consequence of the English spirit of individualism. He argues that there is no evidence of the existence in England of a class of 'peasants', like those in Russia, Poland, France and China – that is to say, cultivators of a plot of land attached by law or custom to a family rather than an individual, people who live in a closed village community on subsistence agriculture. If a peasantry did exist it disappeared at some date before we have reliable records. The earliest records that we do possess suggest a very different form of rural society, in which villagers bought, sold and inherited land as individuals. Macfarlane's hypothesis – and it cannot yet be more than that – is 'that the majority of ordinary people in England from at least the thirteenth century were rampant individualists, highly mobile both geographically and socially, economically "rational", market-oriented and acquisitive, ego-centred in kinship and social life'.

It is true that the English upper classes all through history had a less market-oriented approach to land than the small proprietors. Of course they possessed far more of it and they were public figures. The idea of the blood and the land going together and its consequence, primogeniture, were deeply engrained – to the chagrin of those younger sons whose portion was often minimal and whose Grace before meals has often been quoted: 'For what *we* ought to have received may the Lord make *them* truly thankful.' But primogeniture was not compulsory, only customary. A high degree of individualism prevailed in those circles too, and there was, as De Tocqueville said, never a caste. The lavish multiplication of hereditary titles on the Continent did not occur in England. The grandson of a duke can be plain 'Mr'. Younger sons either faded into obscurity or, stimulated perhaps at the thought of being only a heart-beat or two away from wealth and grandeur, carved out careers for themselves in commerce and finance or, uninhibited by quarterings, married the daughters of rich merchants.

In his chapter on 'The Medieval Centuries', George Holmes points out another feature of the fluidity of English society. Although Parliament was, it is true, divided into two houses, the nobility, abbots and bishops receiving their separate summons to the Lords, in the Commons the burgesses, chosen by the towns, and the knights of the shire, chosen by the counties, sat cheek by jowl with no social differentiation. Unlike the principal continental countries, England from an early stage avoided the rigid stratification between the merchants of the cities and the rural seigneur. Squires and burgesses thought of themselves as part of the same political 'interest'.

England has been richer than most countries since the 13th century for many reasons – the wool trade, cloth-working, merchant adventure, exploration and the Industrial Revolution. It may well be that the mild climate and fertile soil were particularly conducive to

The English gentleman was already defined by 1630: well born, well educated, accomplished, courteous – 'hope in heaven, feet on the ground'. The elements of the knightly ideal look back to Henry VIII's revival of chivalry; those of social responsibility (he holds a rod signifying the office of Justice of the Peace) look forward to the Victorian age.

the success of farming in terms of sheep, cattle and crops. Certainly English agriculture has led the world for many centuries and, arguably, leads it still. England has also been more libertarian, egalitarian and socially mobile than the rest of Europe. Nor can one seriously doubt that the immense technological and economic explosion of the mid-18th century – that peculiarly English achievement – has some connection with the earlier, perhaps much earlier, structure of a society which happened to be particularly conducive to such a development.

One of the most significant aspects of this trend towards a highly competitive and socially (though not economically) egalitarian society was the impetus it gave to the English colonies of the 17th century in America. The people who went out to that apparently remote and perilous continent were not the grandees of the upper class. They were individualistically minded members of the 'anti-establishment' – Puritan merchants, shopkeepers and small landowners. America's heritage of libertarianism, hostility to government, scepticism about the role of the state and hatred of interference, stems from this highly characteristic stratum of English society. De Tocqueville was convinced that by the 17th century England and America had an entirely different social system from that of continental Europe. The English situation 'passes finally to America', and that country's 'history is that of democracy itself'. The English spirit of mobility and liberty became sharpened and heightened by its

27

passage across the Atlantic. After breaking the link with England herself and opening up a continent, that spirit was to reflect back upon the whole of Europe and to become one of the most potent factors of change in the 20th century. If the differences between the English world and Western Europe are not what they were in De Tocqueville's day, it is because the Anglo-American attitude has largely triumphed. If that outlook is still heretical in the vast and gloomy domains governed from Moscow, it is because of the brute force of a privileged army and a secret police, not the attraction of a totalitarian ideology which is intellectually on the wane and is heading for economic catastrophe.

There have been other significant features in the development of England which mark it as a country to some degree separate from the Europe whence its people and culture largely originated. One of the most important is the language. It is of Germanic origin but, as Professor Muir observes in his chapter, 'Language and Literature', half the words come from other sources, and the result is an astonishingly wide vocabulary acquired quite early in its history. Whereas Racine had to choose from a vocabulary of only 3,000 words, Shakespeare used over 29,000 words, many invented by himself. The result is a language of unparalleled richness, subtlety and variety, which unlocks the treasures of a literature second to none in the world. English has another distinguishing feature. Although Anglo-Saxon was an inflected language, the English which derived from it gradually shed most of the inflections. This makes it, despite oddities of spelling and pronunciation, basically an easier language to learn than almost any other. If there is ever to be an international language it will not be Esperanto, Ido, Antido or even Nov-Esperanto. Nor will it be Russian or Chinese despite the numbers involved. Thanks to Britain's imperial expansion English is the language of North America, Australia and New Zealand. It is the second language of India and large areas of Africa. In the vast majority of non-English-speaking countries it is the first foreign language taught to those who learn other languages at all. It is by far the strongest candidate for a universal method of communication.

Another highly distinctive feature of English history is the impact of the Reformation. This affected England more decisively than any other country in Europe. There is much historical dispute about the motives and character of Henry VIII and the exact nature of the changes that he wrought, but one can hardly deny that they were immense. The Act of Supremacy breaking the age-long link with Rome and substituting the king's authority for the pope's was a fairly revolutionary step, although it can be argued that it was the culmination of an anti-papal tradition of long standing. Far more revolutionary was the dissolution of the monasteries. Everywhere in Western Europe the monastic orders had constituted for eight centuries past a major feature of the social and spiritual structure of society. The life of contemplation, prayers for the souls of the dead, the ascetic rule, the giving of alms at the monastery gate – all these were characteristic of the Catholic world, and were respected in principle throughout Europe. Practice was another matter and no doubt it was true, not only in England, that the system had become in many respects corrupt, scandalous and hypocritical. It could, however, have been reformed and in many countries it was. But in England alone, whatever the original intention, events led to total abolition. The monastic world vanished as if it had never been, leaving behind only imposing ruins, those magnificent shells such as Fountains and Tintern which, like the Greek temples at Agrigento or Selinunte, still astonish the sightseer.

The revolution was traumatic. There has not been a comparable transfer of land in English history since the Norman Conquest. Only in modern times in Eastern Europe has there been any parallel – the expropriations in Russia after 1918 and in its communist-conquered satellites after 1945. However, the revolution begun by Henry VIII was not only economic but also religious, social and ideological. It resulted in a profound defensive mistrust not only of Rome but of Catholic practice and doctrine which has coloured English life ever since and is only now beginning to fade, although it is still strong in many places, among them atavistic Ulster. As late as 1850 the pope's decision to create Catholic dioceses in England could produce a major political uproar both in Parliament and in the country. The Henrician Revolution separated England from Europe spiritually even as the sea always has geographically. It was responsible, although not in Henry's day, for the Church of England – that remarkable amalgam of religion and étatisme, compromise and conviction, reform and tradition – essentially the product of Queen Elizabeth I, herself one of the most remarkable of all English monarchs. By a strange turn of events this most parochially English invention, this Anglican communion of the *via media*, whose Prayer Book was a schedule annexed to an English Act of Parliament and which seemed one of the least likely of churches to make converts, became an international denomination. The reason was the rise of the Second British Empire. The church, like trade, followed the flag, but the decline, indeed disappearance, of empire has not resulted in a parallel decline of the Anglican communion which continues to hold its own perhaps better in the English-speaking world outside England than it does in the country of its birth. Moreover, it gave to that world one of the greatest literary, as well as religious, publications of all time – the Authorized Version of the Bible.

England's geographical separation from Europe has been, until recent advances in communications abolished the Channel, as important as her cultural separation. One of its most significant by-products is the relatively small amount of fighting which has occurred on English soil. Certainly there have been invasions: successive incursions by Romans, Saxons,

Now a peaceful and picturesque scene, the crumbling remains of Furness Abbey in Lancashire, like those of the hundreds of other

ruined monasteries of the English countryside, still bear silent witness to the catastrophic impact of the Reformation.

Norwegians, Danes and Normans have created the English world. But thereafter the sea has proved an effective barrier. Of course there have been wars of conquest – waged on the Welsh and the Irish successfully and the Scots unsuccessfully. But England has never endured anything comparable to the strife which, largely because of English royal ambitions, raged off and on in France for a hundred years. Nor in England has there been anything remotely comparable to the Thirty Years War. It is true that there have been internal struggles – the Wars of the Roses and the Civil War. But when the latter broke out in 1641 there had been no war in England for nearly a hundred and sixty years – a period during which Europe had been convulsed by almost continual fighting.

Macfarlane quotes John Aylmer, later bishop of London, who from exile wrote a pamphlet in 1559 urging his fellow-citizens to defend themselves against foreign invaders:

Oh England, England, thou knowest not thine own wealth because thou seest not other countries' penury. Oh if thou sawest the peasants of France, how they are scraped to the bones and what extremities they suffer: thou wouldest think thy self blessed. . . . The husbandman in France, all that he hath gotten in his whole life loseth it upon one day. For when

so ever they have war (as they are never without it) the kings' soldiers enter into the poor man's house, eateth and drinketh up all that ever he hath.

He went on to comment on the heavy taxation in France – another respect in which the English were fortunate (until modern times). The Italians only wore sacking, 'and in Germany though they be in some better case than the other: yet eat they more roots than flesh'. But England was in a very different state:

Now compare them with thee and thou shalt see how happy thou art. They eat herbs: and thou Beef and Mutton. They roots: and thou butter, cheese, and eggs. They drink commonly water; and thou good ale and beer. They go from market with a salad: and thou with good flesh fill thy wallet. They likely never see any sea fish: and thou hast thy belly full of it. They pay till their bones rattle in their skin: and thou layest up for thy son and heir.

Somewhat in the spirit of the famous song by Flanders and Swann ('The English, the English, the English are best./I wouldn't give twopence for all of the rest'), the author ended:

Oh if thou knewest thou Englishman in what wealth thou livest, and in how plentiful a country: Thou wouldest vii times a day fall flat on thy face before God and give him

29

thanks that thou wert born an Englishman, and not a French peasant, nor an Italian, nor German.

Macfarlane observes that although the contrast may have been heightened for effect, the author was a man of intelligence who had been tutor to Lady Jane Grey. He was unlikely to have been writing complete nonsense.

This separation from continental Europe gave a special position to the navy which protected England from battles on her soil. It produced a sense of security and led to a prosperity which the major rival countries did not enjoy. In general, until the present century the army was neglected and distrusted. True, the soldiers of New Model Army were held in respect but the rule of the 'major-generals' at the end of the Protectorate was highly unpopular and became a part of folk memory. For more than two centuries afterwards the army had a low place in public esteem. Its officers who were of the upper class, since they had to have private incomes to supplement their pay, commanded a certain social prestige, but it was not until the First World War that the rank and file approached the status of Oliver Cromwell's troopers. 'He has gone for a soldier' was a condemnation, and the duke of Wellington's remark about 'the scum of the earth enlisted for drink' corresponded all too closely to reality. In continental Europe the situation was quite different. There the ever-disputed frontier lines drawn on the map, but invisible on the ground, gave armies a position of far greater importance. There was no moat to which the European rulers could look.

England's moat gave a protection possessed by none of the countries with land frontiers. The Norman Conquest was the last successful invasion which did not depend upon a well-disposed fifth column within the country. England has not always been a great power, although she was under the three Edwards and became so again in the 18th century. For much of her history she has belonged to the second rank, as she does today and did from the death of Henry V through the Wars of the Roses and the rule of the Tudors and Stuarts. But England has always been a very difficult country to conquer. The knowledge of this imprinted on the national consciousness a strong sense of security. Combined with that spirit of libertarian individualism which, whatever its origins, has long been an undoubted feature of English society, it made possible the creation and survival of a system of 'limited government'. Other countries besides England had parliaments in the Middle Ages, but everywhere else in Europe the rise of the nation state and the fluidity of land frontiers produced an uneasiness which led to absolutism and the suppression of parliamentary institutions. People prefer liberty to despotism but not if they believe that national survival requires an authoritarian regime. Only in England did Parliament survive; and limited government is one of the great legacies of the English world.

Shorn of its monarchical element, it was transmitted into the American Constitution. When in the latter part of the 19th century some European countries cast off their absolutist regimes it was to the English parliamentary tradition that they looked, not to the atrophied and long-forgotten institutions of their own past.

Security at home, naval power, libertarianism and a quasi-industrial society established very early (partly through the widespread cloth-working trade) may explain two notable developments which will always be associated with the English. One of these was empire. It has now vanished in the sense that British sovereignty over great areas of Asia, Africa and America, and the whole of Australasia no longer prevails, but this does not alter the immense historical effect of the First and Second British Empires upon a world which was to be permanently altered by their impact. The other development was the Industrial Revolution. The literature purporting to account for that astonishing and unique experience is vast and controversial. No agreed solution has ever been achieved. But it is hard to believe that the orthodox economic and technological explanations account for its occurring in England rather than anywhere else in Europe. Historians are coming round to the conclusion that there was something about English social and property relationships – something dating back a long way, although how far is a matter of argument – which made the industrial 'take-off' more likely to happen in England than elsewhere. There are those who do not go back beyond the 17th century to discover this divergence from continental Europe; some find it in the 16th century or in the years following the Black Death. Yet others believe that the differentiation already existed at latest by the end of the 13th century. There are fascinating problems involved in the historiography of the Industrial Revolution, but this is not the place to resolve them. One can, however, safely assert that it was one of the major contributions of the English world and its impact had greater consequences for the rest of the world than any other English achievement. For good or ill – and mostly for good – mankind was launched on a course which was irreversible.

Enough has been said to show that the English people at an early stage developed on different lines from the rest of Europe. This is not to deny the importance of continental European influences on English art, architecture, music, literature, culture and thought. What is surely hard to deny, however, is that the English influences on Europe were just as great, and on the world outside Europe even greater. The purpose of this book is to describe the most important of those influences and to analyse their history. It is an outline of a vast subject on which many volumes could be written. But one hopes that at the end the reader will gain a clearer idea than he had before of the nature of English civilization and of its impact upon the rest of the world.

I
The Making of a Tradition

1 Who are the English?
Migration, conquest and the mingling of races

2 The Medieval Centuries
The foundation of English institutions
up to the Tudors

3 Ruling Dynasties and the
Great Families
The historic role of the monarchy
and aristocracy

THE ENCIRCLING SEAS, England's protection once she became a united kingdom, had opened her to invasion and colonization in earlier times. Of the first settlers we know little. The Celtic 'ancient' Britons left no written records and few material remains, although some of their rural traditions and practices passed on into later ages. The Romans, arriving in the 1st century AD and departing in the 5th, left their impress more on the land than on the people. But with the coming of the Angles and Saxons the story of the English people begins: language, literature, topography, religion and art must all trace their ancestry to this period. Subsequent Danish raiders in the 7th and 8th centuries caused disruption and bloodshed but were eventually absorbed into the existing fabric. The Normans (racially related to the Danes but culturally and linguistically French) made their impact at the top of the social scale, determining the whole future of the English nobility, law and administration in spite of being a tiny minority in terms of numbers. Since then there has been no conquest, although the racial mixture has continued, a gradual and in general peaceful process. It is a curious fact, however, that the ruling dynasties have always originated outside England – Normans and Plantagenets in France, Tudors in Wales, Stuarts in Scotland and Hanoverians in Germany. Such a peculiar amalgam of continuity and change, of internal stability and innovation from outside, has surely been a contributing factor to the unique quality of the English character. In the following pages we look at the fluctuating fortunes of the monarchy, its vicissitudes and transformations, and consider the role of the great families that grew up by its side.

The first map of Britain
was one drawn by Matthew Paris in the middle of the 13th century (*opposite*). Its basis is an itinerary from Dover to Newcastle, shown as a vertical line of towns ending just below Hadrian's Wall. The rest of the country is outlined in more summary form, with rough indications of distance and direction, but with no thought of geographical accuracy in the modern sense. The south of England is more recognizable than the north: Cornwall stands out on the left, Norfolk and Suffolk on the right. Wales, with the Isle of Anglesey at the top and the Severn estuary at the bottom, is also fairly clear. Most of Scotland, however, was believed to be an island, connected to England by a bridge at Stirling. (1)

Dramas of history

Violent, spectacular and often tragic, the high points of England's story have always powerfully appealed to her novelists, painters and, more recently, film-makers. Their imaginative recreations are useful in bringing the meagre documents to life, as long as one does not begin to think of them as documents themselves.

The Descent of the Danes, by William Bell Scott. Panic-stricken, the people of Northumberland take refuge behind rough stone walls as the Danish raiders appear on their coasts. *Above*: a coin of Alfred the Great, who organized English resistance to the Danes. (2, 3)

The Death of Bede, another of Bell Scott's paintings. Bede, the first great scholar of the English church, died as he was finishing his translation of the Gospel of St John into Anglo-Saxon. *Below*: the first page of his *History of the English Church and People*, from an 8th-century illuminated manuscript. (4, 5)

The field of Hastings: Ford Madox Brown imagines the end of the battle, when the body of King Harold is brought before William the Conqueror. It was a day that determined the course of English history for centuries to come. *Left*: the death of Harold from the Bayeux Tapestry, which was made only a few years after the event. *Right*: a coin of William I. (6, 7, 8)

35

Power and chivalry

The orders of knighthood were originally founded with practical as well as symbolic intent. Symbolic in their revival of legendary glories, they were also instruments of military policy, welding together a warrior élite.

The Round Table still preserved at Winchester (*right*) linked the medieval monarchy to the mythical court of King Arthur. The painting now to be seen on it is Tudor, but the table itself goes back to the days of Edward III. (9)

Feudal rights all stemmed from the king, who in theory owned the whole realm. This 15th-century miniature showing the enfeoffment of Count Alan of Brittany looks back at the origins of the whole system when William I distributed land among his family and barons. (10)

Edward III's long reign of fifty years (1327–77) marks a high point of English prestige, when the victories of Crécy and Poitiers consolidated English control over large parts of France. *Right*: Edward III in the Garter robes. (11)

The Order of the Garter was founded about 1348 and originally consisted of the king, Edward III, his son the Black Prince and twenty-four members. This miniature of about 100 years later shows the king (here Henry VI) with his knights and ladies, kneeling before the altar of St George. The numbers remained constant until 1786, but long before that the Order had become merely honorific. The loss of France in 1453 began a change in the character of the English aristocracy. Deprived of their military function, they became a privileged ruling class, though at the same time looking back with nostalgia to a chivalric past. (12)

Henry V, most successful and most popular of Plantagenet kings, was also the most English. He was the first monarch since the Conquest to use English officially, a decisive point in the growth of national identity. In this miniature (*right*) Thomas Hoccleve presents him with his poem *De Regimine Principum*. (13)

37

Manor, town and church

In the Middle Ages England shared with the rest of Europe a rigidly stratified social system. Beneath the king and his nobles was a class of landowning squires living on estates worked by peasants. Slightly outside the system stood the towns (ruled by autonomous guilds), the universities and the church.

Lords, farmers and fishermen: three details from manuscripts of the 14th and 15th centuries. *Top*: a page helps his lord to dress. *Centre*: a sower. *Bottom*: fishermen with their catch. (14, 15, 16)

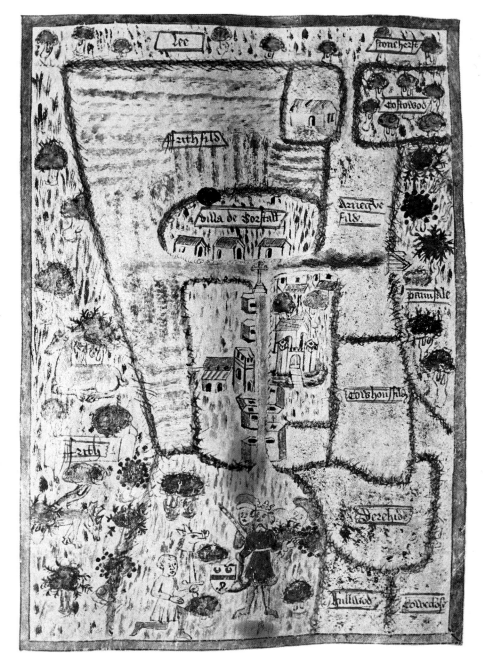

The village of Boarstall in Buckinghamshire consisted in 1444 of a few houses, a church and a gatehouse tower, surrounded by large communal fields (showing strip farming), each of which had its own name. (17)

'Sheep', in the words of a 15th-century epitaph, 'paid for all'. The wool trade not only enriched the merchants of East Anglia and Somerset but, through taxation, enabled a king such as Edward III to play a major role in European politics. (18)

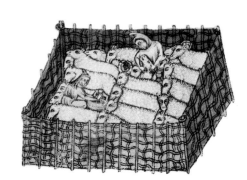

Intellectual life was geared to the requirements of the church. William of Wykeham, bishop of Winchester, founded both New College, Oxford, and the boys' school that was to prepare students for New College – Winchester College. This schematized view shows it in 1463, with the bishop, teachers and pupils in the foreground. Medieval England produced two great theological thinkers in Duns Scotus and William of Ockham and even began to probe the physical sciences. (19)

The towns were largely free from feudal constraints thanks to the guild system. *Above*: Simon Eyre, draper and Lord Mayor of London (1445–6), who built Leadenhall granary, later a famous market, and endowed a chapel and a school. (20)

The end of medieval England came when the old system broke up under new economic and religious forces. This financier (*left*) is portrayed to represent the sin of covetousness, but sophisticated banking methods, largely introduced from Italy, were already important in the 14th and 15th centuries and heralded the ways of the modern world. In the 16th century came a redistribution of land when the great property-owning abbeys were dissolved, creating a new social fabric. *Right*: Henry VII, in one of the last such transactions in England, establishes a chantry with Benedictine monks, headed by the Abbot of Westminster. (21, 22)

The Tudors: a new order in England

In retrospect, the reign of Henry Tudor – Henry VII – represents more of a break with the past than it probably seemed at the time. Though lacking any dynastic claim to the throne, he was able to end the civil wars and establish strong central control financially and politically.

When Henry VIII succeeded, the Tudor dynasty seemed secure; it was to last, however, only one more generation. This group portrait, painted in the reign of his daughter Elizabeth, shows him with his three children: Mary, on the left, with her husband (who became Philip II of Spain); the boy Edward VI, who died aged fifteen; and Elizabeth herself. Allegorical figures attend them on either side. (23)

The Queen's ministers. Robert Dudley, earl of Leicester (*above*), was Elizabeth's first favourite, notable more for his personality and charm than for any special abilities. William Cecil, Lord Burghley (*below*), on the other hand, was a statesman of genius, upon whom the queen leaned for much of her reign. (24, 25)

The Stuart succession

Elizabeth died in 1603, and the throne passed smoothly (chiefly through Robert Cecil's efforts) to the next legal heir, James I, the great-grandson of Henry VIII's sister. The Stuart family had reigned in Scotland since 1371; the two Crowns were now united, but separate Parliaments remained for the two countries.

James I (*left*) brought to his new task experience, caution and shrewdness; but the working relationship with the House of Commons established by Elizabeth became eroded. James filled the House of Lords with his own followers and promulgated a doctrine of 'divine right' that was to be the downfall of his son. This portrait, 'The Lyte Jewel', was given by him to Thomas Lyte as a reward for drawing up a genealogy connecting James with Brut, the legendary Trojan founder of Britain. (26)

Charles I lacked his father's sense of political reality, and the breach between him and Parliament widened until relations broke down completely. Van Dyck's genius preserves, and in some respects created, the image of a tragic figure whose qualities were out of touch with his age. *Below*: Charles I, his queen Henrietta Maria, and their elder children, including the future Charles II. (27)

Monarchy restored. After the revolutionary experiment of the Commonwealth, Charles II returned in 1660 amid general acclaim (*above: The Sea Triumph of Charles II*, by Antonio Verrio). But the dynasty was destined to be short-lived. Charles had many illegitimate children (*right*, a daughter by Barbara Villiers) but no heirs. His Catholic brother, James II, was deposed, leaving a son and grandson ('Bonnie Prince Charlie', *far right*) to assert the Stuart claim well into the 18th century. (28, 29, 30)

The rise of a great family

Social mobility has been a feature of English life since the Middle Ages, and there were numerous paths by which a commoner could climb into the aristocracy: by royal favour, by success in business, by political talent or by military service to the realm.

John Churchill, ennobled by Queen Anne for his victories over Louis XIV, took the title of duke of Marlborough, with the immense palace of Blenheim as his seat. He and his duchess, the formidable Sarah Jennings (*below*), produced five children, but only one of them was a son, who died childless. The title passed through the female line to the Spencer family, who adopted the name Spencer Churchill and remained one of the leading English families through the centuries. The ninth duke (*right*, with his American wife Consuelo Vanderbilt, a portrait by John Sargent) was a secretary of state. Far more eminent, however, was his nephew, Randolph Churchill, whose son was Winston Churchill. Churchill was born at Blenheim and himself painted this view of the Great Hall (*left*). (31, 32, 33)

The house of Hanover

The Hanoverians came to the English throne by a devious route. James I's daughter married the German Elector Palatine. Their child was Sophia, electress of Hanover, and when the Stuart succession failed – apart from the Catholic branches, which were unacceptable – it was her descendants who became kings of England.

Sophia would have been queen of England had she lived another seven weeks. She died on 8 June 1714, Queen Anne (the last of the Stuarts) the following August. This detail is from a vast allegorical painting of the succession. (34)

England and Hanover now shared a king – George I – but in every other way they remained separate. The arrangement lasted until 1837. On this commemorative medal, a leaping horse, the badge of the house of Hanover, joins the two countries. (35)

The Georges succeeded each other throughout the 18th century (skipping one generation when a prince of Wales was killed by a cricket ball). In this scene by John Zoffany, portraits of Stuarts and earlier Hanoverians look down on two sons of George III, George (later George IV) and Frederick duke of York. (36)

With Victoria the monarchy acquired a popularity and prestige that it had not enjoyed since the Tudors. In an age when England briefly took over the leadership of the Western world, she epitomized the nation's pride. She was also a dynastic focus, since her children and grandchildren married into all the royal families of Europe. This group portrait by Laurits Tuxen shows her with her extended family at the time of the Golden Jubilee in 1887. (37)

The future Edward VII (*left*) found his friends largely outside the circle of the old nobility. Here he relaxes with the industrialist Lord Armstrong at his country retreat of Cragside. (38)

1 Who are the English?

Migration, conquest and the mingling of races

FRANK BARLOW

◇

IN THE EARLY YEARS OF THE 8TH CENTURY the Venerable Bede, a learned monk at Jarrow in Northumbria, began to write his last and greatest work, the *History of the English Church and People*. In order to describe how God had arranged for the conversion of the heathen English and brought about a united church under the guidance of the apostolic see of Rome, he opened with a description of Britain and a brief review of Roman rule of that province which had finally collapsed when Germanic troops were recruited by a native chieftain to repel the attacks from the north of Picts and Scots. Bede did not seem, however, to have been quite sure who the auxiliaries were. First he related that it was agreed that Saxons should be brought in; then he stated that in the year 449 King Vortigern enlisted three warships of 'the race of the Angles or Saxons'; next he added that the Saxons won a victory against the king's northern enemies; and finally, in a famous passage, he explained that the recruits came from three very powerful Germanic tribes, the Saxons, Angles and Jutes.

Bede was writing some two hundred and fifty years after 'the coming of the Saxons' he described, and he had little beyond tradition on which to base his story. This can now be amplified from other literary sources and from archaeological and philological evidence. Before the end of Roman Britain, soldiers of Germanic origin were being settled in small numbers in the provinces. Then in the 5th century, as part of the general movement of Germanic tribes across the Roman frontiers, Britain was penetrated at many points on the eastern and southern coastlines by war-bands. Some of these came at the invitation of local warlords who had seized power as Roman government collapsed; some entered simply as marauders, colonists or would-be conquerors. Besides Bede's Saxons, Angles and Jutes, traces have been found in Britain of Frisians, Swedes and Franks; and with Britain at the flotsam edge of the tide of barbarian migrations a racial mixture is to be expected.

The monarchy's place in present-day England seems safe and secure: the royal family rises in popular esteem and is constitutionally indispensable. At both levels it is the links with the past that count, and it is hard to think of any other occasion that would have delighted the whole country as did the wedding of the prince of Wales in July 1981.(39)

'The English nation'

The earlier history of these Germanic peoples is obscure. At the end of the 1st century AD the Roman historian Tacitus gave some account of the nations or tribes living in the regions to the north of the Rhine and Danube in his *Germania*, a book not entirely innocent of the desire to castigate the decadent morals of imperial Rome by painting an idealized picture of the simpler warlike virtues of the barbarians. And in his *Agricola*, a biography of his father-in-law who governed Britain from 77 or 78, he provided us with a view of the island which the Germans were to overrun. Tacitus mentioned the Angles among the most northern tribes, but ignored the Saxons and Jutes.

The Saxons were first noticed by Ptolemy in his *Geography*, compiled about 140 but based on 1st-century sources. They were then located in modern Holstein. In the 3rd century they seem to have moved south-west and conquered and perhaps absorbed the Chauci, a more famous west German tribe living between the Elbe and the Ems, and then, following behind the Franks, occupied Frisia and the lower Rhine, with settlements as far south as Boulogne and Bayeux. In the east they penetrated to Swabia and Thuringia and even to Italy (568). Roman writers also regarded them as the fiercest pirates on the northern seas.

By the 5th century, as a result of their migration, the Saxons had brought under their rule or attracted into their allegiance parts of other tribes, including perhaps the Angles and Jutes. Although a large number of Saxons remained on the Continent, and gave their name to Saxony, nothing more is heard of mainland Angles or Jutes. And the position is further complicated by the habit of the victims of Germanic marauders in the West of calling them indiscriminately 'Saxons'. The epithet 'mongrel' is one which can be applied to even the earliest English. In the 5th century parties of these 'Saxons' set off for Britain from many points on the continental seaboard from the mouth of the Elbe to the Channel ports, with the mouth of the Rhine and Frisia at the centre of the movement. In Britain rebel Germanic garrisons and mercenaries, reinforced or followed by these new waves of invaders, pushed inland and made conquests and settlements. Although there was sometimes stout local resistance, setbacks to the advance and long periods of stability, over the centuries the frontier between the new kingdoms of the

'English' (as they began to be called) and those of the British moved inexorably west. By the end of the 7th century the newcomers had brought under their control most of what later was to be known as the kingdom of England. They had reached northwards up to the Firth of Forth and westwards as far as Cornwall, Wales and Cumbria; and only a few pockets of native rule remained behind.

When the Highland zones and less desirable lands were reached, progress became even slower. Cornwall was brought under English rule in the 9th century, southern Cumbria at the end of the 11th. The lowland areas of Wales were subdued bit by bit after the Norman Conquest and the whole region annexed by Edward I in 1284. Ireland was largely conquered in the late 12th century. In none of those countries, however, except for parts of south and north Wales, was English colonization heavy. In contrast, the kingdom of Scots, based on an English, or at least an anglicized, Lothian, and later adopting many of the governmental practices of its Anglo-Norman neighbour south of the Tweed and Cheviots, was never for long subjected by force to English rule. It kept for centuries the character of a hybrid marcher kingdom placed between the Sassenachs and the Celtic-Scandinavian west and north.

The Germanic invaders of southern Britain in the 5th century were never under the effective command of any one great leader, as sometimes happened on the Continent, and as a result campaigns were uncoordinated and the conquests piecemeal. In the 6th century, however, a number of petty kingdoms were created by war leaders, who either conquered the native population or imposed their rule over Germanic settlements. By the time of Bede these principalities had been given names, some of which, such as Kent, probably the earliest conquest, and Deira and Bernicia beyond the Humber, were Romano-British; others, such as Essex, Middlesex, Sussex, Wessex (the East, Middle, South and West Saxons) and East Anglia, had an ethnic significance; while Mercia in the north midlands was the marcher kingdom, although whether between the South and North Humbrians or between the English and the Britons is not clear. In whatever circumstances these distinguishing titles may have arisen (and in some cases they were not the original names), they cannot be regarded as a completely accurate guide to the race of the inhabitants. Although Bede tells us that the Jutes settled in Kent and round Southampton Water, and it is likely that Angles predominated in the north and Saxons in the south, archaeological evidence suggests that few if any of the kingdoms were composed exclusively of people from a single tribe.

There is also the complication of the nationality of the royal families. While the kings of Essex traced their ancestry back to Saxnot, a specifically Saxon deity, all the rest put Woden at the head of their genealogy and sometimes shared with others several of his descendants. It would seem, therefore, that all the dynasties

50

except the East Saxon were of Anglian origin. In the case of Mercia its great 8th-century king Offa believed that he was the descendant of an earlier Offa, king of Angeln in Schleswig before the migration, a famous hero commemorated in the poems *Widsith* and *Beowulf*. It is possible, however, that the bulk of the population came from the largest of the Germanic nations taking part, the Saxons. This dichotomy would help to explain the otherwise puzzling fact that, although most observers called the invaders Saxons, the rulers themselves preferred to call themselves and their people 'Angelcynn', the English nation; and Bede, as we have seen, chose to write the *Historia ecclesiastica gentis Anglorum*, the history of the *English* people.

It is still the name in use among the inhabitants: only outsiders call them Saxons. But 'Anglia' as a geographical term is rarely found before the 11th century; those writing in Latin preferred to employ the more classical 'Britannia', although it could also mean Brittany. And when in modern times the British Isles became politically united, the English not only joined forces with their largely Celtic neighbours but also became, with the others, British citizens.

The contribution of the 5th- and 6th-century Romano-British people to the English nation is, however, a difficult problem. The 'ancient' Britons belonged to the large family of Celtic peoples living in north-western Europe. Physically, they impressed the Romans by their tall stature, fair skin, blonde hair and blue eyes, whereas many modern 'Celtic' populations are much darker. They were farmers, living in hamlets and small villages; and in Britain there was some agricultural continuity, for the Germanic settlements often further developed areas already under cultivation in the late Roman period. Their religion invested many local features, such as rivers, mountains and groves, with magical significance. This too was the custom of the German tribes; and rural ceremonies associated with sacred places may have continued through Roman into Anglo-Saxon times. There may even have been a Celtic origin to some of the superstitious practices which persisted for centuries beneath Christianity.

How deep the Romanization of Britain went it is difficult to say, but judging by subsequent events it was in many areas relatively superficial. During the decay and collapse of the imperial province, the Romano-Britons lost much of their Latin culture, and at the time of the invasions were probably not greatly different in economic and political organization from the newcomers, who themselves had often had some contact with Roman civilization, even if only at second hand. One difference was that many of the Romano-Britons were Christian, while the invaders were heathen; but the only grounds the conquerors could have had for despising the conquered was their alleged cowardice or 'degeneracy'. The failure of the native tongue to leave any impression on the English language, the widespread replacement of geographical names and the disappearance of almost all Roman institutions have been taken as evidence of the wholesale extermination or displacement of the natives. But the history and pattern of the settlement and the value of the Britons, if only as slaves and concubines, to the newcomers suggest that nothing so drastic could possibly have occurred. Archaeologists are finding more and more evidence of peaceful co-existence and continuity. Personal names are sometimes revealing. The Christian poet so admired by Bede, the cowherd Caedmon, had a Celtic name. And so had most of the early West Saxon kings: Cerdic, Ceawlin and Caedwalla, to name the most famous. They must have been at least partly of British origin.

It is possible that in areas of dense English settlement, while the invaders remained monoglot, the surviving natives, soon bilingual, then abandoned their ancestral tongue. Moreover, although the survivors could have had something to teach their conquerors, what little remained of their Roman veneer proved to be of small value in the changed circumstances. There is reason to believe, therefore, that a proportion of the British population, increasing in density from east to west and from south to north, was silently incorporated into the new society. Whereas in a few areas the invaders cleared the land of its former inhabitants – there must have been a substantial retreat before the advancing marauders – in others, and especially where there had been ancient co-existence or land was plentiful, the natives suffered a variety of fates ranging from enslavement to the intrusion of new foreign settlements. There must have been from the beginning some interbreeding; and in the frontier regions the relations between the two nations had eventually to be defined. Because there were graded ranks in both social systems, it was easy to slot the natives in at lower points on the scale; and in the West Saxon laws of the early 8th century the Welsh (as they were beginning to be called), who must have been numerous in the south-west peninsula, were given the full protection of the law, but at reduced rates. At the end of the 9th century King Alfred of Wessex seems to have been on good terms with the Welsh in Wales – his biographer was Asser of St David's – but by the 11th century racial prejudices had arisen which hindered intermarriage. More stable boundaries and regular conflict across a frontier may have polarized the two peoples. A similar situation developed in western Gaul.

One reason why the Germanic invaders were so uninterested in the few rags of Roman culture still on display in Britain was that they were soldiers and farmers, notoriously averse to town life and possessing strong social customs of their own. One of the main features of Germanic society was a caste system which, because the value of a man's life (his *wergild*) and of many other of his parts and attributes was determined by his class, was expressed in the law codes in monetary terms. At the apex was a royal family, which had arisen out of the nobility and was distinguished from it only by its greater sanctity. Companions (*gesiths*) or servants (*thegns*) of the kings formed the nobility, a wide and

usually disparate class which sometimes was sub-divided. The ordinary freeman, the *ceorl* or churl, normally had a *wergild* only a sixth of the value of the highest nobleman's (in Wessex, 200 shillings), a rate much lower than was general in continental Germanic society, and a peculiarity which has never been convincingly explained. Finally, at the base of society were the slaves, comprising subject races, prisoners-of-war and the victims of the law and other disasters. Although in those violent times, with so many opportunities for making and losing a fortune, there was a good deal of social mobility, legally defined status was still of fundamental importance as late as the 11th century. It was always a hierarchical society, with the agricultural population organized to maintain king-ship, the nobility and the priesthood (later the Christian church) through services, food renders and other taxes and dues.

The coming of Christianity

Between the 5th and the 10th centuries the English nation experienced great changes in religion, political organization and, no doubt, although these are more difficult to perceive, social customs. By the end of the 6th century the English kingdoms had become isolated pockets of heathenism in western Christendom. The Christian church in Britain had survived and flourished in Wales and spread to Ireland and thence to Scotland. In the 6th century there were close relations between the churches in Britain, Ireland, Brittany and Gaul. Although the Britons – among their other 'unspeakable crimes', according to Bede – did no missionary work in English areas, the other churches did not share their reluctance; and when, some time after 560, King Ethelbert of Kent married the Christian Merovingian princess Bertha, daughter of King Charibert who ruled from Paris, this was recognized as the signal for evangelizing to begin. And so from Scotland, Gaul and Rome brave men brought the good tidings to communities still deeply attached to their Germanic gods.

Pope Gregory I's mission in 596 of a party to Kent under the leadership of the Roman abbot Augustine was not only an improbable event but also one which greatly affected later English history. Although Irish-Scottish missionaries, operating largely from Iona and then Lindisfarne in Northumbria, converted the greatest part of England in the 7th century, it was this Roman mission based on Kent which in the end was recognized as the repository of the most authentic tradition. When King Oswiu of Northumbria accepted the customs of the Roman church at the Synod of Whitby in 664 he ensured that the English would for centuries receive a stream of cultural influence from the remnants of the Roman empire. The new situation is shown dramatically by the arrival in England four years after Whitby of a Greek monk, Theodore of Tarsus, to be archbishop of Canterbury. A refugee in Rome, he was the eccentric choice of Pope Vitalian to govern an outpost church. He came with an African abbot, Hadrian, and a former Northumbrian nobleman, Benedict Biscop; and by his death in 690 he had reorganized the English bishoprics, established a great and influential school at Canterbury for the education of the clergy, and given the church a form and culture which it was to preserve for centuries. The English had entered at last into the fellowship of civilized nations.

England was not, of course, Christianized in a day. Sussex and the Isle of Wight were not converted until the 8th century and formal renunciation of the old gods was not always followed by a real change of heart. The message of the New Testament was so much at variance with the mores of the Germanic warrior that most men regarded the new ideals as an alternative way of life, to be followed only when necessary, particularly just before death. But a few, including some kings, renounced the world in their prime, and entered monasteries, became hermits or went on pilgrimage. Visits to Rome and Jerusalem became an English habit; and for some it was soon changed into missionary work on the Continent, especially among the Frisians and Saxons, their own people. Women took an important part in these activities, for they enjoyed a high position in Germanic society. Double monasteries, in which monks and nuns lived together, although in separate buildings, were ruled by an abbess; and the Anglo-Saxon church calendars were strewn with female saints. Christianity created new paths for the English to tread; and they brought back with them the treasures of both Rome and of the Holy Land. Among these were books – the classical and the patristic authors, all in Latin versions. Latin was from the beginning the language of the English church, and Bede was the first, and for centuries the greatest, monument to this traffic and learning. At Jarrow he tried to produce for his countrymen an encyclopedia of Christian knowledge. With the teaching of an even more eclectic and practical curriculum at Canterbury in the days of Theodore and Hadrian and the diffusion of Irish learning through Wessex, England became for a time more a great entrepôt for the exchange of knowledge than a shadowy outpost on the very rim of the world.

A common religion, hierarchically organized, may have reinforced the bonds of race in the movement towards political unity. The English church as seen by Bede was the model for a united English nation. In the 6th and 7th centuries, as a result of warfare and marriage alliances between the kings, the number of small Germanic kingdoms was greatly reduced. By the 8th century only three of actual or potential importance remained, Northumbria, Mercia and Wessex, all of which had retained their pioneering, competitive and expansionist nature, with Northumbria looking to the north, Wessex to both east and west, and Mercia, centred in the midlands, in all directions, but mainly to the south-east. In the 8th century Mercia was the dominant power, and King Offa (757–96), by his conquests and his destruction of rival dynasties, and by

extending his lordship occasionally over all the other regions, laid the foundations of a united kingdom of England. His achievements also included the introduction from Kent of a new type of penny and the construction of the great earthwork between his own kingdom and the Welsh, known as Offa's Dyke. But his illustrious dynasty did not long survive his death, and even before then the Northmen or Vikings were raiding the English coast, so that unity was achieved only much later, and by West Saxon kings.

Invaders from the north

The Scandinavians, among the most northerly of the Germanic tribes, differed from most of the rest by not migrating during the 'folk-wanderings' which seem to have started in the 3rd century AD. Indeed, they still live substantially in their earliest known homelands. They became instead traders and explorers, and from the 7th century onwards spread astonishingly across the seas and lakes and along rivers, establishing trading posts and small settlements throughout a good part of the northern hemisphere. No one comprehensive reason can be given for this expansion. Growth of population, the love of adventure among men bred to the sea, an ancient habit of trade, the development of suitable ships and the great success of their enterprises sent them radiating in all possible directions. The Swedes, whose ships had been described by Tacitus, and who were the most easterly of the three Scandinavian nations, travelled through Russia to Constantinople, which they reached in 865, and traded with the caliphate of Baghdad. Their involvement in Western Europe was small. The Norwegians followed three main routes. The first was across the arctic seas. They discovered Iceland about 680 and colonized it after 870, discovered and partly settled Greenland at the end of the 9th century, and briefly reached the North American mainland. The second was round the north of Britain. They explored and colonized the Shetlands, Orkney, the Hebrides, west Scotland and the inlets of Ireland. In 795 Iona was plundered, in 798 the Isle of Man was reached, and by 853 there was a Scandinavian kingdom of Dublin. From these western islands they spread in the 10th century to Westmorland, Cumberland and Yorkshire. The third Norwegian route was across the North Sea. In 787 they attacked Dorset, and in 793–4 plundered the monasteries of Lindisfarne and Jarrow. At different times and in different places the Norwegians were agricultural settlers, lords of subject peoples, traders and robbers.

It was, however, the Danes, who in the 8th century inhabited the lands around the entrance to the Baltic, who most affected England, although Norwegians sometimes took part in their expeditions and were occasionally the leaders. Danish Vikings had by 865 swept round the western seaboard of Europe into the Mediterranean and were raiding the countries on both sides. The English calamities arose out of the Danish reaction to Frankish imperialism. Charlemagne completed the conquest of Frisia and campaigned against the Saxons, the two buffer states, in the last quarter of the 8th century, and the Danes retaliated by attacking the Frankish empire by land and sea. When they occupied Frisia, and especially after 840 when the Frankish empire began to break up, England was in danger. Between 835 and 865 there were at least twelve Viking raids on the south-east coast and we do not know what was happening in Northumbria. Raids were succeeded by armies of conquest, and conquest by settlement. By 878, when King Alfred drove Guthrum's army out of Wessex, the Danes had conquered the kingdoms of Northumbria, East Anglia and Mercia and had begun to divide up the spoils, including the land. Probably in 886 Alfred and Guthrum, by then settled in East Anglia, made a treaty by which the boundary between the two kingdoms was to run up the Thames, then up the Lea (to leave London in Alfred's hands), thence to Bedford and along the Ouse to Watling Street. The regions to the north were outside the power of both: Danish *jarls* (earls) ruled over eastern Mercia, the area of the Five Boroughs (Derby, Nottingham, Lincoln, Leicester and Stamford), Rutland and Northampton, and in Northumbria the Viking Halfdan was king. Hence the 'Danelaw' covered an area south of the Tees and north-east of a line from London to Chester.

The area of Danish conquest in England can be roughly defined; but the extent and nature of Scandinavian settlement are harder to discover. No one now believes that the Danelaw was inhabited exclusively by Danes; but recent attempts to minimize the density of the colonization and posit an aristocratic domination rather than a peasant migration seem, in their more extreme formulations, to have failed. The pattern of settlement probably varied a good deal, with areas of heavy colonization, areas where Danes brought new lands under the plough between or outside surviving English villages, and areas where the newcomers merely replaced the former landlords and collected the customary rents and taxes. Danish immigrants were probably most numerous in East Anglia, the Five Boroughs and parts of Yorkshire, with the greatest density of all in Lincolnshire. In Yorkshire the existence of a Norwegian kingdom between 902 and 954 attracted a new wave of colonists from Scandinavian Ireland. But after that, even when Viking raids were resumed at the end of the 10th century and England was incorporated for forty years into the Danish empire, mass immigration seems to have ceased. Danish kings brought in new *jarls* rather than more farmers.

Alfred's son, Edward the Elder, and his grandsons, Athelstan, Edmund and Edred, in an unparalleled series of successful campaigns, reconquered the Danelaw between 909 and 954; and by absorbing western Mercia as well they created for the first time a single kingdom of England. The unity was fragile and occasionally broken in the next century, with England

Offa, King of Mercia in the late 6th century, might have succeeded in uniting England under his rule but for the Danish invasions. In the later Middle Ages he was seen as a knight of chivalry: here he is being invested by his father with sword and spurs. Among Offa's numerous achievements was the establishment of a new type of penny.

usually splitting on the line of the Thames–Severn. It remained until 1066, and in some ways for many years more, an Anglo-Danish kingdom, with the eastern and northern parts susceptible to Scandinavian adventurers and cultural changes alike. But the English traditions were dominant. The Anglo-Saxon Chronicle, written in the vernacular, continued after its foundation in Alfred's reign to record national history from the English standpoint, and even if its initial notes of triumph were to turn in the 11th century into lamentations, it preserved and fostered among the nobility and church a sense of continuity and of patriotism.

The last years of the Anglo-Danish kingdom

For the best part of a century, however, the English monarchy went from strength to strength. By 975, when Edgar, Edmund's son, died prematurely, the kings had become overlords of almost the whole of Britain. In 920 Edward the Elder on a northern campaign had received the submission of the king of York, the ruler of Bamburgh and the kings of Scots and of Strathclyde. In 975 Edgar, after his belated coronation, was acknowledged at Chester as their lord by the kings of Scots, Strathclyde, Cumbria, the Islands and North Wales. Kings of the English and emperors of Britain, these descendants of Alfred were, like their ancestor, much more than just military conquerors. They reorganized the administration of their enlarged kingdom, dividing it into shires and these into hundreds (or wapentakes in the Scandinavian areas); and the unusual sophistication of their government is amply demonstrated by their having in their household a secretariat which could issue their very impressive diplomas or land charters. Drawing on Flanders and Fleury on the Loire, they also patronized a far-reaching reform of the English church. Starting with the monasteries, they eventually improved all its parts and lent royal power to a reformation of the morals of the clergy and laity alike. Even the Danes, by then

Christians, were involved in this movement. Among the leaders were Oda archbishop of Canterbury and his nephew Oswald bishop of Worcester, both of Scandinavian descent. Oswald founded an influential monastery at Ramsey in East Anglia. His colleague, Æthelweald bishop of Winchester, re-founded monasteries at Ely, Peterborough and Thorney.

With Edgar at the apex of both the secular and ecclesiastical hierarchies in the kingdom, deeply respected by both, and acquiring a great reputation in Europe, the Old English monarchy reached a new peak. The descent, however, was precipitous. The kingdom's notorious wealth, the succession of Edgar's two young sons in turn, Edward the Martyr and Ethelred 'the Redeless' ('Unready'), and the existence of a large unassimilated Scandinavian population once again aroused Danish cupidity. The Danish invasions of England from 980 onwards during the reign of Ethelred, leading to its capitulation to Swegn king of Denmark and his son Cnut in the years 1013 to 1016, were a direct consequence of the earlier settlements. England had become part of the Scandinavian world before Cnut incorporated it into his empire which, at its most extensive, also included a reluctant Norway and parts of Sweden. And it retained its Anglo-Danish character under Edward the Confessor and Harold II, after the direct line from Cnut had failed in 1042.

Two features of this hybrid kingdom need to be noticed: firstly, the persistence of Danish culture among the settlers, together with its influence on the native English; and second, the Scandinavian features of the monarchy. As the Scandinavian peoples were, like the English, Germanic, the Danish settlements and conquests were of a different nature from both the English in 5th-century Britain and the Norman in 11th-century England. Although Danish culture was recognizably distinct, it was of the same kind, and its barbarity should not be exaggerated. The Scandinavians had been in touch with the Roman empire and the Vikings had world-wide experience. From the beginning the Danes and the English regarded each other as equals. Alfred and Guthrum in 886 fixed the *wergilds* of the two races in the Danelaw on the basis of equality. In the 10th century the English conquerors of the Danish kingdoms confirmed to their new subjects their native laws and customs. Hence Danish colonization profoundly affected not only the racial composition of a wide strip of England but also its law, language and social customs.

Danish law, with its clearer concept of crime and heavier penalties, persisted as a provincial custom for centuries and also influenced English development: 'law' is itself a Scandinavian loan-word. The Danish language had a major influence on all dialects of the English tongue in all its aspects: vocabulary, grammar and pronunciation. Scandinavian place names, from towns to fields, are dense in some eastern areas, and personal names, especially when Danish kings were in power, spread widely among the English. The last Old English archbishop of Canterbury, who came from Norwich, bore the Old Norse name of Stigandr; but his brother had the English name, Æthelmaer. The settlers also brought in their art styles and court poetry of the northern type. There is no evidence that they introduced new methods of husbandry or even of land tenure, but they liked to live in fortified towns and may have stimulated trade and even widened England's connections. England became very much a part of the northern world, and in general the Scandinavian settlement reinforced the Germanic side of English culture.

It is also clear that the Vikings were admired, and some of their habits imitated, at all social levels. King Edgar himself was said to have loved their customs too well; and his son Ethelred behaved increasingly like a Viking. In Gunnlaug's Saga we are told that the poet travelled from Iceland to the king's court at London, probably between 1001 and 1005, and recited a lay which he had composed in his honour and had the refrain: 'The whole host of the warrior king fears the lord of England as a god, and the race of men submit to Ethelred.' In return he received a scarlet cloak lined with the best skins and ornamented at the bottom hem with lace, and at the king's invitation stayed with him for the winter. When in 1012 Ethelred recruited the great Jóms-Viking Thorkell Hávi and his forty-five ships and in 1014 Olaf Haroldsson, the future king of Norway and famous saint, and his Norwegian warband to fight for him against Swegn of Denmark, the situation was becoming close to civil war. It is symptomatic of this period that the last English king before the Norman Conquest, Harold, a son of the English Earl Godwin and his Danish wife Gytha, should have a Danish name, like his brothers Swegn and Tosti and his sister Gunnhildr, and should have named his own children Godwin, Edmund, Magnus, Ulf, Harold, Gytha and Gunnhildr. Harold fought his last battle at Hastings, under the standard of the fighting man, surrounded by his bodyguard of Scandinavian housecarls armed with the Danish 'bearded' axe. He was almost as much a member of the Viking world as the legendary Harold Hardrada, king of Norway, whom he had just defeated and killed at Stamford Bridge.

The Norman invasion

The background to the Norman invasion of England in 1066 is mostly political. Ever since Ethelred had allied with Duke Richard I of Normandy at the end of the 10th century, in an attempt to deny Norman harbours to the Danes, and married his daughter Emma in 1002, the ducal family had acquired an interest in the English Crown, which was reinforced when Emma married *en secondes noces* Ethelred's supplanter, Cnut, in 1017. It was to prosecute his slender legal claim to the English throne that William the Bastard invaded when Emma's last surviving son, Edward the Confessor, the second of her offspring to wear the crown, died childless in

January 1066 and was succeeded by his brother-in-law Harold, a nobleman whom William had not managed to attach to his side. Because of Edward's failure to produce a son and because of the confusion in English affairs since 1014, when Ethelred had been driven into exile, there were many pretenders with colourable claims; and it is more than likely that Edward had on different occasions promised the succession to different relatives. In England there was the young Anglo-Hungarian Edgar Ætheling, a great-grandson of Ethelred, who had some appeal to the English, but sacrificed ambition to survival, and for long, when not on some more distant jaunt, flitted between the Scottish, English and Norman courts. In 1066 the contest was not for boys. Besides Harold Godwinson and William, Harold Hardrada of Norway and Swegn Estrithson of Denmark (both representing a claim derived from Cnut 'the Great') decided to intervene. And the issue was decided by war.

After Harold Godwinson had eliminated the king of Norway at Stamford Bridge and William (the Conqueror) had in turn defeated Harold and his brothers at Hastings, Swegn of Denmark was left as the main outside threat to William's security. But his invasions in 1069 and 1070, and that of his son Cnut in 1075, although doing much harm, were militarily indecisive. William was greatly alarmed in 1085–6, when Cnut, by then king of Denmark, organized a naval coalition, including Olaf III of Norway (Harold Hardrada's son) and the count of Flanders. But before the invasion fleet could sail Cnut was murdered in the church at Odense and the last great Viking adventure against England came to nought. England was to remain for seventy years in the power of the Norman ducal family, and after that in the hands of its continuation through females.

Political and diplomatic events had given William a claim to England. The spirit of adventure among the Norman aristocracy, possibly due to their Viking origins, and the efficiency of Norman battle tactics, castle building, and general military organization allowed him to press it home. Normans had been seeking their fortune in Italy since early in the 11th century, and the most famous of these, the sons of Tancred of Hauteville-le-Guichard, had by 1066 risen from the ranks of brigands and *condottieri* to create the Norman principality of Capua and the duchy of Apulia and Calabria. William, another who had fought his way out of his initial handicap and difficulties, was no less ambitious.

The Normans, or at least the Norman nobility, were, as the name proclaims, originally Northmen, Vikings who had settled on the south side of the Channel at the turn of the 9th century when the Danelaw had been formed in England. Both colonies were part of the same movement. But the Norman kings of England addressed their writs to their vassals both French and English. Although French served as a blanket description for Normans, Bretons, Flemings and the other Francophones whom William planted in England, it also seems that the Normans viewed themselves officially as French; and this is indeed what they mostly were by 1066 owing to their intermarriage with the natives of their new homeland in Neustria and their adoption of Frankish culture. Possibly because the Viking settlement on the Continent was even more aristocratic than in England (more soldiers and fewer farmers), probably because the environment was more foreign and no accommodation could be made between the language of the settlers and that of the natives, the Northmen gradually adopted the French tongue and most other French customs, and abandoned their own. There is little to distinguish William in 1066 from his rival the count of Anjou, his father-in-law the count of Flanders, his future sons-in-law the count of Blois and the duke of Brittany, or his ally the count of Boulogne. Normandy became feudalized like the rest of northern France, and the Norman church, although under ducal control, was French in its customs. It was no Germanic, or even particularly provincial culture that the Norman aristocracy carried to England, but one as close to the French ideal as it could achieve.

The Norman Conquest was not, therefore, the final Viking success in England. It was a conquest by a French duke, in English eyes much more of a stranger than had been the Danes Swegn and Cnut two generations before. Nor was it the last chapter in the Age of Migrations. In order to share the spoils with his friends and vassals and favoured clerks and monks, William had to eliminate what remained of the higher Anglo-Danish nobility after the battles and revolts and secure the deposition of bishops and abbots. But a good number of English nobles of less importance managed to retain at least part of their estates, or obtain fresh endowments, and survive as tenants of the new magnates. Quite a few abbots, but fewer bishops, were left in their posts. And the lower ranks of society, both lay and clerical, were not greatly disturbed. There was no peasant immigration. Some traders followed the flag and a few Jews from Rouen found a place in some of the largest cities. But that was all. The new high French aristocracy had its followers of all kinds: vassals, knights, household servants and clerks; and on the evidence of Domesday Book, a survey of the king's tenants and their lands and men made in 1086, it can be estimated that some 1,500 foreigners had been endowed with land. The influx, therefore, could have been of the order of five to ten thousand men and women out of a total population of one or two million, that is to say half of one percent.

The newcomers were, however, in the seats of power, a new aristocracy; and became, once the initial hostility had died down, the models for imitation by their social inferiors. Most were from Normandy; but there were important minorities. Among the baronage were some distinguished Bretons; and although they suffered losses because of implication in the rebellion of 1075, Henry I brought new Bretons in. The count of

Boulogne was given by William a large estate. There were also nobles from Flanders, Maine and Aquitaine. And followers were usually of the same race as their lord. A few of the clergy were even more exotic. The first two archbishops of Canterbury were Italians; but when Henry I proposed to appoint a third, Fabrice abbot of Abingdon, his doctor from Arezzo, the barons and bishops demurred. It was time, they thought, that the office should go to a compatriot. The foreign clergy, since they were supposed to be celibate, had no great effect on the racial composition of the kingdom; but they did have some, for they too had households and even the most saintly usually had nephews.

The medieval kingdom

From 1066 until 1144, except for two breaks, England was part of a cross-Channel Norman kingdom, and from 1154 onwards a small piece of a very large Angevin empire. Until the accession of Henry II England was decidedly the weightier part. The kingdom was more important and wealthier than the duchy, the archbishopric of Canterbury more illustrious than that of Rouen. William I emphasized his kingship at the expense of his French titles. William II never, and Henry I rarely, used the ducal title. They were all anxious to appear as kings wherever they were in their dominions. Under the early Angevins, however, although the importance of England and the royal title remained, the kingdom was heavily outweighed by the continental duchies which extended with Aquitaine to the Pyrenees. Moreover, Henry II and his sons reinforced French aspects which had been waning a little in England because of a re-emergence of English culture encouraged both by the passage of time and by the occasional separation of the kingdom from the duchy. The Angevins not only temporarily arrested this process but also reopened England to a French culture much more potent than of old. The exciting new learning to be found in the schools of Paris, exemplified by Peter Abelard, and the resurgent Capetian monarchy were irresistibly attractive.

There was not, however, much change in the racial composition of England after the 1070s. As king, Stephen of Blois employed Flemish mercenary soldiers; the Angevin kings introduced a few of their relatives, nobles and soldiers from other parts of their dominions; under the Angevins the Jewish colonies became more numerous and populous, but remained ghettoes. The absence of further large-scale immigration and the usually strong royal government allowed the country to settle down, and a new English nation came slowly into being. Some racial tension, however, persisted for a long time. The existence of a French-speaking aristocracy with close family and emotional ties with the duchy of Normandy and a prelacy attracted to French schools undoubtedly created a cleavage in English society. By 1100 none of the greater barons, bishops or more important abbots was of native stock, and it was the policy of the Norman kings to deny high

office to the English. After a short time the system became self-perpetuating. This discrimination was greatly resented by those natives, especially clerks and monks, who suffered from it.

Nevertheless, it is doubtful whether the situation was all that different from before. In Anglo-Saxon and Anglo-Danish England there had been a caste nobility, defined by the law, and the nobles had often been foreign – Danish *jarls* over English villages and English earls in the Danelaw. And such racial intensification of class divisions was by no means unusual in other parts of Europe. More important was the absence of racial antipathy in the Anglo-Norman kingdom. The English nobles with their good looks, long hair and excellent manners were well regarded by the Normans and there was some intermarriage among the aristocracy from the beginning. William the Conqueror gave his niece in marriage to Waltheof earl of Northumbria. Lucy, probably the daughter of Earl Ælfgar of Mercia, married successively Ivo Taillebois, a royal steward, Roger fitzGerold of Roumare, and Ranulf le Meschin, lord of Cumberland, and carried the lordship of Bolingbroke to her husbands. Through her second and third marriages she became an ancestor of the earls of Lincoln and of Chester. At lower levels in free society intermarriage was from the beginning common and unremarkable. Even kings took brides of partly English descent. Henry I married the daughter of Malcolm III of Scots and Margaret, Edgar Ætheling's sister, and Stephen married Matilda of Boulogne, their granddaughter. English blood, if only in a trickle, had re-entered the English royal dynasty.

There was also accommodation in the matter of language. The newcomers held on to their French tongue, but in the second generation became mostly bilingual. And those natives who came in regular contact with Normans learned to speak French. The ground was being prepared for an extraordinary enrichment of the English language. As a result of intermarriage and bilingualism, by Henry II's reign the distinction between the two races in free society was being obscured. In the *Dialogue about the Exchequer*, written by the royal treasurer, Richard fitzNeal, in 1177, the pupil asks his master about the murdrum fine, imposed on the neighbourhood when a Norman corpse was found and the murderer could not be identified, a measure introduced by William the Conqueror in order to protect his followers. Was it, the pupil inquires, also levied for the secret death of an Englishman? 'Not originally', replies his mentor; 'but nowadays, when English and Normans live in company and intermarry, the two nations are so mixed that there is no way of telling, in the case of the free classes, who is English and who Norman by birth.' In the case of the unfree, the villeins, however, the presumption was that they were English.

To see the situation in all its dimensions we should notice the two extremes. From 1154 until the end of the 14th century the kings married foreigners exclusively, and thereafter as a rule. In contrast, as Richard fitzNeal pointed out, the bulk of the kingdom's population, the agricultural classes, the farmers and their dependants, had been little affected by any racial changes since the early 10th century. They remained English or Scandinavian, or a mixture of the two. They were mostly bound to the soil and rarely moved from their ancestral home. They spoke a dialect of English and observed provincial customs. These dialects, of course, were also spoken by the gentry and nobility. It was noticed that Samson of Tottington when abbot of Bury St Edmunds in Suffolk (1182–1211) had kept his native Norfolk accent.

A manifold society

English society was manifold. There were both horizontal and vertical divisions, and most were accentuated by racial differences. It is not easy to decide at what point after 1066 one can speak again of English nationality or patriotism. There may never have been much sentiment of that kind among the agricultural classes, with their immobility and close horizons. Village patriots they may always have been. The royal family became increasingly international. But the members of the nobility seem not to have been able to follow in its wake and to have become, by European standards, increasingly provincial, speaking the French not of Paris but of Marlborough or 'the scole of Stratford atte Bowe'. In the course of the 12th century they, together with the country gentlemen, may be considered to have become Englishmen. The church, although 'universal' and using three languages, soon became again the *ecclesia anglicana*. It was indeed the historical writers in the church who gave expression to the continuity of English history. The Anglo-Saxon Chronicle, begun during Alfred's reign, continued without interruption until 1154, and broke off, paradoxically, at the very time when the English language was beginning to recover some of its respectability. Nor were the pre-Conquest English saints forgotten in hagiography. In this way much of England's heroic and spiritual past was recovered and the cleavage of 1066 minimized.

Historians of the 12th century, almost all of mixed Anglo-French blood, continued the same tendency. William of Malmesbury wrote two companion volumes, one on the deeds of the kings of the English, the other on the prelates, drawing upon Bede and the other Anglo-Saxon sources and giving full attention to the earlier centuries. And he was not alone. By seeing English history as a single unbroken line, other writers too were giving their readers a firm emotional link with the past.

In 12th-century Europe, beneath the internationalism of the Latin church and the pervasiveness of French culture, new nations were being formed; and the Celts began to raise their heads again. The Norman bishops in Wales manufactured histories of their dioceses, replete with claims to primacies and independence from Canterbury. Geoffrey of Monmouth, in the 1130s, invented a Welsh history in which are to be found the seeds from which the Arthurian cycle was to grow, and quoted prophecies foretelling the future greatness of Wales. In Henry II's reign, the monks of Glastonbury, quick to exploit a new fashion, found by excavation under an ancient funeral monument the bodies of King Arthur and Queen Guinevere, neatly labelled in their graves.

Even more remarkable was the reception of this British past by medieval English historians. Geoffrey started his pseudo-history with the story of Æneas fleeing from Troy to Italy, where he became the founder of Rome. This hero's great-grandson Brutus, who had accidentally killed his father and been exiled to Greece, after great adventures landed at Totnes in Albion, which he renamed Britain and his companions Britons. Later he founded a city on the Thames which he called New Troy, in after years corrupted into Trinovantum and finally called Kaer-lud, London, after King Lud. After Geoffrey has run through the history of Britain under the Romans we reach, in Book VI, King Vortigern and the Saxon adventurers, Hengist and Horsa. All this and the rest was far more exciting history than writers tied to the more conventional sources could produce. The book was immensely popular from the start, and in the middle of the 12th century first Gaimar, a Norman clerk from Hampshire or eastern England, and then Wace, a Channel Islander, turned it into French verse; and later there were English renderings. Geoffrey had produced one of the most influential romances of all times. Not the least of his achievements was the creation of a new first chapter in the history of England, for after him the story of Æneas and Brutus the Trojan, the founder of Britain, became prefaced in most English histories to the previous opening, 'In the year 449...'. By the 15th century continuations of these vernacular versions of Geoffrey of Monmouth, known as the *Brut* chronicles, had become the standard English history, which had in effect been turned into the history of Britain. The acquisitive English had not only absorbed Celts, Scandinavians, Normans and other Frenchmen but also drawn profitably on the legacies of Rome and Troy. The expansion of Bede's English nation had never ceased for long.

A scene from that great document of early medieval history, the Bayeux Tapestry, showing weapons and mail shirts being transported by Norman soldiers preparing for the invasion of England.

57

2 The Medieval Centuries
The foundation of English institutions up to the Tudors

GEORGE HOLMES

◇

DISTINCTIVE national characteristics were not prominent in high medieval England. The ordinary Englishman of 1300 belonged to a highly centralized European church and was ruled by a government which conducted its correspondence in a foreign tongue. Over him reigned a very powerful king who aspired to control substantial parts of France, as well as the rest of the British Isles. The story we have to tell in this chapter is the process by which this kingdom was transformed into the much more separate, withdrawn society, the politically weaker but more distinctive England of the Tudors, out of which the characteristics of the modern nation grew.

The reign of Edward I (1272–1307) represents the high point of the medieval English monarchy. A contemporary would have regarded Edward as one of the two great princes of the Western world – the other was the king of France; they were without rivals because there was at that time no dominant monarchy in central Europe or Spain. Edward was, as it happened, a masterful, aggressive ruler, but his pre-eminence resulted also from the fact that the state which he inherited was reaching a summit of institutional development.

To begin with, Edward did not rule only over England. He completed the conquest of Wales and instituted the tradition that the king's eldest son should be prince of Wales. The Welsh became for over two centuries a subject people ruled either by marcher lords or by the king or prince. Edward also had a substantial foothold on the Continent. He had inherited his ancestor's lands in Gascony, a fluctuating and disputed area centring on Bordeaux, already a metropolis of the wine export trade. His deputies governed from Bordeaux and the accounts they sent home are still stored among the public records in London. Like his ancestors again, Edward ruled an uncertain area of Ireland. But the greatest venture of his reign was his attempt to unite the whole of the island of Britain by becoming king of Scotland. The opportunity was offered by the extinction of the Scottish ruling house in the main line. Edward tried to go beyond arbitration between candidates to assert his own sovereignty as overlord. In doing so, he came up against the resistance of the Scots gentry to a foreign king, and Scotland produced its national hero, Robert Bruce, a leader of genius who humiliated the English more effectively than any other Scots ruler (his greatest victory,

Bannockburn, was won against Edward's much less effective son, Edward II, in 1314) and ensured that the kingdoms would never be united by English conquest. In spite of his failure finally to subdue Scotland, however, Edward ruled over a vast empire stretching from the Pyrenees to the Scottish Highlands.

Machinery of the state

Within England herself some national institutions were indeed already assuming forms which would persist for centuries, in some cases into recent times. It was characteristic of England, an exceptionally united monarchy at that stage, that it enjoyed a largely unified judicial system and a distinctive law. As everywhere in the medieval world there were, of course, separate church courts and many lords administered lower forms of justice on their manors, but for free laymen justice in general meant the law administered in the king's courts. Royal judges travelled the country holding assize courts in the county towns. In most parts of Europe Roman law was widely in use; in England the 'common law' consisted of the legal principles which had been evolved pragmatically in the practice of the king's courts. The common law was not based on a code but essentially on precedent, modified only to a limited extent by legislation. This peculiarly English approach to law, quite separate from the legal codes of continental Europe although it was later to be exported to the English-speaking countries of North America and Australasia, already had a full century of development behind it.

Another result of the highly unified English monarchy was the practice of holding 'parliaments' – the word was already acquiring a fairly precise meaning as the description of a distinct institution – in which the politically important classes of the whole country were regularly represented. Parliamentary institutions of one kind or another were common in medieval Europe. The modern pre-eminence of the 'mother of parliaments' is due not to any original priority but to its survival through later ages when parallel institutions were widely suppressed in absolute monarchies. But, as Robert Blake describes in more detail in Chapter Four, the forms of a modern Parliament do display a remarkable continuity from its 14th-century predecessors. Essentially a Parliament was attended by three kinds of people. The great lords – a few dozen earls and nobles, the bishops and greater abbots – were

adjunct of monarchy, but even more because his vast apparatus of war depended on heavy taxation. Taxation took various forms but the reason why Edward was a rich king who could confront the king of France on something like equal terms was the enormous profitability of the wool export trade. The mild, damp climate and the green sheep pastures made medieval England the greatest wool producer in the world. Every village common supported sheep and in some parts of the country flocks of many thousands were profitably maintained on extensive sheep runs by the great monasteries. Every year huge quantities of this essential raw material were shipped from Hull and London to the looms of the textile cities of Flanders and Tuscany. Like the oil of modern Arabia, wool was a product for which the industrial world of that time had an apparently insatiable appetite and it was, therefore, a perfect object for heavy taxation. On the basis of its agriculture and its relatively backward industry, Edwardian England would not have been a dominant power – wool made the crucial difference. As a later poet wrote anonymously ('The Libelle of English Policy', c. 1437): 'Of Brutus' Albion his wool is chief richesse', neatly incorporating in one line the romantic claim of the kings of England that their monarchy was established by the legendary Trojan heroes of antiquity and the modern economic reality that the power of their kingdom was based on the wool trade.

Medieval England was, to a degree remarkable perhaps even in that warlike world, a society geared for war. Apart from the permanent problem of the Scottish border, England and France confronted each other in poses of traditional hostility. The standing reason for this was the position of Gascony: the king of England was its duke, the king of France in that respect his feudal overlord, anxious to assert his sovereignty over the whole land of France and, if possible, to drive out the intruder. Edward I fought the French for many years in Gascony and attempted an unsuccessful invasion of France through Flanders. A period of weak kingship in both England and France in the reign of Edward II (1307–27) was followed by the reign of the most fortunate of all warrior kings, Edward III (1327–77), and the beginning of the series of conflicts known as the Hundred Years War (1337–1453).

Edward III added a new and more ambitious war aim, the Crown of France, which he claimed by right of his mother, a French king's daughter. He had a gift for

individually summoned as the peers and bishops are to the modern House of Lords. A great many towns were each represented by two men chosen from their burgesses. Rural society supplied two 'knights of the shire', chosen in each county by the gentry and farmers who attended the county court. The characteristic division of a Parliament into two houses, one containing the lords, the other the county and town representatives, emerged in the course of the 14th century. This is an important characteristic of the English political system because it placed the country squire and the city merchant side by side in the same assembly. Although Englishmen have always been class-conscious, sharp distinctions of caste between noble and commoner, between rural seigneur and town burgess, have always been strikingly absent from English society. The formalities of the medieval Parliament encouraged gentry and merchants to think of themselves as belonging to a single political community.

It is safe to assume that such a dominating and ambitious king as Edward did not hold these assemblies because he was unduly sensitive to the interests and wishes of his subjects. He was compelled to summon them because a forum for the expression of grievances and the presentation of petitions was a necessary comradeship in arms which made him an extraordinarily successful leader of the nobility and gentry. His court became a famous centre of chivalric manners, both in their military aspect and in the form of courtly behaviour to ladies. He sought to recreate King Arthur's legendary company of knights: the round table made to his command survives to this day at Winchester. An incident of courtly gallantry led to the foundation of the Order of the Garter, an order of chivalry which embraced the king's most trusted brothers-in-arms and which became immediately the inner social élite of the English lay world.

These romantic institutions were not merely adornments of aristocratic life. The members of the Order of the Garter were the spearhead of a powerful military machine which defeated French armies at Crécy (1346) and Poitiers (1356) and controlled large parts of France for long periods. The English nobility and gentry, the knights and squires who led the armies, became addicted to warfare in the rich lands across the channel. For decades scarcely a year passed without some English expedition to France. Warfare, which was justified by legal claims, became a way of life in which individual glory and plunder (which Jean Froissart, the French chronicler of these wars, said that the English loved more than other men) was as important as the ostensible political aims. The English upper classes became a plundering and marauding nobility perhaps to a greater extent than ever before.

Faith and reason

The aggressive society which produced the archers of Crécy was also, however, very much united with continental Europe in the Catholic Church. In many respects England before the time of John Wycliffe was a model of orthodoxy, scarcely touched by the heresies which disturbed the prelates of other parts of Europe. In part we must attribute this to relative social backwardness. England was less urbanized than other major countries of Western Europe; London was its only genuine city and London was a commercial and administrative rather than an industrial metropolis. It was a society in which the characteristic institutions of the Western church flourished to a large extent in undisturbed seignorial grandeur: the bishop ruling over his largely rural diocese, the monastery lavishly accommodating its little group of privileged contemplatives. Something of the splendour and power of the medieval diocese can easily be recaptured by a visit to one of the smaller cathedral cities – say Salisbury, Wells or Ely – where the towers and spires built in the 13th and 14th centuries still dwarf the town. The monasteries of medieval England are in ruins but some of them – Benedictine St Albans and Bury St Edmunds, Cistercian Fountains – were among the mightiest and richest in Europe. There were few English cardinals and, after the 12th century, no English pope, but the integration of the English church into the European church was complete.

With no pope and very few saints, the church of high medieval England was extraordinarily successful in producing scholars and scientists. If Paris was the scholastic capital of Europe, Oxford ran it a close second. Little of pre-Black Death Oxford survives. The richly endowed and architecturally splendid colleges were mainly a later phenomenon, starting with William of Wykeham's New College in 1377; the students of high medieval Oxford lived in less grand private halls of residence. But Oxford was in the early 14th century already, by medieval standards, a large university with perhaps about 2,000 students. It was part of the international life of Europe, although its main function was to prepare aspirants to careers in the upper levels of the English church. It also produced a remarkable series of thinkers, outstanding in the main European stream of philosophical theology, culminating in the two great names of Duns Scotus, a synthesizer of reason and faith whose ideas are still sometimes regarded with approval by Catholics, and William of Ockham. Like Scotus, Ockham was a Franciscan, unlike him he was a rebel by temperament who rejected the rational demonstrations of religious truth and was summoned to the papal court to answer for his errors. It was not so conspicuous at the time, but historians now recognize the peculiar importance of the Oxford tradition of physical science which led up to the Merton College school in the 14th century in which some of the antecedents of the theories of Galileo are to be found. These men place Oxford at the heart of the medieval intellectual tradition in the early 14th century. Not until the days of Isaac Newton and John Locke, centuries later, was England to re-enter and dominate the main stream in this way again.

The Black Death and its aftermath

This society was partly shattered and largely transformed by the effects of one of the great natural catastrophes of history: the Black Death and the further outbreaks of the bubonic plague which followed it. The plague reached England in 1348 and in that and the next year killed an enormous number of people, perhaps as many as forty per cent of the population. There were further large-scale epidemics later in the century. Thereafter plague remained a continual, although less spectacular, hazard of life and did not disappear until the 1660s. It was in the period from 1350 to 1470 that its effects were most strongly felt because the early epidemics led to a massive distortion in the age-structure of the population which prevented the normal replenishment of numbers while the depressive effects of minor outbreaks was still continuing. The result of this was that England was much more thinly peopled in the 15th century than it had been in the 13th. There are places such as the margins of the fens in south Lincolnshire where it can be shown that the population did not return to its medieval density until the 19th century. England in 1300 had been a rather heavily populated country, precariously fed by the primitive

High medieval society had been steeply hierarchical. At the top a few earls and bishops controlled vast estates: from some of their lands they collected rents, others they farmed, encouraged by the abundance of labour and the scarcity of food, as great ranches and plantations. At the bottom the village was often a 'manor' over which a lord held petty jurisdiction exercised in his court. The villagers were divided between freemen and villeins or serfs, the latter bound to their tenements and liable to be sold with them by the lord or obliged to do regular compulsory labour for him – similar in fact to 'souls' who made up the patrimony of a Russian nobleman before the Emancipation of the Serfs. The fall in population was a massive blow to this social structure. However much parliaments tried to fix wages by Statutes of Labourers, they could not prevent them rising. However much landlords tried to tie down their serfs, they could not prevent village families dying out or survivors fleeing to more profitable employment elsewhere. The result of this was a general levelling effect on society and a general relaxation of seignorial control. Serfdom, universal and normal in 1300, was becoming rare by 1500. Great landlords, such as the bishop of Winchester, gave up trying to farm their own estates. The manorial court had less and less influence over the village. Low food prices made the 15th century a golden age for the English wage-earner. The magnates of the Wars of the Roses period in the 15th century, Warwick the Kingmaker and his like, dangerously powerful as they might seem, actually had much less control over their subordinates than their ancestors had had two centuries earlier.

The English spirit revives

The beginning of this social transformation coincided with an equally profound intellectual and spiritual change. The age of the Black Death was also the age of the revival of English. Nothing, of course, is more crucial to the sense of identity of a nation than the possession of a common language. Medieval England was in this respect a peculiar society because its own language was submerged below two others. In the first place, there was the universal use of Latin as the language of the church and of scholarship: that was common to the whole of Europe. But, in addition, England had been conquered by a French-speaking Norman nobility. These nobles continued to use French and, in this respect at least, did not for centuries become entirely assimilated to the Englishmen whom they had conquered. When noblemen and gentlemen wrote to each other they wrote in French. More than this, they imposed upon the conquered English a government conducted in the conquerors' tongue. The language of parliamentary records and of pleading in the law courts was French – to this day many of the key words of English law are of French origin. Precisely because of the ubiquity of French as the official language wherever Latin was not used, it is difficult to

William of Wykeham, lord chancellor and bishop of Winchester, was the founder of two great centres of learning, New College, Oxford (1377), shown here in the background, and Winchester College (1382) for '70 pore and needy scholars' (see p. 39).

methods of agriculture; it has even been suggested that it was subject to Malthusian checks by famine like densely peopled parts of South Asia in modern times. In the 15th century, in contrast, cultivation was cut back, some villages disappeared and the 'park', an enclosed area of grass and woodland in which herds of deer could roam freely for the landlord's delight, became a characteristic feature of the English landscape. A Venetian visitor to England about 1500 commented on the great profusion of animals both wild and domestic, but also said that on a journey from Dover to London and Oxford he found the country thinly populated by humans.

The era of plague certainly had profound physical results. Whether it had direct psychological effects – so that, as has been suggested, the 15th-century poem with the monotonous refrain *timor mortis conturbat me*, 'the fear of death troubles me', reflects a general heightened sense of life's transience under the impression of the prevalence of disease – is much more debatable. Its social effects on the character of English society, however, were as remarkable as its impact on the aspect of the land. The prolonged change in the general relationship of land and men had the simple economic result that food became cheap, labour became expensive and tenants became scarce. This affected the structure of rural society from top to bottom by weakening the power of landlords.

Chivalry in matters of war and matters of love was the required characteristic of the medieval knight, vividly portrayed in Chaucer's 'Canterbury Tales' for which this woodcut of c.1490 is an illustration.

discover just how much the use of English survived or how quickly it climbed back up the social scale. As early as 1258 an important state document, the Provisions of Oxford, was circulated in English, presumably so that it could be widely understood by the lesser gentry and farmers, but this was very unusual. A subterranean stream of literature in English flowed through the three hundred years of French supremacy. Works of devotion such as *Handlyng Synne* show that English was used by monks, stories of romance chivalry such as *Guy of Warwick* show that there were gentry households in which polite literature was read in English rather than French. Official letters and documents in French must often conceal the actual use of the English tongue.

The revival came in the century from 1350 to 1450. It took two forms. Firstly, English crept up into the upper levels of administration and formal correspondence. Externally the take-over was far from complete. For example, the Exchequer continued to keep its records in Latin and the law courts in Latin or French. On the other hand, the language of parliamentary records and of much routine government correspondence was English by the early 15th century. This certainly makes a difference to the historian. When we read a letter by Henry V to one of his councillors in 1417: 'Tiptoft, I charge ye, by the faith that ye owe to me, that ye keep this matter, hereafter written, from all men secret save from my brother th'Emperor own person', we hear him speaking as we have not heard any English king before him. It must also have made a considerable difference to the sense of a common nationality in Englishmen, transcending class and separating them from other nations across the Channel.

The other form which the English revival took was the complete ousting of French as the language of imaginative literature. This was decisively achieved when the court of Richard II patronized an esquire writing in English for the delectation of his social

superiors, a man now reckoned among the great European poets, Geoffrey Chaucer. Chaucer's impact on the English-speaking mind has been so great that it is now almost impossible for us to visualize medieval England without reference to his gallery of portraits in the Prologue to the *Canterbury Tales*. Chaucer's characters are types but they are presented with such a complex indication of the ironies of their social position that the nuances of English life spring suddenly into view. The Franklin, a rich farmer, sure of his material security but unsure when it comes to handling the courtly ethos which is natural to the knight and the squire, appears to us with scarcely less realism than the people of Henry Fielding and Jane Austen. The marriage of the English language with the literary inspiration of the Italian Renaissance achieved an immediate identification of the national scene and enrichment of the imagination. In contrast, Chaucer's contemporary William Langland in *Piers Plowman* gives us a picture of English society from below, illuminated by the mind of a visionary with his eyes fixed on the ultimate Christian purpose of life. How much of the English mind we can see already established in the writings of these two giants!

The same generation saw the first emergence of distinctively English religious movements. The orthodoxy of religious life in medieval England was compatible with a strong tradition of anticlericalism. Kings and magnates persistently quarrelled with bishops and with the pope. Edward III's great son, the Black Prince, renowned as a model of piety and chivalry, was a hammer of the church when it came to questions of taxing clerical incomes to support his wars. At lower levels laymen resented the parson's demand for tithes or the pope's interference in the appointment of parish clergy. Was there a subterranean current of heterodox lay piety similar to that of the English language? The records of the church do not tell us. On the surface everything was changed by John Wycliffe. This learned, laborious, ambitious Oxford theologian, an unattractive man but unquestionably one of the creators of the English spirit, was employed by the court as an anticlerical spokesman and then emerged in the years 1376 to 1384 as a heretical writer on a grand scale, denouncing the pretensions of the priesthood, asserting the supremacy of the Bible and the lay conscience. Wycliffe was hounded out of Oxford and his learned writings were effectively suppressed. But his ideas and followers provided a focus for much more widespread discontent with the existing structure of the orthodox church and its doctrine. The only serious attempt at this period to overturn the church, the march on London of a heterogeneous rabble led by Sir John Oldcastle in 1414, was put down in a few hours. The importance of the Lollards, as the unorthodox of the 15th century were called, was the unspectacular infusion of independent attitudes to religion among a wide variety of classes of ordinary people. Lollard culture was based on the English language, so here are the roots of the identification of national religion with certain kinds of individualistic protest. Wycliffe's disciples translated the Latin Bible into English, so providing an essential tool for Lollard lay piety and evangelism. Many fragments of Lollard writing in English survive showing that a religious movement of this kind was necessarily linked with writings in the vernacular.

Lost empires

While French and Latin loosened their grip, the medieval English state was also being undermined to make way for the emergence of the rather different monarchy of the Tudors. Edward I and Edward III had been great potentates ruling over the toiling masses of a heavily populated land. A century later the picture was somewhat changed. The most measurable aspect of the change was the decline in the Crown's command over material resources, which was to a large extent the result of social and economic evolution. The wool trade, which had given earlier kings marvellous financial strength, declined. It was replaced by a cloth-exporting industry. The result must have been an economic benefit to a large section of the king's subjects but it was almost sheer loss to the king because cloth could not bear a heavy tax.

The monarchy of the 15th century was also crippled by an obsolete system of property taxation: the village tax assessments made in 1334 were still being used a century and a half later when they were, of course, hopelessly out of date. One of the more ill-judged attempts to replace that system was the poll tax which sparked off the Peasants' Revolt of 1381. For a few days a rural mob occupied London, terrorized the courtiers and slew the archbishop although it failed to cow the boy king Richard II. The politically conscious were more wary of tax experiments after that experience.

Perhaps the 15th-century monarchy was weakened most of all by the smaller numbers and higher living standards of its subjects. No longer could the king call on masses of impressed infantry from the English and Welsh counties to swell the numbers of his armies in Scotland and France. The armies of Agincourt (1415) and other battles of the 15th century were smaller and better paid and a higher proportion of the soldiers enjoyed the luxury of riding on horseback.

If we look at the reigns in long perspective through the century of Edward III (1327–77), Richard II (1377–99), Henry IV (1399–1413), Henry V (1413–22) and Henry VI (1422–61) what we see, in spite of the meteoric achievement of one of these kings, Henry V, is the decline of an impressive monarchy into a state of relative impotence. Henry VI founded King's College Chapel but he would have been utterly incapable of carrying out Edward I's majestic enterprise of building Caernarvon and all the other great castles in North Wales. He could not pay his soldiers or stop his nobles resorting to arms to settle their private quarrels. It is true that Henry VI in his later years was 'simple', but his

powerlessness was also the result of a structural weakness in the state.

Yet it was in this period that the English established and held for a generation an empire in northern France. That surprising achievement can be explained by two factors. First, the weakness of France which happened to be divided by warring factions and open to relatively easy invasion. Second, the military genius of Henry V. Henry is outstanding among English monarchs as a ruthlessly efficient prosecutor of war. He devoted himself to the extension of his power with a puritanical single-mindedness and skill which place him among the great conquerors. Perhaps, as he promised, he did intend eventually to lead Europe on crusade. What he achieved in only five years before his early death at the age of thirty-five in 1422 was to conquer north-western France and establish a government at Rouen and Paris. Henry's aim was not merely to plunder France but to subdue it and rule it as king. He died leaving as heir a child less than a year old so that the chances of realizing that plan were greatly reduced, but the child, Henry VI, was eventually crowned at Paris and for about fifteen years a dual monarchy genuinely existed. It is difficult to imagine how that monarchy could have developed into a viable state if it had survived, but for some years it seemed strong. Then the inevitable revival of the Valois monarchy, initiated in popular legend by Joan of Arc, gradually squeezed the English out. In 1428 they had controlled most of France west of Paris and north of the Loire. By 1445 they were out of nearly all except Normandy and Gascony. By 1453 those too were gone. The Hundred Years War ended with the king of England ousted even from those territories which Edward III had started by trying to safeguard. Only Calais remained, a strongly fortified English outpost, retained because it was the home of the Company of the Staple. The taxation of the dwindling wool trade paid for its ruinously expensive upkeep, until Mary lost it in 1558. The expulsion of the English from France in 1453 was both the end of a dream and a turning point in English society. The implications of this change extended further than the loss of Henry V's conquests. The end of British rule in India springs to mind as a remote but not totally inappropriate parallel. A great field of activity for the English upper classes was closed for ever. From 1066 to 1453 there was no time when the English nobility were not involved to a lesser or greater extent in soldiering in some part of France. For the last hundred years the nobility and the state had been exceptionally absorbed in this activity. That was all ended. It was impossible that the character of the state and of the nobility should not as a result be transformed. Never again would an English king invade France with an army led, in effect, by his earls as Edward III and Henry V had. The end of continental warfare reduced the importance of the nobility in England in the long run because they ceased to be the main beneficiaries of a system of taxation designed primarily to pay soldiers. It also banished the chivalric way of life to the realm of nostalgia. Naturally, the English empire in France had encouraged a revival of interest in the knightly arts. Among the humble knights who were attached to one of the great commanders, Richard Beauchamp, earl of Warwick, was – if he has been identified correctly – Sir Thomas Malory, the author of *Morte d'Arthur*. That book was composed in prison at the end of an extremely turbulent life and during the Wars of the Roses; its tale of disastrous treachery and turmoil aptly marks the end of the age in which the ethos of courtly romance had predominated in society and politics.

A changing land

Below the romantic surface of nobility and chivalry, humbler folk were changing the character of the English economy in the most fundamental way by the extension of industry. A country which essentially exported a raw material, wool, was being slowly changed into a country which exported a manufactured product, cloth. The change was fundamental because the cloth industry was soon to be found in so many English counties, widely spread and woven into the fabric of English rural society. This is the origin of one of the characteristic features of English society and one of the preconditions of the Industrial Revolution which was to follow three centuries later. The great industrial centres of the high Middle Ages in continental Europe had been cities and even in England the embryonic small-scale cloth industry of an earlier period tended to be concentrated in towns such as Leicester and Oxford. The forces of the post-Black Death era not only encouraged the textile industry to expand greatly but also diffused it. While some towns, Coventry for example, famous for its caps in the 16th century, continued to be textile centres, the industry spread to a greater extent over the countryside, attracted by local wool, purer streams and unorganized labour. The typical English weaver – the last of the line is George Eliot's Silas Marner – was an independent cottager, not a factory worker, not even a member of a town guild. The great areas of the new industry were the West Riding of Yorkshire, the Cotswolds and East Anglia. Typical successful clothing centres, such as Lavenham in Suffolk or Castle Combe in Wiltshire, still display the characteristics of overgrown villages – these, not the cities, were the industrial centres of the new age. This development did not carry with it a general industrial growth. In many sectors – mining and metals for example – England was backward in 1500 in comparison with the advanced areas of continental Europe. But the ubiquity of the cloth industry and its integration into rural society meant that a whole nation was being involved in manufacture and commerce.

Even at the end of the 15th century the English were far from controlling their own overseas commerce and shipping. Quite a lot of the cloth that flowed into London was carried to the Continent by Hansards or Genoese or in Dutch ships: a further sign of relative economic backwardness. But there were also important signs of commercial enterprise. The largest and most promising outlets for English cloth at this period were to be reached through the trading metropolis of Antwerp at the mouth of the Rhine. There was, therefore, a growing commercial link between London and Antwerp. The chief operators in this trade were the Merchant Adventurers of London who already had an organization in Antwerp at the beginning of the 15th century. The great names of English commerce in this period belong to this group. One of them, William Caxton, introduced printing into England from the Low Countries in 1468. Another, who lived at a time when the trade was in decline, was Thomas Gresham, financial adviser to Elizabeth I and founder of the Royal Exchange, credited with the principle that 'bad money drives out good'. Between Caxton and Gresham was a century in which the Antwerp cloth trade was England's main economic strength.

If London was by far the greatest, Bristol, on the other hand, was the most completely English of the major ports and, through its ancient trade with Spain, the most likely to develop an interest in the Mediterranean and the wider Atlantic. Bristol merchants had tried without much success to break into the Mediterranean long before the 15th century was over, but it was from Bristol that the Genoese John Cabot sailed to the New World with Henry VII's licence in 1497. It was from a still more English and much more obscure harbour, Plymouth, that William Hawkins traded with Brazil in the 1530s. The oceanic expansion of England was in the future but its seeds were hidden in the pirate-infested creeks of the West Country.

How far were the hierarchies of high medieval society levelled by the social movements of the post-Black Death era? The most perceptive writer on late medieval England in recent times, K. B. McFarlane, popularized the term 'bastard feudalism' to describe the prevalent networks of relationships between laymen in the English countryside. The phrase indicates that they lived within a looser framework of dependence on or deference to great lords, but one which still gave the magnates considerable power. As late as the reign of Elizabeth it was possible for John Aylmer, bishop of London, to write:

'If there be any noble man dwelling in the country, either a duke, a marquess, an earl or a baron, he shall lightly have in his retinue all the cobs in the country. . . . And if any matters be touching him, his man or his friend, whether it be a crime capital or *nisi prius* sent down for lands the case shall weigh as he will.'

Later overmighty subjects – such as Warwick the 'Kingmaker' in the Wars of the Roses or Protector Somerset in the mid-16th century – did not, however, command the relative wealth and power of their ancestors such as Thomas earl of Lancaster in the reign of Edward II. Wealth had shifted somewhat down the social scale to the gentry. It is in the 15th century also that the English gentry first appear to us as real people in the English letters of the Paston family. The Pastons were East Anglian lawyers and landowners of the middle rank. Their class is in many respects the dominant one in early modern English society. It was they who ruled the country from their manor houses as justices of the peace, who represented it in Parliament as MPs; it was from their class that the nobility and the officialdom of the king's court were endlessly replenished.

England turns inward

The prolonged crisis of the English state in the later 15th century, usually known as the Wars of the Roses, has an exaggerated reputation as a watershed between the medieval and modern worlds. The wars were a series of disputes about who should be king, settled in the end by the effective seizure of the throne by the Tudor Henry VII in 1485. The more important underlying change in the character of the state, the shrinkage of the power of the medieval monarchy and nobility, which we have already mentioned, was neither the cause nor the result of the Wars of the Roses.

Nevertheless, it is true that the new dynasties which emerged out of the wars, York and Tudor, did set the English monarchy on a different path. They were compelled to do so by the undermining of the old bases of power. It was a path, on the whole, of narrower and more modest aims, less grandiose power, more consideration for the interests of a wider section of the king's subjects. The Yorkist and Tudor kings for the most part managed to avoid expensive entanglements on the Continent. Both Edward IV and Henry VII allowed themselves to be bought off by French bribes. The exception was Henry VIII, whose ambition for European glory carried him into war with France as a young man in 1512 and again as an old man in 1544. The second enterprise was financially disastrous: it resulted in the king selling his estates and debasing the coinage. What these wars showed was that, given the economy of the country and the system of taxation, the early Tudor state was quite incapable of fighting on equal terms with the dominant Valois and Habsburg monarchies. England was not quite a first-rank power. With the exception of Cardinal Wolsey's brief, skilful management of European diplomacy, England tended to stand slightly apart from the battles of the two giants. Modern England begins as something much more like an 'offshore island' than medieval England was, withdrawn because of the more modest development of its wealth and state power.

The Tudors did not attempt any very radical improvement of their taxation system. They continued to rely on a parsimonious House of Commons for subsidies which were sparingly doled out for the emergencies of defence, although in practice used to keep the machinery of state going in peace as well. Yorkists and Tudors made more of an effort than their predecessors to live off the proceeds of their lands and they made this slightly more possible by snatching other people's lands. Henry VII was notably unwilling to let go of estates which fell to the Crown as feudal rights. Henry VIII carried out the last great land-grab in the dissolution of the monasteries (1536/9) which temporarily swelled the landed wealth of the Crown considerably – temporarily because it was soon dissipated to pay for war. The Tudor state also remained restricted in its personnel, almost a skeletal state in comparison with the expanding bureaucracies of the continental monarchies. The monarchy had few local officials apart from sheriffs, estate managers, collectors of customs and assize judges. It depended for the execution of its wishes on the co-operation of nobility and gentry. It was essentially a regime which depended on consent, in the broadest sense, rather than imposed power. Occasionally – as in the Pilgrimage of Grace of 1536 when northern gentlemen rose in anger against excessive meddling in their affairs, or in Kett's Rebellion of 1549 when Norfolk countrymen rose in despair about their social depression – the system of consent broke down. For the most part it worked because the Crown did not demand very much of its subjects and allowed a large autonomy to local society. This characteristically limited nature of English government was largely the result of the weakness and self-abnegation of the late medieval monarchy. It is a very important long-term feature of English history. English government remained simple and limited until 1914 along lines established in the 14th and 15th centuries.

Only within this perspective can one judge properly the ambitious efforts of reorganization which are associated with the three major figures of the reign of Henry VIII: the king himself, Cardinal Wolsey and Thomas Cromwell. Henry was certainly larger than life but he was also a good delegator, not anxious to be immersed in the details of administration himself. He allowed Wolsey to carry out an impressive reform of some aspects of the central law courts. Cromwell has been credited by Professor G. R. Elton with a 'Tudor revolution in government' because of his establishment of a properly organized Privy Council and a more effective administration of the various courts which managed the king's revenues. Cromwell was a new – and for a long time to come unique – figure in the management of the English state, a businessman of humble origins without the usual qualifications, either lay or clerical, which the court demanded of its administrators. He gave shape and purpose to the institutions of monarchical government, but he did not overcome their essential limitations. The most fundamental change which English society suffered in the Tudor period was, of course, another matter – the Reformation.

Although the Reformation was eventually to lead to the creation of a national church which defined many of the limits of the modern English mind, its original intellectual inspirations were mostly imported from abroad. Pre-Reformation England was remarkably barren of intellectual or aesthetic life. Lollardy was a widespread state of mind but primitive and incoherent in its doctrines. Oxford in the 15th century was passing through one of its periods of stately torpor. The brightest star in the spiritual firmament of the early Tudor period, Sir Thomas More, was an exotic in the English landscape: a man who practised conservatively severe asceticism but had been deeply touched by the ideas of the continental Renaissance emanating from Erasmus and the Italians. Renaissance influences introduced a new kind of idealism, the conception of a simpler and purer religious life and impatience with the stale luxuriance of ritual and scholasticism. So far as the court of Henry VIII was animated by an ideal, it was this. Although the reformers martyred More, they shared some of his ideas. This enlightened stream of thought persisted through the terrorism and persecution of the Reformation period to be found in the circle of Henry's last queen, the pious and intellectual Catherine Parr and in the courts of his children, all of whom were in different ways strikingly well-educated and serious-minded princes. A quite different mode of religious thought combined with a rejection of papal authority sprang from Luther's reformation in Germany. Henry earned the title 'Defender of the Faith' by attacking it, but his own later Reformation owed a good deal to it. And finally, by the 1540s England was beginning to be touched by the more radical religious doctrines associated with Calvin which aimed rationally to sweep away much medieval doctrine and organization. These strands of thought, rather than any native ideas, provided the materials for early Anglicanism.

The act of state which constituted the Reformation, making the King in Parliament, instead of the pope, the ultimate authority in the English church, was in some ways a natural consummation of the tendencies of the previous two centuries. Since the Great Schism of the late 14th century, papal authority had been greatly restricted. Even Henry V, who was notable for his orthodox piety, refused to allow his uncle to be made a cardinal for fear of the infringement of Canterbury's, and his own, authority in the church which might result. Papal powers to tax and appoint were, in practice, much more limited than they had been. Nevertheless, the Act of Supremacy of 1532 was a very sharp institutional break. At a blow it destroyed papal control over doctrine and jurisdiction. From one point of view, and perhaps this is historically the most important, it was a further cutting of the links between England and continental Europe. The typical Englishman of the later 16th century would regard the whole Catholic world with fear and distrust.

The most decisive feature of the Reformation was negative: the abolition of the monasteries, the mendicant orders and the chantries. The implications of this revolution are incalculable, not only or indeed primarily because of the economic change involved in

the seizure and transfer of property on such a vast scale but because of the total removal of certain features of life from the English scene. With one stroke the contemplative life ceased to be assumed as a necessary function of society; with another stroke the function of continual prayer for the souls of the dead was abolished. These were social amputations to which there is no parallel in English history, at least since the devastating aftermath of the Norman Conquest of 1066.

The most lasting achievement of English monasticism, taken in the broadest sense, is the remarkable group of 14th-century mystical writings which includes the anonymous *Cloud of Unknowing* and the *Showings* of Lady Juliana, the recluse of Norwich. It may be possible to maintain that the monastic life was a rather exotic importation from the Mediterranean but these writings show that it had taken deep root and spread widely. It is difficult to point to any more fundamental distinction between the societies of modern England on the one hand and France, Italy and Spain on the other, than that resulting from the extinction of the religious orders and all they stood for.

In place of Catholic Christianity with its strong emphasis on the distinction between the spiritual (represented by monastic asceticism and priesthood) and temporal, the Reformation established a religious framework which in many ways conformed to the attitudes of the medieval lay critics of the church. It confirmed the alliance between the parson and the squire, the archbishop and the king. It emphasized the biblical side of Christianity. It produced a doctrine in which compromise and ambiguity allowed a fairly wide spectrum of opinion. The two basic documents of English Christianity are the English Bible and the Prayer Book. The introduction of the general use of an English Bible, in the version compiled by Miles Coverdale, was essentially the work of Cromwell in the 1530s. The new orders of service reached maturity in the second Prayer Book of Thomas Cranmer, the first Anglican archbishop, which was published in 1552. Cromwell and Cranmer rather than Henry VIII were the creators of the new Church of England. An oddly assorted but complementary pair, the ruthless intriguer and the sensitive intellectual, jointly established the framework of a national religious style. By mid-century – or to be more precise by the accession of Elizabeth I in 1558 – England was totally severed from Catholic Europe.

Part of the title page of the first printed English Bible, Coverdale's translation.

3 Ruling Dynasties and the Great Families

The historic role of the monarchy and aristocracy

MICHAEL MACLAGAN

◇

WHEN DARKNESS FELL over the bloodstained hills of Sussex on 14 October 1066, few people can have had any idea of what had happened. A king of England had been slain; another invading force had won a great battle, but the future was as obscure as the night. In the event, Anglo-Saxon resistance crumbled and the Norman victor was able to establish himself as King William I. By the time of his death he had set up a new Anglo-Norman society and linked the fortunes of England with those of his own duchy of Normandy.

For generations 1066 has been regarded as a crucial date in English history; to contemporaries it probably appeared less startling. William was an alien conqueror: so had been Cnut. No hereditary principle had been established about the succession to the throne; indeed, between 1016 and 1216, only one person became king (Richard I) whom we would todày regard as the proper heir of his predecessor. Before 1066 there was a preference for an adult, competent member of the house of Alfred; since 1066 all English rulers have at least boasted the blood of William the Conqueror.

No royal house has reigned in Britain for long, and none has been of mainly English descent. The Normans could be described as Vikings with a touch of French polish. They were followed by the Plantagenets who originated in Anjou in northern France. In 1485 the last Plantagenet king, Richard III, was overthrown and killed by the upstart Welshman, Henry Tudor (Henry VII), but the family of the latter endured a mere three generations. From 1603 to 1714 England, as well as Scotland, was ruled by members of the Scottish house of Stuart, whose earliest origins were Breton. The reign of the last Stuart, Queen Anne, witnessed the welding of the two realms into the kingdom of Great Britain. On her death, she was succeeded, in the interests of the Protestant religion, by the Elector George of Hanover, a German of mainly Teutonic ancestry, whose descendants all married German princesses. Queen Victoria, in her turn, married Prince Albert of Saxe-Coburg-Gotha and our present Queen is her great-great-granddaughter. The Duke of Edinburgh stems paternally from the royal house of Denmark; accordingly the ascending male ancestry of Prince Charles derives from Danish sources.

The Norman Conquest

William the Conqueror laid great stress on his position as the heir of Edward the Confessor. He found much to admire and preserve in the late Anglo-Saxon system of government. His followers, who were drawn from the full length of the north coastline of France, naturally expected reward in the form of land. The former nobility amounted to perhaps four or five thousand nobles, generally described as *thegns*; they were not necessarily of ancient lineage, for many must have achieved their position during the Danish invasions of the past century. This old Anglo-Danish aristocracy was eliminated or depressed: many had no doubt fallen in the three great battles of 1066; some may have become agents of the alien newcomer or clung to a tiny corner of their ancient territory. When, at the end of his life, William I compiled the massive land survey which has been known as Domesday Book since the 12th century, the new position was clear. Under the king were rather less than two hundred tenants-in-chief holding substantial fiefs of him by feudal tenure, normally the production of a fixed number of mounted knights. It was a world of cavalry and the castle. Only two of these tenants-in-chief were Anglo-Danish. Moreover, among the newcomers eleven of the close associates of the Conqueror had been given exceptionally large estates; between them they held about a quarter of England. However, in many cases, the Saxons rose again to wealth and power. Among others, the great houses of Berkeley, Neville and Stanley, all extant today, derive from native founders.

In the first half of the 11th century, England had been divided into a number of great earldoms, each comprising several counties. William had been familiar in Normandy with counts or *comtes*, drawn from his own kindred, and usually controlling border areas. In England he followed a similar scheme. Only a few of his close followers were honoured with the rank of earl; these lived at danger points, such as Kent or the Welsh border, and were only in control of a single county. For more general administrative purposes he preserved the Anglo-Saxon office of shire-reeve or sheriff. Earl is still today a peerage title, although by a pleasing quirk of language the wife of an earl is styled by the Norman-French word 'countess'. A sheriff is still appointed by the Crown for each and every county once a year, although the duties are no longer arduous, dangerous or profitable.

Potentially the powers of the king were enormous. In the first place, he possessed vast estates and the revenue derived from them. However, the throne of

England in the Middle Ages was not a soft option. There was a large and ill-defined frontier between the prerogatives of the sovereign and the rights of the land-owning nobility. Much depended upon the personality and upon the techniques of the monarch. A tough king could tamper with the succession to estates and limit the degree to which he took counsel from his nobles; but in general he needed to command their support and loyalty. The nobility, most of whose lands were fairly widely dispersed, expected a measure of consultation but were not well situated for active opposition or rebellion unless there was a widespread reaction to royal activity; a noble needed to command the active support of the smaller landholders, who held land from him, and of the peasantry who constituted the rank and file. The general failure of aristocratic revolt in the century and a half after 1066 underlines these factors.

At his death William I divided his domains; Normandy went to his eldest son, England to the next. When William II was killed in the New Forest, the youngest brother seized the throne by a coup-de-main and became Henry I. His acceptance was reinforced by the fact that his wife was descended from the old Saxon dynasty. However, at the end of his reign he had only one legitimate child, his daughter Matilda, now married to Geoffrey count of Anjou. Henry sought in vain to make her his successor, but on his death the throne was boldly seized by his nephew, Stephen of Blois, who already possessed large English estates. Matilda pressed her claims, and there ensued a period of spasmodic civil war, often mis-styled as 'anarchy'; ultimately a compromise was achieved by which Matilda's son succeeded as Henry II in 1154.

Naturally the nobility profited from the discord and the less vigorous government of Stephen's reign. In particular the title of earl was freely bestowed by both rivals; it was still associated with a territorial shire, from which a small profit was derived, but sometimes the earl had scant estates therein or none at all. The family of de Vere, whose main strength was in East Anglia, thus became earls of Oxford, in which county they had no land; they long outlived their fellows, for the last earl did not die until the days of Queen Anne. In all over twenty new earldoms were created by Stephen and Matilda: from being a rarity the rank became relatively common.

The Plantagenets

Henry II succeeded by hereditary right, as the heir of his grandfather. He had already conquered Normandy; he inherited his father's county of Anjou; by a spectacular marriage with Eleanor of Aquitaine, he added control of that extensive duchy. His frontiers stretched from Berwick to the Pyrenees, but of course for all his lands south of the Channel he was the vassal of the king of France. His father's ancestors had been counts of Anjou, and may originally have come from Brittany; the name Plantagenet, which has become attached to the dynasty, derives from their traditional use of broom

(*planta genista*) as a badge or device. Henry II was a strong, as well as a mobile, king with a powerful interest in all forms of law and government; his judges toured the land and by the end of his reign there was what could be called a 'common law'. None the less his rule was often exercised by force and favour; there were occasional risings against him and at the end of his life he had troubles with his sons, but he furnished a fine example of constructive royal authority which received general approval.

Henry was duly succeeded by his eldest surviving son, Richard I, an expensive and unrewarding absentee, whose chivalry and crusades have perhaps gained him an undeserved reputation. At his death his brother John secured the throne, despite the claims of their youthful nephew Arthur of Brittany. Circumstances did not aid John, and flaws in his own character added to his problems. He was unpredictable and at times inactive, although gifted with considerable ability, and faced prepotent adversaries in Philip II of France and Pope Innocent III. By 1204 he had lost Normandy and by 1213 had accepted the pope as his suzerain for England. What mattered more to the aristocracy of England were the stiff financial demands, admittedly in an age of inflation, made by John in his long effort to regain Normandy. A feudal monarchy was two-sided: the ruler had obligations to his subjects, even as they had to him. A shattering military defeat at Bouvines in 1214 brought discontent to the boil. A powerful group of the barons (although by no means all) threw off their allegiance. In June 1215, the king sealed Magna Carta: ostensibly a charter of liberties, it can also be seen as the terms by which the revolting barons returned to their loyalty or as a statement that the king had to be under some sanction.

Opinion and the bulk of the nobility rallied to the infant Henry III. After him Edward I and then Edward II succeeded peacefully. However, while the passage of the Crown was becoming simpler, its political status was coming under discussion. Already in the 12th century John of Salisbury had distinguished between a king who rules according to the law and a tyrant who does not; the latter, he thought, might properly be killed. A century later, the great English jurist Henry de Bracton had stated that 'the king ought to be subject to God and the law, since law makes the king'. It was, however, less clear to him what should be done about an irresponsible ruler.

One of the duties which the nobles of the realm conceived as their right was that of giving advice and counsel to their overlord. Henry III found himself facing a crisis in 1258, partly because he had relied too exclusively on his foreign kinsmen and servants. His generous rewards to them from a limited stock of good marriages, wardships or offices had also aroused antagonism, as had his disastrous foreign and financial policies. Assemblies which can be regarded as embryonic 'parliaments' were a feature of his long dispute with the barons and with his brother-in-law, Simon de

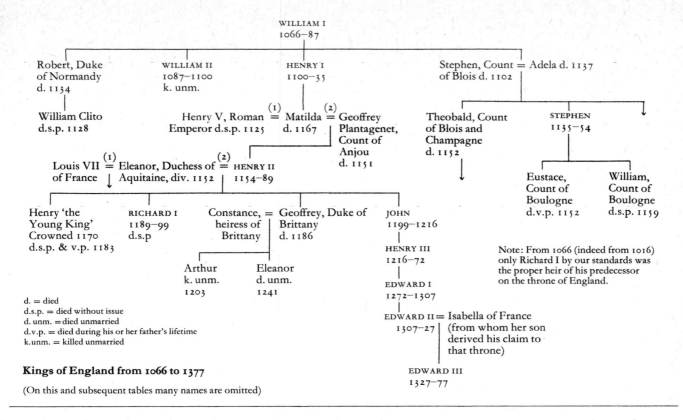

WILLIAM I
1066–87

Robert, Duke of Normandy d. 1134	WILLIAM II 1087–1100 k. unm.	HENRY I 1100–35	Stephen, Count = Adela d. 1137 of Blois d. 1102

William Clito d.s.p. 1128

Henry V, Roman (1) = Matilda (2) = Geoffrey Emperor d.s.p. 1125 | d. 1167 | Plantagenet, Count of Anjou d. 1151

Theobald, Count of Blois and Champagne d. 1152

STEPHEN 1135–54

Louis VII (1) = Eleanor, Duchess of (2) = HENRY II of France | Aquitaine, div. 1152 | 1154–89

Eustace, Count of Boulogne d.v.p. 1152

William, Count of Boulogne d.s.p. 1159

Henry 'the Young King' Crowned 1170 d.s.p. & v.p. 1183	RICHARD I 1189–99 d.s.p	Constance, = Geoffrey, Duke of heiress of Brittany Brittany d. 1186	JOHN 1199–1216

Arthur k. unm. 1203

Eleanor d. unm. 1241

HENRY III 1216–72

EDWARD I 1272–1307

EDWARD II = Isabella of France
1307–27 | (from whom her son derived his claim to that throne)

EDWARD III
1327–77

Note: From 1066 (indeed from 1016) only Richard I by our standards was the proper heir of his predecessor on the throne of England.

d. = died
d.s.p. = died without issue
d. unm. = died unmarried
d.v.p. = died during his or her father's lifetime
k.unm. = killed unmarried

Kings of England from 1066 to 1377

(On this and subsequent tables many names are omitted)

Montfort. These meetings, developed and enlarged by Edward I, brought about a new relationship between the dynasty and the great families, a relationship which in the course of the 14th century crystallized into the House of Lords and a concept of peerage. The initiative lay always with the Crown, but to each full Parliament would be summoned by a personal letter (or writ) between forty and a hundred important landowners. They would join the two archbishops and the bishops, some abbots, the surviving earls and a group of the king's judges and officers of state. Later doctrine asserted that the receipt of a writ, followed by attendance, created a peerage, and there are members of the Upper House today (for example, Lord Mowbray) who owe their presence there to a 13th-century summons.

The number of earls had stood at over twenty when Henry II came to the throne, but by the time of Edward I the figure had shrunk to a dozen, although by fortunate alliances some of these held more than one earldom. It has been suggested that Edward I had a conscious policy to reduce this number even further. Certainly he was slow to promote his own servants or the great families whose extensive estates might have seemed to warrant it. This attitude was reversed in the next two reigns. Edward II was prepared alike to confer earldoms on a worthless royal favourite (Gaveston) and on a loyal and successful servant (Harcla) whose elevation might be regarded as the first for merit alone. Edward III was more generous still and in 1337 advanced no less than six men to comital rank and declared in their wordy charters that this was a matter of policy. He also more or less stabilized the list of those barons who received parliamentary writs.

The claim to France

Edward III did more than increase the number of earls: he instituted the rank of duke. His grandfather, Edward I, had conquered Wales and united that country with England, an event which he emphasized by conferring the style of prince of Wales in 1301 on his eldest son, the future Edward II. Henceforward this designation was regularly given to the eldest son of a reigning monarch, usually as he approached manhood. Now, also in 1337, Edward III bestowed upon his son, already earl of Chester and popularly known as the Black Prince, the title of duke of Cornwall. Later in the reign (1351), the king raised his cousin Henry earl of Lancaster to a dukedom of the same name. Nor was this all. Through his mother, the only surviving child of Philip IV, he had a claim to the throne of France. Now he began to call himself king of France and to combine on his shield the fleurs-de-lys of France with the leopards of England. From this arrogant claim by the English king, strongly resisted in France, developed the Hundred Years War.

The position of the ruler continued to be central to all activities of the state; his participation and direction in government were essential. A minority or an incompetent king spelled danger to the kingdom. At his coronation the new king swore an oath to govern justly and to maintain the liberties of the land. He was anointed with holy oil. He was believed to cure scrofula, the 'king's evil', by the act of touching the afflicted (a practice which can be regularly traced from the time of Edward I and may be older). It is sometimes dangerous to divide history into reigns, and yet the *persona* of the ruler had an effect which cannot be ignored: two reigns during the 14th century ended in disaster and the murder of the king. Edward II was just not interested in the machinery of administration and he gave his attention and patronage to favourites who were disliked or despised. In the end he was deposed as a result of a conspiracy between his wife and her lover Roger Mortimer. There was no question of any successor other than his son, Edward III.

The fate of Richard II was more complex. He came to the throne in 1377 as a boy of ten. Minorities were always dangerous, and his was troubled by a losing war, a financial crisis, social unrest and active royal uncles whom Edward III had lavishly endowed. The upper level of the aristocracy was shrinking in number, but growing in wealth and in royal blood. The young king was provocative. His friend, the earl of Oxford, was given the new rank of marquis (of Dublin) and later made duke of Ireland. These elevations and also the unpopularity of other members of Richard's circle excited strong antagonism among the nobility. A coalition attacked ('appealed') the king's friends in the 'Merciless' Parliament (1388). It was a severe rebuff to the position of Crown and dynasty. In effect the king was reduced to the tutored position of a minor, while the coalition governed. It is easier to view the appellants as power-hungry and jealous than as defenders of the constitution.

Gradually, and with more skill, Richard built up a second group of supporters and servants, endeavouring not only to restore but to enhance the powers of the monarchy. In some ways he anticipated the methods of the later 15th century. In 1397 his former enemies were condemned, and he celebrated the triumph with profuse peerage promotions. So many became dukes that they were known contemptuously as the *duketti*. In 1398 he exiled his cousin Henry of Bolingbroke, earl of Derby (and now duke of Hereford). A few months later Henry's father, John of Gaunt, duke of Lancaster, died and the king by a doubtfully legal manoeuvre sequestered the entire, extensive lands of his dead uncle. It was a measure which made every landowner, large or small, tremble for his own heirs in their turn. The king then departed for Ireland. When Henry of Bolingbroke returned to claim his inheritance, Richard was in a poor position and was betrayed by many of the nobles whom he had benefited. Henry was able to secure his person, engineer his deposition and become king. Richard died in prison, probably by violence: he was childless.

Two more of Richard's actions deserve attention. In 1387 he made his steward, Sir Thomas Beauchamp of Holt, a baron by letters patent (as opposed to summoning him by writ), with limitation to his male heirs. The precedent was not followed for over fifty years, but from the second half of the 16th century it has been the normal method for the ennoblement of commoners. During his second marriage (to Constance of Castile) John of Gaunt had diverted himself with Katherine Swinford, governess to the children of his first marriage to the heiress of Lancaster. Half a dozen children resulted who were given the name of Beaufort:

all were begotten in adultery. After Constance's death John married Katherine and himself died soon after. But in 1397 Richard II declared the children legitimate 'by the plenitude of our royal power and the assent of our Parliament'; it was however explicitly added by Henry IV that this did not extend to the succession to the Crown.

Lancaster and York

It was not easy to justify the succession of Henry IV. He was, of course, the nearest relation by *male* descent, but Lionel duke of Clarence, elder brother of John of Gaunt, had left descendants through his daughter: her son, Roger Mortimer, earl of March, had been recognized as Richard II's heir, but he died in 1398 and his heir was Edmund, aged only seven. No one wanted another minority. Henry IV was accepted as king without any very clear public statement of how this had happened. The doubtful manner of his succession was to haunt his descendants: behind their triumphs and disasters lurked the ghost of Richard dead in Pomfret Castle.

With regard to the kingdom of France, Henry IV was in a still more anomalous position. It was, after all, indisputable that Edward III had based his claim on his mother. The French countered his pretensions by asserting the Salic law which limited the descent of their Crown to the male line. If Edward III had inherited France from Isabella, then beyond doubt his heir in 1399 was young Mortimer. The Lancastrian kings remained conspicuously silent on this point, but it was not ignored by French chroniclers and polemicists.

There were three main routes by which an aspiring family could increase its wealth and enhance its status: royal favour, the French war and successful marriage alliances. When he became king, in addition to being duke of Lancaster, Henry IV boasted no less than five earldoms, all of which had once been independent honours. Similarly the 15th-century dukes of Buckingham could claim three earldoms. Land and power were concentrating in fewer, more potent hands. Attitudes were changing as well as affluence. The military side of the old feudalism was dead: the battles of Edward III and even Edward I had been waged by a more professional, and therefore paid, army. Equally it had become less important to the smaller men that they held their land of such and such a magnate; if they were ambitious, they would rather attach themselves to one by an indenture and be 'of his livery'. Great men needed badges to identify their retainers, the crescent of the Percys or the sun in splendour of the house of York.

It has been estimated that the average medieval noble family lasted through direct male descent for about two hundred years. Naturally old names vanished and new ones took their place. At the start of the 15th century, the Percy line had achieved a dominant position in the north of England with two earldoms to its name (Northumberland and Worcester). But rebellion checked its fortunes. Often in rivalry was the other

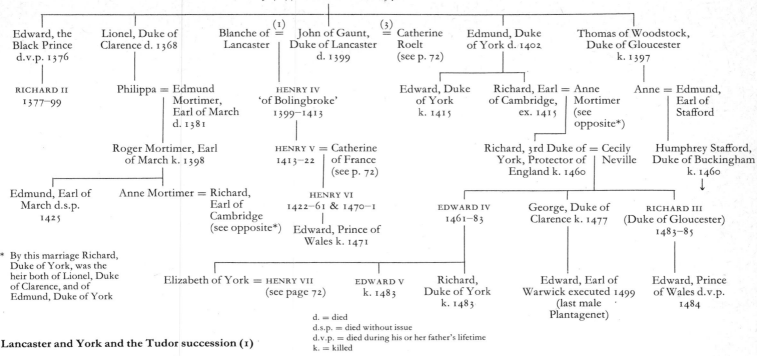

EDWARD III
1327–77. Claimed France 1340

Edward, the Black Prince d.v.p. 1376	Lionel, Duke of Clarence d. 1368	Blanche of Lancaster =(1) John of Gaunt, Duke of Lancaster d. 1399 (3)= Catherine Roelt (see p. 72)	Edmund, Duke of York d. 1402	Thomas of Woodstock, Duke of Gloucester k. 1397

RICHARD II 1377–99

Philippa = Edmund Mortimer, Earl of March d. 1381

HENRY IV 'of Bolingbroke' 1399–1413

Edward, Duke of York k. 1415

Richard, Earl = Anne of Cambridge, Mortimer ex. 1415 (see opposite*)

Anne = Edmund, Earl of Stafford

Roger Mortimer, Earl of March k. 1398

HENRY V = Catherine 1413–22 of France (see p. 72)

Richard, 3rd Duke of = Cecily York, Protector of Neville England k. 1460

Humphrey Stafford, Duke of Buckingham k. 1460

Edmund, Earl of March d.s.p. 1425

Anne Mortimer = Richard, Earl of Cambridge (see opposite*)

HENRY VI 1422–61 & 1470–1

Edward, Prince of Wales k. 1471

EDWARD IV 1461–83

George, Duke of Clarence k. 1477

RICHARD III (Duke of Gloucester) 1483–85

* By this marriage Richard, Duke of York, was the heir both of Lionel, Duke of Clarence, and of Edmund, Duke of York

Elizabeth of York = HENRY VII (see page 72)

EDWARD V k. 1483

Richard, Duke of York k. 1483

Edward, Earl of Warwick executed 1499 (last male Plantagenet)

Edward, Prince of Wales d.v.p. 1484

Lancaster and York and the Tudor succession (1)

d. = died
d.s.p. = died without issue
d.v.p. = died during his or her father's lifetime
k. = killed

---

great northern house of Neville, which by a series of brilliant marriages was to spread to the midlands when it acquired the earldom of Salisbury and the greater prize of the Beauchamp earldom of Warwick. On the margin of Wales the Mortimers were predominant, but their formidable assets passed to the royal house of York. Another leading family was that of Stafford, whose members became dukes of Buckingham and respresented the youngest son of Edward III; their influence continued to grow into the 16th century. Also influential were the Mowbrays, who held the dukedom of Norfolk, still more the new clan of the Beauforts and the rising house of Bourchier. Talbot and Hastings were winning the earldoms (Shrewsbury and Huntingdon) which still figure on the roll of the House of Lords today. Younger sons of significant families, such as Cardinal Beaufort or Archbishop Stafford, often filled the see of Canterbury or the richer bishoprics.

The monarchy in the 15th century saw one fleeting moment of triumph and one period of disaster. Henry V was the greatest warrior king, perhaps even England's greatest king. At Agincourt (1415) he overwhelmed the forces of France. Several successful years of campaigning resulted in the Treaty of Troyes (1420) by which Henry recovered sovereignty of Normandy, bound himself to marry Catherine, the daughter of the French king, Charles VI, and was to inherit the Crown of France on his death. It seemed as though England had finally triumphed in the long dynastic war. It was not to be so, for Henry died near Paris in August 1422, aged just thirty-five. A few months later Charles VI followed him; the Crowns of England and of France devolved upon the tiny head of Henry VI, not yet one year old.

The minority of the child king was marked by disputes between his kinsfolk, especially his two uncles, John duke of Bedford and Humphrey duke of Gloucester. His majority merely revealed his inadequacy: he was partisan and indecisive and eventually lost his reason. There was a steady diminution in local law and order as men resorted to violence and above all to patronage; in this decay there was little royal intervention save to the advantage of the king's favourites. Gradually the situation deteriorated into what are called the Wars of the Roses. Opposition to the king found a leader in Richard Plantagenet (the first regularly to use that name) duke of York. On his father's side Richard was descended from the fourth son of Edward III, but through his mother he represented Lionel of Clarence, an *elder* brother of John of Gaunt, and the Mortimers. However, he did not positively claim the throne until 1460, by which time Henry's capacity had seriously degenerated but he had achieved a son, Edward prince of Wales.

Among those honoured by Henry VI were John Beaumont, who became the first viscount in England (1440), and the king's two half-brothers Edmund and Jasper Tudor, raised to be earls of Richmond and Pembroke in 1453. They were the children of Henry V's widow, Catherine of France, and Owen Tudor, a Welsh squire in her service. It is widely assumed that the couple must have been privily married, but the Tudors could not find any evidence for this after they attained the throne, nor has any ever been discovered.

Civil strife began in 1455 and lasted intermittently until 1487. The term war gives too harsh an impression for spasmodic campaigns whose duration was in months rather than years. None the less the Crown

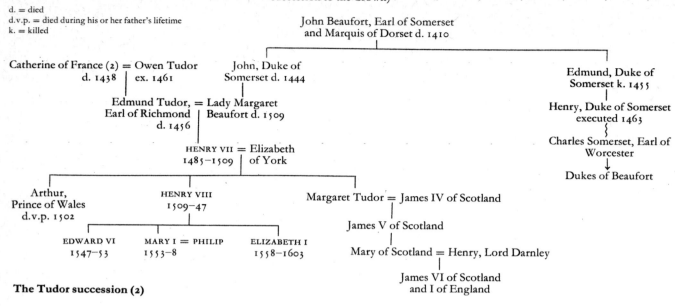

Issue of John of Gaunt by Catherine Roelt (born out of wedlock and legitimated but *not* for succession to the Crown)

The Tudor succession (2)

d. = died
d.v.p. = died during his or her father's lifetime
k. = killed

---

twice changed hands by battle, and finally the Plantagenet dynasty was overthrown. Up and down the country, however, the wealthy were building manor houses rather than castles. In the wise words of K. B. McFarlane, 'the war was fought because the nobility was unable to rescue the kingdom from the consequences of Henry VI's inanity by any other means. It does not follow that they liked the task.'

York was slain in 1460 but his son, the earl of March, gained the throne as Edward IV. His marriage, seemingly for love, with Elizabeth Woodville, a Lancastrian widow, was not universally popular – he was the first crowned king to marry an Englishwoman since 1066. Although briefly deposed in 1470–1 (when Henry VI reigned again) Edward did much, especially in the second half of his reign, to improve the position of the monarchy: royal agents put down local disorder; royal finances were reorganized; the royal council comprised qualified advisers rather than well-born aristocrats. Some of his expedients looked back to the unsuccessful experiments of Richard II: in 1478 he encompassed the death of his feckless brother, the duke of Clarence. All seemed set fair, when Edward IV died unexpectedly at the early age of forty-one, leaving two sons of twelve and nine. The king's will appointed his youngest brother, Richard duke of Gloucester, hitherto the most loyal of supporters, as protector.

Few can have looked forward to another minority. Within a few months the 'Princes in the Tower' had disappeared and Richard III had assumed the throne. His abilities and determination were undoubted, but he soon discovered that his position was precarious. His most powerful initial supporter, the duke of Buckingham, rebelled and was executed. Fear and insecurity were widespread. In 1485, fighting valiantly, the king was overpowered and slain at Bosworth, while two valuable contingents, those of Stanley and Percy, watched cautiously from nearby. In the middle of the battle, the former joined Henry Tudor. With a little more loyalty Richard might have been a successful ruler: but the roll of blood in his short reign was formidable, and he was probably responsible for the deaths of his inconvenient nephews.

It is no longer believed that the Wars of the Roses were responsible for the extinction of a great proportion of the medieval peerage, but their effect on the dynasty of Plantagenet can indeed be regarded as cataclysmic. Of the descendants of Edward III in the male line (including the Beauforts), seven were killed in battle and five executed or murdered, including Henry VI himself. As a consequence, when the banner of Lancastrian revolt came to be raised in 1485, it was by the unlikely hands of Henry Tudor, earl of Richmond. On his father's side he stemmed from the union of Owen Tudor and the dowager-queen Catherine; his mother was indeed Lady Margaret Beaufort, who could be regarded as the heiress of her family, but a family expressly excluded from any rights of succession. She was now married to Lord Stanley, who watched and waited at Bosworth.

The Tudors: a new dynasty

The grandeur of the Crown of England had been sorely buffeted. Between 1461 and 1471 there had been two anointed kings alive at the same time; the usurpation by the last Plantagenet king had been 'justified' by a series of arguments which were at best specious. Henry VII had no claim at all: his only connection with Edward III was through his Beaufort mother; if such a descent had any value, his mother ought to have been queen. Moreover, there existed a surviving son (Edward earl of Warwick) of the late duke of Clarence, who was a direct male descendant – the last – of Edward III. It is true that Clarence had been attainted, but so for that matter had Henry himself. The fact was that Henry VII had achieved his position by conquest, and Parliament endorsed this fact by declaring him and his heirs, 'avoiding of all ambiguities and questions', kings of England and France with no positive reason given. The records of Richard III's accession were to be destroyed. As soon as papal dispensation for their kinship could be obtained, Henry married Elizabeth of York, eldest daughter of Edward IV. The white rose of York and the red of Lancaster were united into a new Tudor rose with petals of both colours.

The Tudors were a family living in Anglesey who boasted descent from the 12th-century Welsh prince Cadwaladr. Henry VII was proud of his Welsh blood and placed the red dragon associated with Cadwaladr on his banner. It came naturally to him to christen his first-born Arthur, who in legend was envisaged as a medieval ruler with a personal following of knights for all of whom coats-of-arms were invented. Henry VII and his family, including Queen Elizabeth, were given to combining these mythical blazons with the accepted arms of France and England.

Once established on the throne, Henry VII naturally aimed to consolidate his position politically at home and abroad and to establish his dynasty genealogically. Yorkist sentiment was strong in Ireland and supported overseas by Edward IV's sister, the duchess of Burgundy. An invasion from Dublin by the pretender Lambert Simnel (crowned there as 'Edward VI', in other words, Clarence's son) was defeated at the battle of Stoke after a tough fight. Only here did the Wars of the Roses terminate. Henry was merciful to the miserable Simnel and gave him a place in the royal kitchen.

To establish a new dynasty, two assets were necessary: a sufficiency of marriageable princesses and an adequate stock of male heirs. Henry had no sisters but, making what use he could of his two sons and two daughters, he achieved connections with Scotland, France and Spain. The full importance of the union of Margaret Tudor with James IV of Scotland was to emerge later: it did not bring peace on the northern border. The marriage of Arthur prince of Wales with Catherine of Aragon was vitiated by his death, still under sixteen and childless, a few months later. Her hapless re-marriage to the second son Henry was mooted at once but not achieved till 1509. Indeed, when he became a widower, Henry VII flirted with various proposals for a second wife for himself. In the course of these he finally deemed it expedient to behead Edward earl of Warwick. Thus, on a scaffold in 1499, ended the legitimate male line of the great house of Plantagenet.

When Henry VII died in 1509 he had gone a long way towards establishing his dynasty. He was secure in England, to which he had brought peace, order and efficient (if rapacious) financial management. Abroad he was recognized and accepted; he could justly lie in the noble chapel whose addition to Westminster Abbey he had personally planned. Yet the future of the dynasty was contained in his one male heir, Henry VIII, and the problems of succession were to shadow the remainder of the century.

Henry VIII and the Reformation

The young king, handsome, vigorous and athletic, was to raise the regality of England to new eminence and splendour. His talents were diverse: by 1521, for example, he had written an anti-Lutheran treatise on the Seven Sacraments, for which a grateful pope awarded him the title of 'Fidei Defensor', Defender of the Faith. Henry's aim to play a kingly role in European politics, however, was to be affected by his lack of heirs. From seven births Queen Catherine had only one daughter, Mary; by 1527 the king was thinking of a divorce, but this depended upon the papacy which was politically influenced by the queen's nephew, the Emperor Charles V. There seems no doubt that Henry was deeply infatuated by Anne Boleyn (whose sister he had already enjoyed) and that she would not yield lightly. To assert that this passion caused the Reformation in England is probably to go too far; there was already a powerful ground-swell of Protestant feeling before this spectacular tempest. None the less the long diplomatic procrastination with the pope eventually sundered the link between England and the papacy. At the end of 1532 Anne was created marquis (the gender was deliberate) of Pembroke and was probably pregnant and married in secret soon afterwards. The following year Archbishop Cranmer pronounced the divorce with no reference to Rome, and Anne was delivered of a daughter, Elizabeth.

Henry became the Supreme Head of the Church in England. The monarchy rose higher on the ruin of the Catholic establishment; this encompassed the executions of Sir Thomas More and Bishop Fisher but did not solve the succession problem. Two miscarriages sealed Anne Boleyn's fate: even her marriage was pronounced invalid. The next queen, Jane Seymour, did produce a son but at the cost of her own life; on this frail child the hopes of the dynasty now rested. The king was to marry thrice more, but not beget any further issue. Complicated Acts sought to regulate the devolution of the Crown, but ultimately full authority was placed by Parliament in Henry's own hands, a further symptom of his royal power and autocracy.

Two tendencies affected the structure of the aristocracy in this reign. Firstly, Henry VIII was more ruthless than his father in eliminating the scanty remains of Plantagenet blood. A series of executions disposed of most of those with a royal ancestry. Secondly, however, despite these fatalities, many medieval names survived unmenaced by royal connections and fresh families arose at their side. This process was accelerated by the huge transfers of landed property which resulted from the dissolution of the monasteries in 1536 and 1539. New and enduring names such as Russell, Paulet and Cavendish joined slightly older ones such as Howard, Herbert, Manners and Spencer.

In the event the three children of Henry VIII followed him in the natural order and as Henry had stipulated in his Succession Act of 1544. The brief reign of Edward VI (1547–53) saw a pronounced move towards a more robust Protestantism in the church and the tenure of actual power by two great nobles, the duke of Somerset, the young king's uncle and then John Dudley, duke of Northumberland. As Edward lay dying, Northumberland endeavoured to stage a coup d'état in favour of Lady Jane Grey, his daughter-in-law – despite the fact that her mother was alive with a superior claim to the Crown.

Popular opinion was solidly behind Princess Mary; the plot failed and England accepted her first queen regnant. Mary (1553–8), already thirty-seven and a pious Catholic, proceeded to marry her cousin, Philip of Spain, who was given the title of king, for Mary's lifetime only. England was indeed briefly reconciled with Rome, but much of the work of the Reformation could not be undone; in particular, the dissolution of the monasteries had vested huge estates in new and secular hands, unwilling to relinquish their desirable properties. From this sad reign public memory recalled the loss of Calais, the last foothold in France, and the burning at the stake of many Protestant martyrs, from Archbishop Cranmer downwards.

In her turn, Queen Elizabeth succeeded without difficulty. The new ruler boasted of being 'mere English'; no other English sovereign, since 1066, has had so little alien blood, and few have been so well educated. With skill and often with feminine guile, she followed a path of moderation. By her ecclesiastical settlement the Church of England remained Episcopalian with the queen as its Supreme Governor, a compromise achieved in the main by Elizabeth and her House of Commons. A Catholic minority, hostile to the Prayer Book and the Thirty-Nine Articles, persisted among the nobility and in parts of the country, especially the north.

We shall never know the whole truth about Elizabeth's attitude to marriage nor with how much sincerity she used her hand as a diplomatic asset. But her continued celibacy kept alive the succession problem. Many names were discussed, sometimes in wordy pamphlets, but nothing could alter the fact that the natural heir was the Catholic Mary Queen of Scots, granddaughter of Henry VII's elder daughter Margaret, who had married James IV of Scotland. Elizabeth's task was made harder by the Scottish queen's flight to England in 1568, which was followed by a serious revolt of the great Catholic families of the north, the Percy earl of Northumberland, the Neville earl of Westmorland, the Dacres and others. Then came the excommunication of the queen of England by Pope Pius V and a lively possibility of her assassination. The rebels were punished savagely and a few years later the

Howard duke of Norfolk, perhaps the richest noble of the land and Elizabeth's close kinsman, went to the block, but not until 1587 could the queen bring herself, despite powerful pressure, to execute Mary of Scotland.

The great triumphs of the reign, the defeat of the Armada and the rich flowering of poetry and literature, belong to its latter half. Had Elizabeth died in, say, 1575, she would seem less impressive. She reigned, however, with splendour. Although her peerage creations were few, she encouraged her subjects to build great houses and there to entertain her lavishly. Burleigh House reflects the successful career of her greatest minister, William Cecil, but Longleat and Montacute were the creation of wealthy commoners. It was through her ministers that the great queen worked; the House of Lords was not influential and the House of Commons (which actually sat for only 140 weeks in 45 years) could generally be controlled or cajoled. The lustre of the closing years helped to conceal the fact that the financial position of the Crown had deteriorated sharply since the prudent management of Henry VII. To the end Elizabeth retained her delicate touch in the management of men; as she declared to the Commons in 1601: 'This I count the glory of my crown: that I have reigned with your loves'. This vital and enigmatic woman was the last, but not the least, of a remarkable dynasty, although it endured but three generations.

The Stuart succession

Elizabeth never committed herself on the succession, probably not even on her death-bed; it was her servants who engineered the smooth arrival of James VI of Scotland as James I of England in 1603. The house of Stewart or Stuart had its origins in an emigré from Brittany: of his descendants, one remained in England to found the great family of Fitzalan who became earls of Arundel by marriage and whose inheritance came (also by marriage) to the duke of Norfolk, beheaded in 1572. A cadet branch acquired the hereditary position of High Steward of Scotland, an office which furnished their surname. Walter, 6th High Steward, married a daughter of the famous Robert the Bruce: their child became king of Scotland, as Robert II, in 1371 and reigned till 1390.

James I had already reigned in Scotland for thirty-six years. Physically unattractive, he was none the less well read and experienced alike in government and in conflicts with Calvinism. Perhaps he was a better judge of books than of mankind. England and Scotland now shared a king, but that was all. Although the border ceased to be a battleground, each kingdom retained its own nobility, its own laws, its own Parliament and its own ecclesiastical establishment. The Kirk of Scotland was Presbyterian and not Episcopalian in organization; but James I was prepared to accept the virtue of bishops in his new kingdom. For he took a very august view of his new position, inclining to the royalist theory of the divine right of kings: 'The state of monarchy', he wrote, 'is the supremest thing upon earth.' To him

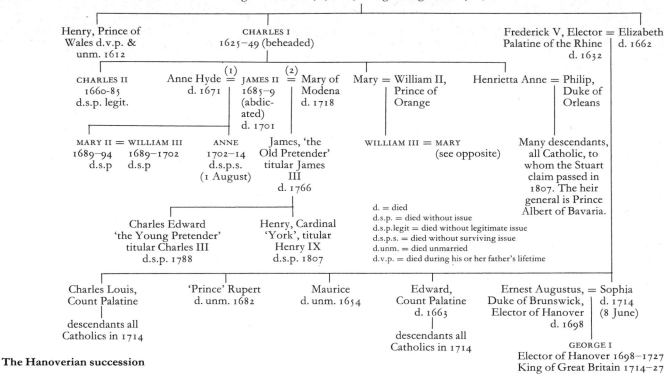

The Hanoverian succession

JAMES I & VI
King of Scotland 1567–1625 King of England 1603–25

Henry, Prince of Wales d.v.p. & unm. 1612

CHARLES I 1625–49 (beheaded)

Frederick V, Elector Palatine of the Rhine d. 1632 = Elizabeth d. 1662

CHARLES II 1660–85 d.s.p. legit.

Anne Hyde (1) = JAMES II 1685–9 (abdicated) d. 1701 = (2) Mary of Modena d. 1718

Mary = William II, Prince of Orange

Henrietta Anne = Philip, Duke of Orleans

MARY II 1689–94 d.s.p = WILLIAM III 1689–1702 d.s.p

ANNE 1702–14 d.s.p.s. (1 August)

James, 'the Old Pretender' titular James III d. 1766

WILLIAM III = MARY (see opposite)

Many descendants, all Catholic, to whom the Stuart claim passed in 1807. The heir general is Prince Albert of Bavaria.

Charles Edward 'the Young Pretender' titular Charles III d.s.p. 1788

Henry, Cardinal 'York', titular Henry IX d.s.p. 1807

d. = died
d.s.p. = died without issue
d.s.p.legit = died without legitimate issue
d.s.p.s. = died without surviving issue
d.unm. = died unmarried
d.v.p = died during his or her father's lifetime

Charles Louis, Count Palatine

descendants all Catholics in 1714

'Prince' Rupert d. unm. 1682

Maurice d. unm. 1654

Edward, Count Palatine d. 1663

descendants all Catholics in 1714

Ernest Augustus, Duke of Brunswick, Elector of Hanover d. 1698 = Sophia d. 1714 (8 June)

GEORGE I
Elector of Hanover 1698–1727
King of Great Britain 1714–27

---

legitimate succession, which had after all brought him England, was a law of nature, almost a law of God; rebellion could never be justified.

It was unlikely that this opinionated, middle-aged man would find the government of England easy. The financial position grew worse: the House of Commons from being an ally of the Crown became an opponent. The House of Lords grew dramatically in numbers, although not in political influence. Peerages were freely given to men of wealth, to Scots favourites and to English minions. George Villiers rose within a decade from cupbearer to duke of Buckingham, to establish a family that would long be eminent in English public life. But royal ministers were also rewarded; the two sons of Elizabeth's William Cecil became earls of Exeter and Salisbury, thus founding another conspicuous political family with two great mansions to its name.

The early death (1612) of Henry prince of Wales, generally regarded as a youth of high promise, resulted in the succession of Charles I on James's death in 1625. Undoubted piety and a fine taste in the arts could not compensate for his lack of judgment, political inconstancy and a Catholic queen. Eleven years of royal rule with no Parliament ended in crisis and civil war. As such contests go, it was not a bitter or revengeful struggle; families were often divided within themselves, but a large majority of the peerage favoured the king, if with varying degrees of enthusiasm. Ultimately the forces of Parliament and Puritanism prevailed, thanks in part to the genius of an East Anglian squire, Oliver Cromwell; they were strongest in the south and east of England, always held London and also controlled the sea. Charles was brought to trial and condemned. On 30 January 1649 he was beheaded in Whitehall 'by no known law and an unknown executioner'. For the next eleven years there was no monarchy, no ruling dynasty in England or Scotland.

The Stuarts restored

The autocratic regime established by Cromwell could only be sustained by its creator. On his death the easiest solution to the breakdown of government was the recall of Charles II from exile. The restored king was perhaps the ablest of his family; above all he was resolved not to go on his travels again. The blighting winter of Presbyterianism was followed by a spring of Anglican triumph and a high summer of a brilliant but licentious court. In the world of politics, the Crown had lost many of its prerogatives for ever and was financially at the mercy of Parliament; it remained, however, the undoubted fountain of honour. Creations and promotions in the peerage were profuse; in particular, Charles II made twenty-nine dukes, more than any other king before him. Some half a dozen of these titles were for his own illegitimate children or their mothers, but many great families also attained the highest rank. Something of a common pattern can be traced. Good service to the early Tudors was followed perhaps by a barony; the estates of the new family were enriched by monastic spoils; an earldom was added by Elizabeth or James I and now the ducal coronet by the last Stuarts. This happened to the families of Russell, Manners and Cavendish. The Montagus did not attain either of their dukedoms until the next century, but they had three earldoms in the time of Charles II and later added a fourth (Montagu, Manchester, Sandwich and Halifax). Nor was this all. The influence and prestige of the House of Lords, and thus of the richer nobility, itself was rising, and an increasing number of heirs and kinsmen of peers were entering the House of Commons.

There was also a fairly rapid rate of peerage extinctions. In at least some cases these were due to the terrifying frequency of miscarriages, still-births and infant mortality. For members of the royal family this dismal record was not improved by the publicity and lack of hygiene attending the actual labour. Charles II had afforded ample evidence of his virility, but his wife Catherine of Braganza never looked likely to produce an heir. This raised once again the problem of the succession and the fate of the Stuart dynasty.

The heir presumptive was the king's brother, James duke of York, who had married an Englishwoman, Anne Hyde. She had given birth to four sons and four girls but only two girls survived infancy. The duke, a devout Catholic, then married an Italian, Mary of Modena; her record was no better, for by 1682 she had given birth to one boy and four girls who had all died. The prospect of a Catholic becoming king haunted the latter part of the reign of Charles II with prejudice, plot and public disorder. None the less, James II mounted the throne in 1685; apprehension was to some degree allayed by the firm Protestantism of his two daughters, Mary (married to her first cousin, William III of Orange) and Anne. Then in June 1688, Mary of Modena produced a son, whose birth offered the prospect of a long line of papist sovereigns. Seven leading Englishmen sent an invitation to William of Orange to rescue the nation.

With considerable courage, the Dutch leader responded to the call and landed late in 1688 at Torbay. The issue was decided less by force of arms than by the craven flight of James and his family; at least in England the 'Glorious Revolution' was bloodless. It posed, however, a deeply serious dynastic problem: who was to be king? Some wished for a regency, some hoped that Mary would reign alone, but Parliament decided that she and her husband should reign jointly, with control in male hands. Moreover, William (unlike Philip of Spain) would continue as king in the event of Mary's prior death. A number of High Tory prelates gave up office rather than swear loyalty to William. A Protestant succession was thus assured for the moment; but William and Mary were childless and only her sister Anne remained of the English descendants of James VI and I. Meanwhile, the exiled James and his son lurked at the court of Louis XIV of France, principal enemy of England and Holland alike.

Parliament had placed William and Mary on the throne; it was thus able further to regulate the succession. In 1701 an heir to Princess Anne seemed unlikely and it was deemed essential not to have a Catholic king; by the Act of Succession of that year the devolution of the Crown was fixed upon the house of Hanover, the nearest Protestant relations of William III and his sister-in-law (Mary had died in 1694). So far had practice travelled since the high theorizing of James I.

The following year, to Jacobite glee, William died after a fall from his horse.

Queen Anne's gynaecological record was tragic. She had been pregnant seventeen times and endured eleven miscarriages: of her children born alive, only the puny duke of Gloucester had lived to the age of eleven. In vain had she laboured to solve the succession problem. The possibility still remained of a Jacobite invasion by supporters of her half-brother after her death; if so, it was likely to be aimed at Scotland. In 1707 an Act of Union was passed which welded England and Scotland into the joint kingdom of Great Britain. The two Parliaments became one; sixteen elected Scottish peers were added to the House of Lords; the first Union Jack was designed. Anne's reign saw also the triumphant wars against France which added the Churchills to the great families and Blenheim to the palaces of England. In the Upper House Marlborough joined with Dutch nobles, Bentincks and Keppels introduced by William III. Anne was the last sovereign (1708) to veto an Act of Parliament, and the last to touch for the king's evil.

The house of Hanover

On 8 June 1714 in Germany, the Electress of Hanover died, granddaughter of James I and until then the designated Protestant heiress to the throne of Great Britain. Accordingly her son became the first king of Great Britain under the new arrangement. George I, already ruler of his electorate for sixteen years, was descended in direct line from Henry the Lion, duke of Saxony and son-in-law of Henry II of England in the 12th century. The new king was a more competent character than has sometimes been supposed; he was a brave soldier, an experienced diplomat and not totally ignorant of English speech. His father's acquisition of electoral status in 1692 ranked less in British eyes than his firm adherence to the reformed faith. There were in all fifty-seven living persons with a closer genealogical claim: every one of them was a Catholic.

The great age of aristocracy

The great families of Britain probably enjoyed a larger political influence in the 18th century than in any other epoch. The actual numbers of the House of Lords did not greatly increase. In 1660 there were 142 peers, to whom were shortly added the 26 prelates; despite quite large creations the total of peers only stood at 145 when Charles II died, an indication of the regular wastage. In 1714 the Upper House numbered 213, including 26 ecclesiastics and 16 Scottish peers; in 1760 the tally was still only 213 and did not much increase till the 1780s. However, the same families were not always involved. George I in fact created no less than eighteen dukedoms, and at his death forty persons enjoyed fifty ducal titles, the apogee of that rank. Casual mortality cannot be avoided, but in 1719 the House of Lords escaped what might have been a greater danger to its survival: a Bill was introduced by Lords Sunderland and Stanhope which would have confined the peerage to its existing number plus six. So ossified a chamber could scarcely have survived the 19th century, let alone the 20th!

Naturally George I remained Elector of Hanover while occupying the throne of Great Britain; the two were not separated until 1837. Even if the new king found his powers in this country substantially fewer than those which he exercised in Germany, they were by no means insubstantial. His civil list was adequate and was voted for life; he had the patronage of a great number of sinecures; he controlled peerage creations and had a large share in the nomination of bishops. Against this must be set a vice of the Hanoverian family, a series of bitter conflicts between king and heir apparent sometimes erupting into political opposition. A large measure of power gravitated into the hands of the great Whig families, influential in both houses, often interlinked in marriage and enjoying an elegance of life based on their superb mansions.

In many respects the English upper classes differed from their continental contemporaries. In France the greater aristocracy was on the whole divorced from rural life and danced protocolled attendance at Paris or Versailles without any political power. In Austria the great estates were tied up more ruthlessly to the advantage of the first-born than was so in England. Although the strict settlement prevailed here, it had normally to be re-enacted at the majority or marriage of each successive heir. In most European realms there were (at least in theory) strict bans on marriage outside a defined noble circle; in England alliances were accepted between peerage families and mercantile families especially if the latter had transferred into land. This is not to idealize the British aristocracy: there were spendthrifts and profligates, great houses begun and not finished, even too many mortgages to endow a plethora of younger sons or unmarriageable daughters. But on the whole the cadets sought places in the church, the army or (particularly in the case of Scotland) overseas, sometimes to the profit of empire, often to the repletion of distant cemeteries. The heads of families in many cases were generous patrons of art, and to an increasing extent of native art.

George I was successful in repelling the Jacobite rising of 1715, serious only in Scotland, ill-led and graced too late by the presence of the nominal 'James III'. Thirty years later the more romantic incursion of James's son, Prince Charles Edward, failed to win any real support in an England most of whose troops were abroad. Henceforward, loyalty to the old dynasty was an affair of sentiment and not of practical politics. Active government had fallen into the hands of a committee of the privy council known as the 'cabinet' and for a generation dominated by the tough Norfolk squire, Sir Robert Walpole; his tenure of office raised him into the aristocracy, endowed his sons with places and contributed to a notable picture collection.

George I had only one son; his wife had spent years imprisoned for a suspected love affair. That son,

George II, only had two sons of whom the younger never married; only gradually did the dynasty begin to look established with the four sons of Frederick prince of Wales, and the nine born to George III. His family had early given the king trouble and was to do so again at the end of his reign. Two of his brothers married non-royal widows, one indeed herself illegitimate. George III was furious and caused Parliament to pass the Royal Marriages Act of 1772; henceforward no member of the royal family who was a British subject could marry without the king's consent in council under the great seal.

United Kingdom

Unhappily, the sons of George III paid scant attention to their uncles' fate. The prince of Wales went through a ceremony with Mrs Fitzherbert which, since she was a Catholic, was in breach of both the Act of 1772 and the Act of Succession of 1701. He was later compelled to marry his cousin, Caroline of Brunswick, but they separated after the birth of one daughter, Princess Charlotte. The death of the last-named (in child-birth) produced a sense of crisis. Only the fifth son, another duke of Cumberland, had any issue, and he was intensely unpopular. The dukes of Clarence and Kent were compelled to discard long-cherished mistresses and espouse German princesses. To the latter was born in 1819 Princess Victoria, the only product of these matrimonial stakes. Meanwhile there had been changes in royal style. In 1800 Ireland was joined with Great Britain by Act of Parliament to form the United Kingdom. The opportunity was taken to discard at last the title of king of France, which now had Napoleon as First Consul. When in 1820 the sad and insane old king died, he had reigned longer than even Henry III.

This period witnessed important changes in the higher ranks of the country. On the one hand, the Industrial Revolution produced new moneyed families which, usually by purchasing estates, could ease themselves into society. On the other, William Pitt the Younger began in 1784 a deliberate policy of enlarging the House of Lords and of promoting existing nobles. Most of his recruits came from landed county families, often with borough influence, but there was also a new ambition to rise a step or two in the peerage. George III (like his grandfather) was reluctant to make dukes, but the title of marquis (which between 1689 and 1784 had only figured on the roll for twenty-six years) was widely re-employed, and many barons rose to earldoms. From about the turn of the century peerages were more commonly bestowed for public service than for territorial influence. Wellington, admittedly the younger son of an Irish earl, was the last man to rise in a lifetime from commoner to duke.

Victoria and after

The death of William IV in 1837 brought Victoria to the throne. The kingdom of Hanover, governed by the Salic law, was inherited by her uncle, the duke of

Cumberland. The United Kingdom, freed of continental commitments at last, was able to exploit its economic and commercial strength. The Victorian age witnessed alterations in the balance of power. The great families were not as potent as they had been; gradually the middle and non-landed classes were reaching a position of influence. The passing of the Great Reform Bill in 1832 did not conspicuously enlarge the franchise, but it was only the first of such measures. Furthermore, William IV had accepted that he might have to coerce the House of Lords by fresh creations, a situation repeated in 1910 to 1911. Victoria could not have sustained a ministry in power, despite defeats in the Commons, as George III had protected Pitt; but she used her long life and her formidable memory to establish the just role of a constitutional monarch, motivated perhaps by empiricism more than by theory. In 1877 she added Empress of India to her titles. If her retreat into deep mourning for her husband brought a temporary slump in her popularity, by the end of her reign she had become an institution.

Victoria was the last Hanoverian sovereign. Her wedding to her first cousin, Prince Albert of Saxe-Coburg-Gotha, brought another Germanic dynasty to the throne. The house of Wettin traced its origin in legend to Wittekind, the opponent of Charlemagne, and in fact to Dietrich count of Hassegau, who died about 982. One main branch ultimately reached the position of king of Saxony; the other subsisted in a kaleidoscopic fragmentation of little duchies including those of Coburg and Gotha. As far as the great families of this country are concerned, the reign of Edward VII might be regarded as their golden twilight. Individuals can however still prosper: the 14th earl of Home became prime minister in 1963.

Queen Elizabeth II is likely to be the last monarch of the Saxon dynasty. Her marriage to the Duke of Edinburgh means that her children descend in the male line from the count of Oldenburg, who in 1448 was chosen king of Denmark. Prince William of Denmark, a brother of Queen Alexandra of England, was selected to be king of Greece in 1863 and reigned as George I. His younger son, Prince Andrew, married Princess Alice of Battenberg; they were parents of the Duke of Edinburgh. In 1917 King George V relinquished the name of Wettin for his family and substituted that of Windsor. At the same time the Battenbergs anglicized their name as Mountbatten and the Tecks as Cambridge. In 1960 Her Majesty decreed that henceforth she and her descendants would bear the name of Mountbatten-Windsor. Her father gave up the title of Emperor of India, and she has assumed that of Head of the Commonwealth.

The United Kingdom has been fortunate in the good sense and constitutional expertise of its rulers in this century. The integrity and devotion of George VI more than compensated for any hesitation occasioned by the abdication and marriage of the duke of Windsor. King George's wife, now Elizabeth the Queen Mother, brought a strong flavour of English and Scottish blood into the ancestry of the present Queen and the marriage of Prince Charles seems likely to continue this process. Elizabeth II has already known eight prime ministers, the first of whom had held cabinet office under her great-grandfather. Between Edward VII and the present Queen there has been a great change in the image of the monarchy. The advent of the popular press and television has lent a new meaning to Tennyson's phrase of 'that fierce light which beats upon a throne'. The 'walk-abouts' which the Queen undertook in her jubilee year must be the envy of many other heads-of-state, elected or hereditary. The life of the individual dynasties of England may have been relatively short, but the continuity and popular prestige of the monarchy and the loyalty to it of the great mass of English citizens are priceless and enduring national assets.

The descendants of Queen Victoria (George I had been succeeded by his son, George II, and his great-grandson, George III. Victoria was the granddaughter of George III and niece of George IV. Many names have been omitted for the sake of clarity.)

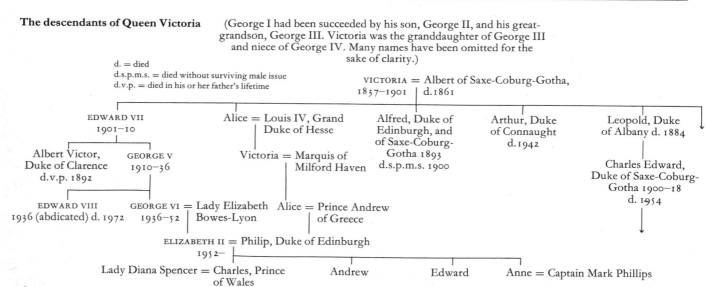

78

II
Power and Survival

4 'Mother of Parliaments'
The development of the Lords and Commons
over seven centuries

5 The Unity of the Kingdom
War and Peace
with Wales, Scotland
and Ireland

PARLIAMENTS were not peculiar to England in the Middle Ages. Other European countries had assemblies of nobles, bishops and commoners to advise the king or to endorse his demands for money. What is unique about the English Parliament is the way in which it has survived in recognizable form until today, without those interruptions, revolutions, and periods of absolute monarchy that have marked the history of its neighbours.

The process by which power has moved first from the king to Parliament and then, within Parliament, from the Lords to the Commons, is a long and complex one, the understanding of which is not helped by the fact that the outward structure of power hardly ever corresponds to the inner reality. Whereas the constitutions of other countries are mostly explicit and embodied in declarations, that of England is riddled with unwritten conditions – either powers that exist on paper but are never exercised (e.g. most of the royal prerogatives) or powers that have no formal existence but which in fact largely determine political events (e.g. those of the party leaders or the trade unions).

Another factor that makes the British Parliament unusual is its progressive enlargement to take in Wales, Scotland and Ireland, all originally independent kingdoms. Wales came first. After its subjugation by Edward I, the Welsh counties and boroughs returned representatives in the same way as the English. Scotland's Crown joined with England's in 1603, on the accession of James I, but she kept her own Parliament until 1707. Ireland's history has been the most complicated of all. Until the end of the 18th

century an Irish Parliament met in Dublin; from 1800 to 1922 Irish members were returned to Westminster; then came partition, leaving Northern Ireland as a still unsolved problem within the United Kingdom.

Parallel with this national expansion has been a social expansion – the widening of the franchise to include first the property-owning middle class, then the whole adult male population and finally women. This process lasted from 1832 to 1928, and was marked by fierce conflicts inside and outside Parliament. Since then the area of controversy has shifted to the House of Lords, whose powers have been progressively curtailed and whose nature significantly changed by the creation of life-peerages. Although voices are still raised in favour of its abolition, the principle of a double chamber has proved valuable and has been imitated, in one form or another, in most other parliamentary systems. The fact that the English Parliament has provided the model for so many democratic assemblies throughout the world will perhaps constitute its greatest claim to the attention of future historians.

At home, the question of separate legislatures for Scotland and Wales revived unexpectedly in the 1970s but after all proved to lack widespread support. In Northern Ireland, five centuries of troubled history have culminated in a situation with which successive governments grapple in vain, a Catholic minority determined to join the Republic, a Protestant majority equally determined to remain part of Britain. Neither the 'mother of parliaments' nor the unity of the kingdom are themes that can be regarded as closed.

Edward I

inherited from his father, Henry III, a parliamentary system that already had many of the features that we know today. It consisted of three bodies – the lords temporal, the lords spiritual, and the Commons who represented the cities, boroughs and shires. By the mid-14th century the Commons met separately in a chamber of their own, but it is not certain whether this custom prevailed from the beginning. They were certainly not thought to be necessary for the enactment of statutes, and Edward I often did not consult them. In this much later view (about 1524) of Edward and his Parliament they are not shown. The lords spiritual (archbishops, bishops and abbots) are on the left, the lords temporal on the right. The kings of Scotland (Alexander III) and of Wales (Llewellyn) are also represented as being present, though they never were. (1)

longtain voyage : quil souffira de porter seulemet vng
las de soye a vng ymage de samct george pendat a icelluj.
Aussi se ledit colier dor auoit besoing de reparacion il pora
estre mis en la main de louurier iusques a ce quil soit
repare. Lequel colier aussi ne pourra estre enrichy de
pierres ou daultres choses / reserue led ymage qui pourra
estre garny au plaisir du cheualier. Et aussi ne pourra
estre ledit colier vendu engaigie donne ne aliene pour
necessite ou cause quelconque que ce soit

Alexander Rex
Scotor̃

Lewellin
princeps
Wallie

Henry VIII used Parliament as an instrument for his own policies. In his quarrel with the pope, most especially in the passing of his Act of Supremacy, he needed all the help he could get, and Parliament seems to have played a willing part. A Roll of Parliament (*above*), showing the king in procession with the lords spiritual going to open the session, dates from 1512, when this struggle still lay in the future. By the end of his reign there would be no abbots left. (2)

James I had to exercise more diplomacy. Many characteristic parliamentary usages became settled at this period. In 1620 (*below*) the lords spiritual still sit on the left, temporal on the right. James himself originated the representation of the universities of Oxford and Cambridge by MPs, a practice that continued until 1948. (3)

King and Parliament

By 1400 it had become accepted practice for statutes to receive the assent of both Houses as well as that of the king. In spite of occasional assertions of royal power (e.g. by Henry VIII and Charles II), the increase of parliamentary rights over those of the king continued steadily until the Glorious Revolution of 1688, when the king became little more than a figurehead.

'**Be gone, you rogues,** you have sat long enough': Oliver Cromwell dissolves the 'Rump' Parliament in 1653. On the wall is the satirical legend 'This house to let'. Though both Charles I and Cromwell succeeded in ruling for long periods without Parliament, it returned in 1660 more powerful than ever. (4)

The Irish Parliament, from which Catholics were excluded after 1691, legislated for Ireland independently of Westminster, though owing allegiance to the English Crown. Here (*below*) it is addressed by Henry Grattan in the late 18th century. In 1800, by the Act of Union, Ireland ceased to have a Parliament of its own and returned members to Westminster. (5)

The meeting place of Lords and Commons was in the old Palace of Westminster, a rambling collection of rooms, halls and courtyards. The Lords sat in the White Chamber, rebuilt in the 18th century as the Court of Requests (*top*: 1809, with the throne at one end); the Commons sat in what had been the medieval St Stephen's Chapel, though remodelled by Wren in 1692. In this view, of 1793 (*above*), Pitt the Younger is addressing the house, while Charles James Fox, wearing a black hat, listens. (6, 7)

Conquest and union

Wales was won by military force – so long ago that a
direct tradition of Welsh independence hardly survives.
Scotland, after centuries of conflict, was united to
England dynastically and peacefully. Ireland was both
conquered and colonized, producing a resentment that
is the main source of the present problems.

Caernarvon and **Harlech,** built by
Edward I to hold down the Welsh, are
among the most impressive surviving
castles in Europe. Caernarvon (*upper
left*) – a symbolic as well as strategic
site, since it was the capital of the old
kingdom of Gwynedd – included a
walled town around the castle. Harlech
(*above*), smaller and more compact,
could be defended by forty or fifty
men. (8, 10)

Berwick-on-Tweed stood guard
against the Scots. The existing walls,
with their Italianate star-bastions, were
built under Elizabeth I. (9)

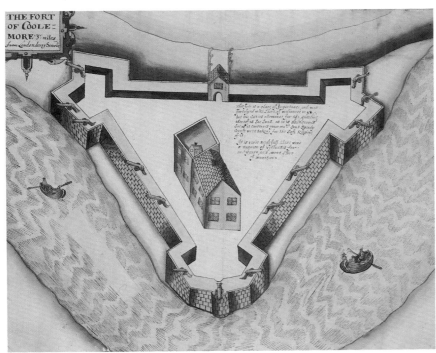

Ireland was never effectively governed from England before the late 17th century. Rebellion simmered throughout Elizabeth's reign, subsided under James but revived under Charles. Culmore Fort (*left*) defended the approach to Derry from the sea. The drawing comes from a report made by Sir Thomas Phillips in 1624. As soon as English attention was diverted by the constitutional struggle against Charles I, the Irish broke out into savage revolt, to be even more savagely suppressed by Cromwell. (11)

A new house

The old Palace of Westminster burned down in 1834.
A competition to design a new one 'in the Gothic or Elizabethan style' was won by Charles Barry, with the detailed drawings by A. W. N. Pugin.

The Speaker's Procession (*right* in 1884) like most parliamentary customs has its origins in pre-19th century history. At the opening of a new session the Commons are summoned to the Bar of the House of Lords to hear the Queen's Speech. (12)

A new Member is introduced to the House of Commons by two sponsors. The man shown here is Lionel de Rothschild, the first Jewish MP, in 1858. (13)

NOBLE LORDS OPPOSING THE TORRENT OF REFORM.

The Lords' chamber was Barry and Pugin's masterpiece and fortunately survived the bombing that destroyed the House of Commons in 1940. As it appeared in 1893 (*above*), which is very much as it appears today, it retained many features of its historic predecessors. The lords spiritual still sit on the left, facing the throne. (14)

The political weight of the Lords has normally been thrown on to the side of conservatism. In this cartoon of 1831 they are shown vainly trying to stem the tide of reform with buckets. The First Reform Bill was actually passed in the following year, the Commons having forced the king to promise to create enough Whig peers to see it through. (15)

87

4 'Mother of Parliaments'
The development of the Lords and Commons over seven centuries
ROBERT BLAKE

PARLIAMENTARY institutions have been the material of one of England's most notable export industries. All over the free world they have been copied, often with variations, but nearly always in a recognizable form. The English Parliament is the oldest in the world and has the longest continuous existence of any of our institutions except the monarchy which is older still. There is a great deal of historical disputation about its exact origins. It has been traced back by some writers to the *witenagemot*, the assembly of the wise which the Anglo-Saxon monarchs summoned from time to time and which consisted of varying and seemingly arbitrary numbers of archbishops, bishops, abbots, ealdormen and *ministri Regis* or king's thanes. Whether there is any real thread of continuity is perhaps questionable, although it is certainly true that the existence of the *witenagemot* and of the later Parliament stem from the same basic political need of the monarch to consult and to obtain the consent of his more influential and weighty subjects. In this sense the *witenagemot* may well be regarded as ancestor of the House of Lords, for the Norman and Angevin kings, like their Anglo-Saxon predecessors, deemed it wise to consult the great magnates in church and state and involve them in their decisions. It was from feudal assemblies or great councils that the House of Lords descended.

The reign of Henry III saw the beginning of something quite different from a feudal assembly, although incorporating elements of it. This was the emergence of an assembly of the three estates – clergy, baronage and 'commons of the realm' – sometimes called the 'third estate'. The first clear instance of the summoning of the latter was in Simon de Montfort's Parliament of 1265. 'Commons', incidentally, has nothing to do with commoners as opposed to peers: the word derives from communities – the French *commune*; the language of the law was still French at this time. What the third estate did was to represent the counties or shires, the cities and the boroughs. But, although it was summoned in this way in 1265, during the next

---

The Queen in Parliament: royal power has virtually disappeared, but the mystique of royalty remains. A painting after Benjamin Constant (*opposite*) shows Victoria in her old age, seated on the throne of the House of Lords and suffused with an almost divine radiance. (16)

thirty years there was no consistent policy. Some of the most important statutes in the first part of Edward I's reign were enacted without the Commons being present. It is not until 1295 that a regular pattern appears and soon becomes crystallized.

The so-called Model Parliament of that year, which met in Westminster Hall, comprised three bodies. The clerical estate, which was summoned collectively on the responsibility of the archbishops and bishops, consisted of their chapter heads, archdeacons and three 'proctors' from each diocese to represent the 'inferior clergy'. The second estate comprised the seven earls and forty-one barons (there being no other rank in the lay peerage), and also the bishops and abbots. All of them were summoned individually by name as baronial tenants. The third estate was summoned by the two sheriffs of each shire or county. They were enjoined to arrange the election of two knights of their shire, two burgesses from each borough in that shire and two citizens from each city ('cities' meant the City of London, virtually a shire on its own, and the seats of the dioceses). The electorate and electoral arrangements are obscure. The shire qualification was settled in 1430 for the next four hundred years – the forty-shilling freeholder. Borough arrangements, depending on particular charters often revoked or reissued over the centuries, followed no consistent rule till the Great Reform Bill of 1832. One has to remember that in the 13th, 14th and 15th centuries – indeed beyond – membership of the Commons was a chore not a privilege, an ungrateful task mainly concerned with endorsing – or not – royal demands for money.

Parliament, which comes from the Latin *parliamentum*, meaning discussion, was not an institution peculiar to England. The notion of the Crown obtaining some sort of support and consent from the principal elements in society was widespread in Western Christendom. So too was the division into three estates – those who pray (which in that outwardly devout era came first), those who fight and those who work. The French States General is the best known to Englishmen because of its resuscitation just before the French Revolution, but there were analogous institutions in many other parts of Europe. Uniqueness was not in the medieval origin but in the survival of the English Parliament. There were, however, two features which differentiated it from the rest of Europe at an early stage. First, the clergy as an estate opted out. They

'A King with his Parliament': an image from the 13th century. The king is receiving counsel from lay lords, bishops and an abbot.

were rich and preferred to tax themselves when necessary through their own bodies, the Convocations of Canterbury and York. They continued to be summoned but their non-attendance was held to give silent consent to Parliament's decisions. The bishops and abbots who had a dual claim, both as leading clerics and as holders of baronies, continued to sit in the Lords. The abbots vanished with the Reformation but the two archbishops and twenty-four bishops are members of the House of Lords to this day – a feature of Parliament hard to explain to foreigners, although perhaps no harder than the continued existence of the House itself.

The other difference was more important. In most European 'estates' the clergy, nobility and burgesses formed distinct categories. The English knights of the shire would have counted as nobility, albeit minor. In England alone they were for parliamentary purposes amalgamated with the burgesses. Those who held land, other than baronial, thus sat and voted with the merchants, tradesmen, lawyers and others who represented the boroughs and cities. Whether this was the cause or the effect of another notable dividing line between England and Europe is arguable, but it is certainly true that in England there never emerged a caste nobility or a nobility of 'blood'. There was a greater degree of inter-marriage and there was much more social mobility (see Introduction, p. 26) than on the Continent.

The origins and qualifications of the 'lords temporal', the earls and barons, have been the subject of controversy, and are far from clear. The most one can say is that the baronage consisted originally of those tenants-in-chief summoned by the king individually because they held estates recognized as territorial baronies – a circular answer which begs a great many questions. It is by no means clear that possession of such an estate ever gave a *right* to be summoned. If such a right ever did exist, the Berkeley peerage case of 1861, a claim to a barony by tenure in virtue of the possession of Berkeley Castle, finally disposed of a notion which would have been absurd in an era when land was freely bought and sold. As Lord Henry Lennox wrote to Disraeli in 1858 before the case was settled, the 'claim would be a signal to deluge the House of Lords with the lowest Parvenus'. But it was much less ridiculous at a time when land could not be bequeathed by will and the Crown's tenants-in-chief needed royal permission to dispose of land to anyone else. Whether or not the baronage was in theory limited to a royal selection within the class of those who held territorial baronies, the Crown in practice issued writs of summons to others who did not possess such estates. It came to be settled law that anyone whose ancestor got a writ of summons and took his seat was entitled to a barony, although it is by no means clear that the monarchs who originally summoned them intended this hereditary right to be established. Such a peerage went to women in default of a male heir, although they could not sit in the House, and it could descend through them to males who could. In the reign of Henry VI the writ of summons fell into disuse and peerages from then onwards were created by letters patent under the Great Seal, which specified the actual title – baron, viscount, earl, marquis or duke – and the mode of descent, normally heirs male of the body. It was held by the Committee of Privileges of the House of Lords in 1856 (the Wensleydale peerage case) that the patent had to confer some sort of hereditary right. Just over a century passed (1958) before life peerages and the opening of the House to women were made possible by Act of Parliament. It is a feature of the English world that change is very slow.

One can forget too easily that in its early stages the House of Lords was far from being dominated by its hereditary members. Throughout the Middle Ages the lords spiritual usually outnumbered the lords temporal who were seldom more than fifty and fell as low as twenty-three in the reign of Henry VI. It is not clear when the Commons began to sit apart from the Lords. Some historians argue that they always did. From the mid-14th century they certainly met separately. The Lords sat in the White Chamber of the king's palace in Westminster which was a royal residence till the 16th century. The modern building is still called the Palace of Westminster. The Commons sat either in the chapter house or the refectory of Westminster Abbey. The two houses, before separating for their independent

A 17th-century view of the Palace of Westminster, a rambling collection of buildings with Westminster Hall, where Edward I's Model Parliament met in 1295, in the centre, and Parliament House (formerly St Stephen's Chapel), where the Commons had sat since 1547, on the left.

debates, assembled in the 'Painted Chamber' of the palace on the first day for which Parliament was summoned – a usage that prevails in vestigial form even today when the Commons, at the opening of a new session of Parliament, go in procession headed by the Speaker to the Bar of the House of Lords and listen to the Queen's Speech.

The development of Parliament into a sovereign law-making body was by no means predictable in 1295. The Model Parliament could well have been a model for nothing. The *Magnum Concilium*, that feudal assembly of clerical and lay grandees in which neither the 'inferior clergy' nor the Commons had any place, continued to enact statutes throughout the reign of Edward I and beyond. For many years no clear line was drawn between its functions and those of the King in Parliament. In the end, by one of those characteristic but indefinite processes of English constitutional change, its powers gradually faded out like the smile of the Cheshire cat. It became a purely consultative body but was consulted less and less. The last *Magnum Concilium* was held by Charles I in 1640. Ironically, its only advice to him was to summon Parliament.

It was not till 1322, towards the end of the reign of Edward II, that Parliament made a clear assertion of its claim as the supreme law-making authority of country. Eight years later a statute was passed declaring that there must be at least one Parliament held every year. This meant annual 'elections', for the device of proroguing Parliament had not yet been invented. In fact the statute was never effective. There were indeed frequent Parliaments under Edward III and his successors – sometimes more than one in a year. In 1328 there were four. But royal need for money rather than obedience to the 1340 statute was the reason, and there were some years in which no Parliament was held. The process required a royal writ, and if the king decided not to summon, there was no means of compelling him to do so. Machinery for ensuring that Parliament met every year was only devised after the Glorious Revolution of 1688. Edward IV, who was rich, only held six Parliaments in twenty-two years; Henry VII, who was richer, seven in twenty-four years.

Parliament's powers are established

The two key functions of Parliament became established by the end of the 14th century – the granting of taxation, and the general power to pass statutes. The story of the former is highly complicated. It is enough to say that at the end of the century it was no longer possible for the king to impose direct or indirect taxes without breaking the law. This did not stop future monarchs trying it on. The great dispute about 'ship money' in the reign of Charles I turned on that very question. In general, however, the power to tax lay with 'the King in Parliament' and not with the king alone, although it was by no means certain that the situation would continue.

The power to pass statutes was equally well established by 1400. The assent of both houses and the king had become essential. In the 14th century the legislative formula was different from the modern one. The king made statutes with the assent of the prelates, earls and barons, and at the petition or request of the Commons – which suggests a subordinate position for the latter. A hundred years later this had been replaced by 'the assent of the Lords spiritual and temporal and the Commons in the said parliament'. The Commons had risen to equality with the Lords; the formula is much the same today. The earlier difference was important. In the first century of Parliament's development there were repeated complaints that the petition of the Commons, although accepted by the Lords and the Crown, was changed into something different when put on the statute rolls. A statute was usually drawn up by the king's Privy Council after Parliament had been dissolved, and it by no means always corresponded to the petition. That is why in the 15th century there was a change of usage and the Commons ceased to make a request but drew up an actual measure – a Bill which, if accepted, would become a statute. Hence the new legislative formula. The Crown of course could veto any Bill, and in theory can still do so, although the right has not been exercised since the reign of Queen Anne. The message transmitted in such cases to Parliament was 'Le roy s'avisera' – the king will think about it – a polite way of refusing. If he accepted, the words were

'Le roy le veut' – in each case a further reminder that French was the legal language of 14th-century England.

The King in Parliament had acquired by 1400 the exclusive right to pass statutes, but there were other forms of law-making. Statutes were serious measures, not readily to be changed or repealed. But the Crown with the consent of the *Magnum Concilium* or of the Privy Council had the power of making ordinances, legislation that was temporary or concerned with details. The King in Council was the real threat to Parliament. Privy councillors were his creatures. He could appoint or dismiss them at will. The ordaining power was hard to define. What are 'details'? What is 'temporary'? No clear frontier could be drawn. There was a further royal power: the Crown could not, even with the Privy Council's endorsement, suspend or revoke a statute, but it could and did exercise what was called the dispensing power – exempt particular individuals from the operation of a particular statute. Here was another area in which it was hard to draw a line. Richard II, who held a theory of royal absolutism, pushed these powers beyond the acceptable limit. In 1399 he was deposed as a result – and probably murdered. The Lancastrian monarchs had a questionable hereditary claim but it was endorsed by Parliament and they were careful to rule through Parliament, partly for this reason and partly from shortage of money. But the ordaining and dispensing powers still existed. They were to produce major disputes under the Stuarts.

Although Richard's bid for total sovereignty failed, Parliament remained very dependent on the Crown. The king summoned it, he later discovered the device of prorogation (suspending its sitting till a date chosen by him for the next one) and he dissolved it at will. He (practically) appointed bishops, although not abbots who were elected by their monks but had long played a less important part. He made peers, although he had to be careful not to elevate dynasties which might oppose him, for he could not get rid of those who claimed by hereditary right nor could he confer peerages for life only. He could create new parliamentary boroughs. He could settle disputed elections. These powers meant that the continued existance of Parliament was far from assured. All over Europe in the 15th and 16th centuries the strength of monarchs against their estates was increasing. From the accession of Edward IV in 1461 Parliament met less and less often, and it has to be remembered that when it did meet the session or sessions were usually very brief. If one can jump forward to the forty-five year reign of Queen Elizabeth I, her ten parliaments only sat for 140 weeks all told. Henry VII, after holding six parliaments in the first thirteen years of his reign, only held one in the remaining eleven. His son similarly held three between 1509 and 1514, and only one (1523) between then and 1530.

Parliament as an accomplice

An intelligent observer scanning the constitutional scene in 1529 might well have wondered what future there was for this ancient institution. True, it had acquired the sole right to grant taxes and consent to legislation (statutes). Neither the *Magnum Concilium* nor the Privy Council could do these things, but the Crown had other resources than taxes, and the limits of its power to make proclamations and ordinances or dispense with statutes were by no means clear. Parliament's role had become less active since the mid-15th century. The last time a minister had been 'impeached' (accused by the Commons and tried by the Lords), was in 1450 – the duke of Suffolk. The last time special auditors had been appointed by Parliament to supervise the expenditure of taxes was in the same year. The last time Parliament had claimed to nominate the Royal Council was during the minority of Henry VI. The first two claims were not to be pressed again till the end of the reign of James I, the third only on the very eve of the Civil War.

Whether Parliament would have survived if events had taken a normal course no one can say. It was in a stronger position to do so than most of its continental analogues, but this was no guarantee. What gave Parliament an immense fillip was the greatest revolution in English history – the decision of Henry VIII to solve his intractable matrimonial problem by breaking with Rome and declaring himself Supreme Head of the Church. To take such a drastic step he needed all the legitimate authority he could lay his hands on. Parliament was the obvious instrument. Given his purpose, there was indeed no other, but his purpose would have been unnecessary if Pope Clement VII had not been a prisoner of the Habsburg emperor Charles V and if Charles had not been the nephew of the queen whose marriage Henry was trying to annul. These adventitious circumstances vastly enhanced the strength of Parliament. Since it did whatever the king wanted, he had no reason to circumscribe the exercise of its powers. The Act of Supremacy formally made Henry Supreme Head of the Church; it informally also made the King in Parliament the supreme lawgiving institution of the realm – or, perhaps one should say, confirmed it in a position already claimed but not yet wholly established. Henry VIII's 'long' Parliament which sat from 4 November 1529 to 4 April 1536 – far longer and more continuously than any of its predecessors – saw the strongest assertion of the sovereignty of the King in Parliament hitherto known.

There is no evidence that this Parliament was especially 'packed' by the king. No doubt there was at times an element of intimidation but by and large the majority of those who constituted the two Houses were in favour of the king's new course: the removal of papal supremacy, the dissolution of the monasteries and confiscation of their lands, and the preservation of traditional Catholic ritual. They supported him too as a bulwark against internal anarchy and external foes.

Henry VIII was a tyrannical monster. His rule echoed Caligula's and prefigured that of Hitler or Stalin. Parliament was his collective accomplice: it blotted out his debts, it carried acts of attainder which deprived his enemies or imagined enemies of land, title and life without even the form of trial, it altered the succession, it allowed the king to bequeath the Crown by will, it gave his proclamations the force of statutory law. In 1589 Sir Thomas Smith, one of Queen Elizabeth's secretaries of state, wrote in his *De Republica Anglorum*:

The Parliament abrogateth old laws, maketh new, giveth orders for things past and for things hereafter to be followed, changeth rights and possessions of private men, legitimateth bastards, establisheth forms of religion ... giveth forms of succession to the Crown, defineth of doubtful rights ... appointeth subsidies, tailes, taxes and impositions, giveth most free pardons and absolutions, restoreth in blood and name as the highest court, condemneth or absolveth them whom the Prince will put to trial ... For every Englishman is intended to be there present, either in person or by procuration and attorneys, of what pre-eminence, state, dignity or quality so ever he be from the Prince, be he King or Queen, to the lowest person of England. And the consent of the Parliament is taken to be every man's consent.

This 'very memorable passage', as the historian F. W. Maitland describes it, sums up the juridical position of Parliament or rather – for the point has always to be emphasized – 'the King in Parliament' ever since. The experience of the Henrician revolution shows that, far from being the guarantee of liberty as 19th-century jurists maintained, it has been the adjunct of ruthless executive tyranny. It could be again. The notion that there was any kind of higher or 'natural' law to which even the King in Parliament had to bow, although pressed from time to time, had no practical significance. The great Chief Justice Coke argued in favour, but there has never been an established case of the judges invalidating an Act of Parliament. Sir William Blackstone in the 18th century seemed to think it could be done. He has had no support. There is, thus, a real problem for those who argue today that there ought to be a Bill of Rights and an appeal to the courts against parliamentary statutes which contravene it. Can Parliament ever bind itself?

King or Parliament: the confrontation

By the end of the reign of James I (1625) many of Parliament's most characteristic usages had been settled: the custom of three readings of a Bill in each house; the right of each to settle its own procedure; the use of proxies in the House of Lords, although not in the Commons; the practice of peers, although not MPs, to enter formal protests in the Journal of the House. In 1547 the Commons were given a new venue, the deconsecrated Chapel of St Stephen – a gift of the boy king, Edward VI. It had originally been built in the 12th century by King Stephen. It was totally reconstructed two hundred years later and remodelled again by Sir Christopher Wren in 1692. The Speaker's Chair replaced the old altar, and the Members sat opposite each other in the stalls. Some argue that the two-party system emanates from this *placement*, which contrasts with the semi-circular habitat of many more modern legislatures, where there can be elaborate and subtle gradations of partisanship. Perhaps the English electoral system, 'first-past-the-post', has continued because of this configuration. No one knows, and it remains something of a puzzle that an electoral procedure, abandoned by almost every European legislature, continues to prevail in almost every legislative body directly derived from the English Parliament, including America, Canada, New Zealand, South Africa and India, although Australia has introduced a minor variation.

The St Stephen's Chapel or Chamber remained the meeting place of the Commons till the fire of 1834. The Lords continued to sit in the White Chamber with a throne for the king who occasionally addressed them, and in front of it the Woolsack where the lord chancellor presided – wool being the symbol of old English prosperity. The chancellor was of course a royal nominee. His position emphasized – and still does – the judicial aspect of Parliament. The king with his prelates and barons always had a judicial role, although the monarch retired from it personally in the 15th century. The Commons, arriving late in the day, never claimed it, apart from the right of impeachment already referred to. The Lords retained till very recently the right to try peers accused of treason or felony. Far more important was their position as a 'court of error' – a Court of Appeal on matters of law, as opposed to fact. It survives to this day, although it is only exercised by a small committee specially appointed for the purpose.

The Speaker too was for many centuries a *de facto* royal nominee, although in theory elected by the Commons. In its early years the office was anything but enviable. In 1381 Sir Richard Waldegrave displayed palpable reluctance when elected to the Chair. A Speaker was actually beheaded in 1410. The formal show of unwillingness has long been part of the ceremony of election although the position is now regarded as a great parliamentary honour. It requires good humour, firmness, alertness and a vast knowledge, not unassisted by the clerks, of Erskine May's *Treatise on the Law, Privileges, Proceedings and Usages of Parliament* (1844). By the time of Charles I the speakership was ceasing to be under royal control. When the king tried to arrest five recalcitrant Members in January 1642 and found that 'all my birds are flown', he occupied the Speaker's Chair and asked where they were. Speaker Lenthall replied in words that have echoed down the centuries: 'I have neither eyes to see nor tongue to speak in this place but as this House hath pleased to direct me, whose servant I am here; and I humbly beg that I cannot give any answer than this to what Your Majesty is pleased to demand of me'. From that day on no reigning monarch has entered the

Chamber of the House of Commons. It should not however be thought that emancipation from royal authority made the Speaker into the quasi-judicial figure that he is today. Until the second quarter of the 19th century he tended to operate in a partisan manner for the party in power.

The 17th century was the crucial period in the history of Parliament. Would the king on his own or the King in Parliament finally acquire sovereign power? The precedents of the Lancastrian kings and the Henrician revolution favoured the King in Parliament, but legal forms masked reality and it was clear that, under Henry VIII, his son, Edward VI, and elder daughter, Mary I, the outward appearance of parliamentary supremacy cloaked a monarchical despotism. Under Elizabeth I there were signs of change in her later years: Parliament was rather more inclined to assert its own claims. The queen's tact, political flair and accumulated prestige avoided a conflict. The situation became far more controversial under the Stuarts. The anarchy of the 15th century had faded away in people's memories; the external threats of the 16th century had been dispelled after the defeat of the Armada. The country could afford the luxury of constitutional debate. The struggle lasted sixty years from 1629, the start of Charles I's period of 'personal rule', to the flight of James II in 1688. In between there was the Civil War, execution of the king, the Cromwellian dictatorship or Interregnum, the abolition of the House of Lords and the Restoration of the Stuarts (in the person of Charles II in 1660). What emerged at the end was a phenomenon unique among major powers in contemporary Europe – the 'limited monarchy' which is one of England's greatest contributions to the art of politics.

Despite the factors that favoured Parliament, the struggle could easily have gone otherwise, as Hugh Trevor-Roper pointed out in his valedictory lecture when he retired from the Oxford Regius Chair. Eleven years of conciliar rule before 1640 had made the political nation more or less used to it; after all, it was the norm not the exception among European regimes. The opponents in the Parliament of Charles I were, on average, eleven years older than his supporters. Time was not on their side. Charles I's follies, however, were. Even so, the battles of the Civil War could well have gone differently; and, after the Restoration, who could be sure that, if James II – an avowed Catholic – had had the sense to put politics above religion (as his elder brother, Charles II, had done), England might not have developed into an enlightened despotism? The fact that these things did not happen is no reason for assuming that they could not have done so. The development of Parliament, like much else in history, depended largely upon the accidents of personality and the contingency of events.

However, given the way events actually did turn out, one can safely say that Parliament after 1689 had won the day. Short of the conquest of England by a foreign state, it was from then onwards bound to be the

William of Orange was offered the English throne in 1688, but on certain conditions. Here the Bill of Rights, ensuring a 'free Parliament', is being read to the prince.

dominant institution of a country already heading for world economic and political supremacy. In the Glorious Revolution of 1688 James II fled after the Protestant William of Orange had been invited to intervene. William promised to defend the liberties of England and the Protestant religion and to call a free Parliament. Although the Crown continued to have real power and was far from being merely the nominal head of the executive, the Glorious Revolution settled all the main points of dispute in favour of Parliament. Machinery was devised to ensure that it met every year and that elections occurred at intervals of not less than three years (changed to seven after George I succeeded in 1714). There was to be no repetition of Charles II's Cavalier Parliament which sat from May 1661 to December 1678, and the king could no longer ensure the indefinite existence of a favourable House of Commons. The Crown's power to suspend statutes, claimed by James II in order to relieve Catholic disabilities, was declared to be illegal in future and to have been so all along. The power to dispense was also abolished for the future, but its past use was made illegal only 'as it hath been assumed and exercised of late'. Too many earlier rights and titles depended upon it for Parliament to pass blanket retrospective legislation. Taxation was put beyond all doubt into the hands of Parliament, likewise the appropriation of monies for the purpose voted.

Two changes not caused by the Glorious Revolution had already affected the House of Commons. The king no longer claimed the right to create new boroughs. Charles II gave Newark two Members in 1677 but there was no repetition. Henceforth it needed an Act of Parliament. The House in 1689 consisted of 513 Members, two each for the 41 English countries (including Monmouth), the 202 English boroughs and the two English universities (an innovation of James I). To these had been added by an Act of 1535 one Member for each of the 12 Welsh counties and 11 boroughs. In 1707 the Union with Scotland added 45 Members and in 1800–1 the Union with Ireland another 100, bringing the total to 658, where it remained till the Reform Bill of 1832. The king also lost his right to settle disputed elections. This now became a matter for the Commons alone and was usually decided on partisan lines.

The other change was of greater significance. The Commons had long claimed the right to initiate money Bills, but they went one further after the Restoration and insisted that the Lords must accept or reject such Bills as they stood and not amend them. It is hard to see on what principle this curious distinction was founded, and in the legislatures which are the progeny of the 'mother of parliaments' it by no means always features, for example, the US Congress which is the most important of all. However, after much bickering the Lords gave way, thus conceding an important engine of coercion to the Commons. By 'tacking' other legislation on to a money Bill, in other words, making a single Bill cover two quite different matters, they could force the Lords to reject or accept it as a whole, and the Lords could not readily reject such a Bill if the effect would be to deprive the Crown of supply. More than any other single development this made the so-called 'Lower' House in reality the 'Upper', and although that nomenclature has never been changed, the House of Commons from then onwards was the body which really counted.

The last quarter of the 17th century saw the emergence of another familiar feature of Parliament – the growth of political partisanship. The struggle was between the Whigs and Tories. Both names were originally terms of abuse adopted as symbols of pride, like 'the Old Contemptibles' in the First World War. The first issue was over the Exclusion Bill crisis of 1679–81. The Whigs who believed, with some reason on past precedent, that Parliament could alter the succession, wanted to exclude James duke of York on grounds of popery. The Tories, supporters of hereditary right, even if they did not all regard it as 'divine', took the contrary view. On this issue the Whigs lost, but the flight of James II in 1688 put them in the better debating posture. In fact, what happened could not be squared with any current theory of the constitution. Parliament had been dissolved before James fled and threw the Great Seal in the Thames. It could only be summoned by royal writ, but the Convention, which offered the Crown to William and Mary jointly, was summoned by the prince of Orange and his wife. It was not a 'Parliament' and its offer could not make them lawful king and queen any more than the Parliament which William and Mary subsequently summoned could legitimize the actions of the Convention. The Whig theory, based on the fall of Edward II in 1327 and Richard II in 1399, held that Parliament was entitled to depose a monarch; but it could not apply if there was no Parliament to do the deposing. Still, it was rather nearer in spirit to what had happened than any theory of hereditary right. The Tories could only console themselves with the thought that the Old Pretender, James II's recently born son, might be spurious and that the succession at least remained in the Stuart line. The fact is that the Glorious Revolution was a revolution, and that there was a gap in legal continuity which cannot be conjured away.

The structure of power

During the reigns of William and Anne, the two factions fought each other furiously in Parliament. Honours were roughly even till Anne's death in 1714. The Act of Settlement, passed in 1700 after there was no chance of descendants from either of them, conferred the monarchy upon the Electress Sophia of Hanover, granddaughter of James I and the nearest Protestant in line of succession. She died just before Anne, and her son became George I. The Tories were anti-Catholic but were divided and caught off balance by the Jacobite rising of 1715. The Whigs, who decisively supported the Hanoverian succession, established what was virtually a one-party system for the rest of the century. Sir Robert Walpole, first lord of the Treasury (1721–42), is usually regarded as the first 'prime minister'. That office was to be silently reshaped and amended over the years, but there has been a discernible continuity ever since his time. The vital point was that the king's first minister now could not survive without the support of the Commons. The Lords were still important but it was the Lower House that really mattered.

One should not imagine that the Commons were a freely elected body. The influence of the Crown was paramount for many years to come. No government in office lost a general election between 1715 and 1830 – and this was no accident. Changes occurred because of Crown decisions, dictated sometimes by policy and personalities, sometimes by the need to reconstruct an edifice which had collapsed; they seldom occurred because of popular demand. The electoral system was anything but democratic. The least undemocratic constituencies were the counties. Inflation meant that the forty-shilling freeholder could be quite low down in the social and economic scale, and the result was the

Sir Robert Walpole (left), the 'first prime minister', talks to the Speaker. Originally a royal nominee, the Speaker became the servant of the House in the 1640s. In Walpole's time he supported the majority party. His impartial role dates from the second quarter of the 19th century.

emergence of something near to a mass electorate. The boroughs each had their individual charter and particular franchise. There was a wide variety. A few, such as Westminster, were relatively democratic. Most borough members were elected by oligarchic close corporations. Both Charles II and his brother had recalled as many old charters as they could, on such legal grounds as seemed plausible, and reissued them in a form that made the electorate more subject to royal control. An elaborate system of 'influence' enabled 'the minister', as he was then called – 'prime minister' was a term of opprobrium – to ensure a majority at the normally septennial elections. This system, which crystallized after 1688, remained frozen till 1832.

An important 18th-century feature in royal influence was the 'placemen' — MPs who held office under the Crown. Their existence was regarded by many people as an abuse. The Act of Settlement in 1700 provided that, after the accession of the house of Hanover, they should cease to sit in the House of Commons. If those clauses had not been repealed, the whole history of English constitutional development would have been different. The Cabinet in the form that we know it would never have come into being. No minister could have sat in the House of Commons. The Act did not apply to the Lords. In Macaulay's famous words: 'the

96

House of Lords, constantly drawing to itself the first abilities in the realm, would have become the most august of senates, while the House of Commons would have sunk almost to a vestry'. The clauses were, however, repealed in 1705, and two years later a fresh Act settled the question for the next two centuries: appointees to 'old' – pre-1707 – offices had to vacate their seats but could be re-elected; holders of 'new' offices were absolutely debarred. But 'new' offices to which this disability did not apply could be – and were – created by later statutes. Parliament can never bind itself. The holders of both old and new offices were to constitute an important element in the oiling of the parliamentary machine from that day to this.

The House of Commons was by now unquestionably the major element in Parliament. Without its confidence no ministry could exist. Its debates were those that really mattered, and already the House of Lords had become in comparison a place not only for hereditary grandees but also for elderly and retired politicians. When Walpole, fallen but ennobled as earl of Orford, met his old rival Pulteney, by then also an earl (of Bath), he is supposed to have said: 'You and I, my Lord, are two as insignificant men as any in England.' The Commons was from the early 18th century onwards the true theatre of politics. Then began the great age of parliamentary eloquence which lasted through the 19th century and is not wholly dead even today – Walpole against Pulteney, Pitt against Fox, Disraeli against Gladstone. Debates were widely reported – although for many years illegally, and the House committed to prison from time to time those detected in the act. By the enlightened thinkers of Europe the British constitution was admired and idealized – the more so since it seemed the foundation of economic growth and, till well after the middle of the century, of success in war as well.

The American interpretation

The admiration for the constitution of England expressed by the avant-garde of Europe was not shared by the expatriate English of another continent – America. The successful war which the North American colonists fought for independence turned on a constitutional point. Often depicted as a struggle against George III personally, the battle was really against the King in Parliament. Taxation without representation was an exercise of parliamentary sovereignty, and the king at no stage exceeded the recognized limits of the royal prerogative. The American Constitution is the earliest important example of the spread of parliamentary institutions outside their country of origin and, since it still remains with little change the juridical framework of the most powerful nation in the world, it is worth examining.

The Founding Fathers, who were steeped in English parliamentary usage however much they disliked its practical application, did not contemplate a *tabula rasa*, rather a reformed version of a system not fundamentally beyond repair. There had to be a chief executive but not, of course, a hereditary monarch who might go on for ever, or go mad as George III later did. The answer was a President elected by a procedure quite separate from that of the legislature for four years and re-eligible. What should his powers be? He would have, like the king, the right to veto legislation but his veto, unlike the king's, could be overridden by a two-thirds majority of both houses of the legislature. He would appoint to all the important offices of state but they would need to be confirmed by the upper house. To prevent undue executive influence the repealed provisions of the Act of Settlement against 'placemen' were revived. No one holding executive office could sit in either house of Congress. This important divergence from English usage has never been changed and it remains one of the most striking differences between the two systems. The American Cabinet is a collection of presidential nominees with no congressional base. If sacked they sink without trace. The British Cabinet is also appointed and dismissed by the head of the executive – theoretically by the Crown, really by the prime minister. But all of them are members of one of the two Houses of Parliament and, if they wish to make trouble after dismissal, they have a sounding board.

The greatest difference between the two systems concerns the legislature. Congress was in many ways an updated version, by contemporary standards, of Parliament. Instead of an archaic hereditary upper house rooted somewhere in the mists of medieval antiquity, there was to be an elective Senate representing the federal principle – two for each state whatever the size of its population. Instead of a House of Commons with a tenure of up to seven years, there would be a House of Representatives elected every two years. Moreover – most important of all divergencies from the English pattern – the legislature would not be sovereign. There was a Bill of Rights which it could not override and a Supreme Court which could invalidate its Acts. Only by an elaborate process of constitutional amendment could these relationships be changed. The need under a federal system to preserve state rights (something that did not apply in England), was only a part of the explanation. There was also behind it a sense born of experience that the sovereignty of King in Parliament could be a dangerous weapon of tyranny, and that there ought to be a system of real 'checks and balances' to avert the peril. It is interesting to notice that in recent times there has been in Britain something of an intellectual move in that same direction. People are beginning to comment, as Lord Hailsham did recently, on the danger of Parliament becoming an elective dictatorship, and the concepts of a written constitution and a Bill of Rights are no longer dismissed from serious consideration.

Reform, rebuilding and reshaping

The 18th-century system carried the United Kingdom successfully through the Napoleonic Wars from which the country emerged as the most powerful nation in the world, but the old parliamentary order could not accommodate the new social and economic forces generated by the Industrial Revolution. It was to the credit of the oligarchical House of Commons that it did

1580 and 1780: in 'old England' the country gentleman was humbly requested by the electors of his county to become their representative; he regarded political duties with some distaste. Now, the 'modern fine gentleman', a dandy and a townsman, is eager for power and bribes the electors of the borough to vote for him. (A cartoon of 1780).

in the end reform itself. The Great Reform Bill of 1832 which produced a uniform if limited borough franchise and extended the county electorate marks the real beginning of our modern constitution. The various property qualifications limited the electorate to about half a million but it could no longer be influenced by the Crown. During the period from 1714 to 1832 the prime minister had to have the confidence of the king as well as the House of Commons, and the support of the former usually entailed the support of the latter. After 1832 it was exclusively a matter of the confidence of the Commons. The Crown could no longer ensure electoral victory for its nominee. The change was made clear to those who had eyes to see when in 1834 William IV dismissed Lord Melbourne and replaced him by Sir Robert Peel. The ensuing election did not give Peel a majority. After struggling vainly in Parliament for two or three months he resigned, and the king had to take Melbourne back. The process had begun whereby the monarch was transformed from an active force in politics to a ceremonial head of state, the neutral hinge on which the constitution pivots; the Crown, incidentally, became far more popular as a result. As so often with such changes, many did not at first perceive the full implications, and in her early years – indeed beyond them – Queen Victoria spoke and sometimes acted as if her position was like that of George IV. But by the end of her reign there could be no doubt.

The disappearance of the old constitution coincided with the disappearance of the old Palace of Westminster. On 16 October 1834 a disastrous fire gutted the St Stephen Chapel, the Painted Chamber, the White Chamber and much else besides. Only Westminster Hall survived. An immense quantity of documents, including the Rolls of Parliament, were burned or irretrievably damaged by efforts to extinguish the

flames. The death warrant of Charles I was one of the few to remain intact. There was, however, a silver lining to the clouds rolling over the embers of these time-hallowed chambers of debate. The accommodation of Parliament had long been a scandal. It was cramped and squalid (Gladstone, elected in 1832, vividly remembered in old age the smell of the lavatories). It was badly ventilated and heated – too hot in summer, too cold in winter. There was insufficient space and a host of ill-lit obscure corridors to which aggrieved members of the public had easy access. In 1812 the prime minister, Spencer Perceval, was murdered in the Lobby by a lunatic. As for committees, they were put into tiny congested rooms of the most inconvenient nature.

It was generally agreed that there should be a new and grand edifice. For the time being the Commons were accommodated in a temporary structure on the site of the White Chamber, and the Lords in the ruins of the Painted Chamber. The choice of architect for the new palace was put out to a competition won by Charles Barry who, after seemingly endless disputes and vicissitudes, produced a great Gothic building of over a thousand rooms – one of the wonders of the world. The internal decoration, carving, gilding and woodwork was largely the work of his appointee, A. W. N. Pugin, who was a decorator of genius and packed much into his brief life which ended when he was forty in 1852. The Lords first sat in their magnificent red and gold chamber in 1847, the Commons on their less ostentatious green leather benches in 1850. Their chamber was to be destroyed by a second fire from a German incendiary bomb in 1941 but the rest of the building survived intact. The Commons sat in the Lords' chamber till their own was restored in 1951; the Lords sat in the Robing Room.

The Reform Bill of 1832 was followed by that of 1867 which gave the vote to all rate-payers in the boroughs and that of 1884 which did the same for the counties. In 1872 open voting was replaced by the secret ballot. In 1918 all men of 21 and women of 30 became electors, and in 1928 all women of 21. The last vestiges of plural voting were swept away in 1948 when the university and business votes were abolished. The age qualification has since been lowered to eighteen. In 1911 the House of Lords lost its co-equal status with the Commons. The Parliament Act of that year – the result of the Lords rejecting the 1909 budget – abolished their power of veto. They could now only delay Bills for two years and could not touch money Bills at all. The Act was carried by the threat of the prime minister to advise the king to create enough peers to swamp the Lords. In 1949 their delaying power was reduced to one year. The hereditary principle, however, has not yet been abolished – strange anomaly though it may seem in the 20th century; but the Life Peerages Act has greatly changed the nature of the House. No hereditary peerages have been created since 1964.

The procedure of the House of Commons underwent a major change in the late 19th century. Till then it had operated much as the House of Lords still does today, with no rules about 'closure', 'guillotine' and so on, and the length of speeches being left to the good sense of Members. The deliberate obstruction exercised by the Irish Nationalist MPs under the leadership of Charles Stuart Parnell after 1880 made this impossible. The modern rules of debate were for the most part devised during the 1880s to meet this challenge. It is interesting to notice that the American House of Representatives is like the House of Commons in this respect with strict rules of procedure. The difference is that the Speaker is still an avowedly partisan figure just as he was in England in the 18th century. In the US Senate, on the other hand, the position resembles that of the House of Lords. Rules are almost non-existent. There can be – and on occasions have been – filibusters, something which could in theory have happened in the House of Lords, although, as far as I know, it never has.

Dr Norman points out in Chapter Eight how that most indigenous and least proselytizing of churches, the Anglican, spread all over the world in the wake of the Empire and the Flag. In a similar way parliamentary institutions, deeply rooted in the past and shaped by the peculiar accidents of English history, proliferated when the Empire grew, or sometimes as in the USA even when it contracted. Everywhere crown colonies had legislatures of some kind based on parliamentary analogies. Being the creation of Acts of the British Parliament they differed from it in one important respect; they did not have sovereignty. Nor did they necessarily have it even after Dominion status had given them virtual independence. The parliaments of Canada and Australia, being federal legislatures, are not sovereign bodies in the Westminster sense. There are matters in both countries which can even now require legislation by the 'mother of parliaments'. The 'patriation' of the Canadian constitution is a case in point. Even in Australia, where an internal amending procedure was built into the Act creating the Commonwealth, the authority of the UK Parliament could be invoked for some purposes. Canada was the first to have its own Parliament. New Zealand followed, then Australia and, last of all, the white settler countries, South Africa.

The spread of parliamentary institutions was not confined to the Empire. After the July revolution in France of 1830 and the widespread revolutions of 1848 they covered much of Europe too. Only Russia, then as now 'the corner-stone of despotism in the world' – to quote De Tocqueville – remained immune to this liberal virus. Some European parliaments were re-animated versions of the ancient estates. Prussia and Austria owed little to the English example. Far more, however, did. The French Chambers of 1815, reshaped in 1830, were clearly modelled on Westminster and had no root in the old States General. The same is true of most of the parliamentary regimes of Europe. Some took permanent root – France, Belgium, Holland, Scandinavia. Some withered away into overt or barely disguised dictatorships – Italy, Spain, Portugal. Today parliaments have no place east of the Iron Curtain but they flourish over free Europe – albeit precariously in one or more places.

The Empire no longer exists in the old sense, but the great wave of decolonization carried parliaments far and wide – sometimes temporarily, sometimes permanently. In the 1950s and early 1960s visiting parliamentary delegations from England seemed to be constantly presenting maces to the fledgling legislatures of newly independent states. Black men in grey wigs learned how to call members to order in the torrid heat of Africa, and high-caste Brahmins in Delhi searched for precedents in the limp pages of Erskine May.

The last battle in the history of electoral reform: with the blessing of Britannia, hundreds of women march towards Westminster in this illustration from 'The Suffragette', 1913.

5 The Unity of the Kingdom
War and Peace
with Wales, Scotland and Ireland
HUGH TREVOR-ROPER

ENGLAND, Wales, Scotland and Ireland were once customarily known as the British Isles. The phrase is still occasionally used as a geographical expression. But even as such the term must be used with caution. It is resented in Ireland. In fact, the people of these islands have seldom been united, politically or culturally. Efforts were made to unite them from the 12th century onwards, but they only came under the same monarch in 1603 and the complete political union, which was at last achieved in 1801, endured only till 1922. Since then the process has been reversed. The greater part of Ireland is independent, and there are political parties which advocate separation and independence for Scotland and Wales.

In these circumstances it seems paradoxical to refer to the unification of the country as if it were a continuous process. In fact, the relations between the various societies in the British Isles have been constantly changing. Only linguistically has the process been continuous: the English language has gradually prevailed over all others. In all other respects unity has been a mirage, often sighted but never completely attained and always liable to dissolve when apparently within reach.

At the base lies a racial difference. The original inhabitants of the islands – or at least the inhabitants first known to written history – consisted of two branches of the Celtic race: P-Celts in England and Scotland (Britons and Picts), Q-Celts in Ireland (Scots). In the 5th and 6th centuries AD, after the withdrawal of the Romans, the P-Celts felt the impact of two invasions which were to become permanent. Anglo-Saxons from Germany settled in England and gradually pushed the original P-Celts (in so far as they did not absorb them) into the mountains of Cumbria and Wales. Almost at the same time, Q-Celts from Northern Ireland, the Scots, settled in the Western Highlands of what is now Scotland and gradually imposed their ruling dynasty, their name, their language and their religion on the major part of the country. The original P-Celts of Scotland, the Picts, fared even less well than their brethren in England, the Britons. Whereas the Britons at least preserved their language and culture in Wales, the language and culture of the Picts, whatever it may have been, was totally extinguished. In those areas where it was not destroyed by the invading Q-Celts from the west, it was destroyed by invading Teutons from the East: Anglo-Saxons, in the south, and

Scandinavians in the north. The Picts, of course, were not themselves destroyed, any more than the Britons had been destroyed in England. They were culturally absorbed. The difference was that the defeated Britons had a receptacle or redoubt in which they could preserve and continue their culture; the Picts did not.

Thus by the time of the Norman Conquest of England, if we ignore the pockets of Scandinavian settlement in northern Scotland, the Hebrides and Ireland, there were three races, firmly settled with their own culture, in the British Isles: Anglo-Saxon in England and south-eastern Scotland; P-Celts in Wales and Cumbria, and perhaps also in Galloway; and Q-Celts in Ireland and in Scotland north of the Firths of Forth and Clyde. An Anglo-Saxon dynasty ruled in England, a Scottish – i.e. Irish – dynasty in Scotland, Welsh princes in Wales. Ireland was in anarchy.

On to this racial pattern, which corresponded to no modern political divisions (the border between England and Scotland was not fixed till the reign of William Rufus), a first form of unity was imposed, not by Anglo-Saxon England, but by the Norman conquerors of England, operating from their new English base. This first unification of Britain was in fact an extension – by varying means – of the Norman Conquest of England; and, as in England, it was achieved in alliance with the Roman church.

At first this extension of the Norman Conquest was peaceful, by social and cultural penetration only. Here the great success was in Scotland. In the long reign of David I, king of Scotland (1124–53), Norman barons and Norman monastic orders advanced into Scotland and obtained lands, for feudal and ecclesiastical settlement, in the borders, in central Scotland, in Aberdeenshire, and even in Inverness-shire and Orkney. Thus the descendants of the Irish kings of Scotland, who still used the Irish language, were surrounded by Norman barons, speaking Norman-French, and the Irish church, which had spread into Scotland from the Irish settlement of Iona, and which had once overflowed into the Saxon kingdom of Northumbria, now receded, in Scotland as previously in England, before the revived missionary Roman church.

The social and cultural conquest of Scotland took place in the 12th century. At that time Scotland was a far more open society than it would be for several centuries afterwards: the internationalism of the

Norman baronage and the Roman church made the political border insignificant. But conquest itself is indivisible and, in the years which followed, the same combination of Norman barons and the Roman church was using other methods to establish itself in other lands. From its base in France it would establish colonies in Syria and Palestine and exploit internal disputes in order to subvert the Byzantine empire; and from its base in Anglo-Saxon England it would invade and conquer the Celtic societies of Ireland and Wales.

The Norman Conquest of Ireland began, like that of Constantinople in 1204, with an invitation to intervene in a local dispute. An Anglo-Norman baron, Richard de Clare, earl of Pembroke, known as Strongbow, accepted such an invitation in 1166, exactly a century after the Norman Conquest of England, and ended, a few years later, by offering a conquered Ireland to the Plantagenet king of England. Henry II already ruled over an empire which stretched from the Cheviots to the Pyrenees. He accepted this new addition to it; and from then on the kings of England were lords of Ireland. As in their conquest of England, so in Ireland, they acted in concert with the international Roman church. In 1172 the Synod of Cashel reduced the Celtic church to the laws of Rome.

In the next century, the Norman kings of England sought to conquer both Wales and Scotland. Edward I succeeded in Wales, and a system of 'counts Palatine' – the marcher lords who guarded the frontier – and huge Norman castles ensured that Wales thereafter, deprived of its native princes, remained a subject province. But in Scotland he failed disastrously. There his forceful measures ended by undoing the cultural union which had been established by peaceful penetration and creating, for the first time, out of the fusion of Irish highlanders, English lowlanders and Norman barons, a Scottish nation.

In Ireland and Wales, the Anglo-Norman kings had conquered Celtic peoples under Celtic princes whose disorderly polity prevented any organized resistance. The struggles there were frontal struggles, between different races. In Scotland, at the beginning at least, the struggles had a different character: for the Scottish Crown and baronage were already Normanized. Therefore what seem, in retrospect, to be wars between two nations were in fact wars between Norman kings and Norman barons – a continuation of the baronial wars which had plagued Edward I's English kingdom under his father Henry III. Such wars were the internal struggles of a foreign ruling class. Indeed, in 1138 when David I – who, though not himself Norman, was an Anglo-Norman baron by adoption, had been educated at the Norman court of Henry I, and had Normanized his own country – invaded England, he was met in Yorkshire by another Anglo-Norman baron who sternly reproved him for using native soldiers – 'Picts of Galloway' – in a gentlemanly baronial war. The Yorkshire baron whose sense of social decorum was affronted by this action was Robert de Bruce, a Norman

A benign and triumphant Britannia symbolizes the unity of Great Britain after the accession of James I. (Title page of Michael Drayton's 'Poly-Olbion', 1612, which was a celebration of the history and the beauty of the British Isles.)

baron who happened also to have feudal lands in Scotland. Thanks to these Scottish interests, Bruce's grandson would compete with another Norman baron, John Balliol, for the Crown of Scotland as a feudal vassal of the Anglo-Norman king, Edward I, and his great-great-grandson would be the national hero of Scotland.

Had Edward I succeeded in Scotland as he had succeeded in Wales a unitary feudal kingdom of Great Britain would have been created. It would not, of course, have been self-contained, for the king of England was a European monarch with hereditary lands in Normandy and Aquitaine. Nor would it have been complete: although Irish chieftains did homage to their English lord, effective Norman colonization of Ireland did not stretch far beyond the 'Pale' of Dublin and the coastal towns. The power of the Norman feudatories in Scotland was similarly confined mainly to the Lowlands of the east. Outside these areas of settlement, in western Scotland as in Ireland, the old Irish culture survived intact. For a time, these areas of Irish culture, which were united, not divided, by the intervening sea, were under Scandinavian domination; but it was a superficial domination which left no deep traces, and was replaced in the later Middle Ages by a native Irish domination: that of the Macdonalds, Lords of the Isles. It was not till the 15th century that the rule of the Macdonalds was broken by the Crown of Scotland, and even then, although fragmented, it remained a force. Finally, there is no reason to suppose that the feudal unity at which Edward I aimed would have lasted. Norman feudalism was a system of exploitation: it was not, like the Christian reconquest in Spain, a system of settlement; and although the Norman barons, in Scotland and Ireland as in England, gradually identified themselves with the natives, this very fact worked against unity. Feudalism itself was anyway liable to disintegration through baronial independence. It foundered, even in England, in the 'bastard feudalism' of the 15th century. It is unlikely that it would have taken firmer root in Scotland than in Syria or Greece.

Such was the first attempt to unite the peoples of the British Isles under one political system. In 1300 it bade fair to succeed. By 1400 it had clearly failed. It had failed not only in Scotland but also in Ireland. There the Anglo-Norman families beyond the Pale, in spite of legislation designed to separate the two cultures and preserve the ascendancy of the ruling class, had gone native: they had taken to wearing Irish dress and speaking Irish. The king of England remained lord of Ireland, but it was a titular lordship which spasmodic punitive expeditions could not render real. Edward I, 'the English Justinian', had not effectively legislated from Wales, which he had conquered: far less for Ireland, whose conquest was nominal; and not at all for Scotland, which had defeated his efforts, as it had defeated those of the Romans, and which, in the 15th century, sank, even more than England, into baronial anarchy. By 1500 feudalism was bankrupt, and the unity of the three countries, which it had once seemed so close to achieving, was further away than ever. Thus ended the first stage of the attempt to unify Great Britain.

'A more perfect union': Tudors and Stuarts

After this failure, a second attempt, on a different basis, was made under the Tudor monarchs of England. If the first attempt had been 'feudal', the second was anti-feudal: it began, at least in Wales and Ireland, as an attempt to break the power of the surviving great feudatories and replace it by that of the new administrative state; and if the ideological basis of the first attempt was provided by the international Roman church, that of the second was supplied by the Reformed Church of England. Two other factors also distinguished the second from the first attempt.

Firstly, the motive force behind it was not merely a

desire, or a need, for expansion. It was defensive. There was the question of security. The Angevin kings, who ruled over much of western France, and were at peace with Scotland, had no fear of foreign invasion through Scotland or Ireland. But after the disastrous attempt to conquer Scotland, and the consequent Anglo-Scottish war, that condition changed. Scotland then became the ally of France; Paris became its cultural centre; and the country was used as a postern gate into England. As Shakespeare was to put it:

> For when the eagle England is at prey,
> To her unguarded nest the weasel Scot
> Comes sneaking, and so sucks her princely eggs.

Later, when Scotland had been reconciled to England, Ireland would replace it as a postern gate for the enemies of England, whether those enemies were Spanish, as in the reign of Elizabeth I, or French, in the time from Louis XIV to Napoleon. The control of Scotland and Ireland thus became a necessity of English defence.

Secondly, in Ireland at least, a new policy of settlement was adopted. For purely English reasons – English insecurity, English land-hunger, English internal revolution – Ireland was to become not a partner but a colony in the united British Isles. From this new development all the later enmity between England and Ireland was to flow.

The Tudors were Welsh, and they began with Wales. Henry VII absorbed the lands of the great marcher lords, and Henry VIII, having executed the last of them, the duke of Buckingham, passed an Act of Union with Wales and caused the country to be shired and governed, like England, by sheriffs. He also set up a Council of the Welsh Marches to impose the will of the central government on the old lordships. Thereafter, Wales was never a distinct problem to the British government. Indeed, the union gave to Welshmen an opportunity which they were quick to seize. Able Welshmen now flocked into England to serve a Welsh court which ostentatiously assumed the Welsh myth of King Arthur. Henry VII's heir was christened Arthur. Arthurian theories formed the propaganda of the Elizabethan court. The queen's greatest ministers, the Cecil family, were Welsh immigrants; and in the next century, when the English revolted against their Scottish dynasty, they did so under the lead of another descendant of Welsh immigrants, Oliver Cromwell, whose real name was Williams.

Ireland was less tractable. Here too the Tudors began by attempting to break the old Anglo-Norman baronage and subject the country to new 'conciliar' rule. Henry VII, by the so-called 'Poynings' Act' of 1495, subjected the Irish Parliament and Council to the English council, and Henry VIII made way on the Anglo-Irish magnates at the same time as on the great English lords. He finally destroyed the power of the Fitzgeralds, one of the original conquering Norman families which had 'gone native'. He then attempted to

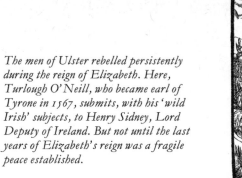

The men of Ulster rebelled persistently during the reign of Elizabeth. Here, Turlough O'Neill, who became earl of Tyrone in 1567, submits, with his 'wild Irish' subjects, to Henry Sidney, Lord Deputy of Ireland. But not until the last years of Elizabeth's reign was a fragile peace established.

bring those families back into subjection by changing the terms of their power. This was the policy known as 'Surrender and re-grant'. The Irish lords were required to surrender their titles to the king and then receive them back on new terms, undertaking to observe English law, to maintain no armed forces without the consent of the king's 'deputy' or governor, and to hold their lands by the same form of tenure as English landlords. In other words, the vague suzerainty of the previous kings was exchanged – on paper at least – for a precise relationship defined by English law. To formalize this change, Henry VIII changed his title. Hitherto the kings of England had been 'Lords of Ireland'; but in 1541, this papal title was repudiated together with the pope. Henry VIII was now recognized as 'King of Ireland', and the English Act of Supremacy, obediently confirmed by an Irish Parliament, made him, there too, Head of the Church.

On paper – the limitation is important. In fact the Tudors never imposed either their secular or their ecclesiastical rule effectively on Ireland. To do so would have required an effort for which they were not prepared. Ireland brought no revenue to England; to impose a policy which was unacceptable to the natives – both to the 'Old Irish', the Celtic natives, and to the 'Old English', the Anglo-Normans who had 'gone native' – was impossible without an occupying army; and the Tudor government was not willing to face the cost of an army except in times of actual rebellion or foreign invasion. There would be both rebellion and invasion during their rule, but the two coincided only at the end of it. That would be the beginning of a new stage.

Meanwhile there was Scotland. Here, too, Henry VIII, who had experienced a Scottish invasion at the beginning of his reign, sought to prevent a recurrence by securing his postern gate. Since Scottish independence was a fact, he attempted to secure the country by a dynastic marriage between his son, Edward VI, and the heiress to the Scottish throne, Mary Stuart. Unfortunately his methods, like those of Edward I, were counter-productive; the religious changes in

England were not yet acceptable in Catholic Scotland; the 'rough wooing' turned to aggressive war; and it was not till the reign of Elizabeth that Scotland was brought – and brought permanently – out of the orbit of France into that of England. This was the effect of the independent Protestant revolution in Scotland, which brought the Scottish nobility and the Scottish Presbyterian church – the two most powerful forces in that anarchical kingdom – into dependence on England. This dependence was achieved by diplomacy under Elizabeth. It was completed in 1603 by the succession of James VI, the ablest of Scottish kings, to the throne of England as James I. In the same year, the most formidable Irish rebellion against the government of Queen Elizabeth was crushed. The Spaniards who had exploited it, and had landed in Kinsale, had been driven out. The rebel earl of Tyrone, who had kept Ulster in revolt, was now forced to surrender; and the new king, as the ruler of three kingdoms, now all at peace, could proudly style himself King of Great Britain.

It was as yet a fragile union, but James was determined to make it real. At the very beginning of his reign, he sought to achieve 'a more perfect union' with Scotland, granting to the Scots the same rights under the Crown as were possessed by the English and importing into Scotland the English system of local justice: government by sheriffs and JPs instead of the hereditary jurisdiction of great nobles. In these large plans, he was defeated by English jealousy: the English disliked the Scots, the 'beggarly blue-caps' who now hurried south to compete for the royal favour, and foresaw, if James had his way, a massive invasion of lean and hungry immigrants. But James, though checked, did not give up his ultimate aim. Thanks to English resources, and to his own distance from that turbulent country, which he perfectly understood, he was able to rule Scotland more effectively than any of his Scottish precursors. He reduced the turbulent barons to order. He controlled the Scottish Parliament through the 'Lords of the Articles'. He was also able to bring the country into some conformity with England.

The decision of Charles I to impose the Book of Common Prayer on the Presbyterian Kirk provoked violent revolt throughout Scotland: here, the 'Arch-Prelate of St Andrewes ... reading the new Service-booke' is assaulted with stools, sticks and stones.

In 1610, by skilful management, he restored the Scottish episcopal church which had been effectively destroyed by the Calvinist revolution of John Knox and his successors. With nobility and church under control, he could boast, at the end of his reign: 'Here I sit; I write and it is done; and I govern with the pen that country which my ancestors could never govern with the sword.'

It was the same in Ireland. Throughout the reign of James I – as in no other reign till the next century – Ireland was at peace. There too the absentee Crown balanced the local factions. There too the Protestant episcopal church was established. There too – thanks to Poynings' Act – Parliament was under control. There too, it seemed, the pacification of ancient feuds would allow economic improvement to follow, and so, as Francis Bacon wrote, the last of the daughters of Europe would be reclaimed from barbarism to civility.

Of course there were strains, as there are strains in any society, however stable it may seem. But the strains were absorbed. The pace was not forced. The political control was not disputed. Above all, religion was contained. The Anglican *via media*, which had been accepted in Elizabethan England, may not have been so perfectly adapted to Scottish or Irish tastes; it may have been a little too conservative for the one and too radical for the other; but it had been established without difficulty. The Catholic church in Ireland, as in Scotland, had collapsed without a blow, and those Irish chiefs who had rebelled against Elizabeth had not thought to consecrate their rebellion by appeal to religion. Nor was the new Protestant church of Ireland a persecuting church: it could not afford to be. Catholics sat in the Irish Parliament: indeed they were a majority there; and although gradually they would lose their predominance, that would be by the creation of new constituencies, not by discriminatory legislation. To an observer in 1620 it might well have seemed that the future was clear and hopeful. Unity and uniformity

– political and religious unity, legal uniformity – might not come as soon as King James had hoped, but it was on its way. Meanwhile minds were being prepared by propaganda. The ablest of Scottish lawyers, Sir Thomas Craig, set out the need for complete legal union with England and one of the most learned of Jacobean scholars, James Ussher, archbishop of Armagh, demonstrated that all three kingdoms, from the time of the Apostles until the Norman Conquest, had equally enjoyed a Protestant episcopal church.

Alas, once again the mirage vanished before it could be grasped. Indeed, it was in the reign of James I that the process of disintegration began. In the next reign, that of Charles I, the whole policy collapsed, and the second stage of the unification of Britain was changed, like the first, from peaceful adaptation to forcible, and ultimately ineffectual, conquest. These first steps were, in Ireland, the Plantation of Ulster and the arrival of Catholic missionaries, and, in Scotland, the disastrous policy of Charles I who contrived to alienate and unite against him the two most powerful forces in the country, by dividing which James I had been so successful: the nobility and the Kirk.

There is no need to go into details of the revolutions which convulsed the relations of the three kingdoms in the mid-17th century; but the Plantation of Ulster has had such profound and lasting consequences that it deserves special emphasis. From the beginning, Ulster was the heart of Ireland: the political heart, for it was the home of its most energetic tribe, who had colonized and conquered Scotland; the cultural heart, for it was the source, and the scene, of its national epics. But its very proximity to Scotland, which had led to that colonization – in the reign of James I Ireland and Scotland could still be described as 'the greater and the lesser Scotland' – meant that communication and colonization could be reversed. After 1600 it was reversed. The Scots of 'the lesser Scotland' then returned to their home in Ulster; but they returned transformed, and in depth, and as conquerors. They are still there today.

The 'Plantation' of Ireland did not begin with Ulster, or in the 17th century. In a sense it had begun with the Anglo-Normans; but the Anglo-Normans had been absorbed and were by now the Catholic 'Old English' landlords. It had been resumed in the 16th century, in the reign of the Catholic Mary Tudor, with Leix and Offaly: the two counties were then named King's County and Queen's County after King Philip and Queen Mary. It had continued under Elizabeth. But even these later colonists, 'the new English', though predatory and resented, had come as individual adventurers, not as a solid nation. If landlords, they were content – indeed, in the end, obliged – to keep Irish tenants. But the Scots came to Ireland, back to Ireland, as they had previously gone to Scotland: as a nation, or part of a nation. That made a lasting difference.

If we are to find an analogy, perhaps we should look

east, to modern Palestine. There too, after many centuries, thanks to a particular, almost accidental political conjuncture, the descendants of the original inhabitants have returned, not (like the Christian crusaders) as a superficial evanescent class, but in depth, as a distinct, inassimilable people. There too, for a time, imperial rule masked their distinct character and controlled the tensions which it caused. There too, the withdrawal of imperial power would reveal that character and present the world with an intractable, perhaps insoluble political problem.

The particular political conjuncture which led to the Plantation of Ulster was the defeat of the Ulster Rebellion in the last years of Queen Elizabeth, followed by the flight, in 1607, of two of the greatest Ulster chiefs, Hugh O'Neill, earl of Tyrone, and Rory O'Donnell, earl of Tyrconnel. London capital and Scottish energy created a new society on the confiscated estates, and this society, continuously reinforced from Scotland, and deliberately strengthening itself after each native revolt, gradually became an implacable, irreducible, unforgivable Protestant redoubt, whose true character, long masked by aristocratic and imperial power, would reveal itself when that power crumbled or threatened to abdicate.

The collapse of James I's hopes of 'a more perfect union' of all three countries under an 'absolute' modern monarchy and a Protestant episcopal church was hastened by the authoritarian recklessness of his son and completed in the violent reaction which followed. In the 1630s the earl of Strafford in Ireland, having begun by balancing between native and planter in order to build up royal power, ended by uniting both against that power. Similarly, in Scotland, the king challenged both nobility and clergy, and ended by uniting them against him. By 1640 all parties alike looked to Parliament for satisfaction. In the summer of 1641, for a brief moment, it looked as if a general settlement would preserve the unity, and the harmony, of all three kingdoms; but the moment was very brief. In their desperate struggle for power in England, both king and Parliament sought assistance from parties in Ireland and Scotland, and thereby increased the tensions which it was the function of statesmen to allay. All hopes of peaceful settlement were then wrecked by the Ulster Rising of October 1641; the rising triggered the Civil War in England; and the necessities of war caused the Parliament to bring a Scottish army into England in 1643. Thus the English revolution was turned, by its own momentum, into 'the War of the Three Kingdoms'.

The legacy of revolution

The Civil Wars of England ended in 1649 with the execution of the king, Charles I, and the creation of a republic; those of Ireland and Scotland with the military conquest of both countries by Oliver Cromwell in 1650–1. Then, for the first time, the British Isles were united, not only under one government and (in theory) one religion, but also under one Parliament, one economic system, and (potentially) one law: for in Scotland Cromwell sought to realize the aims of James I, abolishing hereditary jurisdictions and reforming the law and local government on an English model. Unfortunately the very method whereby that unity was attained ensured that it could only be formal. It was also brief. On Cromwell's death, it crumbled again. When Charles II was restored, the formal constitutional position reverted to that of 1640, but in fact there was a significant difference. Twenty years of civil war had inevitably inflamed old tensions and bred new interests and resentments. To crush the Irish rebels, to punish them for 'that execrable massacre' – the Ulster Rising of 1641, which (greatly exaggerated) would remain part of the Protestant folklore for more than a century – the English Parliament (and Cromwell after it) had been ruthless in its methods. It had financed the war by a policy of expropriation which Cromwell's victory would enable it to realize. The Irish, left without effective political leadership, turned, like other oppressed and leaderless peoples – like the Greeks under Ottoman or the Poles under Russian and Prussian rule – to religion. They declared the pope to be their king and accepted his nuncio as their general. The Scots similarly turned to the Presbyterian church. At the Restoration of the monarchy in 1660, all three countries consecrated their mutual revulsion by resuming their national religion in an intolerant form. The national Church of England became intolerantly Anglican, that of the Scots intolerantly Presbyterian, that of the Irish intolerantly Catholic. Although the Protestant Episcopalian church was maintained by authority in both Scotland and Ireland, it was a frail thing, the mark of English supremacy. It was not a national church. The ideal of James I, of a tolerant uniform religious system in all three countries, had gone for ever.

This intensification of distinct religious loyalties was carried further after the second stage of the English revolution, which began with the Glorious Revolution of 1688. James II, like his father Charles I, had sought to build up his power in all three countries and, again like Charles I, he precipitated a revolution in all three countries. But this second revolution was simpler than the first because its base was narrower, and more clearly defined. It was not merely a struggle for power, for a return to autocracy, which might perhaps have been won. It was also an attempt to re-establish Catholicism, which proved its ruin. Because of this simplification, the revolution triumphed easily in England and Scotland, but was resisted firmly in Ireland. By supporting the Stuarts the Catholic Irish hoped to recover their lost lands and lost rights; and so Ireland became the last redoubt of the Catholic king. When William of Orange followed James to Ireland, he came, like Cromwell, to save the Protestant English establishment from a native Catholic revolt, and to ensure that Ireland would not be used by a foreign power as a means of counter-revolution. His bridgehead was the Protestant north-east; his victory on the Boyne, and the relief of Londonderry, opened the way to the reconquest of all Ireland just as Cromwell's victory at Drogheda had done; and the conquest, once again, led to still further discrimination in order to guarantee that the revolt would not, once again, be repeated. After each revolt, for the last century and more, the result had been the same: confiscation and plantation, the replacement of natives by planters. Increasingly, too, the power of the planters was reinforced by discriminatory legislation. After the revolt of 1641, Catholics had been excluded from the Irish Parliament and, although they returned after 1660, they were again finally excluded in 1689. By the Cromwellian reconquest they had lost, irrecoverably, nearly half their remaining land. After 1689 they suffered further discrimination, designed to prevent them from ever acquiring, or recovering, possession of land. The Catholic church hierarchy, which had existed alongside the Anglican hitherto, was now abolished. Although not actively persecuted, in every respect the Irish Catholics became second- or third-class citizens. Politically, for over a century, the Irish nation was confined to the Protestants: that is, very largely to the English planters; for in the North even the 'Scots of Ulster' chafed under the dominance of the landed class. So Ireland, which in 1625 had been a distinct kingdom with its own native, or assimilated, ruling class, became a colony: a colony of conquest, expropriation, discrimination.

Such was the terrible legacy of the 17th century to Ireland. To Scotland it was very different. For Scotland, even under English conquest, was never 'planted'. Under Cromwell, Scotland and Ireland both sent Members to the British Parliament; but whereas the Irish Members were English officers or English planters, the Scottish were Scotchmen. At one time, indeed, a 'plantation' of Scotland was suggested. In 1657, exasperated by the obstinate nonconformity of the Scots under English conquest, Cromwell's commander in Scotland, General Monck, wrote that, if all else failed to pacify the country: 'I think it were just reason to plant it with English.' All else did fail, but luckily the Protectorate of Oliver Cromwell failed too. Otherwise, Scotland might have been 'planted', and the history of Anglo-Scottish relations might thereafter have been very different.

As it was, in the long run the Scots remembered the economic benefits rather than the political compulsion of Cromwell's conquest. Only a few years after the Restoration of the monarchy, and with it of Scottish independence, the Scots petitioned for that 'more perfect union' with England which had been set forth by 'His Majesty's royal grandfather King James'. The project was killed by the English, who rebelled against the proposed over-representation of Scotland in the British Parliament. But as the political and economic condition of independent Scotland worsened, Scottish politicians came more and more to seek a full union with England, and after the Glorious Revolution of 1688, when the exiled Stuarts sought to recover power

by means of native revolt and French invasion in Scotland as in Ireland, the English politicians came to accept the same view. So, while Catholic Ireland was made secure by the forcibly imposed and unbreakable monopoly of a Protestant landed class and a Protestant episcopal church, Protestant Scotland was made secure by an equal union, in which the Scots preserved their own law and their own church and Scottish merchants and manufacturers gained equal access to the markets of the British Empire.

The result was remarkable. While Ireland, under the rule of a foreign caste, remained sunk in helpless poverty, Scotland in the 18th century enjoyed an extraordinary economic and cultural efflorescence. For centuries the Lowland Scots – that mixture of Pict and Gael and Saxon which had been moulded by European institutions – had been a defensive society cramped between two other societies which it distrusted. To the south was the historic enemy, England, from which all threats of conquest had come. To the west was the primitive tribal society of the Highlands, the source indeed of the Scottish dynasty and people, but now arrested in its own 'Irish' culture, inaccessible in its valleys and islands, despised and sometimes feared. Even Cromwell's army had not penetrated those tribal areas which the most ambitious governments in Scotland sought only to cordon off. But after the Union of 1707 the fear of invasion from the south ceased and, after the suppression of the last Highland revolt in 1745, the whole Highland society was broken up and dissolved. The united British government had resources which the independent Scottish government had lacked; and Scottish society, enriched and excited by new economic opportunities, entered into that remarkable phase of history known as the Scottish Enlightenment.

One of the most important effects of the defeat of the

1707: the Duke of Queensberry presents the Act of Union between England and Scotland to Queen Anne.

last Highland revolt was the statute which finally abolished the hereditary jurisdictions of the nobility. It was these jurisdictions – or at least so it was believed – which had enabled the Jacobite aristocracy in Scotland to raise armies against the Hanoverian government. James I had sought to abolish 'all these unjust powers' which he had seen as 'the greatest hindrance to the execution of our laws'; but in vain. Cromwell had abolished them during his brief period of power; but they had been restored in 1660. Now at least they were effectively abolished and, with the opening up of the Highlands, the rule of law extended, for the first time, over the whole country. It was with reference to this change that David Hume wrote, in the 1750s, that although the Highlanders of Scotland had long been entitled to all the rights of British subjects, it was only in the last few years that they had been able to enjoy them.

The third unification

The Act of Union with Scotland in 1707 marks the beginning of the third attempt effectively to unite all three kingdoms; but it also illustrates the complete divergence which the revolutions of the 17th century had caused between English policy in Scotland and English policy in Ireland. While the Act of Union with Scotland was being negotiated, the Irish House of Commons passed a resolution requesting a similar union, but the English government declined to consider it: it preferred to exercise direct control over Irish affairs through the appointed viceroy and the operation of Poynings' Act. In any case, a similar Act of Union could not, at that time, have led to similar results; for the Irish Parliament was now as unrepresentative as the established Church of Ireland: it represented the Protestant establishment – effectively, the English 'planters' – only, and a parliamentary union would not have been a union of independent representative legislatures but merely – as under Cromwell – the inclusion in the British Parliament of the nominees of a colonial élite.

This essential fact vitiated all Irish politics in the 18th century. As the century progressed, the Protestant landlord class – the Protestant Ascendancy as it was called – felt itself secure, and, feeling secure, began, like the English colonists in America, once they were relieved of anxiety, to demand legislative independence. That is, they wished to be freed from the control which the British government exercised through Poynings' Act. Such independence had been demanded in the reign of Charles I, when the Irish landlords had still been mainly Catholic and the Irish Parliament had still contained Catholic Members. But now it was demanded for the Protestant colonists only. In 1782, when the British government was about to yield to the American colonists, and leave them free to perpetuate a society based on slavery, it yielded also to the Irish colonists, and left them free to perpetuate their 'ascendancy'. Poynings' Act was effectively abolished, and 'Grattan's Parliament' was able to pose, for a time,

'*No power on earth but the king, lords and commons of Ireland is competent to bind Ireland*': in 1782, thanks to pressure exerted by the Protestant Ascendancy, Ireland, '*Hibernia*', was delivered from Poynings' Act (a contemporary cartoon).

as the independent legislature of a sister kingdom. In appearance, it was a move away from unity, towards separation. In fact it led, within a few years, to complete union.

For in fact the parallel with the American plantations is not complete. Both in America and in Ireland, in the mid-18th century, the planter class felt secure; but the security of the former was more real than that of the latter. After 1763 the American colonists had no fear of their previous enemies, the French in Canada. That chapter of history was closed. But the security of the colonists in Ireland was temporary only: their most dangerous enemy was not the external enemy, who had been defeated, but an internal enemy, the native Catholic population; and that population, though cowed, was still resentful. It was also far more numerous than they. Moreover, in time of war, there was always the danger that a foreign enemy might exploit that resentment. The Spaniards had done so in 1601, and the French in 1690. In time of peace, that danger might recede; but within a few years of Grattan's triumph, its hollowness was shown. The French Revolution kindled the hope of revolution everywhere, even in Ireland, and the Napoleonic Wars raised again the spectre of a foreign landing to exploit local resentment. In such circumstances the Protestant Ascendancy realized that it could not exploit – could not be allowed to exploit – the luxury of independence. For it was not in fact independence. It owed its position to British support: support not only against the resentment of the Catholic peasantry but also – and in the 1790s this seemed an equal threat – against the radicalism of Protestant artisans in the North.

Moreover, that support was not unconditional, although the planters too often assumed that it should be; as their successors in Ulster have long continued to do. For by now the mood in England had changed. In the 17th century the English government had feared, above all things, a Catholic reaction, or an invasion by Catholic powers exploiting the Stuart cause. After 1745 such fears dissolved, and in that liberal, sceptical age the sectarian zeal of the previous century went out of fashion. In such circumstances, discrimination on grounds of religion became, to educated men, indefensible. In the 1790s, in England, Catholic Relief Acts were passed, and in Revolutionary France the discriminatory laws against Huguenots were swept away. Even in Ireland the 'independent' Parliament accepted a Bill, dictated from England, to allow Catholics to vote in parliamentary elections. But where, it might be asked, would such a process end? If religious discrimination was indefensible, why should Roman Catholics be allowed merely to vote? How could they (if otherwise eligible) be denied the right to sit in Parliament? And if that should happen, where would the Protestant Ascendancy be?

At present, admittedly, they held the reality of power. They had closed every breach in their monopoly. They had made themselves independent. But these were mere mechanical devices. In a conquered country, where an alien aristocracy, imposed by force, controls the entire mechanism of government, and the natives are denied any means of participation, the only resort left to them is force. In the 18th century the Irish peasantry, organized in secret societies, took to systematic violence against Protestant landlords and thus began a tradition which would soon be transferred to politics and has never ceased. Under the restricted 18th-century franchise, the new Catholic electors could only be men of some property; but in the years after 1790, under the pressure of 'revolutionary principles', electoral reform was in the air, and indeed was being demanded more vigorously by the radical Protestants of the North than by the cowed Catholics of the South. The combination of possible Catholic emancipation with possible electoral reform and the real resentments of the Irish people were thus an alarming prospect to the English landlord class; and it was this prospect which, against the background of war, fear of revolution and an actual insurrection backed by a French landing, put a quick inglorious end to the 'independence' of Grattan's Parliament and, at last, in 1800, led to the third stage in the unity of Britain, the parliamentary union of all three countries, under the title of 'the United Kingdom of Great Britain and Ireland'.

The Union of Britain with Ireland in 1800–1 was based on the Union of England with Scotland in 1707. Indeed, it was then that the documents of the Anglo-Scottish Union were published, as a model to be followed. And in fact, the two unions had something in common. Both were imposed by immediate need. In 1707 it was the need to secure the English Revolution and to guarantee the Protestant succession. In 1880 it was the need to resist the French Revolution and to preserve the Protestant Ascendancy in Ireland, and thereby the British control of Ireland. In both cases also there were strong local motives for union. But there was also local resistance. The Protestant landlords in Ireland, like the lairds of Scotland, were not enthusiastic to be saved, and now, as then, a good deal of manipulation and lubrication was necessary to persuade them. They enjoyed their 'independence' and the Irish Parliament which they seemed to control; they did not wish to exchange status in Dublin for insignificance in London; and they reckoned that they could best defend their own interests in their own Parliament. But the politicians perhaps saw further. They saw that in the new era, with or without Catholic emancipation, only union could secure, and perhaps restrain, the Protestant interest. Some saw union as a substitute for emancipation – and having secured union, they contrived to postpone emancipation for a generation. Others saw union as a condition of emancipation: for the Catholics, who would then dominate an 'independent' Parliament in Dublin, would be a minority in a British Parliament at Westminster. In any case, union was a necessity. Only thereby could the Protestant planter-élite be secured, now that its *raison être* had gone, against the threat of 'a popish democracy'.

Luckily for the Unionists, the circumstances of the time gave them other allies. With revolution in the background, conservatives of whatever religion supported the established order. Moreover, the threat of a new order had broken up an old alliance. When the rule of English landlords had seemed unshakeable, the Presbyterian traders and artisans of the North had joined with the Catholics of the South, as 'United Irishmen', to challenge it. But as the form of an alternative society became apparent, the divergences within it also appeared. It was in the 1790s, in the years of threatened revolution, that the radical Protestants of Ulster began once more to look at the Catholic peasants of the South not as oppressed brethren in a present struggle but as rivals for the ultimate spoils, and to hate and fear them. It was then that the Orange Order was founded, then that Catholic sectarianism was mobilized against it. Therein lay a new source of division: a division which would not merely separate Ireland from England, but fragment Ireland itself.

Britain has never been a completely unitary state. It has never had, under the same Crown, effective all over three kingdoms, one legislature, one established church, one law. Under James I there was one established church, but not one Parliament or one law;

but under Charles I that unity was atomized. The Cromwellian union, though theoretically complete, was never effective. After 1800 there was one Parliament but not one established church or one law, for the Scots had preserved their own; and soon the Protestant Church of Ireland would be disestablished too. Nevertheless, the period 1800 to 1922 is the period during which unity was most nearly achieved. Even so, it was a fragile unity, and the cracks were not long in appearing.

Perhaps they would have appeared sooner, but for a time they were obscured. One of the veils which obscured them was romanticism. In the 18th century, 'improving' Scotchmen looked with contempt or shame at the barbarous condition of their country before the Union and the Protestants of Ireland did not allow the Celtic Irish to speak. But after the defeat of the last Highland rebellion, and the opening up of the Highlands, the Celts of Scotland ceased to be dangerous and became picturesque. At the same time, the opening out of Lowland Scotland enabled a later generation to look dispassionately, even indulgently, on the cramped lives and internecine feuds of their ancestors. This was the mood that was captured by Sir Walter Scott. But Scott was not the first novelist to exploit that vein. In her Irish novels, published from 1800 onwards, Maria Edgeworth, the daughter of an Anglo-Irish landlord in Ireland, similarly depicted the rural life of Ireland in a manner which softened its harsh lines. Afterwards, in acknowledging his debt to Miss Edgeworth, Scott remarked that nothing had done more than her novels to disperse popular prejudice against the Union of Ireland, and he added that he hoped, by his novels, to achieve the same result in Scotland: for although the Scottish Union was never seriously challenged until the 20th century, popular prejudice in Scotland had always been quick to blame it for any inconvenience. Romanticism generally is a conservative force and can provide a useful safety-valve for nationalism where real grievances are not strong. Real grievances were not strong in Scotland. It was different in Ireland. There, even in the life of Miss Edgeworth, the movement to repeal the Union would be under way.

The struggle for Home Rule

There is a certain irony about the Irish Union. It had been imposed on the reluctant Irish Parliament by a British government which had to resort to wholesale bribery in order to achieve it: for the Protestant landlords of Ireland believed that their own 'independent' legislature was the best guarantee of their power. But once the Union had been achieved, the terms of politics changed. The demand for 'Home Rule now' came mainly from the Catholics of Ireland, who saw the revival of the independent Irish Parliament as the only means of overthrowing the Protestant Ascendancy. The explanation is obvious. It lies in the transformation of the British Parliament, first by Catholic emancipation, blocked in 1800 but ultimately achieved in 1829,

then by the gradual widening of the franchise from 1832. Thus it was entirely logical that the great Irish demagogue, Daniel O'Connell, whose agitation finally secured the Act for Catholic emancipation, then moved on to demand repeal of the Union. It is arguable, of course, that the Irish landlords were wise in their own generation: that the independent Irish Parliament would never have agreed to the Catholic emancipation or the widened franchise and would thus have preserved the status quo. No doubt such conservatism would have led, like the conservatism of the Southern planters in America, to a civil war. Perhaps therefore the Act of Union, seen by its architects as the only means of preserving the Protestant interest in the new age, could have been defended at the time as the most promising means of dissolving that interest and thereby effecting, by legislation, a revolutionary change.

The change duly came, and it came by legislation. In spite of the terrible famine of 1845 – as critical to Ireland as the Jacobite rising of 1745 to Scotland – and this constant, counter-productive force of sectarian strife and agrarian violence, by the close of the 19th century Ireland had been transformed. If Gladstone had been able to carry his policy of Home Rule through the British Parliament, the Irish would have recovered their 'independent' legislature under native – that is, Catholic – control. It would not have been entirely independent, for Home Rule was not separation; but then it had not been entirely independent in 1782: there had always been the viceroy and the castle. However, Gladstone failed, as Asquith after him failed; Home Rule was never tried, and we cannot say whether it would have been successful. The forces which broke it were many and complex; but they were not, in the end, the English 'planters'. Their power, dwindling through the century, was effectively destroyed by the English Tory government of the 1890s, and by the 20th century they were content to merge into Irish society. The last and most resolute and most successful defenders of the Union, those who were prepared to face and prolong civil war rather than accept Home Rule, were the descendants not of the Anglican landlords of the South but of the Scottish Presbyterian settlers in Ulster.

When the battle-lines were drawn, after the last Home Rule Bill of 1912, neither side thought in terms of partition. The Unionists fought for the Union of all Ireland with Britain: the Home-Rulers for the autonomy – and ultimately the complete independence – of all Ireland. Even today, the Irish Republic does not recognize partition: its constitution explicitly claims authority in all Ireland. Partition is the result of deadlock. But such partitions, if the result of ideological or social antithesis, can be permanent. In the mid-16th century, the seventeen provinces of the Netherlands were united under the heirs of the Burgundian dukes. Those who fought on each side – the king of Spain to preserve the union, William of Orange for Home Rule – always claimed obedience or freedom for all the provinces. Their heirs had to settle for deadlock and partition; and once opposite religious systems had become established on either side of the frontier, no reunion was possible. It was tried in 1815 and lasted only fifteen years. The division of modern Germany and Korea is similar. Partitioned Ireland today satisfies no one except the Ulster Protestants; but it may nevertheless last – unless the British government, weary of a too imperious loyalty, disowns the planted society of the North as it previously disowned the planter élite of the South.

The failure of the last Home Rule Bill through the refusal of the Ulster Protestants, the Easter Rising of 1916, the civil war and the Treaty of 1922 marked the final failure of the Union of 1800; the grant of Home Rule, and its own Parliament, to six counties of Ulster, was its unexpected result. The Parliament at Stormont has not been a great success. Whether a similar Parliament for all Ireland, at Dublin, as envisaged in the Home Rule Bills, would have been any more successful is an open question. It has never been tried.

The present state of the Union

Recently, the scene has moved from Ireland to Scotland. All through the 19th century, the Union of England and Scotland was unquestioned. The advantages for Scotland had been immense, and the Scots who, thanks to the Union, exploited the commerce of the Empire and peopled Canada and Australia – unlike the Irish emigrants who carried their long-lasting resentments to America – remained loyal subjects of the United Kingdom. So pleased were educated Scots by the Union that, in the late 18th century, they sought to forget the name of Scotland, preferring to call their country North Britain: a usage which was still regarded as natural in the 1920s but is now resented by Scottish nationalists as an English insult. (I am told that the sharp-eyed workers in the Scotch Post Office now maliciously redirect letters containing the once usual abbreviation N.B. to New Brunswick.) Even in the 1890s, an Englishman could be appointed secretary of state for Scotland without exciting comment. (To make it worse, he was a Northumbrian.) But recently Scottish nationalism has raised its head and what began as a party of tartan romantics has, thanks to the discovery of North Sea oil, become a force in Scottish politics sufficiently formidable to frighten the British Labour Party into a programme of 'Devolution' – that is, of Home Rule for Scotland similar to that offered to Ireland and secured by Ulster. Of the policy of Devolution it is not necessary to speak here. Its origins lay rather in the fears of the labour Party than in the demands of Scots – for Scotland was an electoral fief of the Labour Party the loss of which would be fatal to its prospects of power in England. But since the Irish parallel was often cited in those debates, it is worth remarking that the parallel has no force. Since the 17th

century, although the policy of England has embraced unity with both countries, and although the stages in that policy have superficial similarities, there is one fundamental difference which renders any pretended analogy meaningless. Scotland was never 'planted'. The whole history of Anglo-Irish relations was conditioned, and those relations vitiated, by the plantations of the 17th century. Indeed, by the earliest of those plantations, the Scottish Plantation of Ulster, they are vitiated still.

To state this is to state the obvious. But still a mystery remains. What is the factor which made the differences between the planters and the natives so acute? It was not merely the acquisition of land, for that happened elsewhere: expropriation and eviction in 16th-century England and in 18th-century Scotland caused less lasting resentments. The early Anglo-Norman settlers in Ireland were absorbed into Irish society. Was it then a difference of race: Saxon against Celt? This is often and easily said but, on examination, difficulties arise. The discrimination in the 17th and 18th centuries was not by race but only by religion, and those who lost most by it were in fact not Celts but Anglo-Normans, 'the Old English' who, in 1600, were still the richest and best-established landlords in the country. Englishmen who were Catholics suffered under the penal laws, Irish who were Protestant did not. It is certainly true that Catholicism became the badge of the Celtic Irish in the 17th century just as Protestantism became the badge of the landlord class; but to treat it as a mere badge is difficult. That is to assume that Saxon and Celt are *a priori* inassimilable. But this was not so in Wales or in Scotland. Wales, like Ireland, was conquered; great castles were built to keep the Celtic population in awe; but it was not 'planted'. The Scottish Highland society collapsed in 1746 more completely than the Celtic society of Ireland before its 17th-century invaders, and yet a new ruling class did not impose itself; not did the Highlanders sink into slavery. Perhaps they were fortunate in their time: racial differences were not then polarized by religion.

However we seek to explain it, the fact remains that the unification of Britain, which was achieved successfully, if unevenly, in Celtic Wales and in Anglo-Celtic Scotland, failed disastrously in Anglo-Celtic Ireland; and it failed because in Ireland, and only in Ireland, the antithesis between conqueror and conquered gradually came to correspond with an antithesis of race, consecrated and embittered by a difference of religion; and because the period in which union was most actively pursued happened to coincide with a period when, in England, passions and fears were flamed by civil war, revolution and threats of foreign invasion. From such accidental convergences of circumstances do long and painful historical experiences flow.

III
Phenomenon of Empire

**6 Exploration and
the First British Empire**
Settlement and colonization in the New World

**7 The Rise and Fall
of the Second British Empire**
India, Africa and Australia

THE RISE OF EMPIRES is a slower, more complex and usually more unplanned process than the critics of 'imperialism' are ready to concede. That of Britain is perhaps the most striking illustration of all. In time it stretches from the first attempts to found colonies in America under Elizabeth I to the annexations and protectorates that followed the First World War. Every step in this 300-year-long saga has a different background and a different explanation. Colonies in North America, South Africa, Australia and New Zealand were mostly seen as simply settling and cultivating unoccupied land for various reasons – to make a profit, to gain political or religious freedom, to escape starvation, to unload surplus population. Any fighting involved was chiefly against other European claimants. In India, the network of trading concessions, administrative controls and indirect intervention through the native princes all arose from private initiatives before the Crown was obliged to take over. But as the role of central government grew, so did a consciously imperialist attitude. The acquisition of Uganda, the Sudan and Burma, the British protectorate over Palestine and similar moves were acts which assumed something like a British 'mission' to rule. By the second half of the 19th century such assumptions had become general in Europe: France, Germany, Belgium and (belatedly) Italy also became convinced that the deliberate acquisition of overseas territory was a means of increasing their material wealth and power. In pursuit of this aim, the last remaining continent to be explored – Africa – was parcelled out between them.

The British Empire was at its maximum extent between 1921 and 1939, although already the most British parts of it had become self-governing Dominions. After 1945 the whole vast fabric collapsed in a matter of twenty years, leaving a legacy of British-influenced institutions and, in some cases, anti-British feelings. The hope that the Empire would be succeeded by a multiracial Commonwealth with many real interests in common is coming to seem too optimistic.

Emigration

was a real and relatively simple option for English men and women up to 1939. The majority of them went to North America, South Africa, Australia or New Zealand, a movement of people that has no exact parallel in other European countries, since the emigrants remained under the British flag. Personal links with the mother-country remained, and still remain, strong. C. J. Staniland's picture *The Emigrant Ship*, painted about 1890, shows the sort of scene that must have been familiar at such ports as Liverpool. The younger generation, with fewer roots at home, leave to seek fortunes overseas. Parents and grandparents sadly watch them go, and in the centre a countryman in a smock waves his stick in farewell. (1)

England renewed

The first colonists in America had no intention of founding an 'empire'. They were re-creating England – without its vices and imperfections. The very names, 'New England', 'Nova Scotia' ... down to tiny villages like Hingham, Massachusetts, preserved memories of their roots at home.

Baltimore began as a 'tobacco port' in the 18th century, but its later prosperity was based on flour. In the earliest known view, in 1752 (*above*), it was still a collection of about fifty households. (2)

Boston by 1801 (*below*) was a thriving town of 25,000 inhabitants, the fourth largest in the USA. Its main square, with the Old State House at one end, is surrounded by dignified classical houses. (3)

The gentry among the early colonists followed the style of their peers at home. Here a hunting party sets out, in a 17th-century painting from a house in New Jersey. *Left*: Mrs Reuben Humphreys of Connecticut, with some of the furniture belonging to her position. (4, 5)

In Lower Canada the English ruling classes tended to be ultra-conservative, partly in reaction against the republicanism of the United States (Canadians firmly refused to be 'liberated', and thousands of discontented loyalists moved north after 1780), partly because of their position vis-à-vis the French majority. Typical of the English establishment is this cultured family of merchants, the Woolseys, depicted there in 1809. (6)

Australasia: the last continent

England's first use for Australia was as a penal colony; voluntary immigration began seriously around 1800. The settlement of New Zealand began later still, starting with missionary expeditions in 1814.

Vice-Admiral Arthur Phillip was appointed first governor of New South Wales in 1787. 'No country', he wrote, 'offers less assistance to first settlers.' But when he left five years later the colony was well established and growing fast, with many ex-convicts in possession of farms. (7)

Sydney, chosen by Phillip in preference to Botany Bay, soon developed into a populous city. In 1888 (*below*) it had all the features of a European capital, including extensive docks. The promontory on the left, Benalong Point, is now the site of Sydney Opera House, that on the right the Harbour Bridge. (8)

COPYRIGHTED SEP 3 1888. THE CITY OF SYDNEY BY M.S.HILL SYDNEY.

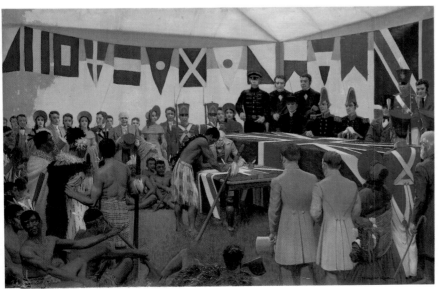

The Commonwealth of Australia
came into being on the first day of
1901, each state enjoying a wide
measure of independence within a
federation. The first federal parliament
was opened in May of the same year in
the exhibition building of Melbourne.
The duke of York, later George V,
reads the inaugural address. (9)

New Zealand's history was always
separate from that of Australia, not
least because the Maori inhabitants
were culturally far more advanced than
the aborigines. The Treaty of
Waitangi, signed in 1840, was designed
– not very successfully – to safeguard
Maori rights: a later painting (*left*)
shows chief Tamati Waka Nene
signing before governor William
Hobson. (10)

Africa

During the early 19th century West and Central Africa were assailed by two kinds of European enterprise: of traders and of missionaries. The flag (i.e. government) followed. After the 1880s the mood changed and in competition with other European countries Britain became a conscious imperialist.

Stanley meets Livingstone (*left*). The engraving was made with Stanley's own advice and according to him 'is as correct as if the scene had been photographed'. (11)

In the south European expansion was challenged by powerful tribes such as the Matabele and the Zulus. First contacts, however, were usually peaceful. *Above:* missionaries meet Matzelikatzi of the Matabele in 1835. (12)

In British East Africa, now Kenya, a reasonable balance was achieved between European farmers and the native inhabitants. Here a treaty is drawn up between Kikuyu tribesmen and a district commissioner, 1889. (13)

Conventions maintained: *wherever* duty led him, the Englishman did his best to behave as if he were at home. *Left*: afternoon tea somewhere in what is now Zimbabwe, *c*. 1920. *Above*: the end of the hunt, Central Africa, early this century. The popular phrase 'big game' is itself revealing. (14, 15)

The missionaries were often the first to penetrate into unknown regions, and their subsequent care was as much physical as spiritual. *Above*: a mission dispensary in (present-day) Tanzania, late 19th century. *Above right*: mass baptism at Msoro, Northern Rhodesia (now Zambia), 1920s. *Right*: teaching country dancing at a central African mission, probably also in the 1920s; note the portable gramophone on the right. (16, 17, 18)

A lesson in empire: this school (*below*) was founded by the London Missionary Society to teach both academic subjects and practical skills. On the blackboards behind are maps of Britain, India and Australia. (19)

The Raj

Much of the Empire consisted of previously empty or backward countries. India was an exception: a high civilization, more ancient than Europe, demanding quite new diplomatic skills.

Robert Clive rose from the clerical ranks of the East India Company to become a brilliant soldier and diplomat. His victory at Plassey gave him the mastery of the whole state of Bengal, ratified by treaties with Meerzaffer Nawab (*left*) and others. Unintentionally, the Company was assuming responsibility for administering large parts of India. (20)

Through Indian eyes: in December 1846 British and Sikh leaders met at Lahore to work out terms for a settlement (*below*). It was an interim stage in British expansion and was soon followed by the annexation of the whole of the Punjab. English attitudes to Indian civilization, however, remained complex and ambivalent. (21)

By proclaiming Victoria Empress of India Disraeli was asserting the British presence there in the face of the rest of the world. At a ceremony at Delhi (*above*) the proclamation was made to the Indians. On the throne sits the Viceroy, Lord Lytton. On the steps stands Major Burns, the Chief Herald. In a semi-circle round them are the assembled British governors and native princes. (22)

To make New Delhi the capital of India in 1911 was a gesture linking British rule with the glories of the Mogul past. There was a curious duality about the way Englishmen thought of India: at one level they knew that self-government would have to come, at another they dreamed of remaining for three hundred years. This gateway leads to the Viceroy's Residence, now the President's home. (23)

The stones of Empire

One result of the Empire was to fill the world with English architecture. Buildings that would be unremarked at home often acquire an exotic air in their alien surroundings.

Victoria Station, Bombay, was built in 1896 in a basically Gothic style, but with concessions to Hindu and Muslim architecture in some of its details. (25)

Victoria Memorial Hall, Singapore, represents the international classicism of the early 20th century. In front of it stands the statue of Sir Stamford Raffles, founder of the colony, who bought the site on behalf of the East India Company in 1819. It quickly grew to be one of the largest cities in Asia, with a population topping a million by 1950. (24)

Church towers that would look at home in Dorset or Gloucestershire still rise above the lush vegetation of the tropics. *Above*: the cathedral of Kingstown, St Vincent, in the West Indies, built in 1820. After being disputed between England, France and Holland, St Vincent became British in 1793. *Left*: 'The Mall', at Simla, a hill town to which the English retired from the heat of the Indian summer. (26, 27)

At Bendigo, Australia, the imposing post office bears witness to the town's prosperity as a gold-mining centre. (28)

Ottawa's Parliament Building (*right*) is in a florid Neo-Gothic style worthy of Westminster. Carvings on the walls are said to depict every plant and animal in Canada, together with the coats-of-arms of the provinces. (29)

From New Zealand to Malaysia architecture provided a sort of rosy reflection of the mother-country. *Below*: Christ's College at Christchurch, New Zealand, an exercise in instant antiquity. *Below right*: a hotel in the Cameron Highlands, Malaysia, complete with half-timbered dovecote. (30, 31)

'A glorious company'

Few Englishmen suffered from doubts about their fitness to rule so vast an Empire. Confidence reached a peak about the time of the Diamond Jubilee. But by the interwar years there were many criticisms.

... A · GLORIOUS · COMPANY · THE · FLOWER · OF · MEN ...

... TO · SERVE · AS · MODEL · FOR · THE · MIGHTY · WORLD ...

BRITISH · EMPIRE EXHIBITION · 1924
APRIL TO OCTOBER ——— WEMBLEY · LONDON

The Wembley exhibition of 1924 was both a serious demonstration of the Empire's prosperity and a symbol of Britain's imperial pride. One of the posters (*above*) showed a procession of empire-builders from Elizabethan to modern times, with the unblushing slogan: 'A glorious company, the flower of men, to serve as model for the mighty world'. *Right*: an emigration poster of about the same time urging British boys to leave the grime and poverty of England for the healthy air of Canada. (32, 33)

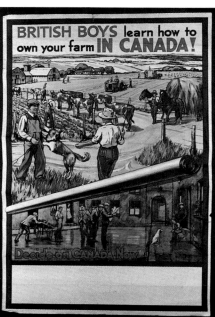

BRITISH BOYS learn how to own your farm IN CANADA!

Decide on CANADA Now

'A Tour through the British Colonies and Foreign Possessions': this Victorian game, played with counters on a board, illustrates how ordinary people at home regarded the Empire – attitudes that were reinforced in popular prints and magazines, children's books and a hundred other ways, and which were still alive in 1939. The prevailing association is with adventure: ships, seas, distant lands, exotic peoples. In the centre stands London, with St Paul's surrounded by a notably industrial landscape. At the bottom, scenes from the five continents. (34)

A TOUR THROUGH THE BRITISH COLONIES, AND FOREIGN POSSESSIONS.

Breaking the chains

It was inevitable that sooner or later the subject peoples would claim their independence. In the case of the white Dominions this was a painless operation. India was a more delicate problem. Elsewhere in the world – Aden, Cyprus, Kenya, Rhodesia – the end of the Empire was a violent trauma, often still unhealed.

India's struggle for freedom was long but relatively bloodless. The Mutiny of 1857 sprang from resentment among the sepoys but was not a national rising and was not supported by most of the princes. *Above*: one of the atrocities that aroused most feeling at home, the massacre of civilians at Cawnpore. In the 20th century, Mahatma Gandhi's campaign was crowned with success in 1947 when the last Viceroy, Lord Mountbatten (*below*), handed over power to the new nations of India and Pakistan. (35, 36, 37)

In **Kenya** a terrorist campaign waged in the 50s against the British by the Mau Mau secret society (*right*: an improvised prison camp) embittered relations between the races. In the event, however, the transfer of power was smooth and Britain's old enemy Jomo Kenjatta (*below right*) took over a country where co-existence seemed actually to work. (39, 40)

Cyprus, occupied by Britain in 1878 and annexed more or less accidentally in 1914, was uneasily inhabited by Greeks with a strong Turkish minority. Agitation for union with Greece was resisted, but in 1960 the island was granted independence under Archbishop Makarios (*above*), not the first or the last opposition leader to step from prison to presidency. (38)

Aden had been acquired in 1839. With the Arab revival of the 1960s came demands for independence and terrorist attacks on British soldiers and civilians, ending in Britain's withdrawal at the end of 1967. Here a suspect is being searched. (41)

The Rhodesian problem lingered longest, mainly because the proportion of white settlers was high enough to prevent an imposed solution from England. After several years of 'illegal' independence under a white government, black guerillas led by Joshua Nkomo and Robert Mugabe (seen on the right *above*) forced a conference in London in 1979, which gave power to the Africans, Mugabe being elected prime minister. (42)

127

6 Exploration and the First British Empire
Settlement and colonization in the New World
HERBERT NICHOLAS

'WHEN WE WOULD ENLARGE OURSELVES, let it be that way we can and to which it seems the eternal Providence hath destined us, which is by the sea'. Thus, Lord Herbert of Cherbury, writing in the mid-17th century, would have us believe that some of Henry VIII's councillors urged his Protestant majesty in 1511. If so, their prescient appeal fell on deaf ears. In 1492 Christopher Columbus had discovered the New World that lay athwart his hard-sought route to the Indies. Only five years later Henry VII had seen something of the implications of his discovery and had engaged the Genoese John Cabot to seek a northerly passage to India. The result was the discovery of North America in the shape, most probably, of Cape Breton, and the opening up to the fishermen of northern Europe of the watery riches of Newfoundland and its neighbouring coast. But the promise of Cabot's voyages was not fulfilled, and the next stage in Britain's empire-building had to wait three-quarters of a century. While the Spaniards settled the Caribbean, raped Mexico and Peru, and even, in the person of Hernando de Soto, pushed up the Mississippi as far as present-day Memphis, and while the French through Jacques Cartier probed the St Lawrence as far as Quebec and beyond, the British were still content to direct their gaze eastward; the trading profits of the Muscovy Company, established in 1555, to traffick with the subjects of Ivan the Terrible at Archangel, were still the brightest manifestations of British maritime enterprise when Elizabeth came to the throne in 1559.

No one has ever satisfactorily explained this time-lag in English response to the challenge of the New World. Something may be attributed to reluctance to cross swords with Spain, and to a lesser degree Portugal, between whom Pope Alexander VI had awarded by papal decree a monopoly of the newly discovered continents. In any case, Elizabeth's accession marked a new stirring of enterprise and acquisitiveness. In the 1560s John Hawkins discovered that there was profit to be made in buying slaves in West Africa and shipping them to the Spanish Main, thus initiating a commerce which brought large profits and criticism for over two hundred years. At the same time Britain began to catch up with and soon surpass her Latin rivals in the arts of navigation. Before long, with a new impudence, marauding mariners were exploiting the opportunities given by the deterioration of Elizabeth's relations with Spain to conduct what was in effect a guerrilla war by sea against Spanish voyagers and Spanish possessions in the middle and south Atlantic. A revival of interest in North American exploration followed, stimulated by the lure of the north-west passage. Martin Frobisher, Sir Humfry Gilbert and John Davis in the 1570s and 1580s mapped out a new geography for Atlantic Canada, while Francis Drake, circumnavigating the globe in *The Golden Hind* and returning loaded with Spanish loot in 1580, demonstrated that the English were now equipped to sail as equals all over the Seven Seas.

Colonization: Hakluyt

However, before exploration and patriotic piracy could develop into colonization and empire, something more was required. The English nation as a whole had to be galvanized into an awareness of the potentialities of the North Atlantic and the lands that lay beyond; both propaganda and staff work were needed. It fell to Richard Hakluyt to discharge both tasks. His *Principal Navigations, Voyages and Discoveries of the English Nation*, first published in 1589, brought together the narratives of British seamen and explorers, with the object of inciting their contemporaries and successors to emulate their pioneering feats. His book was, as the 19th-century historian J. A. Froude rightly called it, 'the prose epic of the modern English nation'; it was also a highly successful exercise in public persuasion. It was Hakluyt who imprinted on the national memory the great legends of Elizabethan seafaring, such as Gilbert's: 'We are as near to heaven by sea as by land', but his value to his contemporaries was no less as a repository of geographic, historical and economic information about the potentialities for British trade and colonization of the marginal areas of the known world. His *Discourse Concerning Westerne Planting*, a private report for Elizabeth and her ministers, was the first sustained argument for a colonizing venture in

---

A returning tide of immigration *into* Britain has been one of the unforeseen legacies of the Empire. Coming as they did from the poorer parts of the world, unprepared for what they were to find and disappointed when they found it, these immigrants were often hard to assimilate. At first the solution was thought to be total integration into English society. More recently it has been argued that to retain some ethnic identity is probably an advantage. The annual West Indian Carnival in London (*opposite*) celebrates an essentially Caribbean way of life in the strangely incongruous setting of Notting Hill.(43)

North America. It failed in its immediate purpose, which was to promote the projects of Sir Walter Raleigh, but its arguments sank into the official mind to shape subsequent policy. Essentially, the case for colonization rested on a belief that North America would provide Britain with the products of a Mediterranean terrain and climate of her own, while at the same time relieving her of surplus population and the unemployment from which she was believed to be suffering. In many ways this was only an extension of the arguments which were being simultaneously adduced for the Plantation of Ireland; Raleigh was not alone in burning his fingers in Ireland before he turned his gaze further to the West.

Colonization: Virginia

The first venture that Raleigh promoted in 1584 did no more than make landfall near Pimlico Sound off North Carolina, make contact with friendly Indians ('such as lived after the manner of the golden age') and return to stimulate interest and investment at home. This led to the establishment the next year of the Roanoke Colony in Virginia with over a hundred men – a short-lived enterprise that petered out in 1586. A second colony under the leadership of John White seems to have established itself in 1587, only to disappear without trace by the time a relief expedition arrived in 1590.

At last, after many false starts and trials, the lineaments of a substantial colonizing venture began to take shape in the form of the Virginia Company, founded in the light of the success of the East India Company, which had been launched in 1600 (although that was a trading venture only). The Virginia Company drew in the hard-headed merchants of London as well as the romantic adventurers. The East India Company, which the City of London had promoted, grew rich on spices and silks; the Virginia venturers saw themselves putting their money into timber, tobacco, fruit, fish and fur, trade with the natives and shipbuilding by the colonials. In 1607 a small band of 143 colonists established themselves at Jamestown, Virginia, and in 1609 were supplemented by six hundred more. At last, under the leadership of Captain John Smith, although not without every kind of vicissitude, a permanent British colony was established in North America.

In the history of Virginia, and indeed of North America, 1619 was a landmark. It saw the meeting of the first legislative assembly on the continent when the governor, six councillors and two burgesses each from the colony's ten plantations met in the church at Jamestown and lost no time in asserting a characteristically 17th-century parliamentary claim – that no taxes should be laid in the province except by the assembly's authority, or expended except as it should direct. And there occurred another event hardly less pregnant with significance for the future, when a Dutch ship arrived with twenty Negro slaves who were sold to the settlers. They were needed, not to produce the Mediterranean delights or the naval stores of the promoters' dreams, but to cultivate a plant which saved the colony's economy by pandering to a novel but fast-spreading addiction, tobacco.

Colonization: New England

The propaganda of colonization had from the start given prominence to the opportunities it would afford for extending the pale of Christendom. However, as it turned out, it was not by the conversion of the 'pagan savage' that this was achieved so much as by the

'The arrival of the Englishmen in Virginia' – the first map of the future colony, showing Roanoke Island. (Drawn by Theodore de Bry, after John White.)

A mill at work in the 'Sugar Islands'; the West Indian natives, supervised by an apparently benign English overseer, bring in bundles of sugar cane which is cut up and fed into the mill.

extrusion of fellow-Christians from the fold of state-established religion in the old country. From Scrooby, Lincolnshire, and the villages around a group of Separatists had in 1607 emigrated to Leyden, where toleration was easier to obtain than at home. For some, however, Leyden still did not provide the full and English liberty they desired and in 1620 they decided to risk everything on a move to America. Along with others from similar congregations in England they embarked, 102 passengers and crew, at Plymouth in the *Mayflower*, 180 tons gross, to make landfall at Cape Cod two months later and to settle for their first bitter winter at what is now Plymouth, Massachusetts. Before landing they executed the mutual Mayflower Compact which applied the principles of their church government to their civil order. By it they combined themselves 'together into a civil body politic', conferring upon themselves in the absence of any charter the power to regulate their own affairs – a seed of autonomy from which some remarkable flowers of American independence were later to grow.

In the wake of these Pilgrim Fathers came other Puritans, most immediately those from the West Country organized by John White of Dorchester. He was a prime mover in establishing the Massachusetts Bay Company, modelled on the lines of the Virginia Company. Together with a group of East Anglian Puritans they organized two well-planned expeditions, the first in 1629 of West Countryfolk, some three hundred strong, who settled mostly at Salem, Massachusetts, and the second in the following year, numbering nearly a thousand, predominantly from East Anglia, under the leadership of John Winthrop, a Suffolk squire, who settled in Boston and its neighbourhood. By an action of questionable legality but of indubitable significance these settlers transferred the entire management and indeed the charter of the colony itself to Massachusetts. In consequence, the colony became practically independent of English control; the emigrant stockholders in the company, the freemen, became the voters who annually elected the governor and his assistants, and a representative assembly evolved which in turn separated into two houses. The theocratic basis of the colony was preserved by restricting the franchise to church members and the influx of 20,000 additional immigrants over the next decade did nothing to impair the dominance of Puritanism and the clergy, since it was from English dissenters that the 'great migration' came.

Colonization: 17th-century developments

The intolerance of Massachusetts Puritanism in turn provoked its own dissent. In 1636 Roger Williams, a believer in the separation of church and state, was driven out to establish at Providence, Rhode Island, what he hoped would become a haven of religious toleration. Out of another variety of religious persecution there emerged in 1634 the colony of Maryland, founded by the 2nd Lord Baltimore, whose father had been expelled from Virginia for his Roman Catholicism. Maryland, a proprietary colony – a quasi-feudal domain – guaranteed religious toleration to its settlers. To the south of Virginia similar proprietary colonies, granted by Charles I to royal favourites, developed into North and South Carolina and Georgia, and displayed a comparable blend of quasi-feudal control and immunity from religious persecution. So too in the West Indies with the proprietary colonies of Barbados and the Leeward Islands.

It was, however, Oliver Cromwell who, by conquering Jamaica from Spain, established the most substantial British presence in the West Indies or, as they were significantly known, the Sugar Islands. The sweet tooth which the British developed in the 17th and 18th centuries became as significant for their colonies in the Caribbean as their addiction to tobacco was for Virginia. The Treaty of Utrecht of 1713, by giving Britain the grant of the *asiento*, the right to trade in slaves with the Spanish colonies, stimulated the introduction of black labour throughout the Caribbean. For more than a century Negroes toiled under the lash to provide the fortunes which enabled plantation owners to buy seats in the unreformed Parliament at Westminster.

Throughout the 18th century the West Indies were the pawns in the recurrent conflicts of the European powers, individual islands changing hands as the fortunes of war and the exigencies of peace settlements dictated. As Spain and later the Netherlands declined, the principal rivals were Britain and France and it was significant of the islands' value that at the Peace of Paris in 1763 it was a nice calculation whether Britain should restore to France Guadeloupe or Canada; only after much doubt was Canada chosen for retention. Not until British maritime supremacy was effectively established by the Napoleonic Wars did the game of island-swapping cease and by that time their economic value had relatively declined. In 1807 William Wilberforce secured the abolition of the slave trade, and a period of apprenticeship for the West Indian Negroes led to their eventual freedom in 1838.

But this is to run well ahead of imperial developments in mainland North America. Here too the British had to compete with European rivals. The French had established a foothold at Quebec as early as 1608 and only a year later Henry Hudson had sailed up the river that now bears his name as far as Albany on behalf of the Dutch West India Company. By 1626 there was a permanent Dutch settlement at New Amsterdam on the tip of Manhattan, soon the hub of a New Netherland colony. With the principals at odds in Europe, this outpost, sandwiched between Connecticut (formed from Massachusetts) and Maryland, obviously could not last, and in 1664 Governor Stuyvesant yielded to an English fleet. New Amsterdam became New York without a shot being fired.

The colonies escaped involvement in the clash at home between king and Parliament, but the effect of the Civil War was no less profound for being negative: for ten years or so each colony was left practically without interference and each continued to develop in its own way and to enjoy an open trade with all the world. Habits were developed which were never wholly lost. In 1650 and 1651 the Commonwealth, in accordance with the prevailing mercantilist theories of the age, passed Navigation Acts which were but lightly enforced; in more vigorous form at the Restoration, as the Acts of Trade and Navigation (1660–72), they represented an attempt to make the Empire a self-sufficient economic unit in which trade would be conducted by English ships, and the bulk of colonial imports and exports – especially such products as tobacco, sugar, cotton and naval stores – would, in the first instance at least, be 'laid on the shores of England', in other words, be handled within the imperial system by the mother-country. Then and subsequently it has been a matter of dispute who lost and who gained by such practices and whether they were justifiable in terms of maintaining the unity of the Empire and contributing to the defence of its component parts.

What is certain is that the enforcement of the system left much to be desired and that it was its loopholes at least as much as its proclaimed benefits that made it initially tolerable.

In general, as unemployment diminished after 1660, emigration from the mother-country declined. Although not actually prohibited, it tended, except for the dumping of malefactors (for example, the estimated 30,000 felons transported across the Atlantic in the 18th century), to be discouraged by British officialdom. There were, however, two especially conspicuous exceptions. The first was that of the Quakers. In 1681 William Penn obtained from Charles II in recognition of 'the memory and merits of his late father' (Admiral Penn, who had conquered Jamaica from the Dutch) a vast land grant, the province of what is now Pennsylvania. For this Penn drew up what he called a 'frame of government', which proclaimed religious freedom as well as the civil requirements of trial by jury, bail and moderate punishment, within a framework of paternalistic government, over which as resident proprietor Penn himself initially presided as governor, with an elected assembly confined to yielding or refusing assent to legislation that governor and council proposed. Penn had remarkable gifts as a promoter and his scheme brought response not only from the British Isles but even from as far afield as the Rhineland. Economic considerations reinforced religious convictions. Colonists flocked in, with capital to support them. Within four years of its foundation the colony, cosmopolitan, adaptable, yet displaying the unmistakable style of a Quaker commonwealth, had almost 9,000 settlers.

The other conspicuous exception to the general British policy of opposition to emigration was provided by the Scotch-Irish. In the reign of James I Presbyterians from the poverty-stricken lowlands of Scotland had been transplanted to Ulster in place of evicted Irish. They had tilled the land and held it, almost as an occupation force, but by the end of the century rack-renting, absentee landlords and mounting disabilities, civil and religious, imposed on them as Presbyterians provoked them to an organized migration. An estimated quarter of a million, mostly as indentured servants, left Ulster initially for New England, then for Pennsylvania and then, as land became more readily available, for the western frontiers of Virginia and the Carolinas. The qualities they had displayed against the Irish were now demonstrated against the Indians. Like some latter-day chosen people they sought their own Zion at any price. 'They kept the Sabbath and everything else they could lay their hands on.' Of such stock were John Calhoun and Andrew Jackson.

A slightly later cycle of migration brought a different kind of Scot to various areas of settlement, to the Mohawk and upper Hudson valleys, to Canada and North Carolina. This was the Highlander, who emigrated initially in the wake of the Jacobite risings of

The growth of the First British Empire on mainland North America up to the eve of the American War of Independence. The revolutionary movement itself grew up, and the issue was decided, in territories that had been English since before 1713.

Map labels: HUDSON BAY · James Bay · R. Albany · LABRADOR · St Johns · NEWFOUNDLAND · CAPE BRETON I. · Louisbourg · L. Superior · Quebec · Montreal · L. Michigan · L. Huron · Ft Frontenac · Kingston · L. Ontario · Ft Niagara · Ft Oswego · L. St Clair · L. Erie · NEW YORK · L. Champlain · MAINE · N.H. · Portsmouth · Salem · Gloucester · MASS. · Boston · Plymouth · Albany · Hartford · CONN. · New Haven · Providence · RHODE ISLAND · PENNSYLVANIA · New York · Ft Duquesne (Pittsburgh) · Philadelphia · R. Mississippi · R. Ohio · Baltimore · DELAWARE · MARYLAND · Jamestown · VIRGINIA · Yorktown · Chesapeake Bay · LOUISIANA · NORTH CAROLINA · SOUTH CAROLINA · GEORGIA · Charleston · FLORIDA · New Orleans · GULF OF MEXICO

Legend:
- British possessions before 1713
- Territory ceded to Gt. Britain in 1713
- Territory ceded to Gt. Britain in 1763
- Spanish territory in 1763
- French fishing rights in 1783

1715 and 1745, but more substantially in the 1760s and 1770s when eviction of the crofters to make way for sheep-farming depopulated whole communities of western and northern Scotland.

Colonial life and growth

It is apparent from the foregoing that there was in Britain no grand imperial design directing expansion and development overseas. Apart from those slaves or malefactors who were almost literally dumped in the colonies, the immigrants were those who for whatever reason were dissatisfied at home and hoped to better themselves abroad. They were, in the expressive New England term, the 'come-outers', those who whether in material, political or religious terms were at odds with the establishment and, either by choice or dire necessity, were making a break with their homeland. Their example and the institutions they created attracted others from continental Europe in analogous conditions; thus French Huguenots came particularly to South Carolina and German sectarians (the so-called Dutch) flocked to Pennsylvania.

The colonies were thus, from the mother-country's point of view, a safety-valve; from their own standpoint, an escape hatch. It was consistent with this that the mother-country should confine her attentions to maximizing the economic advantages which possession of these territories conferred and that the colonists should nurse a determination to run things their own way as much as possible. By the turn of the century they had become substantial communities, some quarter of a million souls distributed between Maine and South Carolina. At the end of another half-century, by 1750, this population had grown, mainly by natural increase rather than further immigration, to over one and a half million, distributed over a vast territory, but also here and there concentrated in substantial towns. Boston was the largest, with Philadelphia fast overtaking it, at around the 16,000 to 20,000 mark each. New York had some 12,000 residents and Charleston in South Carolina some 8,000. A diversity of cultural institutions had developed – Harvard, Yale, Princeton and William and Mary, a tax-supported school system throughout New England, theatres in New York and in Charleston. The merits of colonial architecture can be seen to this day in Charleston and Philadelphia and, exquisitely restored, in Williamsburg. If New England maintained a learned and, after the Great Awakening of the 1730s and 1740s, increasingly diversified ministry, the Southern colonies developed a plantation aristocracy with serious pretensions to taste as well as to sport and politics. Social stratification, indigenous in some degree in any 18th-century society, developed more in those states where the spread of slavery (conspicuously for the cultivation of cotton, rice, indigo and tobacco) encouraged the rise of a planter class. But it was always held in check by the mobility of American life, by the proximity of the frontier where all social discriminations came under the acid test of utility and survival, and by the fact that the supply of labour always fell below the demand.

The society – or to speak more accurately, the societies – of the colonies did not enjoy, save at fortunate points along the seacoast, an altogether tranquil existence. From the beginning there were clashes with the indigenous Indians and at various times and places these assumed serious proportions. Thus in Virginia in 1622 and 1644, in New England in 1637 (the Pequot War) and (very extensively) in 1675–6 (King Philip's War), in North Carolina in 1711–12 (the Tuscarora War) and 1715–16 (the Yamasee War), stern and costly struggles for land and pacification had to be resolved. But it was the rivalries of Europe, projected across the Atlantic, that most frequently and extensively brought the clash of arms to North America.

Imperial conflicts with France

All the time that the British colonists were striking westward from the eastern seaboard another power was seeking to establish a large presence in North America. France, indeed, was in Canada before England was in Virginia. Initially hers was not a colonizing presence: fishing and fur-trading, coupled with a strong Jesuit missionary drive amongst the Indians, accounted for the modest population of 'New France', a little over 2,000 by 1660. But then the French Crown developed an interest in colonization and over 3,000 further settlers of both sexes were dispatched with a clear expectation that they should increase and multiply. This they did, to such purpose that eighty years later their peasant settlements up the St Lawrence river totalled over 40,000 souls. There were three points at which these settlers came into conflict with the English – at the fisheries (Newfoundland, Cape Breton Island and Nova Scotia), in Hudson's Bay (where in 1670 the Hudson's Bay Company had begun to enter from the sea and compete in the fur trade), and finally to the south and west of the St Lawrence valley where the French and the English encountered each other's westward movements. In this last area in particular, the practice grew up of each side mobilizing 'its' Indians against the others, thus injecting an extra touch of savagery into an already fierce contest. The almost continuous conflict in Europe that went by the names of the War of the League of Augsburg and the War of the Spanish Succession had its counterpart in the ding-

dong warfare in North America. It involved, among other things, an encircling movement by the French down the Mississippi, and the establishment of a new French colony, Louisiana, at its mouth. South Carolina's efforts to nip this development in the bud were a failure, and the end of the war brought about by the Peace of Utrecht in 1713 saw a return at most points to the status quo, save that Britain acquired possession of Nova Scotia as well as being confirmed in Newfoundland and Hudson's Bay.

Thirty years of tolerably peaceful coexistence followed, until the War of the Austrian Succession (1740–8) and the Seven Years War (1754–63), more accurately called in North America the French and Indian War, brought sweeping changes in the disposition of power. A conflict was launched upon Europe, Asia and North America in which, to quote Macaulay's famous apothegm, in order that Frederick the Great 'might rob a neighbour he had promised to defend, black men fought on the coast of Coromandel, and red men scalped each other by the Great Lakes of North America'. Behind Macaulay's exaggeration lay the inescapable fact that the war was a conflict for imperial mastery not just in Europe, but across the world, with Spain's historic power in the decline and Britain's swelling ambitions at odds with France from the Mississippi to the Bay of Bengal.

Initially the French enjoyed the advantages that went with a highly centralized imperial administration able to dispatch substantial armies to energize a docile colonial population. Their strategy was to confine the English settlements within the Appalachians by a chain of forts and fur-trading posts that would run along the Ohio and down the Mississippi and link with the new French capital of New Orleans at its mouth. Had they succeeded, North America might have been governed from a French-speaking metropolis on the junction of the Ohio and Monongahela rivers, Fort Duquesne (the present Pittsburgh), which the French established in 1754. In hopes of forestalling such a move, Virginia's governor had dispatched a young lieutenant-colonel, George Washington, with a handful of militia to the frontier, but after a brief encounter he found himself worsted and had to retire. A larger force under the British General Braddock suffered a worse fate a year later. This exposed the whole range of western frontier settlements to French attack and soon a devastating French offensive drove a wedge between New York and New England along Lake Champlain. However, in 1758 William Pitt's organizing genius took control of the British war effort and by degrees the advantages Britain derived from command of the sea and the vastly larger population of British North America compared with that of New France began to make their weight felt. In successive years Louisburg, which commanded the St Lawrence from Cape Breton Island, fell to Jeffrey Amherst, and Quebec, which was the key to Canada, fell to James Wolfe. Under the terms of the peace signed in 1763 in Paris, French Canada, the Spanish

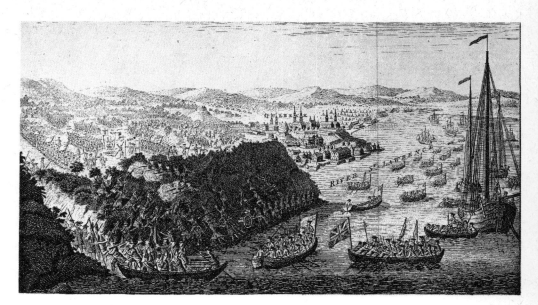

After some earlier setbacks in the British campaign against the French, Quebec, the key to Canada, finally fell to General Wolfe in 1759. This illustration from the 'London Magazine' shows the large and highly organized British force taking the French town.

Floridas and a range of West Indian islands were ceded to Britain; French Louisiana and French claims west of the Mississippi went to Spain. With the further acquisition of Bengal in India, the British Empire was, in relation to the known world of the time, at its furthest point of territorial expansion. 'Rule Britannia' was at last a realized ambition.

Strains between England and her colonies

However, it was not territorial expansion as such which was the prime objective of imperial policy. Trade and, in particular, trade which would support naval supremacy, was still, as it had been for two hundred years, Britain's main concern. This meant an order of priorities surprising to modern eyes, with India (still in form the responsibility of a mere trading company) and the West Indies, with their predominantly slave population engaged in the production of sugar and molasses, assuming an importance that often exceeded that of North America with its English-speaking population and its fast-developing skills and cultures. Significantly, Nabobs from India and planters from the West Indies bought seats in Parliament from which to reinforce these claims, while the North American colonies had to rely upon agents to lobby for them in London. North America found its main role in the imperial scheme of things as a market for British manufactures and as a producer of materials which could not be found at home. In a purely rational economics this could work also to North America's advantage, as an assured market and a reliable and cheap source of supply both of manufactured goods and capital. This was demonstrated when, after the great rupture, Adam Smith's economics took over both in Britain and the USA and the trade of each with the other continued to increase. Unfortunately in the 1760s neither side was wholly rational in its economic or its political thinking.

The British, in general, were the insensitive innovators, the colonists, the hypersensitive defenders of the status quo. Thus it was the British who felt constrained, despite the defeat of the French, to keep a force of 10,000 men in North America (there were, after all, still belligerent Indians) and who felt that towards this (and the debt left after war) the colonies ought to make their contribution. At the same time, to avoid unnecessarily provoking the Indians, it was the British who wanted a curb on westward expansion (to London it was the fur trade and not free land that the term 'frontier' suggested). So in 1763 a royal proclamation forbade settlement west of the Appalachians. And in 1764 the Sugar Act was imposed to tighten up the notoriously loose collection of customs duty in North America, and by so doing to guarantee that the colonials got their molasses from the British West Indies and not by smuggling from the Spanish and French. It was a piece of administrative tidiness that touched a sensitive colonial nerve. As John Adams said later: 'It is no secret that rum was an essential ingredient in the American Revolution.' Protest was immediate and it fastened on the argument that Parliament was improperly seeking to tax colonial commodities for revenue: hence the cry 'no taxation without representation'. To supplement the still inadequate revenue thus raised, Grenville at the British Treasury devised a stamp duty on newspapers, licences, legal documents and so on, a measure almost perfectly calculated to irritate the 'talking classes', the journalists, bankers and lawyers, who constituted the most politically sensitive element in colonial society. The reaction to the Stamp Act was even more immediate and intense than that provoked by the Sugar Act. In Virginia a brilliant young lawyer and orator, Patrick Henry, swung a rump session of the House of Burgesses into endorsing resolutions that claimed that Virginia's legislature had the exclusive right to levy taxes in the colony. Massachusetts took the issue to the streets, where a Boston mob (the legislature being prorogued) forced a terrified stamp distributor to resign his post, while they gutted the governor's mansion and threw his library into the street. In New York delegates from nine colonies met a few months later in an unprecedented Congress to adopt resolutions only slightly less emphatic than those of Virginia.

London's defence to the 'no taxation without representation' charge was to contend that the colonists enjoyed 'virtual representation', that like the new conurbations of Liverpool or Sheffield they were represented by spokesmen for like-minded interests or classes not necessarily drawn from their own locality. To colonists already suspicious of corruptibility and class bias in the British political system, this was no argument at all and they resorted to more forthright ripostes. Respectable merchants adopted non-importation agreements and boycotted British goods, while slightly less respectable 'Sons of Liberty' took to the streets and kept the pot of violence at boiling point. Parliament bowed to the economic pressure thus generated and repealed the Act in 1766, insisting however on replacing it with the Townshend duties. These, it was said, respected the colonies' protest against internal taxation and confined themselves to an external levy. They imposed on the colonies a new range of import duties, tightened up the loose system of collection, but also, worst of all, proposed to utilize the resultant revenues to pay the salaries of royal governors and judges, previously dependent on votes by the colonial assemblies. When in 1768 Massachusetts and Virginia by circular letters organized a country-wide protest against the Townshend Acts the governors dissolved the assemblies. The colonials' worst fears were now confirmed. Had not Charles I treated his Parliament in equal style? Troops had to be sent to see that the Acts were enforced. The inevitable consequence was bloodshed. In March 1770 four Bostonians were killed in an open clash between the redcoats and a Boston mob. At the hands of Samuel Adams and his propagandist friends this became known as the Boston Massacre, ironically perpetrated on the very day that Lord North's ministry repealed the Acts.

'Blows must decide'

The repeal profited nothing. Characteristically North offset whatever benefits his action might have brought by retaining the duty on tea, and so identified that harmless beverage with the cause of tyranny and the provocation to revolt. Simultaneously the ministry gave a monopoly to the East India Company on the sale of tea to North America. It thus by one and the same stroke reaffirmed the principle of imperial taxation and helped to bale out a sinking imperial agency; the East India Company was on the verge of bankruptcy. To the colonial agitators the measure presented an opportunity to add the issue of monopoly to the complaints about taxation. The Boston Tea Party of December 1773, when a group of the Sons of Liberty, disguised as Indian braves, threw consignments of tea into the harbour, dramatized the protest in an unmistakable way. Their action had predictable consequences: in the colonies it made it harder for moderates to control events, and in England it intensified the official disposition to meet violence with repression.

Massachusetts was judged to be in revolt. The port of Boston was closed to commerce. The colony's charter was revised to substitute an appointed for an elected council and to give sweeping powers to the governor. Since local courts could no longer be trusted, powers were taken to transfer cases to Britain for trial. To the colonists these were the 'Intolerable Acts', which precipitated the calling of a Continental Congress at Philadelphia, to which all but Georgia sent representatives. The Congress advocated resistance to the Acts, agreed to stop all trade with Britain and all consumption of British goods as long as they remained in force, and set up an 'association' of committees in every district designed to enforce the boycott and penalize its violators. It endorsed the resolutions passed in Suffolk County, Massachusetts, to pay no taxes to Britain and to prepare for self-defence if British forces attacked. In Britain, meanwhile, the friends of America – the Chathams, the Shelburnes, Rockingham and Burke – were out of office and helpless. The king and his stubborn and loyal first minister, North, were determined that, as George III put it, 'blows must decide'.

In the spring of 1775 General Gage, the military governor of Massachusetts, tried to seize the patriots Sam Adams and John Hancock, but was foiled by Paul Revere. The first blow had been struck and the first legend of the revolutionary war created. At Lexington the militia put the redcoats to rout. Two months later, at Bunker Hill, the king's forces lost over a thousand men. The Continental Congress recognized the irregulars of Massachusetts as the nucleus of an army and appointed George Washington as commander-in-chief. Meanwhile, a force under General Schuyler, a New Yorker, invaded Canada in hopes of making it the fourteenth secessionist colony. In this they were disappointed. The French Canadians stayed loyal to their new masters and the Americans had to withdraw with heavy losses. But the offensive hardened support in Britain for North's unyielding stance while it did nothing to arrest the movement of opinion in America. Despite all the efforts of last-minute conciliators such as John Dickinson, sentiment moved inexorably towards independence. In June 1776 a committee of Congress consisting of Thomas Jefferson of Virginia, John Adams of Massachusetts, Benjamin Franklin of Philadelphia, Roger Sherman of Connecticut and Robert Livingstone of New York prepared a Declaration of Independence. On 4 July, after amending Jefferson's critical passages on Negro slavery, Congress adopted it as 'the unanimous Declaration of the thirteen united States of America'. A nation had been born, an empire riven, a war begun.

Accepted with reason as one of the great credos of western civilization, the Declaration of Independence, if closely examined, impresses one as much by the non-revolutionary character of its claims as by its political universality. Except for the splendid but obscure (then as now) right to 'the pursuit of happiness', there is nothing in the document which would have been novel to the Parliamentarians of the 17th century, to the readers of John Locke or to dissenters or radicals such as John Wilkes in the England of its time. The strength indeed of the signers' claims derived from their very familiarity, from their place in an evolving tradition of English constitutional liberties that went back to Magna Carta. Significantly, the Declaration drew not only on fine and sonorous phrases – 'the Laws of Nature and of Nature's God . . . our lives, our fortunes and our sacred honour' – but also set out in the true tradition of Anglo-Saxon legalism a Bill of particulars itemizing the respects in which the king had broken the social contract with his people. This was not, like the 1789 French Declaration of the Rights of Man which borrowed heavily from it, a blueprint for a new state or society. It was a justification for the establishment of a new and separate nation on principles which had been violated or ignored by the contemporary custodians of the British realm. It was not even explicitly republican; it simply asserted that 'a prince whose character is thus marked by every act which may define a tyrant, is unfit to be the ruler of a free people'. To this one might add that when the time came, as it did in 1787, to draw up a constitution for this free people, the principles upon which it was built were essentially those of John Locke and the Whig tradition, save of course for the need to adapt them to the needs of a people which had 'thrown its sovereign across the Atlantic'.

With the Declaration, American independence became an established fact. There could be no going back now. Observers then, and historians two hundred years later, have been hard put to it to explain this rupture of the English-speaking world. At the heart of the problem is the seeming disparity between the scale of colonial grievances, and the desperate remedy, civil war no less, which was taken in order to rectify them. Scholars impressed by the latitude which the First British Empire allowed to its constituent elements in most matters other than trade, have been puzzled to make out why a trading system that brought benefits to all its component parts should have generated so much American resentment. Undoubtedly the Americans *felt* themselves to be unfairly treated under it, but why? Partly because the closing of loopholes removed an element of elasticity that had made the system tolerable. Partly because the spirit of entrepreneurial individualism which was rising in the colonies was, as it were, anticipating Adam Smith without realizing it. (Independence was not the only event of 1776: the publication of Smith's *The Wealth of Nations* took place in the same year.) Partly because of the Puritan suspicion that venality, great fortunes and political corruption lay behind England's enforcement of the system – as indeed they did.

That mutual suspicion played a disproportionate part in precipitating the explosion cannot be denied. Sundered by 3,000 miles of ocean that could take months to cross, each side held exaggerated views of the intentions of the other and was determined to

The Stamp Act (1765) was one of a series of Acts of Parliament providing for the taxation of the American colonists without their consent. In protest the Boston mob burnt bundles of stamped paper arriving from England.

prevent (in both meanings of that term) whatever it judged the other to be intending. Mass hysteria is not too strong a word for some of the manifestations of the Boston mob; master propagandists, such as Samuel Adams and Joseph Warren, stoked up the theory of a conspiracy against American liberties to the point of generating a national paranoia. At the same time there was a pervasive short-sightedness and stupidity in Westminster and Whitehall, such as alternately coercing and conceding, displaying an incompetence in the arts of imperial management which exactly reflected the corruptness of electoral and administrative processes.

It is no longer fashionable, as it is indeed no longer practicable, to see the debate in terms of a class struggle within the American colonies themselves. In most of the colonies, especially Massachusetts, political power was widely diffused, and no clear lines of economic fission can be detected by which to distinguish loyalists from insurgents. That the movement to independence went hand in hand with a general trend to democratic liberalism cannot be denied, but it was the urge to win independence that was the primary animating motive of Bostonians, New Yorkers, Virginians and Carolinians alike. That secured, they could – and did – go their several ways in the measure of domestic 'revolution' that they sought; generally, it was a very controlled and peaceable revolution.

In a sense, the search for a cause or causes of the separation is a mistaken one. Instead one ought to ask how, given the circumstances of the time, separation could have been avoided. Over the previous century and a half the colonies had been developing very much on their own, peopled by immigrants who had, for the most part, left Britain by deliberate choice and who had established in America modes of life and government matched to their personal preferences. That they should react kindly to attempts to bring them back within the control of a distant government, particularly one in whose establishment and operations they had no share, was an intrinsically improbable idea. Add to that the fact that, for the most part, the government and society of these colonies still reflected the circumstances of their inception as the radical spill-over of the 17th-century conflicts in church and state, and you have a situation in which only an inconceivable display of statesmanship in London could have averted a split. Until 1763 the threat of New France was a restraining influence; that removed, the colonials were free to assert themselves. Relying upon the arguments of 17th-century constitutionalism in its purest form, they claimed the 'rights of Englishmen'. The placemen of George III's parliaments had no effective reply. The consequences were predictable.

The war that ensued upon the colonists' breakaway was, since this was still the 18th century, comparatively civilized. Although there were hardships a-plenty – so that Washington's winter at Valley Forge passed into legend – it was in no sense a total war. Armies still went into winter quarters, prisoners were exchanged, and for the common soldier there was always, especially on the American side, the available palliative of desertion. None the less, casualties were high and feelings were bitter. There were as many loyalist refugees and property confiscations as there were emigrés in the French Revolution, in proportion to the populations involved. But what astonished contemporaries – European contemporaries at least – was how much better the American volunteers stood the strain than the British (and Hessian) professionals. In the end it was the astonishing resilience of Washington's forces that won the war – that, and the invaluable assistance of the French and Spanish fleets which were able to threaten the very shores of England as well as, at the end, precipitate the collapse of the British forces at Yorktown.

After the war

To the infant United States the war brought the self-confidence and determination which only a victory against odds can provide. To the Empire the loss of the colonies was a humiliation, but a humiliation moderated by the navy's defeat of the pride of the French line in the naval battle of the Saints, which saved the West Indies and recovered for Britain control of the Atlantic. When peace was made at Paris in 1783 Shelburne, who had displaced the discredited North, gave terms which were none the less generous for being the only rational alternative to further hostilities. He ceded everything in North America south of the St Lawrence and the Great Lakes and hoped to reconcile the Americans by admitting them to all the rights of Englishmen in matters of trade, making them in effect partners in a North Atlantic co-prosperity sphere. Into the mouth of his sovereign, making the speech from the throne, Shelburne put a statement of his aspirations: 'Religion – language – interest – affections may, and I hope will, yet prove a bond of permanent union between the two countries.'

The aspirations were premature. Mercantilism and wounded pride were still too strong. Although Shelburne's peace was ratified, the silences and ambiguities of its terms, which might have been the basis of a constructive *rapprochement*, survived as the breeding ground of mutual irritation. The attempt, in 1794, to tie up loose ends in Jay's Treaty still fell short of what was required for reconciliation. In particular, Britain's insistence upon her right to search American ships and impress any British deserter stuck in the throat of the young republic.

What lay behind the apparent outrageousness of the imperial claim was the fact that since 1793 Britain had been involved in a war with Revolutionary France which, even more than the Seven Years War, was a life and death struggle across the globe. In this America was neutral, but split two ways. Memories of the War of Independence encouraged sympathy with France. Yet French misfortunes could be turned to America's advantage. In 1803 Jefferson effected the Louisiana Purchase which eventually secured for the USA possession of a vast continental hinterland. Yet, Franco-phile as he was, even Jefferson realized that America's opportunity had been secured behind the protection of the British hearts of oak. As both Britain and France resorted to the economic weapon in their total war and sought to impose a blockade even against neutrals, America found that neutrality offered her no protection against infringements of sovereignty from both sides. It was indeed almost an accident that in 1812 it was against Britain that she turned her guns. Almost an accident, but not quite. The War of 1812 was also a final assertion of independence, a reminder to the mother-country that Yorktown had, after all, been an American victory, an insistent demand for equality of treatment in the comity of nations. As such, although in some respects a buffo conflict in which peace negotiations were begun almost as soon as hostilities, the war contributed its own invaluable quota of patriotic legendry to the young republic's store – for example, 'Don't give up the ship' and 'Oh say, can you see by the dawn's early light?'.

To a third party as well, the infant Canada, the war was an initiation ceremony of manhood. When, to the discomfiture of the USA, Canadians declined to be 'liberated' and gave a good account of themselves at Niagara and Detroit, they were asserting an otherness which eventually flowered in a nationhood independent of both the USA and the mother-country, although closely related to both. This was the beginning of the Canadian miracle, the achievement of a two-culture nation capable of extending itself to the Pacific and resisting the magnetic pull of a vastly more powerful USA. Two factors contributed to the shaping of Canadian self-determination. The first was the British decision, when Quebec was acquired in 1763, to guarantee to its inhabitants the free exercise of their Roman Catholic religion and enjoyment of French civil law. Embodied in the Quebec Act of 1774, this became paradoxically a contributing factor to the loss of English America, since the New England colonists in particular saw it as blocking western land development. The second factor was a direct consequence of the War of Independence, the emigration to Nova Scotia and Ontario of the United British Loyalists, some 50,000 strong, those Americans whose loyalty to the Crown transcended their attachment to the colonies of their birth or emigration. Their militant anti-Americanism gave a distinctive cast, not quickly lost, to the Canadian national identity.

Rapprochement

The War of 1812 was over by 1814 and peace was signed at Ghent the following year. But although it took years for various points of difference – western boundary lines, fisheries, disarmament on the Great Lakes (an invaluable concordat) and so on – to be fully resolved, the natural affinities and the inescapable undertow of mutual interest gradually asserted themselves in the relations of Britain and the USA. When, almost in imitation of 1776, the Latin American colonies broke away from Spain, President Monroe was provoked to assert in 1823, in the Doctrine that bears his name, that the USA was opposed to any European recolonization or interference. Yet for all its seeming unilateralness, the Doctrine was in fact grafted on to the resolution which Canning, the British foreign secretary, had already taken to resist any such reassertion of Spanish rule. And it was the British fleet which provided the bulwark of naval power without which the Monroe Doctrine would have been an impotent form of words.

When the USA in turn fell victim to internal conflict in the Civil War of 1861 to 1865, each side had its sympathizers in the British public and government. It was then, in the face of incidental clashes like the Trent affair, that the basic good sense and fundamental liberalism of Abraham Lincoln's Union and John Bright's Britain asserted themselves. The country which in 1833 had taken the lead in slavery emancipation throughout its colonies could not deny the validity of the North's cause in a war which, whatever the constitutional niceties involved, was ultimately fought on the issue of slavery extension. The fact that the North's victory meant dearer cotton for the mills of Lancashire and a high tariff for the North's developing industries did not hinder the admission of the martyred Lincoln to the Victorian pantheon or the swelling flood of British emigrants (over 2 million between 1830 and 1890, to say nothing of the 3½ million, with rather different background and sympathies, from impoverished Ireland), or the intermarriage of American wealth and British nobility which peopled the pages of Henry James, refurbished any number of ancestral seats and created such Anglo-American dynasties as the Churchills and the Astors. No less important were the alliances, marital, intellectual or commercial, of the middle class, whose philanthropies, literary tastes, political ideas and aspirations, business interests, academic concerns and religious affiliations wove a web of attachments that made the Atlantic of the ocean liner narrower than the Channel of the packet-boat.

It is doubtful whether this Victorian and Edwardian transatlantic amity would have developed without the concomitant rise of democracy in Britain and the revision of old ideas of empire that attended it. The passage of the British North America Act in 1867 was a crucial date in this evolution. Its recognition of Canadian nationhood and its provision of federal institutions of self-government not so very different from the USA's own removed a vital weapon from the armoury of American annexationists and guaranteed that the Canadian connection with Britain would acquire the additional strength derived from a free and equal relationship. In contrast, Britain's failure to evolve a viable relationship with Ireland created persistent problems with the United States. The large Irish immigrant population nourished a suspicion of Britain amounting to intermittent hostility. More frequently, it helped to stoke the fires of isolationism, in any circumstances a natural enough corollary of America's historical and geographical evolution. In the First World War a Scotch–Irish Calvinist and internationalist president broke the classic mould of American diplomacy by defeating the isolationist forces which saw the conflict between the Allies and the Central Powers much as Madison had seen the issues of 1812. Even so, Woodrow Wilson's zeal for a world League of Nations was not enough to persuade his fellow-countrymen to accept the Treaty of Versailles and the League membership that went with it. A decade of sterile withdrawal from the outside world was followed by the Great Depression and a gradual reacceptance under Franklin Roosevelt of America's inescapable involvement in the fate of the European democracies. Even before the Japanese struck from the east at Pearl Harbor, the United States had accepted Britain's lonely resistance as an outpost of her own defence. When outright hostilities were precipitated the two countries joined in the closest fighting alliance in history: 'The British Empire and the United States', in Churchill's famous understatement, were once more, 'somewhat mixed up together'. Whatever else has happened since, this process has not been reversed.

7 The Rise and Fall of the Second British Empire
India, Africa and Australia
MAX BELOFF

THE PEACE OF VERSAILLES in 1783 ending the international conflict that had arisen out of the revolt of the American colonies and confirming their recognition as the independent United States, is usually taken as marking the beginning of a second British Empire. It was this 'Second Empire' that evolved during the 20th century into what was first known as the British Commonwealth of Nations and later on as simply the Commonwealth. Yet, although much territory was added to the area under British rule or influence between 1783 and 1921 when the system attained its maximum extent, the foundations in conquest, commercial penetration and settlement had been laid before the American rebellion.

The transformation of the Empire from an English into a British enterprise was also in progress. Wales was already part of the home base before the period of overseas expansion began in the reign of Elizabeth I, the last monarch of the (Welsh) Tudor dynasty. Access to the fruits of imperial trade was one of the inducements that brought the Scots to accept the Union of 1706/7. The opportunities opened up by the Union were fully exploited and, whether as entrepreneurs, soldiers, administrators, settlers or missionaries, Scots play so essential a role in the imperial story that to talk of the 'English' Empire would clearly be absurd. The case of Ireland is different. Ireland would be seen by many as having been the first country to be colonized by the English and the Scots. While Ireland had for long been part of the domains of the British Crown, her institutions had not been assimilated to those of the larger island. After the Act of Union in 1800 the Irish like the Scots had full access to imperial markets and imperial opportunities. But in Ireland itself the Union was never fully accepted, and Irish nationalism continued to present a series of challenges to the imperial system from close to its commercial and political heart.

The Empire as it existed on the morrow of the peace of 1783 consisted of Canada and Nova Scotia, Newfoundland, the islands and small mainland possessions of the Caribbean, trading posts on the West African coasts mainly engaged in the slave trade to the New World and the possessions of the East India Company. The extension of the eastern trading empire was being sought through further exploration in the South Seas and the Pacific Ocean. For it was as a trading empire rather than an empire of settlement that its future was viewed. From the loss of the American colonies most English statesmen had derived the opinion that Englishmen overseas would not readily accept regulation of their affairs by a Parliament at Westminster, and that the expense of holding colonies of settlement by military force was unlikely to yield a profit. On the other hand, trade with other continents was clearly profitable and investment in naval forces and in the provision of naval stations for the fleet's support appeared to be a justifiable expenditure of the country's resources.

During the next half century new ideas and attitudes gained currency as Britain itself underwent the major changes of the first Industrial Revolution. Ideas of free trade gained ground at the expense of mercantilist notions, although never completely winning the day; evangelicalism brought with it new attitudes towards relations with subordinate peoples, leading to the expansion of missionary endeavour and more specifically to the onslaught first against the slave trade and then against the institution of slavery itself. The justification of imperial rule by the notion of trusteeship and that of bringing the benefits of western civilization to non-European peoples was the secular counterpart of evangelicalism. The purely exploitative ventures of the 17th and 18th centuries required some other justification if they were to be accepted into the Victorian Englishman's world picture – although this did not prevent new forms of exploitation from developing along the Empire's expanding frontiers.

Imperial policy after the American Revolution intruded itself only intermittently upon the British political scene. It was still much affected by Britain's relations with other major powers, some of whom possessed or might aspire to an imperial role – above all with France and Russia and, much later, Germany. But what continued to be true was that the impetus for expansion and development was only to a limited extent the result of decisions taken by government. It was the individual energies of British citizens seeking to acquire fortunes or simply as settlers to better their own condition that determined the course of events. Even the underpinning of the system through the military and civilian services, the supply of proconsuls for minor as well as major posts, depended upon the men being forthcoming: no younger sons, no empire!

Canada and the Caribbean

Another Anglo-American war, the War of 1812, was the prelude to a new Atlantic trading system. But the United States had not abandoned her hope of incorporating Canada, and friction continued over boundary disputes and border raids by Irish exiles. But Canada's links with Britain were strengthened by the loyalist migration from the United States to Upper Canada and Nova Scotia, and paradoxically by the ability of the French Canadians to consolidate their own hold on Quebec through natural increase alone. Upper and Lower Canada became separate colonies each enjoying a measure of self-government. The maritimes retained their own distinct interests separate from those of the commercial empire of the St Lawrence with its potential for westward expansion and from the remoter fur-trading outposts of the Hudson's Bay Company.

The British West Indies entered on a long decline. Sugar became less important, the slave interest more unpopular and its representatives less courted in Parliament. By 1807 abolitionist feeling was strong enough to enact the abolition of the slave trade and the Royal Navy became the principal instrument in putting it down. Slavery itself was not abolished until 1833 (and lingered in the territories of the East India Company for another three decades). The West Indies themselves lost their competitive position as protectionism gave way to free trade, and the islands, although enjoying in some cases old forms of representative government, increasingly figured as museum pieces in the imperial structure. Race relations could still give rise to outbursts of violence such as swept Jamaica in 1865 when public opinion in England was polarized over the degree of force used in its suppression. Not till the 1930s did British governments begin a policy of active intervention to ameliorate economic and social conditions.

India and the Far East: the beginnings

If the mainland colonies in North America form the pivot of the history of the First British Empire, it is India that provides the centre-piece of its successor. Yet Britain's acquisition of political power in India was not only unplanned but even resisted by many members of the governing class. In seeking to trade and plunder in the eastern lands, important originally for their spices and later for other commodities ranging from tea to textiles, the English in the 17th century faced competition from earlier arrivals – the Portuguese and the Dutch. Indeed, had it not been for their defeats at the hands of the Dutch which excluded them very largely from the Spice Islands (modern Indonesia), they might have shown less interest in the Indian sub-continent and its coastal and inland trade. By the end of the 17th century the British East India Company had acquired three positions of importance – on the Coromandel coast which developed into the city of Madras; in Bengal, most important of all, what became

Josiah Wedgwood, one of the campaigners in the crusade against slavery, made and distributed cameos like the one above as propaganda.

the city of Calcutta; and finally, on the west coast, Bombay, originally obtained by Charles II as part of the dowry of his Portuguese bride.

The 18th century witnessed three new developments. The first of these stemmed from the fact that trade between India and Britain – the raison d'être of the East India Company – did not give scope for the personal profit which could alone reconcile its servants to the climate and fearful mortality rates of the subcontinent. As compensation they secured privileges which could assist them to get rich through internal trade and monopolies. Secondly, the condition required for such trade – political stability – could not be guaranteed by the local rulers who succeeded each other with bewildering rapidity as the Mogul empire entered upon its period of decay. Lastly, the attempts by the French to profit by intervention in local Indian politics stimulated the British to do likewise. In the end the British command of the sea proved too much for the French, and their superiority in the use of artillery too much for the Indians. The decisive events were packed into the career of Robert Clive, the outstanding figure among the 'nabobs', whose incursion into British political and social life was widely and deeply resented. His principal successor in charge of the company's affairs, Warren Hastings, faced similar obloquy at home.

It was clearly an anomaly that a commercial company should have acquired what was virtually a territorial empire even if covered by the shadowy sovereignty of the Mogul emperor, but the idea of abandoning the positions that had been won and so permitting the French to reassert themselves could not seriously be contemplated. Instead, Parliament increasingly intervened to exercise control; the governors-general were drawn not from merchant adventurers but from the core of the aristocratic ruling class and, aided by continuous strife among the Indian rulers, the British consolidated their territorial power and began to exercise a conscious role as masters of the subcontinent.

India also offered a base for commerce with the Far East, although this met with the formidable resistance of the Japanese and Chinese authorities. The territorial nucleus of further expansion was created. Ceylon, conquered from the Dutch, was finally annexed in 1814. Penang, the first outpost in Malaysia, had been acquired in 1796. Most important of all, the island of Singapore, almost uninhabited but, like Madras, Calcutta and Hong Kong (founded in 1841), to be yet another great new oriental city arising out of British imperial rule, was on the initiative of Stamford Raffles ceded to the East India Company in 1819. Lower Burma was annexed in 1862; Upper Burma not till 1886.

The British in Africa

Contacts with the west coast of Africa began early in the history of British maritime enterprise but the trade did not give rise to settlements other than fortified posts along the shore or up the rivers. The first colony was Sierra Leone, founded as a refuge for liberated slaves. Elsewhere the trading companies themselves exercised authority and, after the last of these was dissolved in 1821, the problems of relations with the local chiefs produced a demand for total disengagement, countered both by merchant interests and by those who wished to see Britain's position used to combat the internal slave trade. Sierra Leone, the Gambia and the Gold Coast remained under British rule which was gradually extended into the interior. Rivalry with the French called forth further efforts in the Niger basin and the new colony of Lagos was established in 1861. A committee of the House of Commons recommended four years later that there should be no further expansion, but explorers, traders and missionaries pushed forward, and the flag eventually followed.

In the 1880s the national mood changed and the idea of Britain's civilizing mission was bolstered by fears of other powers establishing exclusive zones of influence. The future of much of Africa was settled at the Conference of Berlin in 1885 and by the end of the century British authority was well established in the interior.

In the case of South Africa, the element of international competition was well to the fore from the beginning, since the Cape of Good Hope, taken from the Dutch at the end of the Napoleonic Wars, was a key point on the route to India. As in Canada, however, the British had acquired an existing white population of another language and culture. Since the new wave of colonization coincided with a thrust southward of Bantu peoples, the stage was set for a triangular contest which lasted until almost the end of the century and in some sense beyond it. Objecting to the British abolition of slavery, the Boers – the descendants of the original Dutch settlers – moved into the interior where the independent or near-independent states they created seemed to menace British control of the Cape itself. After a short period of direct rule, autonomy was restored to the Boers in 1881, but Cecil Rhodes used the Cape Colony as a basis for an outflanking movement which created what eventually became the protectorates of Southern and Northern Rhodesia.

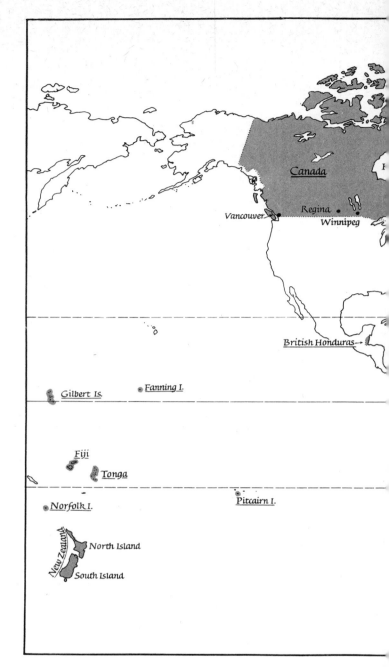

The British Empire on the eve of the First World War.

A similar blend of humanitarian and strategic considerations lay behind the acquisition of the Sudan which arose directly from the occupation of Egypt in 1882 which itself was connected with the British interest in the Suez Canal – the new route to the East. The first conquest of the Sudan ended catastrophically with the death of General Gordon in 1885; but in 1898, General Kitchener was victorious over the Mahdi at Omdurman and the French were forced to withdraw at Fashoda. Following on Livingstone's explorations, much of East Africa was also acquired for the usual mixture of commercial, missionary and strategic considerations. It looked as though the British idea of an all-red Cape to Cairo route had triumphed over French hopes of an equatorial empire stretching across the continent from east to west.

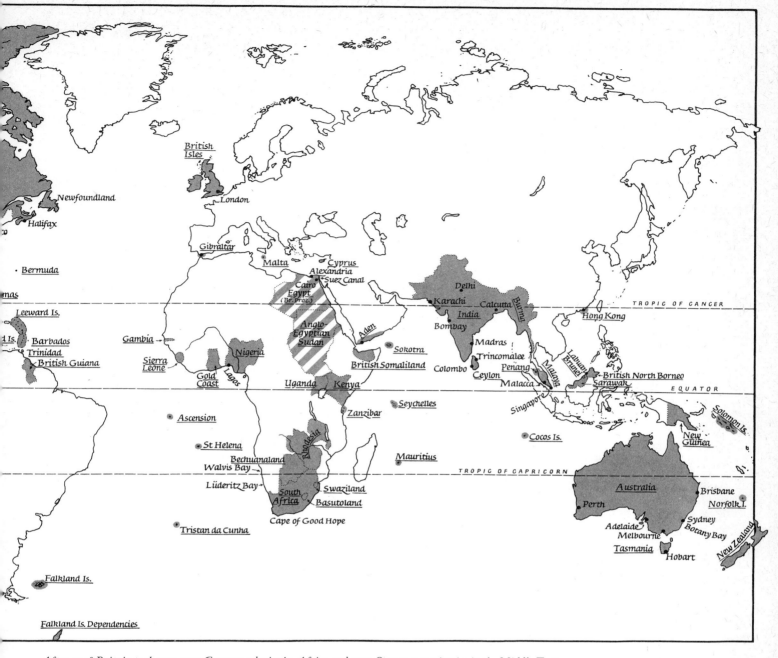

After 1918 Britain took over some German colonies in Africa and some Ottoman territories in the Middle East.

The foundations of the British Raj in India

The division of responsibility between the home government and the East India Company and the effects of distance gave considerable scope to the men on the spot when, like the Governor-General Wellesley, they felt inclined to take advantage of India's internal discords to extend the frontiers of British rule. India was the arena in which generations of British soldiers from Wellesley's brother, the future duke of Wellington, to Field Marshal Auchinleck and Field Marshal Wavell in the last days of the Empire established their reputations. The development of British industry meant that the textiles which had been so important an import from India in the 18th century now gave way to plantation products, cotton, jute, indigo, tea – and opium much in demand further east. The invasion of the Indian home market itself by British textiles made home-spun and home-woven cloth the most effective symbol of India's nationalist movement later on.

After the Napoleonic Wars expansion slowed down although it continued in the north-west where the 'great game' of rivalry with the Russians was at its beginning. The annexation of Sind and the Punjab in the 1840s took place at a time when the two dualities in Britain's position were becoming established. 'British India' organized into provinces directly administered was contrasted with India of the Princes where Britain practised a minimum of intervention in domestic affairs. In British India the Indian Civil Service, recruited almost wholly in Britain itself, was trained to

'Here . . . and there; or, Emigration a Remedy'; at home, unemployment, poverty, even the threat of revolution (the year is 1848, one of revolution in the rest of Europe); emigration is held up as the panacea.

administer justice, collect revenue and at times to initiate public works. Small in numbers, it depended upon a large subordinate Indian bureaucracy to make its orders effective.

The general assumption was that such an empire could not be permanent and that ultimately Britain would have to hand over government to an indigenous authority. Meanwhile the twin but rival currents of evangelicalism and utilitarianism produced much conflicting argument as to how the British should behave in the meantime – should India be 'westernized' or should Indian religious custom be left intact and Indian education be based upon India's own linguistic and literary heritage? Most of the issues were settled by compromise. Missionary activity was tolerated, but Indian religious practices were mostly left unmolested. Higher education was in English and along Western lines, otherwise in the vernacular languages. In the legal sphere, Western codes were dominant, though largely administered by Indian judges. On the whole, the British remained aloof from Indian society, dispensing justice in paternalistic isolation. Officers and civil servants had their wives with them, although children were sent home to school. The contacts of the common soldiers with Indian women were exclusively mercenary and temporary.

Australia, New Zealand and the Pacific

The first British colony in Australia was at Botany Bay (or rather the neighbouring Sydney). Established in 1788 it was the outcome of a purely domestic need – where to transport criminals now that North America was no longer available.

Voluntary settlers soon followed and, by 1820, New South Wales and its dependency Van Diemen's Land (Tasmania) could boast a population of some 30,000: convicts, 'emancipists', political deportees and free

settlers. A further impetus was provided by the belief that the problem of unemployment at home could be solved by organized emigration, and schemes for financing this movement out of land sales in the colonies were advanced by the group of colonial reformers of whom the most notable was Edward Gibbon Wakefield. Their most important impact was in the Australasian colonies, beginning with the foundation of South Australia in 1836. Transportation as a punishment for crime was reduced after 1840 and came to an end in 1868.

Australia had begun to attract settlers for the familiar reasons of economic self-betterment – wool and gold playing important roles in the story – and new colonies came into being on the rim of the island continent: the Swan River Colony (Western Australia) in 1829; Moreton Bay (the nucleus of the later Queensland) in 1833; Port Phillip (Victoria) in 1835. Relations with the indigenous population were, as so often in imperial history, an element of contention with the imperial government. The Australian record was a dismal one and included the complete extirpation of the indigenous population of Tasmania.

In accordance with the current preference for holding colonies on a loose rein, representative institutions were granted between 1846 and 1852 to all colonies that enjoyed financial independence, and by 1859 the Australians enjoyed full responsible government in their internal affairs on the Canadian model. In contrast to Canada, however, there was no immediate move towards consolidating the separate colonies into a single dominion. After the renewal of international rivalries in the region in the 1880s, twenty years of negotiation were required before an agreed federal constitution, accepted in a national referendum, was submitted to the Westminster Parliament. The Commonwealth of Australia came into being on 1 January 1901.

New Zealand refused to become part of the new Dominion, and indeed its different history fortified the argument from distance. In the years after 1820, European contacts with the Maori people of New Zealand were almost wholly limited to successful missionary enterprise. In 1839, the first colonists, the fruit of one of Wakefield's schemes, arrived at what was to become Wellington, but very soon afterwards, by the Treaty of Waitangi between the Crown and the principal Maori chiefs, British sovereignty was extended to the entire island grouping, and an official capital established at Auckland. The government's action had been taken largely to protect the Maoris and this came up against the ambitions of the settlers. After warfare between 1843 and 1846, the North Island was pacified, and in 1846 the first representative institutions were granted to the settlers. Two years later, the New Zealand constitution was inaugurated, creating a federation of six provinces, five of them the product of Wakefield's enterprises. The Crown had reserved relations with the natives to itself but this did not prevent further Maori wars waged intermittently from 1861 to 1871. In 1876, the provincial divisions were abolished and the Dominion of New Zealand acquired a unitary frame of government on the British model. The problem of the Maori minority (diminishing in numbers until the turn of the century but growing thereafter) was met by the allocation of reserved seats in the legislature.

New Zealand, the most British of the colonies of settlement, established itelf in the final decades of the century as a pioneer in democratic forms of government and measures of social welfare. It also (as did Australia) sought to extend its influence into the ocean to its north; so that Britain's reluctance to add to the number of Pacific island possessions (of which Fiji acquired in 1874 was the most important) was balanced by the local imperialism of the two Pacific Dominions highly sensitive to their security requirements.

India: the Mutiny and after

The ambiguities, fragilities and strengths of Britain's position in India were thrown into relief by the uprising among the sepoys (native troops) in 1857, known to the British then and since as the Indian Mutiny but looked back to later on by nationalist historians as the Great Rebellion. While its immediate cause was the belief among sections of the Indian army that their religious taboos were being violated, other elements in Indian society – both princes and peasants – who had recent grievances against particular acts of British rule were recruited to the rebel cause. But there was little contact between the mutineers who concentrated on the urban centres of Delhi, Lucknow and Cawnpore, and the peasant risings; and when a political symbol was sought it was found in the shadowy Mogul emperor still living under British protection.

On the British side, the mutiny had the effect of sharpening some existing attitudes and of bringing about a rationalization of the political structure. The East India Company was swept away and British India became a direct responsibility of the Crown, exercising authority through a secretary of state, aided by a council composed of men of experience in Indian government. The governor-general, now also viceroy, received increased authority – though the steamship and cable made it easier for Whitehall to convey its wishes.

The idea of handing India over to native rule became increasingly difficult to reconcile with the growing awareness of India's key role in the British imperial system and the sensitivity to Russian pressure; and this awareness was given symbolic content with Queen Victoria's adoption of the title of Empress of India in 1875, and the first visit of a reigning monarch, that of George V for the Durbar of 1911.

Railways and industrialization changed the traditional face of India. New pressures developed for a literate class seeking opportunities for public employment and politically inspired by Western liberalism. Its principal voice came to be the Indian National Congress founded in the 1880s. Yet the old Hindu-Muslim division was not extinct. The transfer of the Indian capital from Calcutta to the old Mogul capital Delhi and the planning of new public buildings to rival the legacy of past glories might have seemed to link the British Raj with India's past (as well as to remove the central government from the pressures of Bengali nationalism); but the lessons of that past were equivocal to say the least.

Canada from Durham to Laurier

The themes of Canadian history after the War of 1812 were still entwined with the affairs of the United States. There was the question of whether the 'commercial empire of the St Lawrence' based upon Montreal could vie for the trade of the interior with the rival system based upon New York and the Hudson valley, and those of the Ohio and Mississippi valleys; there was the question of whether the interaction of the American and Canadian economies on a north-south axis would prove too strong for the creation of an independent nation along the narrow belt of country capable of close settlement north of the border. Would 'manifest destiny' result in Canada's absorption into a single North American Republic as many Americans, until well into the present century, believed it would and should? Finally, there was the question as to whether the idea of Canadian nationhood could in the long run be reconciled with the highly developed sense of a unique identity retained by the French inhabitants of Lower Canada separated from what became the majority by language and religion.

From the point of view of the British Empire, it was the early phases in the resolution of these problems that most concerned the government at Westminster. Local issues in Upper Canada and somewhat different problems in Lower Canada reached a head in two separate rebellions in 1837. Neither movement had a clear set of objectives; each was suppressed without too much difficulty. But the warning was clear to a British government, with the history of the American Revolution as its point of reference. The Radical Lord Durham was sent out as governor-general and to produce suggestions for reform. His suggestions on the constitutional side took the form of a far-reaching extension of self-government in all internal matters; but he attached more importance to the conflict of the two races, and saw as its only possible solution the merger of the two Canadas so that the French would eventually be assimilated into a predominantly British culture. The amalgamation took place in 1841 and over the next ten years Canada gradually acquired the constitutional status which he had recommended.

Two new sets of circumstances now intervened. The coming of the railways and the demand for more land for settlement after the exhaustion of the agricultural possibilities of Upper Canada meant a westward push to link eastern Canada across the prairies with the earlier beginnings of settlement on the Pacific coast in what became British Columbia. The other factor for change was the impetus given to American expansionist intentions by the slavery contest in the United States, and the exacerbation of Anglo-American relations to which its Civil War gave rise. But the solution this time was not a matter for British but for Canadian statesmen; so far had a sense of Canadian nationhood developed. A group of Canadian statesmen not inferior in ability to, if lacking in the panache of the American Founding Fathers, contrived the device of 'confederation' – in fact a rather tight federation – which enabled the Canadian provinces, both those existing and those still to be created (including long afterwards in 1949 the ancient colony of Newfoundland), to form a single political unit, enshrined in the British North America Act of 1867 and taking shape in 1873. In confederation, Lower Canada recovered its separate status as the Province of Quebec.

The growing agricultural and later industrial importance of Canada made the distinction between internal self-government and the continued responsibility of the United Kingdom for external affairs difficult to maintain, since Canadians naturally pressed for their own inclusion in commercial negotiations, as 19th-century laissez-faire gave way to various forms of protectionism. The issue had not been fully resolved by 1914, but Canada's association in dealing with all that concerned her was increasingly seen to be inevitable.

For the first generation after confederation, Canada was led by a Conservative Party whose strength lay in Ontario (as Upper Canada was now known). But in 1896, Wilfrid Laurier, a French Canadian, inaugurated an important period of Liberal rule. The Liberals were more questioning of the imperial tie, and less hostile to close co-operation with the United States than the Conservatives.

The new imperialism and the Boer War

The new period of imperial expansion in the last fifteen years of the 19th century was not without contradictions. While there was talk of the economic importance of the newly acquired territories the economic conjuncture was such that little capital was available for their development. Although there was a more positive attitude towards imperial responsibilities – typified by Joseph Chamberlain's tenure of the colonial office from 1895 to 1903 – there remained a strong disinclination to spend money upon them. Hence the attempt to use the old instrument of the chartered company for Borneo, Nigeria, East Africa as well as Southern Africa (Rhodesia), so as to minimize the direct involvement of government. In no case was this successful. In the new conditions only government could run empires. In some areas climatic conditions made the building up of a permanent and consistent British administrative presence virtually impossible. It was only the medical advances of the last years of the century that made it possible to contemplate forward-looking policies in West Africa.

Arguments about the role of the Empire were now at the heart of British politics, and important historical and political writings and even imaginative literature – Seeley, Dilke, Kipling – buttressed the arguments of statesmen. Two issues were paramount. In the first place, there was the question of the extent to which the Empire could enable Britain to hold its own in the increasingly harsh economic and political clime of the period. Could the self-governing colonies of settlement be persuaded to enter into some form of federal arrangement or imperial tariff union so that the Empire's total resources could be managed to the common benefit? Secondly, the new interest in the natural resources of the dependent Empire, notably in Africa, raised the whole question of combining responsibility to the world at large for developing these resources with policies directed towards the material and moral betterment of the indigenous populations – the doctrine of the 'dual mandate'. In particular in Africa much attention was paid to the possibility of fulfilling the latter duty by making the maximum use of the local tribal authorities – 'indirect rule'.

The new imperialism received a major blow in the failure to solve peacefully the continued problem of the Boer republics. The continued independence of the two countries was particularly hard for Britain to accept for two reasons in addition to the old friction over 'native policy' – the arrival in the Transvaal of non-Boer migrants drawn by gold and diamonds and not easily assimilated into the Boer's rural paternalism, and the fears of foreign and particularly German influence getting a foothold. After the plans of Rhodes – the embodiment of the new imperialism – had failed to bring about annexation through an internal uprising by way of the 'Jameson raid' in 1895, it was left to the cooler and more deliberate imperial strategy of Sir Alfred Milner to force the issue in such a way as to lead to war. While British opinion had accepted wars against native rulers as part of the price of empire, war against a white people who enjoyed the vocal sympathy of Britain's rivals was another matter. The long-drawn-out nature of the struggle (1899–1902), once it had entered the stage of guerrilla warfare, cast doubts upon the efficacy of Britain's military machine and, even more important, helped to animate an anti-imperialist body of theory and sentiment that was powerfully to influence the subsequent course of imperial history.

It is true that the aftermath of the war gave some grounds for optimism; the presence of contingents from other parts of the Empire had helped to sustain a belief in its durability; the army and the navy underwent important reforms; and the Boer republics converted into provinces in a new Union of South Africa seemed to have been reconciled to its equality of status with the older self-governing Dominions, although, as it proved in the end, this had not altered the determination of their people not to be assimilated into a British-dominated society. Liberalism was not a panacea for the problem of nationalism.

The Empire and the First World War

The long-drawn-out struggle of the Great War – as that generation knew it – was mostly confined to Europe, once the German colonies in East and south-west Africa had been conquered, largely by South African troops. But other forces of the Dominions played an important military role – Canadians on the western front, Australians and New Zealanders at Gallipoli and in the Middle East. Australia, with a population one-twentieth of that of the United States, suffered more fatal casualties. It is not surprising that the Dominions should have demanded a greater say in the running of the war and should have insisted that the peace treaties did not return to Germany colonies they believed to menace their own interests. Indian military participation was on an even more massive scale, not only in Mesopotamia, which could be regarded as an outpost of India itself, but on almost every fighting front. This participation was particularly important early in the war before the British themselves were fully mobilized. In the autumn of 1914, the Indians held one-third of the British line. When Lloyd George became prime minister, he made a point of associating leaders of the Dominions and representative Indians with the conduct of the war and the disposition of the post-war world. But the same basic differences that had hampered the pre-war movements towards some form of imperial federation were still present. If the Dominions wished for consultation when their own interests were involved, they did not wish this to involve any lessening of their own autonomy or any commitment to support Britain's policies in areas remote from their own interests. Although interested in preserving the British market for their own primary commodities and in access to British capital, they were not prepared to put a check on their autonomous industrial growth through any imperial *zollverein*. While the war brought home to the British the importance of their Empire and while in framing the peace treaties, notably in respect of the Middle East, they even sought additions to the Empire so as to strengthen its communications in any era in which air transport was likely to play an increasing role, the Dominions and India derived from it a further spur to their own independent development.

From Empire to Commonwealth

The international status of the Dominions (and potentially of India) was recognized in their individual signatures of the Treaty of Versailles. Their constitutional position as autonomous members of the Commonwealth was set out in the Balfour Declaration of 1926 and the Statute of Westminster of 1931. The common Crown and to a diminishing extent the right of appeal to the privy council were the main surviving links between them and the mother-country. India might, it was felt, one day join them. What was now the Empire was a series of colonies all over the globe some with limited measures of self-government about which

'*The Scapegrace of the Family*': Ireland, here a terrorist with rifle and dynamite, was seen as the misfit and troublemaker in the otherwise serenely happy family of the Commonwealth, comparing ill with the other dutiful sons and daughters of the Empire.

people were once again beginning to think in terms of positive development after the more or less benign neglect preferred by the Victorians.

Each Dominion had its own problems: Ireland which had acquired Dominion status (at the price of partition) in 1921 regarded its status as at best transitional and sought to weaken Commonwealth ties, finding in South Africa – increasingly dominated by the Afrikaner elements – a ready ally. Canada, unable to solve the constitutional problems of amendment, had retained the British Parliament as the final constitutional authority but was more concerned to prevent entanglement in Britain's European concerns; Australia and New Zealand, worried about the rise of Japanese power, still looked to Britain to provide both security and markets. The Great Depression and the growth of Italian and German threats alongside that from Japan, together with the general spread of economic autarky, gave a new lease of life to the idea of the Empire-Commonwealth as an economic unit – an aim very partially achieved in the Ottawa agreements of 1932. Inter-imperial relations were made more intimate by the speed-up in communications and by emigration which was a two-way affair as economic fortunes fluctuated. Improvements in tropical medicine extended the areas in which British men and women could work or settle. Interest in the Empire – for and against – was more conspicuous in British politics and political thought.

The crucial weakness was in defence. The main threat to Britain was in Europe; its armed forces were traditionally organized for imperial needs – hence the strong preference of the Dominions, with the partial exception of New Zealand, for the 'appeasement' policy. If it failed, the naval forces that Britain could provide were insufficient to guard at once the North Sea, the Mediterranean, the Indian Ocean and Far Eastern waters. Ground troops were also in short supply. A high proportion of the British army was needed for the defence of Egypt and the Suez Canal and to keep the peace in Palestine where the Arabs rebelled against the British commitment made in 1917, and confirmed by the League of Nations, to assist in the creation of a Jewish national home.

India: towards self-government

The upsurge of nationalism in India during the war produced a response in the shape of the Montagu-Chelmsford Report in 1917 and its proposals for a measure of representative government in the provinces known as dyarchy went ahead, although not before the country had undergone a period of civil disobedience and violence during which the impact of the Russian Revolution was not unimportant. The disorders provoked repression and the massacre at Amritsar on 13 April 1920 was an important stimulus to the nationalist cause not merely because of the loss of life but also because of the reaction in Britain to the disciplining of the officer responsible, General R. E. Dyer. A strong minority in the House of Commons and a majority in the House of Lords assented to the view that he had been unfairly treated, and in so doing voiced sentiments of racial superiority wounding to Indian pride.

It was clear both that political India would press for much more rapid constitutional advances and that Britain's place in India's future was now in doubt. The India Act of 1935, put into effect partially in 1937, gave some experience in executive government in the provinces to the nationalist leaders until the Congress-sponsored executives resigned when Britain in 1939 declared India to be at war. The federal part of the Act never came into being, since the princes refused to take up their allotted role fearing for their positions in an India in which the Congress would be dominant. At the same time, the Muslims who had briefly aligned themselves with the main body of the nationalist movement between 1916 and 1924 became increasingly anxious about their future and increasingly inclined to seek it through some form of territorial separation. The importance of the Muslims in the Indian army made it possible for the British to ignore their wishes. Furthermore the very nature of the Indian national movement made its full comprehension by British statesmen and administrators by no means an easy task. Leaders such as Pandit Nehru spoke the language of Western democracy, in his case with some Marxist overtones. But Mahatma Gandhi, who seemed to make the most direct appeal to the Indian masses and whose moral authority seemed so widely entrenched, embodied a repudiation of much of what Britain had seen as its mission of westernization in favour of a return to philosophical and social concepts of a much earlier age.

The Empire in the Second World War

The role of the Empire in the Second World War was superficially not unlike that which it had filled in the first. Despite the greater display of autonomy exhibited by the Dominions in their separate decisions to go to war – Ireland marked a further stage in its separateness by maintaining a sullen and dangerous neutrality – Canadians, Australians, New Zealanders and South Africans again fought on distant battlefields. So too did soldiers from parts of the Empire whose participation was decided upon in London – Indians, West Africans and Rhodesians. The economic resources of the Empire played their part.

Yet the differences were greater than the apparent similarities. Parts of the Empire were over-run – Hong Kong, Malaya and Burma. Indeed the fall of Singapore in 1942 and the discovery as to how illusory was its fortress role might be taken as marking the moment when the writing appeared on the wall. India was threatened with invasion and to other nationalist arguments was now added the doubt as to whether Britain could protect her. Egypt and the Middle East were also threatened; at moments the outlook there was bleak indeed. Australia found its troops committed to campaigns in the Western Desert at a time when its own territories seemed open to a Japanese descent.

In the end all seemed well: the British returned; the flags were raised again. But the victory was not unequivocal. Some had seen the possibility of using the war to seek their own nationalist anti-colonialist ends – seeking reinsurance with the Germans or the Italians or the Japanese. The prestige of the white race and its own self-confidence had been badly dented. A sense of effortless superiority would no longer substitute for material strength. That India would get independence after the war was a common assumption of policy from 1942 onwards.

The victory itself was owed in large measure to two countries whose leaders, Roosevelt and Stalin, if they had little else in common, shared a profound animus against the British Empire. In the interests of national survival, the Russians had put anti-imperialist propaganda and subversion into cold storage for the duration; Roosevelt had no such inhibitions. Nehru was to be for him the 20th-century George Washington. The importance of the American contribution to the victory also meant that, among the independent members of the Commonwealth, Australia and New Zealand now followed Canada in seeking American military protection. Relations with Washington rather than with London would henceforward bulk largest in their diplomacy.

The Labour government elected at the end of the war had many calls on its depleted resources and little to spare for transforming the Empire into an extended Commonwealth in an orderly fashion. However robust its sentiments it could not resist the pressures from below. The British did not wish to be an imperial people. The most any government could do was to make the best bargains it could; some of these lacked lustre.

The end of the Empire in India

Britain's failure to reach agreement with the Indian nationalist leaders during the war had been partly due to the belief that it was not safe to transfer the ultimate control of the war effort into Indian hands and partly to the increasingly assertive claims of the Muslim minority for a state of their own. On the other hand, the risks of partition were increased by the fact that no simple geographical line could be found that would separate the two communities and not involve partition of two of the historical provinces of the existing federal system – Bengal and the Punjab. The post-war Labour government was conscious that while Indian politicians argued, the material resources to hold the country together and preserve the minimum of law and order were being drained away.

In the end it was decided to impose agreement by stating a date for Britain's withdrawal which in February 1947 was fixed to take place in June 1948. The new Viceroy, Lord Mountbatten, decided to bring the date forward, and partition and the abandonment of British sovereignty took place simultaneously at midnight on 14 August 1947. The British were thus unable to intervene in the subsequent movement of populations across the borders between the two new Dominions of India and Pakistan or to prevent the massacres that accompanied them. It was also impossible to prevent the forcible incorporation of the princely states into the new Dominions, despite the hopes their rulers had placed in their direct relationship with the Crown.

It was not to be expected that Britain would wish to exert authority for long in neighbouring countries which had been drawn into the British orbit by proximity to the Indian Empire. In September 1947, Burma assumed the status of an independent republic outside the Commonwealth. In February 1948, Ceylon became like India and Pakistan an independent member of the Commonwealth. Malaysia followed in 1957 and Singapore, which had broken away from the original federation of Malaya, in 1965. Only Hong Kong remained; its anomalous position stemming from its role as an outlet to the world for the new Communist rulers of China.

British possessions in the Mediterranean and the Middle East had largely been acquired and defended as stepping-stones on the route to India. Now the responsibilities and expense of ruling them did not seem to be justified. Cyprus became independent in 1960 although Britain retained a military base on the island itself, and Malta followed in 1967.

In Palestine, the effort of balancing the scales between Jewish and Arab claims could no longer be justified, it was held, by the need to retain a British presence. As with India, an attempt was made to force agreement on the warring parties (or to get, in this case, international action) by giving a date for withdrawal. The tactic was even less successful than in India. On 15 May 1948, the Palestine mandate came to an end, and the political future of the area was left to the arbitrament of force. The relaxation of control over Egypt took longer to effect, but after the overthrow of the Egyptian monarchy in 1953, an agreement to evacuate the Canal Zone was achieved on October 1954 – only to be called into question by the abortive Suez expedition following the Egyptian nationalization of the Canal in 1956. The final stage in the dismantling of the Middle Eastern route took place in November 1968, when Aden which had been under British rule for 128 years was evacuaed and transformed into the Soviet-oriented Republic of South Yemen.

The wind of change in Africa and the Caribbean

The dissolution of the Empire in India involved changes in the Commonwealth since the new Dominions insisted upon republican status as the price of remaining within it. They then used their new role to prevent South Africa from remaining a member when it decided to end the link with the monarchy in 1961. The touchstone of membership was henceforth not participation in British modes of government – military rule and one-party states became the norm – but a formal dedication to racial equality.

British withdrawal from Asia and the Mediterranean had been the result of the pressure of circumstances rather than of some major change in British attitudes. But there seems to have been general acceptance of the view that although self-government and even independence were appropriate for countries with old and sophisticated societies, it was too early to apply the same principles of self-determination to the less advanced peoples of Africa (where in some cases white settlement provided another brake on the process of political change), or to the impoverished colonies of the Caribbean which also faced problems arising from the multiracial character of their populations. It was therefore assumed in the immediate post-war years that Britain would have a colonial empire for at least one more generation; and young men were duly recruited and trained for its service, while limited forms of representative government were introduced.

All this proved to be an illusion, as did British attempts to meet the economic difficulties facing these communities by federal devices in Central and East Africa and in the West Indies. To retain control in the face of nationalist movements, stirred into activity by the war, and fostered by external precept and example, would have been possible, but only through a commitment of military manpower that Britain was unprepared to face. Ghana (the Gold Coast), the most advanced of the African colonies, became an independent member of the Commonwealth in 1957; Nigeria the largest and most important one in 1960. Others followed at a rapid pace including in 1963 Kenya, the scene during the Mau Mau rising of Britain's major military effort of the transition period (except for the help given to the new Malaysian Dominion to cope with communist insurgency). By 1968, the British Empire in Africa had disappeared. All its former components were now ruled by governments speaking in the name of their indigenous majorities except for Southern Rhodesia which, having repudiated British rule in 1965, remained until 1979 under the rule of its white minority, and the Republic of South Africa.

The principal islands in the Caribbean and Guyana also achieved independence within the Commonwealth in the 1960s, and somewhat more gradually a similar process took place in the smaller islands, not only in the Caribbean but in the Indian and Pacific oceans as well. No consideration was now given to size, or economic or political viability, and where an old-established colony such as Bermuda was unwilling for good local reasons to face the future on its own, the pressure from London was all for cutting the link. It was only the firmly expressed preference of the local inhabitants that prevented the British government from ceding Gibraltar to Spain and the Falkland Islands to Argentina.

The English and the imperial experience

To discuss the modern history of the English people with no reference to their imperial experience would clearly be absurd; yet nothing is harder on the morrow of the ending of that experience than to assess its importance for the home country. One reason is that the transition from having an empire to not having one was not merely very rapid but was carried through without a long-drawn-out rearguard action such as that which marked the French, the Dutch and the Portuguese withdrawals. Where there was serious violence, as in India and Palestine, the reasons lay in the conflict over the succession and not in any British desire to hang on. Where, as in Rhodesia, a white minority strove to cling to power it got little help or sympathy from home.

It was perhaps because of the relative ease of the transition that it proved difficult to take in the impact of the very real changes that had occurred in the quarter of a century following the Second World War. If the Empire had originally owed its foundation to a seeking for commercial satisfactions, it had in turn affected the channels of trade and the choice of commodities to produce. Once it became a Commonwealth of independent sovereignties, with some former imperial possessions not even members of that shadowy association, other considerations would operate more powerfully. Britain's entry into the European Economic Community was the counterpart of imperial retreat. Nevertheless it was difficult for a former world power not to think globally, nor had Britain ceased to have major interests in maritime trade. The uneasy reconciliation of these calls on resources with new worries about home and European defence reflected itself in the successive rounds of cuts in the armed forces, each of which evoked some of the old arguments and old imperial echoes. In the 1970s Britain was still using Gurkha mercenaries from the mountains of Nepal to protect the jungle frontiers of the sultanate of Brunei.

Of greater direct significance to British citizens no longer brought up at school on imperial myths was the change in the make-up of the population of England due to immigration from former imperial possessions. As with the original outpouring of English energies overseas this reflux was not a matter of government planning but the result of the same individualist motives of self-betterment and of corporate interests, in this case of public bodies such as the health service and transport authorities seeking to make up for labour shortages at home at a time of full employment. But the imperial legacy was involved in three ways: it was the former common status of subjects of the Crown that made such immigration relatively simple and also made efforts to curb it without injustice extremely difficult; it was the use of English as a lingua franca that made it natural for an ex-colonial to see England as the most obvious European country in which to seek one's fortune; it was elements of a common legal administrative and cultural heritage that encouraged immigrants to believe that they could at once assume an equal status.

As in the experience of the English overseas there was more in the differences than colour alone. Not all the new Britons wished for assimilation and some had, or rediscovered, strong, cultural traditions of their own. England became in the third quarter of the 20th century what students of European empires overseas had conceptualized as a 'plural society'. The English had left behind them in India and elsewhere churches in Victorian Gothic style incongruous in those climes. Now in Regent's Park in London, the Nash terraces, built when the British Raj was being consolidated in India and when the Prince Regent was illustrating his country's new links with the East in the oriental fantasies of the Brighton Pavilion, were overshadowed by a gilded mosque. The wheel had come full circle.

As former colonies of Great Britain achieved Dominion status the idea of the Commonwealth as a family grew in popularity. In this cartoon from 'Punch' (1897) the British Lion takes his young cubs on a patriotic trip to watch the Portsmouth Naval Review.

IV
The English Spirit

8 Religion in the Life of the Nation
The churches in the political
and social texture of English development

9 Art and Popular Taste
Architecture, painting, decoration
and fashion

10 Language and Literature
The English heritage
of poetry, drama and the novel

SOMETHING upon which both foreign observers and native Englishmen seem to be agreed is that moderation, the avoidance of extremes, the choice of a middle way, are among the essential qualities of Englishness. In this section we shall try to see how this characteristic has shown itself in three important aspects of English culture: religion, the visual arts and literature.

English Christianity, even in the Middle Ages, was inclined to pursue a path of its own and when, in the age of Luther, every country in Europe seemed faced with a choice between Wittenberg and Rome, England typically chose both – or neither: a Protestant church with a hierarchy of bishops, a Catholic church without a pope. The *via media* worked out by Henry VIII and Cranmer, whatever its drawbacks from the doctrinal point of view, has evidently suited the English temperament, since it survives with little change until today. Structured and yet flexible, undemanding yet capable of accommodating deep spirituality, it exhibits the supreme merit of English institutions: it works.

Is there a *via media* in the arts? Certainly England has avoided some extremes here too, some would say to her detriment. There is no English Michelangelo, or Bernini, or El Greco, nor even an English Dante or Dostoevsky. Only rarely has a social élite or a court been the centre of patronage; even more rarely has there been an intellectual élite setting the standards by which art and literature were to be judged. In England the appeal has always been to the experience of ordinary men. Themes and values have been predominantly bourgeois; people have been more interesting than ideas; and humour has percolated into almost every genre in a way that has often puzzled foreign critics. The great exception to all this, of course, is Romanticism, which the English helped to invent; but even here they refused to go too far – there is no English Wagner.

Most of what has been quoted as typically English, it will be noted, is post-Reformation. That event cut England off from the mainstream of continental culture and accentuated the individualism that had been merely latent before. English medieval art was universal as no subsequent art has been; Chaucer was a European in a sense that Shakespeare was not. It is arguable that this phase is now coming to an end, and that in religion, in the visual arts and in literature, the gap between what is English and what belongs to Western civilization is narrower than at any time since the Middle Ages.

English work –

opus Anglicanum – was the name given in the 14th century to a type of embroidery in which England excelled. It is a frail art and only a few complete examples survive, but they are of the highest quality. The Syon Cope (*opposite*) belonged to the Brigittine convent of Syon, near London; possibly it was made by nuns, but more probably by professional craftsmen in the service of the church. A series of quatrefoil panels tell the story of man's fall and redemption; here St Michael defeats the Dragon of Evil. (1)

Catholic England

England made her own unique contribution to medieval Christendom. Often the impetus came from abroad – notably from France. But just as often the native genius produced styles that had no counterpart elsewhere.

Durham Cathedral on its rock, with the castle guarding its approach in the foreground, is one of the great sights of Europe. Like most English cathedrals, it combines work from various periods, from Romanesque (the nave) to Perpendicular (the central tower). (2)

At Ely the Norman tower collapsed in 1322 and was replaced by something without precedent – an octagonal crossing surmounted by an open octagonal lantern. It was the great age of the Decorated style, when England momentarily took the lead in architecture. This watercolour of the Ely octagon (*right*) is by Turner, 1796. (4)

The alabaster carvings of Nottingham were, like *opus Anglicanum*, a prized export and most of the best examples are now outside England. This expressive study of the Resurrection dates from 1310. (3)

Before the Reformation and the
Renaissance spelled the end of Catholic
Europe, England produced one more
luxuriant architectural style, the
Perpendicular. Parish churches (like
March, in Cambridgeshire, *above*)
blossomed into hammer-beam roofs,
rich with golden-winged angels; while
in cathedrals and royal chapels the fan-
vault crowned five centuries of
structural experiment. *Below*: King's
College Chapel, Cambridge, vaulted
1512–15. (5, 6)

Contrasts in worship

First the Reformers and then the Puritans had left the Anglican church physically denuded, hostile to imagery and suspicious even of ritual. It was one of the achievements of the 19th century to revive colour, symbolism and a sense of the supernatural.

A rational faith was the ideal of the 18th-century church. The clergy's task was to give sound moral guidance while abjuring excess, emotion, superstition and idolatry – in a word, Popery. In Gibbs's St Martin-in-the-Fields, London, depicted here about 1810, the nub of the service is the sermon, to which congregations were happy to listen for hours on end; there is no altar, no cross, no painting, no imagery of any kind except the royal arms over the eastern arch. Beneath it is the elaborate baptismal font. (7)

'The Light of the World', Holman
Hunt's vivid, and very Protestant,
image of Christ's call to the Christian
conscience. *Below*: stained glass angel
by Edward Burne-Jones, one of the
leaders of the revival of ecclesiastical
craftsmanship. (8, 9)

Mystery came back in the mid-19th century when, with
the Middle Ages as their model, churchmen and architects
were again ready to put art at the service of faith. Crucifixes,
statues of saints, screens, choir-stalls, sculptured altars,
candles and incense reappeared in English churches. This
sketch by William Burges shows the interior of his church at
Studley Royal, Yorkshire, glowing with stained glass,
coloured stencilled decoration and painted sculpture. (10)

Religion of the people

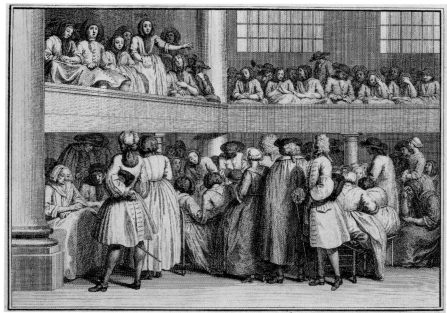

English Christianity from 1660 onwards (like most other areas of English thought) has been notably undogmatic. Anglican clergy make no claim to special authority; the laity are free to criticize and, if need be, to defect; Nonconformity itself has virtually attained the status of an establishment.

The Quakers – properly the Society of Friends – represent the extreme of a self-sufficient laity. Founded about 1650 by George Fox, they dispensed with priests and clergy altogether, every member of the congregation bearing Christian witness equally. Here, in an assembly of 1727, a woman addresses the meeting from the gallery. (11)

John Wesley saw himself as rejuvenating the established Anglican church, not as rejecting it. The first Methodist Conference (*below*) was held in London in 1729. (12)

Prayer and charity: the most lasting legacy of Puritanism was the idea that religion is at bottom a private matter, capable of sustaining itself within the individual or the family. J. van Aken's *Saying Grace* is wholly typical of English piety. The official church was, however, part of the social fabric at every level. Here a dinner for destitute women is served by the chapter of Durham Cathedral, 18th century. Each gets a parcel of food and a clay pipe. (13, 14)

The poor cleric and the rich, a comment on Anglican life-style by Peter Paul Marshall, 1861. The poor cleric works at a bare table furnished only with tea and bread; on the floor a Bible – and an income-tax demand. The rich cleric has a beautiful young wife, a well-stocked library and fine furniture (note *The Light of the World* on the screen). He grasps a copy of *The Saturday Review* while a petition has been thrown away at his feet. (15, 16)

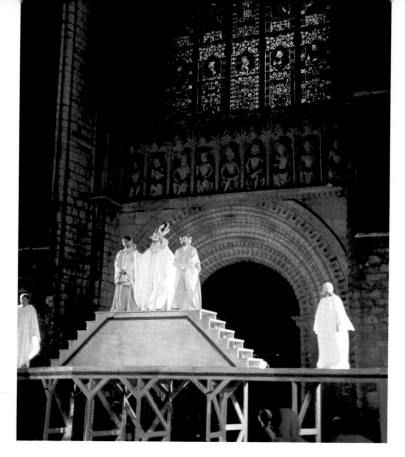

The world a stage

Drama too began as part of religion, only slowly freeing itself to treat secular themes. It has indeed been argued that an element of ritual is inseparable from theatrical performances – an idea that has recently been applied to stage productions with striking success.

The Mystery Plays of the Middle Ages dealt episodically with the whole history of the world as recorded in the Bible, beginning with the Garden of Eden and ending with the Last Judgment. They were performed in the open air by members of the trade guilds ('mystery' means craft or skill) and took the whole of Corpus Christi Day. Modern revivals show them to be still theatrically effective. Here (*left*) a scene is acted in 1981 in front of Lincoln Cathedral. (17)

'O Lord, let me be gone!' says the lawyer Buckram in Congreve's *Love for Love*, faced with Valentine's feigned insanity. Congreve helped to revive English comedy after the interregnum of Puritanism. (18)

'The Beggar's Opera' (*right*: Hogarth's painting of the last scene) belongs to no genre, yet is archetypally English – a mixture of satire and comedy, set to traditional folk tunes. (19)

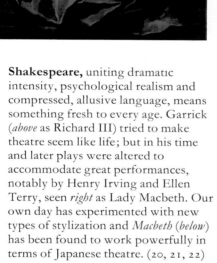

Shakespeare, uniting dramatic intensity, psychological realism and compressed, allusive language, means something fresh to every age. Garrick (*above* as Richard III) tried to make theatre seem like life; but in his time and later plays were altered to accommodate great performances, notably by Henry Irving and Ellen Terry, seen *right* as Lady Macbeth. Our own day has experimented with new types of stylization and *Macbeth* (*below*) has been found to work powerfully in terms of Japanese theatre. (20, 21, 22)

Romantic realists

In the second half of the 18th century two currents began in England, apparently quite separate yet both representing deep strains in the English character, and both destined to influence other European literatures to a crucial degree. The first, realism, became embodied in the novel; the second, Romanticism, in lyric poetry.

Duke Frederick enters the Castle of Otranto, a scene from Horace Walpole's sensational 'Gothic' novel, by John Carter, 1740. The Gothic novel made no claims to psychological truth, but its combination of medievalism, terror and unrestrained emotion, was to mould writers from Scott to the Brontë sisters. (24)

'Pamela' by Samuel Richardson is the first modern novel – the first long fiction, that is, that seeks to reproduce the thoughts and feelings of the characters at the moment they are experiencing them. It is a first-person narrative (told in the still awkward form of letters) of a maidservant sexually persecuted but eventually married by her master. This episode (*above* by Joseph Highmore) shows his attempt on Pamela in a summer house. (23)

'The Eve of St Agnes', Keats's richly sensuous evocation of the Italian Middle Ages, dates from 1819. Here, in a later painting by Holman Hunt, the lovers Porphyro and Madeline steal away while her family revels and the porter lies in drunken sleep. (25)

The doom-laden rhetoric of dramatic poems like *Manfred* captured the imagination of Europe and set a fashion in aristocratic melancholy that is still associated with Byron's name. John Martin's *Manfred on the Jungfrau* catches the authentic atmosphere – demonic passion plus sublime natural scenery. (26)

With Charles Dickens the English novel reached that mass audience that was now, with the spread of literacy, hungrily waiting for it. Some of the qualities that made Dickens so loved in his own day – the elaborate plots, the simplified characters, the sentimental moral tone – have been held against him; but his humour is still irresistible and new, darker, more complex sides to his genius are coming to light than were previously suspected. *Right*: 'Kit's Writing Lesson' from *The Old Curiosity Shop*, by R. B. Martineau. (27)

Figures in the landscape

Realism and Romanticism are present also in English painting. That interest in the individual and the particular (which in literature informs psychological fiction, intimate biography and empirical philosophy – all English inventions) helped to make portraiture one of the two dominant art forms. And love of nature (which lies at the heart of Romanticism) helped to make landscape the other. Here we have a favourite English synthesis, the portrait in a landscape.

Mary Robinson by Gainsborough (*opposite*). Known as 'Perdita' after her success in Shakespeare's *Winter's Tale*, Mrs Robinson was renowned as an actress and a beauty. Gainsborough places her, in her delicate finery, amid the fleeting shadows of a spring day. (30)

Sir Brooke Boothby elegantly reclines in a wooded landscape (*below*). Painted by Joseph Wright of Derby some two centuries after the Hilliard, this picture is remarkably similar in mood, and very unlike any counterpart abroad. In his hand he holds a work by Jean-Jacques Rousseau. (29)

Henry, earl of Northumberland leans on an elbow, reading poetry in a flowery setting. The art of the miniature reached its peak in the Elizabethan age; this portrait is by one of its greatest masters, Nicholas Hilliard. (28)

Who sets the standards?

The English are not easily swayed in their literary and artistic tastes by the voice of authority. 'Academic' has become a term of disapproval.

The Academy had the backing of royalty but did not carry the kind of prestige that an absolute monarchy like that of France could give it. *Above*: William Hunter lecturing to the R.A. on anatomy, *c.* 1775, by Zoffany. *Right*: the Council of the R.A. selecting pictures exactly a hundred years later, by C.W. Cope. (31, 32)

Horse painting was an English speciality. It was not an academically recognized genre, but it was something that many patrons wanted. Stubbs's *Hambletonian* is now seen to be one of the greatest, as well as one of the most English, works of art. (33).

Sir Joshua Reynolds, as the first President of the Royal Academy, dutifully propounded orthodox classical doctrine in his lectures and writings. But his heart was with the natural presentation of real life and real people. *Right*: General Sir Banastre Tarleton, a war hero and incidentally a lover of 'Perdita' Robinson. (34)

An everyday scene – but given glamour by being transported back to the days of the Roman Empire: Lord Leighton's *The Music Lesson* of 1877. (36)

The favourite subjects of English painters around 1890–1900 were strikingly different from those of their French counterparts. Instead of religion, the nude and military glory, they went for landscapes, animals and scenes from daily life. *Right: Cutting Bracken*, by H. H. La Thangue. (37)

'Trial by Jury' by Sir Edwin Landseer belongs to a type of painting that seems unlikely to return to popular favour – animals posed in playful parody of a human gathering. (35)

'The Fish Sale' by Stanhope A. Forbes (*right*). Realistic scenes from modern life, with or without a social message, accounted for a large proportion of paintings at the Royal Academy exhibitions. (38)

The two giants

Turner and Constable represent the high point of English painting, and it is entirely fitting that both should have excelled in the most characteristic English genre, romantic landscape.

Turner dissolves the solidity of objects into pure light, suggesting rather than describing, and delighting most in scenes of sublime and terrible beauty like *The Burning of the Houses of Parliament* (*above*). He is the painterly equivalent of Shelley. **Constable** is more Wordsworthian. Nature for him is something to be observed, studied and loved in her everyday moods. But nature is incomplete without nan. In Constable's art, as in the English garden, architecture forms a harmony with landscape, exemplified in *Salisbury Cathedral* (*opposite*). A more limited but equally original artist, **Samuel Palmer** in some ways combined both ideals. His watercolours of Kentish scenes (*below*) are faithfully observed, yet have an unearthly magic that makes nature supernatural. (39, 40, 41)

The Augustan century

In the spheres of architecture and design, England and continental Europe were probably closer together during the years 1660–1800 than before or since. Yet the two currents never really merged.

Hanc Tabulam invenit & incepit Anton: Verrio, Perfecerunt Gothofredus Kneller & Jac: Thornhill Equites.

Sir Christopher Wren was a scientist before he was an architect, and his buildings, however 'Baroque', are always lucid and rational. In this portrait (*right*) he holds the plan of St Paul's while in the distance rise the spires of the City churches which he built after the Great Fire. *Above*: the 'Great Model' of St Paul's, a design which Wren preferred but which was never built. *Below*: the wings of Wren's Greenwich Hospital frame the earlier Queen's House by Inigo Jones, precursor of English classicism (42, 43, 44)

After Wren English Baroque architecture took a highly original, even eccentric, path, but was never so emotionally charged as in southern Europe – possibly because England was Protestant instead of Catholic. Nicholas Hawksmoor's church of St Anne, Limehouse (*below*) remains monumental in spite of many bizarre details. (45)

As the Stuart age turned into the Georgian, as Lely was succeeded by Gainsborough and the Restoration wits by Pope, Swift and Johnson, English design renounced opulence and ornament for chastity and restraint.

The cherubs and flowers of Grinling Gibbons at Petworth (1692) constitute a sort of miniature Baroque. *Below*: teapot (1719) and sauceboat (*c.* 1780) exemplify the severity of English classical taste. (46, 49, 50)

Sculpture and furniture of the late 17th century share the same exuberant energy. *Above*: tomb of Lord Mordaunt by John Bushnell, 1675, in All Saints, Fulham. *Below*: walnut chair of *c.* 1695. (47, 51)

Neo-classicism. *Above*: Flaxman's monument to Joseph Warton, 1804, at Winchester. Inside the home, Thomas Chippendale's Rococo curves were now rivalled by Robert Adam's graver allusions to the antique (*below*) (48, 52)

Designs for living

The evolution of the ordinary English middle-class house has been illustrated earlier in this book (p. 18, 19). Here we look higher in the social scale and show rooms built for the upper classes through three centuries.

Knole, in Kent, has the rambling charm of a house put together at various periods. Its Cartoon Gallery was decorated in the first decade of the 17th century with a fine plaster ceiling and painted pilasters. (53)

Wilton, near Salisbury, is a masterpiece of the period of Charles I. Inigo Jones designed the Double Cube Room (*below*) for the earls of Pembroke. (54)

The Adam style took its motifs from ancient Rome but reduced them to an elegant domestic scale. The Anteroom of Syon House, Middlesex (*right*), is perhaps the most lavish room Robert Adam ever built; faced in marble and decorated with gilded statues and stucco, it is clearly intended for public show rather than private comfort. (55)

As Victoria's reign drew to an end, a new style – lighter, more practical, looking both to vernacular traditions and to ideas from outside Europe altogether – arrived under the aegis of William Morris and his friends. Standen, in Sussex (*below right*) was designed by Philip Webb for a successful solicitor between 1892 and 1894. (56)

Painting in our time

In the 20th century English painters have tended to follow movements that originated abroad, chiefly in France. But, as in the past, they have endowed them with qualities that subtly change them from their originals.

Wyndham Lewis turned to Cubism and Futurism, founding a movement that he called 'Vorticism' and in 1912 a magazine to publicize it called *Blast*. This is the cover of one of its later numbers. (57)

Duncan Grant and his fellow artists of the Bloomsbury group took the same stream of French painting as their point of departure, but applied it later in a different way. (58)

Walter Sickert's art could hardly have existed without the example of Impressionism. Like Degas, he was fascinated by the theatre. His *Old Bedford Music Hall* (*above*) irresistibly evokes the atmosphere of that uniquely English institution. (59)

Paul Nash experimented with several styles. Here (*below*) he was clearly influenced by Surrealism, but the landscape is entirely, even assertively, English. (60)

With **Graham Sutherland** English art began to free itself from dependence on overseas models. His *Entrance to a Lane* looks back, if anywhere, to the art of Samuel Palmer. (61)

Peter Blake in the mid-1950s was responding to the arrival of Pop art from America. His *On the Balcony* (*right*), however, brings together images that could not be American, including the royal family – twice. (62)

Stanley Spencer's religious paintings (*below*: detail from *Christ Preaching at Cookham Regatta*) give the traditional Christian story a startling but wholly convincing English setting. (63)

David Hockney (*below right*) returned to bourgeois themes realistically portrayed (here his own parents), and is predictably the most popular English artist now living. (64)

With the art of Henry Moore there is no need to search for continental sources or precedents, but it is equally difficult to trace any ancestry for him in England. To find his true forerunners we must look further back: to Romanesque sculpture, to early Greece, to Mexico, to prehistory – and beyond art to natural rock formations and the bones and sinews of living creatures. Rooted as they are in the landscape, his works appear most at home in the wild settings that he chooses for them. The bronze *King and Queen*, generalized figures of authority, quasi-divinities but closer to naturalism than was usual with him at this time, were cast in 1952. (65)

8 Religion in the Life of the Nation
The churches in the political and social texture of English development
EDWARD NORMAN

THE ANGLICAN CATHEDRAL of St George in Jerusalem, planned by Bishop Blyth at the end of the 19th century, is unambiguously English. Here are all the external components of English religiosity, transported as if miraculously to the Middle East – like the movement in reverse of some latter-day Holy House of Loreto – and sitting exotically among the domes and minarets of the city, a monument to English Gothic taste. To St George's, on Sundays, come the English pilgrims: many are baffled by the shrines they have visited, unable to cope with the styles and worship of the historic churches of Christendom. The stained-glass windows and the hymn-boards of St George's are, for them, the very evidences of a right order of things, just as the glowing icons and the votive candles are for their co-religionists in the Orthodox and Latin churches. But they experience no sense of insularity: to English Protestantism it is the greater part of the Christian world whose religious practices are foreign and bizarre. This circumstance illustrates the intense particularism of English Christianity, itself a symptom of what is perhaps its major characteristic – its close proximity to the values and social customs of English life in general.

It has always been so. In the very earliest period of Christianity in England there was an almost comparable detachment from the mainstream developments of Europe. For a time it looked as if English Christianity would become permanently integrated with the Celtic church. Ireland itself remained outside the development of Roman Christianity until the Synod of Cashel in 1110. The English church, however, ended its isolation by conformity to the jurisdiction and practices brought to these shores by St Augustine of Canterbury, an Italian who landed in Kent in 597, charged by Pope Gregory I with bringing England into the regular ecclesiastical discipline of Rome. The ultimate sign of his success was the Synod of Whitby, held in 664. For almost a thousand years thereafter English Christianity was linked to Europe.

The medieval English church
Outwardly uniform, and institutionally modelled upon the prevailing religious authority of Rome, the church of the European Middle Ages can hardly be said to have represented a single, universal Christianity, however. Local and national practices were abundant, and the English church was especially resistant to anything that could be represented as an unwarranted intrusion by the pontiff. By the end of the 12th century anti-Roman sentiment had reached down from the court and the governing families to have a widespread popular appeal. The practical power of the Crown over episcopal appointments was greater than in other countries; most bishops and ecclesiastical dignitaries were named by the king in some way or other. From the 13th century the English church had its own provincial council of Canterbury, a real measure of autonomy. The church also had its own distinctive liturgy: the Sarum Use. The popes frequently travelled in the Middle Ages, but England was not visited on a single occasion.

The popes did, however, actually believe that they had a special relationship to England. The Donation of Constantine had given them jurisdiction over islands, and England had, additionally, been converted by a papal mission. It was the rejection of these claims in the Tudor Reformation which gave such a nationalist ring to the rhetoric of ecclesiastical independence then employed with such decisiveness: 'This realm of England is an empire, and so hath been accepted in the world, governed by one Supreme Head and King having the dignity and royal estate of the imperial Crown of the same, unto whom a body politic, compact of all sorts and degrees of people divided in terms and by names of Spiritualty and Temporalty, be bounden and owe to bear next to God a natural and humble obedience.' These words are from the legislation of 1533 forbidding appeals to Rome. The English church, the Act declared, was sufficient of itself, 'without the intermeddling of any exterior person'. When the supporters and apologists of the English Reformation projected the notion of an independent *Anglicana Ecclesia*, which had fallen under the illegal usurpation of papal authority for a millennium, they were in many things, therefore, merely formalizing an existing tradition of thought and practice. Just as the medieval English church had been orthodox in doctrine and institutionally integrated within mainstream Christendom, so it was, of course, intended that the church fashioned by Henry VIII's changes should remain attached to Catholic practice. The church was to be separated from Roman authority, yet it was to remain the same church, with the same liturgy, theology and ecclesiastical hierarchy. Henry did not regard himself as indulging in religious novelties, but as restoring an ancient institution to its place in the body politic.

Even religious dissent had, in the English Middle

Tension between the autonomy of the state and the claims of the church was no new thing. The quarrel between Henry II and Rome reached a sensational climax in 1170, when Archbishop Thomas Becket was murdered in his own cathedral.

Ages, been characteristically national in type. There was not much of it, and it was – again characteristically – lacking the extravagances and Antinomian excesses which characterized so much of the heresy of the continental European countries. The most significant thought was that of John Wycliffe and the Lollards, at the end of the 14th century. Lollardy comprised a simple Biblicism and a rejection of what its adherents regarded as the corruptions of the Roman priesthood. The influence of Wycliffe, however, was much greater in Bohemia, where the Hussite movement was in some large measure a result, than it was in England. In the transitional phase of the English Reformation, under Edward VI, it was the penetration of the European theology of religious dissent which, in an unusual exposure of the English church to external ideas, upset Henry VIII's notion of a Catholic church under domestic management and began to replace it with the beginnings of Protestantism. As a sign of this, in Archbishop Thomas Cranmer's second Prayer Book, of 1552, the mass was transformed into a service of holy communion. With the accession of Elizabeth I the swing to a thoroughgoing reconstruction of the church was arrested – some of the reforms were even reversed – and the national establishment of religion began to take on the form that is still familiar: a compromise of Catholic and Protestant, equipped with formularies and liturgical practices which are sufficiently generous (or ambiguous) to accommodate quite divergent ecclesiastical and theological positions. It became a church which its friends regarded as a pragmatic and sensible

conciliation of extremes, where the conscience was eased over doctrinal complications that elsewhere produced enormous civil strife. Blood was spilled in the English adjustment but it was, compared with other European countries, in modest quantities. The famous *via media* was ushered in with the usual English veneration of moderation and precedent; differences elsewhere settled by force were here patched up in a series of stages by an undramatic reasonableness. It was the fact that this low-key procedure issued in a sort of custom-built version of Christianity, as much as the assertion of political over religious authority, which once more removed the English church from external influence.

Via media

Yet the intellectual exponents of the *via media* within English Christianity have given it a theological basis which has also been rooted, as they have contended, in the doctrinal constructions of the early fathers of the church. Richard Hooker in the 16th century, and John Cosin, Jeremy Taylor, Henry Hammond, John Bramhall and Herbert Thorndike in the 17th, provided a theoretical justification for the religious settlement which its basis of authority might otherwise appear to lack: the Prayer Book of the church is actually a schedule annexed to an Act of Parliament. However, the great expansion of Anglicanism in the 19th and 20th centuries, when the church of the *via media* suddenly became an international denomination, cannot be said to have been the result of its inherent reasonableness or its spiritual force. The English church simply followed English people overseas; where they settled and colonized and where they encountered native peoples, the institutions of Anglicanism were faithfully reproduced. The modern extent of the Anglican communion is a chance by-product of the expansionism of English society in a particular historical moment. Its Englishness sometimes achieved a startling priority over its religious characteristics. In the 1870s, for example, an archdeacon, Robert McDonald, set up an Anglican church among the Tukudh Indians at Fort Yukon in an area to the north-west of Canada, which subsequently passed, with Alaska, to the sovereignty of the United States. When, many years later, an American bishop arrived, he found the Indians still fervently praying for Queen Victoria – who had by then been dead for a decade. 'Archdeacon McDonald taught us to pray for Queen Victoria', they stubbornly insisted, 'and we shall continue to pray for Queen Victoria.' Before its expansion, the English church was, in the scales of Christendom, of negligible weight. Robert Curzon, travelling through the Middle East in the 1830s, discovered that the patriarch of Constantinople had never even heard of the archbishopric of Canterbury.

The Anglican churches overseas were at first simple copies of the English original. As with the cathedral of Jerusalem, Gothic edifices encased the cool tones of Cranmer's English and the resonances of Victorian hymns. The extent of England's ecclesiastical expansion was astonishing; and in the lives of its missionaries and teachers it disclosed heroic qualities only exceeded in the Spanish and Portuguese evangelization of South America or the spread of Orthodoxy by the eastward movements of Russia. In most places to which it was transplanted, the English religious establishment remained closely related to the governing classes – and this obscured, for a time, the difficulties involved in adjusting institutions and ideas put together in the peculiar historical development of England to quite different circumstances. As colonial societies developed governmental autonomy in the second half of the 19th century, the connections of church and state were at first loosened and then altogether abandoned, and the Anglicans were obliged to evolve systems of ecclesiastical authority for themselves. What is so remarkable is that the church of the *via media*, with its insular culture and its finely balanced ambiguities, was so successful in surviving in relative isolation from the parent body. And despite later adaptations to local sentiment and national practice, it is still remarkable to see – as one may almost anywhere in Africa – black prelates dressed in Tudor convocation robes, radiating the urbane confidence of Anglicanism. But it is also impossible not to conclude that the overseas success of Anglicanism in the present century is due to the abandonment of its more specifically English qualities. The impressive vitality of contemporary African Christianity owes more to its revived African than to its inherited Western practices.

In Quakerism, Methodism and the Salvation Army, England has produced three major Christian influences, each now of international distribution, which grew up outside the religious culture of the national church. The Quakers represented the spiritual dissatisfaction of George Fox and his followers, in the mid-17th century, with the ecclesiastical infrastructure of the established church. Theirs was an appeal to an immediate relationship to God experienced through inner-direction, free from the intervention of worldly religious authority. It was, in a sense, a post-Reformation version of the spiritual psychology of English medieval Puritanism, of the instincts which had inspired the Lollards. The Quakers avoided the excesses associated with other movements of religious independency in their day – the Diggers, Levellers, Ranters, Seekers, Fifth Monarchy Men, and other millennarians and antinomians – and survived to modern times as an increasingly respected section of English and American Christianity, noted for sober judgment and philanthropic enterprise. Methodism began in the middle years of the 18th century as a reform movement within the established church, and it was only with reluctance that John Wesley (who always regarded himself as a loyal minister of the Church of England) made arrangements in 1784 for a separate conference of his followers. Early in the 19th century Methodists persisted in considering themselves as still

Many of the classic texts of Anglicanism were written in the mid-17th century, in the atmosphere of heightened theological debate that accompanied the Puritan revolution. Jeremy Taylor is here represented on the title page of his 'Rule and Exercise of Holy Living'.

within the establishment, and continued to use the Book of Common Prayer in their worship. By the middle years of the century, however, Methodism had fragmented into a number of rival bodies, each of which evolved separate denominational identities. In some parts of England Methodism acquired some classically sectarian characteristics – especially in the mining villages of Cornwall, Yorkshire and Durham, and in South Wales. Here it gathered up the social aspirations of the poor into a religious exclusivity and a stern culture: represented in the austere grey chapels which are still a feature of those areas, but which gave dignity and hope to those who were depressed in the circumstances of industrial change. However, because of its middle-class leadership and because of its very success, Methodism did not become a sect. In the second generation, members organized churches on a denominational scale, whose extension in the English-speaking world has rivalled that of Anglicanism. In the United States, in fact, where Thomas Coke and Francis Asbury had already set up Methodist churches at the end of the 18th century, Methodism became much larger than in England itself.

The Salvation Army, formed by William Booth in 1878 from his Christian Mission, was neither a sect nor a denomination. It was, and is, a mission to all those outside the ministrations of the churches – rather than the expression of religious or social awakening. It did not come into existence as a social or religious protest against the existing institutions of religion, but as a way of reaching those whom those institutions did not reach, whose lives were untouched by any sort of Christian illumination. Although numerically small, compared with the historic churches in England, the Salvation Army has lodged itself deeply into the popular affection. The clarity of its message, its lack of social pretension, the proximity in social-class terms of its leaders and members to those whom it seeks to address, and its practical good works, have exactly suited the image many Englishmen have of what religion should be like. 'Why all this apparatus of temples and meeting-houses to save men from perdition in a world which is to come, while never a helping hand is stretched out to save them from the inferno of their present life?' asked Booth in his book *In Darkest England*, published in 1890. Yet his religious purposes were extremely orthodox; he did not raise the priority of practical philanthropy to the exclusion of Christian conversion. Both went together in a vital movement to which very many have looked for solace and personal elevation. The Salvation Army is something very rare in England's religious history: a genuinely proletarian religious organization.

A mystical tradition

The balance between faith and works has not always prevailed so evenly in the thinking of English Christianity. In modern times it has often been notable for its preoccupation with right moral conduct – usually, it is true (and especially in Victorian England), by insisting upon its relationship to repentance and to divine grace, but increasingly, in the present century, by allowing an emphasis on ethicism and the priority of human rights and material needs which scarcely distinguishes Christian discourse from the surrounding secular moral seriousness of educated opinion. It is not to be supposed that this is unpopular. It corresponds, in fact, to the widely diffused English supposition that religion is about doing good, and that doctrinal or dogmatic definitions are unnecessary refinements. The churches, again, have demonstrated their proximity to general qualities in the national outlook.

The comparative absence, in the last two centuries, of a mystical tradition within English Christianity also corresponds to the pragmatic, commonsense religion that English people value. Among them there is not the light and dark in juxtaposition, the contrast of the flesh and the spirit, of corruption alloyed to virtue, which has been the experience of those who, in the Christian centuries, have witnessed to the ecstatic and transcendent dimensions of the faith. In England there are no Baroque Christs in agony, as in the churches of southern Europe or Latin America, no guardians of timeless liturgy or exemplars of vicarious suffering, as in Russian Orthodoxy, and (except in the new black immigrant churches of England's cities) no spontaneous exuberance of song and dance. For this, if for nothing else, visitors from an earlier time would find contemporary English Christianity unfamiliar. The religion which Bede described in his great *History of the English Church and People*, completed in 731, was full of miraculous occurrences and mystical experiences. In the Middle Ages England had a distinct tradition of spirituality with a coherent history. It had little contact with contemporaneous European mysticism; even its literature was in the vernacular. The country was especially noted for its devotion to the Virgin, and was known, indeed, as the 'dowry of Mary'. Perhaps the most moving and beautiful of the many lives of Christian mysticism was that of the Lady Juliana of Norwich, an anchoress whose series of visions in 1373 – which she recorded twenty years later – comprise a classic of the spiritual life. After a revelation of the Holy Trinity, she received a vision of Mary: 'I saw her ghostly, in bodily likeness; a simple maid and a meek, young of age and little waxen above a child, in the stature that she was when she conceived.' Marian

'Enthusiasm displayed': an 18th-century print showing a Methodist preacher in front of St Luke's Hospital, London. The Methodists relied on mass emotion in a way that alienated conventional churchmen, but what their opponents laughed at as 'enthusiasm' was for them the essence of religious experience.

William Booth's 'Salvation Army' helped to mobilize the social mission of Christianity, giving it impetus and appeal in the new industrial towns of the 19th century: 'Happy Eliza on active service in Marylebone', April 1880.

devotions had their centre, in medieval England, at the great shrine of Walsingham, also in Norfolk. According to legend, in 1061, during the reign of Edward the Confessor, the widow (whose name was Richeldis) of the lord of the manor of Walsingham Parva was taken up by the Virgin, during a mystical ecstasy, to Nazareth, and was there shown the place of the Annunciation. The Virgin told her to build a reproduction of the Holy House at Walsingham, and this she did – mysterious events indicating the exact spot. According to historical probability, however, the shrine dates from around 1130. Even more pilgrims came to this place than visited the shrine of St Thomas Becket at Canterbury. Its fame was such that popular opinion held that the Milky Way itself pointed to Walsingham. The constellations did not deter Henry VIII's commissioners from dissolving the shrine in 1538, however, and it was not until 1922 that the present sanctuary was re-established: a red-brick structure unhappily resembling the crematoria which were the religious buildings most commonly constructed in the years between the wars in England. It is, today, the nearest thing in the country to the shrines that adorn the historic churches of Christendom – the dark interior of the church illuminated by the glowing tapers beneath a new image of the Virgin, a doll displayed in gold fabric and silver crown, installed in 1922. It is, surprisingly, Protestant. For Walsingham today is not a monument to a sustained tradition of English Catholicity but to the Ritualist Movement that succeeded the Victorian high church revival. The Roman Catholic shrine – an austere affair some little way off – is also a revival.

Before its decline the English tradition of spirituality was not exclusively Marian. At Little Gidding, in Huntingdonshire, is the tiny church where Nicholas Ferrar and his household – a company of thirty souls – formed a religious community in 1625. Theirs was a combination of regular devotions and good works. An infirmary was established for the sick, and food was distributed to the poor. But the spiritual life of Little Gidding was Laudian in style. The community was visited by Charles I in 1642; and during the Civil War, in 1646, the house and church were sacked and despoiled by the Puritan soldiers of the parliamentary army. The church remains, in the tree-shaded corner of a quiet field: an enduring link with one of the last evidences of England's mystical tradition. The association of devotional symbols with daily life and common objects has also largely disappeared from English custom and vocabulary, in a way that it has not in the Catholic nations. The small yellow wayside flower known in Spanish as 'St James's grass', for example, is in England called ragwort.

Clergy and society

English religion has always contained a generous measure of anticlericalism. Distrust of the pretensions of the clergy, and dislike of ecclesiastical jurisdiction, contributed a rich vein in the folklore of the Middle Ages, and the English were no more enamoured of their Protestant clergy than they were of their predecessors. The subject of ridicule and popular distrust through many centuries, the parson is still, in caricature, regarded as a figure either of clumsy if well-meaning ineffectiveness or of humorous inconsequence. The English clergy have not, however, ever been particularly notable for neglect of duty or for immoral living. They have shared the manners and expectations of the society in which they were set – probably more so than elsewhere – and this has made them look worldly in a worldly age, such as the 18th century, and redundant in a secular one, such as the present. At the top of the church, the national establishment, especially, has produced a succession of fine scholars in an uninterrupted sequence to the present time. The parochial clergy have tended to be unexceptionable men of earnest intention and rather circumscribed intellectual ability. Many have shown real heroism of character in their thankless task of seeking to illuminate the most dispiriting of urban parishes with the lamps of Christian truth.

James Woodforde's *Diary of a Country Parson* (which chronicles personal events of the years between 1758 and 1802) is enjoyed for its rich descriptions of comfortable living: '... sat up the whole night and played cards until 6 in the morning' (23 December 1778); '... what with laughing and eating hot Gooseberry Pye brought on me the Hickupps with a violent pain in my stomach which lasted till I went to bed' (18 May 1779); '... I dined with the Farmers in the great Parlour ... Wine drank 6 bottles. Rum drank 5 bottles besides Quantities of strong Beer and Ale' (3 December 1782). The reader easily forgets the frequent side-references to the pastoral care of the simple people amongst whom Woodforde lived: '... Bitter cold day again with high wind ... sent Ben round my Parish with some money to the Poor People this severe Weather, chiefly those that cannot work at this time' (6 January 1789).

The closeness of the clergy to the values and life-styles of the lay world has considerably assisted what is in fact one of the greatest achievements of English Christianity: the performance of educational and social work. The clergy have been acquainted with social need and with social expectations in a manner which a more sacerdotal caste could never have been. The ministers of the national church, distributed across the land in their parishes, provided a network of local services which left no section of the population – however isolated or small – outside its attentions. The larger part of this work was so much an accepted part of the normal life of the nation, and was performed with such anonymity, that it has passed from memory. It is commonly remembered that the medieval church undertook charitable works: hospices for the sick, the establishment of monastic and collegiate schools, the distribution of alms, the encouragement of lay guilds and fraternities for charitable as well as for mutual benefit services. It is also frequently supposed that these were swept away during the Reformation; there was a powerful later myth, still current in our day, that with the dissolution of the monasteries under Henry VIII the entire social welfare arrangements of the nation were terminated. 'The Reformation robbed the poor of their patrimony,' said William Cobbett in 1825, 'taking from the higher all compassion for the lower classes.' In a less romanticized form the intellectual debate about the relationship between the rise of Protestantism and the development of capitalism, associated with the writings of Max Weber, Ernst Troeltsch and R. H. Tawney, has also emphasized the replacement of social paternalism by attitudes and practices more conducive to self-help. The orthodoxy of Political Economy in the 19th century had strong Christian support in England, and some of its most influential theoreticians – such as Archbishop John Bird Sumner and Bishop Edward

Copleston – were also leading churchmen. But the Christian exponents of Political Economy were not inattentive to social welfare; it was simply that they believed the poor would be better served by sound economic practices able to eradicate the sources of poverty rather than by the mere palliation of its symptoms. The popular contrast, nevertheless, between the romantic depiction of the medieval church, with its charitable institutions, and the Victorian church, with its supposed indifference to social suffering, has endured. In reality, of course, the 19th century was the great age of philanthropic and charitable enterprise – most of it directly conducted by the church or by laymen inspired by the moral seriousness of Victorian Christianity.

Parish clergymen and their wives – for the ministers of the national church were permitted to marry after the Reformation – have undertaken social welfare work as part of their normal duties. The large numbers of clerical witnesses who appeared before parliamentary select committees or royal commissions into social conditions in 19th-century England were an indication not only of the extent to which the clergy were actually involved in social work but also of the preparedness of public men to accept their expertise in the various fields of need. The parishes contained dispensaries for the sick, youth clubs, clothing clubs, orphanages, refuges for the fallen or the destitute, and schools – all under the management of the priest. In the vast new slum areas of the industrial cities it was often the clergy who first sought to draw public attention to the harrowing conditions of peoples' lives. 'You possess,' the bishop of London told his clergy in 1847, 'from the nature of your duties, a larger experience than almost any other persons of the actual state of the dwellings of the poor.' It was, indeed, precisely this link between Christianity and social improvement that the English missionaries conveyed to the underdeveloped parts of the world in the 19th century: it was this which made them associate the work of religious conversion with the establishment of what they considered to be enlightened social practices and attitudes – an association which, because it resulted in the destruction of native social custom and the disruption of traditional society, particularly in Africa, has seemed so insensitive to later observers.

The educational work of the church since the Reformation has been one of its most impressive social achievements. In local charity and endowed schools (the grammar schools) and in the learning of the universities (which were under clerical control until 1871), English Christianity sustained a tradition of attention to intellectual inquiry which, despite occasional lapses, has served the nation well. Unlike some European and South American countries, where there was a bitter ideological clash between religion and the emergence of modern intellectual disciplines, there was in England, generally, a harmonious transition. The famous debate of 1860, between the bishop of Oxford and Thomas Huxley, about the nature of evolution and the conflict of science and religion it apparently provoked, was in fact an unusual departure from the norm. It was the universities under Christian control which, because of their tradition of free inquiry, laid the foundations for the scepticism and relativism of modern knowledge. It was a paradoxical tribute to the educational interests of the church that it fashioned the means of its own decline.

The social and educational work of English Christianity was largely conducted by the established church and, in the 19th century and subsequently, by the Catholic church. The expansion of the latter, the result of Irish immigration, impelled it into the foundation of schools in order to avoid the proselytism of children in the institutions conducted by the Church of England. There was also, as in the state church, a Catholic tradition of cultivating learning for its own sake, which English Catholicism in the 19th century, stimulated by the conversion of Newman, heightened. The Protestant Nonconformist bodies were oddly inattentive to the provision of educational facilities. Very few schools were set up by them – a negligible number, anyway, when compared with the enormous investment in education made by the establishment and the Catholics in the last two hundred years. It is difficult to see why this was so. The financial resources available to Nonconformity may have been more limited, but as so many of the rich industrial entrepreneurs professed religious dissent it can hardly be supposed that economic considerations were decisive. Victorian Nonconformists looked to the state to establish schools – the education to be free from the influence or direction of the Church of England – and their campaign for this, which achieved a partial success in 1870, constituted a major reason for the alliance of religious dissent with liberal and radical politics, so providing one of the most important dynamics in the emergence of popular politics in the 19th century. As is often remarked, the socialism of the English working classes has its roots in the Nonconformist chapels rather than in the pages of Karl Marx; it is Christian in sentiment, unlike the atheism which has frequently attached to the bourgeois socialism of the intelligentsia. Where popular political movements have assailed the churches, and especially the established church – as the Victorian Chartists did – it was because the churches seemed to have become the repositories of alien class values. They were attacked because they were not considered to be Christian enough.

The established church

The reduction in the importance of the relationship between church and state in England, which has occurred during the last century and a half, has again been unlike comparable changes in other European societies – where the separations of religion and public life have in general resulted from the hostility of secular political forces to ecclesiastical institutions. In England the relative separation of church and state was carried

The satire of cartoons like Rowlandson's 'Sleepy Congregation' of 1811 encouraged the belief that the contemporary church was worldly and moribund. In fact the 19th century was an age of considerable dedication and achievement.

out by Christian opinion for what were considered to be Christian reasons. It was the thoroughgoing nature of English Erastianism, of lay control over religion, which enabled this transition to proceed within the existing constitutional framework, so that a major change of national policy was achieved without political disruption. When the Act of Supremacy in 1534 declared that the king was 'the only Supreme Head in earth of the Church of England', and the clergy made their submission, the priority of the civil over the ecclesiastical, which had existed de facto in the Middle Ages, was given a legal basis. The convocations of the two provinces of Canterbury and York continued to meet, and the medieval canon law continued to provide for the discipline of the national church; but the Crown exercised the real governmental powers of the church, the king in Parliament assuming ultimate responsibility for the interests of religion. The relationship was intended to be – and usually actually was – expressed in terms of mutual interdependence. Parliament was, for this purpose, considered as an assembly of the Christian laity. The bishops sat in the Upper House. When Parliament departed from its obligation of guarding the ecclesiastical settlement, which it did during the English Civil War, it was the king who contended in person for the historic episcopate – as well as for a number of political practices from which the religious question appeared to be inextricable. The execution of Charles I in 1649 provided the Church of England with its only formally recognized saint: for two hundred years the Prayer Book contained a special order of service to commemorate the royal martyr.

During the 18th century the relationship of church and state became extremely intimate; the parochial clergy and the higher dignitaries of the establishment faithfully and happily integrated with the society from which they had been called. The convocations ceased to meet in 1717 and parliamentary government of the church became absolute. During the same century, however, the survival of Independency and the appearance of Methodism meant that the basis upon which the establishment rested – the religious homogeneity of society, so that membership of church and state was co-extensive – became gradually less like the ideal which legitimized Erastianism. When, early in the 19th century, first Protestant dissenters and then Roman Catholics were admitted to Parliament and to public office, anomalies began to stack up against the logic of the national church's position. The enormous multiplication of dissenting congregations, in the first half of the century, made it seem as if the established church could not even be defended on a numerical argument. By the 1840s the more militant dissenters had begun a vociferous campaign for complete disestablishment. Both in that, and in their attempts at particular concessions – such as entry to the ancient universities, or exemption from church rates – the Nonconformists argued on grounds of civil equality and ordinary justice: that they should not be disqualified from public benefits because of their religious convictions. But they also developed a more fundamental position: that the relationship of church and state was corrupting to both. They held that the religion of Christ should rest on free assent and on voluntarily supported institutions; that the state should be Christian in its moral identity but uncommitted to any particular denomination, because Christ had not entrusted the preservation of religious truth to the civil power. These contentions, of course, were rejected by most members of the establishment and by most public men in Parliament. The actual means by which the ties of church and state were in practice loosened were characteristically pragmatic and expediential. One by one the different grievances of the Nonconformists were conceded; stone by stone the edifice of state religion was dismantled, without any renunciation of the principles involved. It was a deeply English process. Those who appealed for a genuinely secular state, such as the Philosophical Radicals of the first half of the century – amongst whom were many freethinkers – were of no significance in the transformation of England's constitution from an exclusively confessional instrument, which it was in 1800, to the liberal guarantor of religious diversity, which it was in 1900.

In 1858 Jews had been admitted to Parliament, and in 1888 atheists. In 1891 the Religious Disabilities Removals Act finally deleted religious subscription from the qualifications required for public office.

Yet still Parliament was the governing body of the national church. Disestablishment was achieved in Ireland in 1869 and in Wales in 1919, but in England the state church has survived in an anomalous form to the present. It has asked for, and got, a structure of quasi-autonomous ecclesiastical government, starting with the revival of convocations in the 1850s, the creation of the Church Assembly in 1919 and the setting up of a full synodical system in 1970. Senior ecclesiastical appointments have recently passed from the Crown to a series of committees on which the church nominees are presumed to have a decisive voice. Yet still, in constitutional theory, the Church of England remains the national establishment, subject to Parliament. Changes which have elsewhere caused sharp conflict and resort to rival political ideologies and theological absolutes have in England been accomplished by a stubborn refusal to go into ultimate matters of principle.

It has to be noticed, however, that this peaceful conclusion also indicates another great change which has taken place in the past hundred years. Had it not been for the progressive secularization of English life, at all levels, an ideological conflict might not have been avoided. It could be said that the religious question was settled so sensibly in England because religion itself had ceased to be a decisive influence in both public and private attitudes. 'The strong but waning tradition of Christian feeling still obscures the general abandonment of Christian principle', Hensley Henson wrote just over forty years ago, when he was bishop of Durham, 'but nothing can finally avert the effect of de-Christianized national habit.' The intervening years have only added to the force of his diagnosis. In all the churches real membership is declining; ninety per cent of the population do not attend divine worship. The frank avowal of secular opinion is still unusual, however – at least outside the intelligentsia. There is a large measure of goodwill towards Christianity in England, and a widely distributed inclination to religious sentiment. But it is as easily rendered as a vague belief in astrology or spiritualism – both of which have enormous followings – as it is in Christian orthodoxy. Most Englishmen are astonishingly ill-informed about the actual doctrines of the faith, supposing that it is more or less summarized as a matter of decent conduct.

Bible and Prayer Book

This is quite a modern development. Knowledge of the Bible was, until within the last century, extremely widespread in all social classes. The church's involvement in popular education, particularly its expansion of educational facilities in the 19th century, was often motivated by the prior desire to enable children to read

184

*The execution of Charles I provided the Anglican church with its
only saint, and a volume of his supposed meditations and prayers,
'Eikon Basilike', was among the most popular royalist books. On*

*this frontispiece, against a background of a rock unmoved amid the
stormy seas and the tree of virtue rising under the weight of
oppression, he looks forward to a crown of glory.*

the scriptures. The sacred words were seen in framed
embroidery upon the cottage wall, and in transfer prints
upon the pottery of Staffordshire. Scriptural texts were
instantly recognized and assisted a kind of universal
culture; a set of references common to men from all
stations – so fulfilling Cranmer's hope, expressed in his
preface to the 1540 Bible, 'that it is convenient and good
the Scripture to be read of all sorts and conditions of
people'. English religion was the religion of the Bible.
The Authorized Version, indeed, is the greatest
spiritual treasure the English church has given to the
world. The first translation of the Bible made in this
country was the work of Bede. He completed his
Anglo-Saxon version of St John's Gospel as he lay
dying at Jarrow in 735. King Alfred translated the
psalms. But it was the Lollards whose association of a
distinct theological tradition of dissent with the
provision of vernacular scripture gave the English
Bible its special place in the development of English
Protestantism. Sometime around 1380 Wycliffe inspired John Purvey and Nicholas Hereford to produce
the translation which subsequently bore his name.
William Tyndale's version of the New Testament,

which appeared in 1526, was the first to be translated
from Greek instead of from St Jerome's Latin text. It
became the basis of all subsequent translations –
including the 'Great Bible', produced by Miles
Coverdale in 1539, and ordered by the Crown to be
available in every church of the realm. This first
authorized version of the scriptures was later succeeded
by another. In 1604, James I instructed the Hampton
Court conference of divines to compile a new
translation. Forty-seven scholars worked on the project
from 1607 to 1611. The result was the English Bible
that is now so familiar – whose phrases and cadences
have been, for multitudes of people, throughout the
English-speaking world, the very essence of the sacred.

The Book of Common Prayer of the Church of
England has, similarly, been a central expression of the
religiosity of many; but whereas the Authorized
Version of the Bible was used by Protestants of all
denominations, the Prayer Book's use has largely
remained restricted to Anglicans. Cranmer drew up the
first and second Prayer Books, in 1549 and 1552, using
materials derived from the old Sarum Use and from the
Roman liturgies. The present book, the fifth version,

Hostility to the Catholic church, written into the Tudor religious settlement, gained ground through the identification of 'Popery' with *treason. The last great outburst was the Gordon Riots of 1780, an obscurely motivated incident that played on the fears of the mob.*

was published in 1662 and has the legal authority of being an appendage to the Act of Uniformity – the statutory basis, until the last decade, of a single liturgical and devotional practice throughout the national church. Translations of the Bible in contemporary English, and new versions of the divine services, are now widely used in the church. Second only to the Authorized Version it has been the great hymns of the English religious tradition that have enriched Protestant Christianity throughout the world. Probably the finest were composed in the 18th century, by such as Isaac Watts, Charles Wesley and Bishop Ken. Victorian hymns, although now more popular, often seem rather too subjective and histrionic, preoccupied more with the sentiments of the believer than with the objective doctrines of Christianity itself. But if that is the case it can scarcely be regarded as surprising: English Protestantism in the last two centuries, both here and in the United States, has been notable for precisely that emphasis upon the feelings of the individual adherent. The phenomenon of Revivalism, on the American frontier and in the industrial cities of 19th-century England, only precipitated in an exaggerated form qualities inherent in the common experience of English-speaking Protestants. Theirs is a religion of individual conviction.

'Popery'

Roman Catholicism has, since the Reformation, always appeared 'foreign' to the Protestant English. Only in the last half-century has it lost its exotic and faintly sinister image. Its history has in fact been noble but

186

unhappy; the Catholic church has been made to look like an intrusion from outside English culture. 19th-century opponents came to call it 'the Italian mission'. Greater accuracy would have been achieved had it been described as the Irish one: most Catholics living in England by the end of the last century were Irish immigrants. Elegant converts from the scholarly and upper classes of England, attracted to the faith by its consistency, or through impatience with the Erastian shambles to which the national church was occasionally reduced, found themselves deposited amongst the odoriferous denizens of the Irish ghettoes. From the time of the Jesuit martyrs under Elizabeth I until Catholic emancipation in 1829 – when Catholics were admitted to Parliament – Catholicism was obliged to pursue a quiet existence in the country houses of the surviving Catholic gentry and among a few literateurs in the towns. 'No-Popery' demonstrations, as in the famous Gordon Riots of 1780, were a recurrent feature of English life, a constant reminder that popular distrust of the Catholic church limited its potential for participation in the national life. The conversions of Newman and Manning (both of whom exchanged their Anglican orders for Catholic ones, and eventually received cardinal's hats), the sudden intellectual respectability of Catholicism, and the restoration in 1850, by Cardinal Wiseman, of a proper hierarchy in England (which had before been a 'missionary district') operated in the second half of the 19th century to allow the re-entry of Catholics to a share in England's evolving religious pluralism. Final acceptance by the Protestant public probably waited more upon the general integration of the Irish immigrants, in the second generation, than it did upon any reassessment of Roman claims and practices.

Jews and Judaism

Christianity is a reformed version of the Jewish religion, and it would be inappropriate to seek a wide view of English religious developments without some reference to the contribution made by the Jewish members of English society. The first immigration of Jews occurred soon after the Norman Conquest. Until 1290, when they were expelled from the country by Edward I, the Jewish settlers experienced alternating sequences of royal protection and public harassment. Excluded from public life and from the membership of the guilds, the Jews remained in some twenty or so cities and provided financial services – being free from the restrictions to which Christians were subject in the taking of usury. As also became familiar in other countries, this made the Jews easily open to attack as a moneyed minority. In 1189 and 1190 some were massacred at Stamford, Norwich and York, until the Crown intervened to stop the outrages. The tradition of religious toleration, which Englishmen now rightly regard as so much a part of their inheritance, is a comparatively modern growth – dating from developments after the Civil War. The resettlement of Jews in England began with the approaches made by Rabbi Menasseh ben Israel to the Cromwellian Council, in 1656, and with the royal protection conceded to the London Jewish community by Charles II in 1664. By the start of the 19th century there was a Jewish population of around twenty-five thousand. Anti-semitism continued to be a characteristic of English popular attitudes until quite recent times, but the 19th-century conviction that civil disabilities should not attach to religious belief allowed a number of Jewish citizens to achieve positions of distinction in public life. In 1855 Sir David Salomans became the first Jewish lord mayor of London. Sir Moses Montefiore was one of the country's leading philanthropists, and es-tablished a family whose names recur in many fields of public service – even furnishing a contemporary Anglican bishop. Baron Lionel de Rothschild was the reformer who helped to secure the entry of Jews to Parliament. Unobtrusive, and both socially and culturally integrated into English society, the Jewish population today practises a version of Judaism that discloses few peculiarly English characteristics.

The Victorian achievement

Regarded from the widest perspective, it would perhaps be correct to conclude that it was the 19th century, the Victorian era, that was the most dynamic and the most inventive period of England's religious history. It witnessed the largest expansion of England's ecclesiastical institutions both at home, in stamping the moral seriousness of the age with a fervent Christian conviction, and overseas, in the missions. So many

features of what are now popularly considered to be timeless symbols of Christianity are in fact of Victorian origin. Christ is drawn from the serene iconography of Holman Hunt's *Light of the World*, painted in 1853; the apostles also correspond to depictions in Pre-Raphaelite art and design, and especially from the sort of illustrations found in Bibles; angels are seen in the ethereal images of Burne-Jones glass. The sounds of worship are the harmonics of Victorian hymn tunes; church furnishings and ceremonial derive more from the Oxford Movement than from their apparent medieval origin. The heroes of English Christianity are the philanthropic activists who thrived in the last century – William Wilberforce, Shaftesbury, Booth – rather than the ascetics or the pietists. The house of God is Gothic, and the chances are that the actual structure of the Englishman's parish church will be Victorian Gothic, and even if it is authentically medieval virtually everything that is still visible will bear the marks of Victorian restoration. It is a collection-bag rather than an icon that is carried in procession to the altars of English churches. There should be no surprise that Englishmen, confronted with the customs of the historic churches overseas, are unable to discover either familiarity or sanctity. But the pragmatism and insularity of English religion closely corresponds to qualities well entrenched in national life – qualities which have also determined the country's social and political developments. Undramatic and adaptable, the English churches have been well-suited to their guardianship of the nation's religious sense. 'Never for a moment', wrote the Victorian theologian, F. D. Maurice, 'let us try to separate, or dream that we can separate our individual life from our national.' There is no better proof of that than in the work of Stanley Spencer, England's greatest 20th-century religious painter. *Christ Preaching at Cookham Regatta*, a series of pictures completed in the 1950s, comprises masterpieces of religious sensibility: the familiar and the numinous, the secular and the spiritual, collectively disclosing eternal qualities in characteristic vignettes of English life.

A village funeral, by Thomas Bewick: the Anglican church quietly fulfilling its part in the fabric of English society.

9 Art and Popular Taste
Architecture, painting, decoration and fashion
QUENTIN BELL

'HURRAH BOYS, NOW'S YOUR CHANCE. The Houses of Parliament are in flames.' The time was 16 October 1834, the place the schools of the Royal Academy, the bearer of glad tidings an Academy porter. I cannot find the source of this story; but I hope it's true. It ought to be.

For centuries English artists had been waiting for some great commission from the state. Other nations had them; other nations had for centuries been painting their churches and decorating their palaces. Now the new Palace of Westminster would need to be adorned. Now painting in Britain would be reborn.

It wasn't. The malady went deeper. From the time of the Tudors until the 18th century the British imported their art. Holbein, Van Dyck and Rubens, together with many lesser but still quite competent foreigners, were imported whenever a fine portrait or a great decoration was needed. The competition was too severe for all but a few miniaturists and lesser portrait painters.

In England, as later in America, the nation first showed its strength in the arts of design through the medium of architecture. Buildings could not be imported. Elizabethan architecture, to be sure, was an odd business: the English simply didn't understand what was happening in Italy and the results were quaint rather than impressive. But in the 17th century Inigo Jones showed that he did understand the Renaissance; he ushered in the golden age of Wren which was followed by the silver age of English 18th-century building.

After two barren centuries, English painting revived with William Hogarth, an aggressively English realist and an enemy of imported Italian painting; and in the second half of the 18th century there was a tremendous flowering of British art led by two portraitists of the first rank, Joshua Reynolds and Thomas Gainsborough, together with a multitude of lesser men; there was a curious and very English flowering of Neoclassicism with John Flaxman, Henry Fuseli and William Blake. And above all, there was a school of landscape painting which stands in the very front of the world's art, the school of Girtin and Crome, of Constable and Turner, a creative excitement which is related to the poetry and the landscape gardening of the time and which, at Norwich, created the only great local school in England. At the same period England took the lead in the applied arts of pottery and furniture.

This great age petered out in the first half of the 19th century and at the same time English architecture set out in a new direction. Already in the 18th century architects had amused themselves with parodies of alien styles: Chinese, Islamic, Indian, Greek Revival; they also built 'gothick' churches. The 19th century made of the Gothic Revival something much more earnest and austere and set a pattern for ecclesiastical architecture which lasted well into our own century. It was not until the mid-19th century that something corresponding to this new and serious spirit manifested itself in painting. Pre-Raphaelitism, realist and poetical in its earliest phase, idealist and poetical in later years, effected a complete divorce between London and Paris and it was not until Roger Fry brought Post-Impressionism to the Grafton Galleries in 1910 that the English realized what had been happening in France. Thereafter, for a generation, they looked steadfastly towards the French or rather to the French avant-garde. Today England looks to America and to herself.

Is there
an English art?

The crucial question remains to be asked: is there, throughout this varied procession of talents, a common quality that we can call English? To give an answer that is more than a series of rather disjointed generalizations would need vast erudition and familiarity with areas of art history that have often barely been studied. I will not pretend that I am equipped for the task; all I can do in this brief essay is to point to the direction in which I think we should be looking. What makes my task even more difficult is that the direction is quite different from the one taken by my great predecessors Roger Fry, whose *Reflections on British Painting* was published in 1934, and Nikolaus Pevsner whose *The Englishness of English Art* was broadcast and subsequently printed in 1955. I have a great respect for both these authors: their books are learned and persuasive, they have some most valuable things to say and I borrow freely from both; but both, so it seems to me, end by leading us up a blind alley. I will direct my fire upon Pevsner, for his account is in many ways the most complete, the most accessible and certainly the best known.

Without exactly defining it Pevsner does very properly begin by pointing to the mutability of his subject – England is something in a continual state of

Inigo Jones was the first Englishman to understand the Renaissance. In a few key buildings and in numerous stage drawings (this one is a variant of the Vitruvian 'Tragic Scene') he looked forward to the classical revival of the 18th century.

change; the nation has undergone drastic alterations. And yet, for his purposes England is seen as something which existed already in the 12th and 13th centuries, and even earlier; he is ready to use evidence from any period, he establishes affinities between the great medieval cathedrals and modern housing estates, between Celtic manuscripts and the art of the 1950s. He is ready in fact to discover Englishness in art at a time when English was not spoken and when England was a non-entity. Nor it is simply that he discovers long and unbroken traditions in English art taking us back to the earliest recorded ages; for him it is sufficient to discover a likeness between that which happened two thousand years ago and that which is happening today, in order to point to a trait in national character.

Nevertheless, one can go a long way with Pevsner and one goes prosperously. The typically English qualities that he finds in English art are: a fondness for moral anecdote and for a rational, commonsensical conservatism; an avoidance of the human body, but a love of nature and of the commonplace details of everyday life; an acceptance of disguise – one style masquerading as another; a tendency towards irregular patterns and repetitive upright forms; a preference for linear design rather than volume; a delight in the refinement of high workmanship and surface quality; and a proneness to speak in a muffled, inarticulate voice. He does not, of course, claim that these qualities are peculiar to England, or even that they are constants discoverable at any period in the history of English art. He maintains, rightly I think, that they are indicative of national character during the past three hundred years and it is only when he tries to discover them in remote epochs that I, personally, feel some doubts.

There is another determinant in the choice of evidence which does seem very questionable. I will illustrate it with a quotation from *The Englishness of English Art*, but before doing so I ought to say that this passage is not typical of the whole book and that usually Pevsner is much more careful in his judgments and circumspect in his methods:

A decent home, a temperate climate, and a moderate nation. It has its disadvantages in art. There is no Bach, no Beethoven, no Brahms. There is no Michelangelo, no Titian, no Rembrandt, no Dürer or Grünewald. There are no vast compositions in the churches, and only bad if vast compositions in the palaces, but there are exquisite water-colours and miniatures, things on a small scale.

Now if – in a discussion of the fine arts – Professor

189

Two examples of 'architectural disguise': St Pancras station (left) hides its train shed behind Sir George Gilbert Scott's Gothic hotel, and Euston (above), where a booking hall assumes the dignity of an Italian Renaissance palace.

Pevsner is going to throw Brahms and Beethoven at our heads we shall reply in kind with Bunyan and Browning and, if we go further down the alphabet to the letter M or to the letter s we shall hurl some quite gigantic names – names quite as massive as Titian or Michelangelo. But this slightly absurd game of name-dropping (both Fry and Pevsner engaged in it) involves a further and more important consideration.

Pevsner cites Dürer and Grünewald; personally I should not have mentioned them in the same breath as Michelangelo. In that I may be wrong; but two hundred years ago it would have been very hard to find anyone to disagree with me. Reputations change. Both Fry and Pevsner are much more severe on English painting in the 19th century than would please most of our younger critics. Pevsner, writing in 1955, discusses the lack of English sculpture but then remembers Henry Moore. He thinks Moore a great man and most of his readers would have agreed with him; but would they have done so if he had been writing in 1945? I doubt it. Moreover, Pevsner admits that Moore 'contradicts all that I have put forward in this chapter'. This is admirably honest; but what are we to say of a theory which can be overset by a single value judgment?

Values and variants

Ought questions of value to enter into our argument at all? If we were writing about 'the best of English art', then I think they might not be out of place. But our brief is different; we are writing quite simply about English Art. It will hardly be denied that all English art

190

is not equally good. Some of it is in my view downright bad. For us the real question should be: is bad art in England bad in some peculiarly English way and is good art in the same way 'nationally' good?

The task, then, of a truly national historian is to amass all the available evidence and to look not only at England's national glories but also at the lesser productions of lesser men, the products not only of craftsmen but of factories, the evidence of shops and hoardings, the innumerable examples of domestic architecture, printed books and postcards. Also to look at our taste both in home products and exotics. It is perhaps relevant that if we go into a stationer's shop and look at the reproductions of works of art that are for sale there, we shall find that the French Impressionists are today almost as popular as Constable's *The Leaping Horse* or *The Hay Wain*, while the Post-Impressionists come a good third? A few years back, one of the greatest favourites was a work by a gentleman called Tretchikoff who painted a picture of a young lady whose face was bright green. Later, the wild fowl of Peter Scott became the cynosure of English taste. Do facts such as these tell us anything about national character?

I ask this because if we English could arrive at valid generalizations concerning our habits both as producers and as purchasers and if we could carry that research back far enough and discover what links, if any, there are between our great masterpieces of painting and architecture on the one hand and our habits as artists and art lovers at a 'lower' level on the other, we might begin to understand ourselves.

Let me begin by looking very briefly at the national character as shown in English architecture. Here Pevsner isolates three elements as typical: conservatism, love of 'reasonable' repetitive forms and grid patterns, all of which are evident in the long-lived Perpendicular style. Contrasting with this is a delight in illogicality, in flamboyant shapes and fantasy, which expressed itself above all in English Decorated; and to this he adds the English affection for gardening, for the *rus in urbe*, and the various English compromises with 'wild' nature. He also adverts, with sorrow, to the English passion for architectural disguise – the hotel masquerading as a Flemish cloth hall, the railway station clad as a Tudor mansion, the clubhouse pretending to be a Florentine palazzo. I think it is evident that all these qualities will be found in English architecture; I suspect the last two ingredients are the most characteristically English.

Can we, by going to areas of architecture that Pevsner hardly considers, add anything to what he says? I think if we look at vernacular styles we may discover something that he does indeed mention, but only in passing: a kind of comfortable solidity, a functional quality which, unlike so much that is called functional today, has nothing aggressive or uncompromising about it. I am thinking here of the farmhouses, barns and other outbuildings of the English countryside. But an examination of vernacular styles is in truth a most discouraging adventure for those who are looking for a consistent national character. The regional differences are immense and become more so as we pass from the rural buildings of southern England to those of the Chilterns and still more to those of Yorkshire and further north. More modern environments show greater consistency. In the suburbs, the high streets and modern shopping centres our native attempts to come to terms with the international styles of the 20th century are perhaps truly national. It does seem that some recent developments might be well worth study; the traveller on English motorways will I think be impressed by the emergence of a style of bridging, engineering and landscaping which is different from that of American or continental thoroughfares and deserves our attention.

Instead of seeking further general parallels and contrasts, let me now change the focus completely and look at a particular locality at a particular time, and the notions about art and beauty that prevailed there and then. It will involve a degree of personal digression, but that is part of the exercise.

Art and industry: a duality of taste

Standing in the very heart of England, the Five Towns – the urban conglomeration centred in Stoke on Trent, Staffordshire, built, I suppose, at the end of the 18th and throughout most of the 19th century – might fairly stand as an example of English art in the industrial age. The Five Towns had been five villages made prosperous by coal, clay and the canal, spreading out without

any sign of plan and purpose, mostly row upon row of little cubic red-brick houses, without anything more impressive than a pompous town hall. A certain charm, a certain beauty was added in the days when I knew them by the bottle ovens which by night emitted blue flames and smoke into the already poisoned atmosphere, but there was little that one would call distinguished architecture. True, the place was very paintable, but paintable mainly by reason of accidental qualities – the ovens, a load of sulphur spilled over the quay beside a lock, and so on. One didn't feel that it was a home of beauty, and yet the inhabitants did so regard it. They were proud, and in a way justly proud, of their fine china. They seldom visited their own museum, which had some good things in it – early Spode, Elers, Chelsea and crudely decorated dishes by Thomas Toft. Even if they had done so, I don't think that they would have cared much for some of the things that I admired. Their own wares they judged by the delicacy of the body, the flawless even tone, the perfectly adjusted glaze and the delicate hand-painted roses, lilies, royalty or whatever it might be that was felt suitable for 'our fine china'. I remember arguing fiercely about the merits of a teapot made in the image of a country cottage, every tile on the roof visible and sprigged bunches of roses around the door. I could not admire it – perhaps it was narrow-minded of me. To me the Five Towns seemed a place of hopeless though picturesque squalor producing objects which varied between the naïveté of the cottage teapot and the vase of pointless though extreme refinement. But it represented something in English art and architecture in the 1930s that was in its own way significant. It stood at least for a high standard of craftsmanship. The girls who so carefully and painstakingly copied someone else's design had their proper pride; they sought a kind of perfection. It was by no means a purely English conception of beauty; but I think that it was English in the complete absence of any other feeling.

The Five Towns themselves were by the same English standards condemned. They were condemned, very properly, as being the result of stupid, acquisitive greed. They were an expression – so it seemed to my friends – of 'free enterprise', the desire of rich men to exploit their less fortunate neighbours and to do it in a hurry. Things had perhaps been little better at Myrina or Faenza or Sèvres – the factory owner must always have been concerned mainly to make money. But perhaps in the past he had done so with a shade more dignity.

The objections that were made by the citizens of the Five Towns to the general standards of architecture were in large part moral; even the lack of planning was perceived mainly in moral terms and set down to a reckless acquisitive spirit, a blind materialism. My own attitude towards the place, my tendency to see beauty in the most squalid surroundings and my inability to find it in the art to which those surroundings gave birth, seemed to my friends highly perverse. Theirs, I think,

One of the areas in which England has undoubtedly influenced European taste is that of dress. The plain black suit was already established in the late 18th century, and after 1815 was taken up in fashionable Paris. Only in his high collar and ruffled stock does Cruikshank's dandy of 1817 (left) make any concession to display.

Right: the 'new man' and the 'new woman', as depicted by Du Maurier in 1895. The man's evening dress remains sombrely austere. The woman has given up the bustle and interest focuses on the sleeves and the corsage.

Far right: the contrast, again by Du Maurier, in 1898, between the 'gorgeous young swells' and the 'aesthetic young geniuses'.

was the more truly English attitude – ever since the Industrial Revolution at all events, utilitarian architecture and applied art have been aesthetically suspect. The apparatus of the factory, the viaduct, the mill, the railway, the gasometer – they all have their friends today, critics who find beauty even in the mining village or the warehouse. But all have been condemned for their ugliness, and the idea that the countryside should remain 'unspoilt' remains entirely respectable. Notice, however, that where a utilitarian building is sufficiently old, condemnation is less severe and may often be cancelled. Even the products of industry, so long as they have achieved a certain degree of antiquity, are not now rejected entirely. The castle erected to repel Welsh invaders has for long been seen as a pictorial asset; the Martello tower is sufficiently antique to be perfectly tolerable, and voices are now raised to preserve the defensive works of the mid-19th century. The launching site for rockets has not yet been sanctified by time.

English cut

Another example of this duality of taste may be found in the history of a minor art, that of dress.

At the end of the 18th century, when British workmanship was rightly respected throughout Europe, a certain British influence was felt even in the capital of fashion, which was then, and to some extent still is, Paris. French admiration for British broadcloth and British tailoring was caught up in a more important complex of emotions which culminated in the French Revolution. In that tempest of change there was no place for the fripperies and artificialities of the old régime. The wigs and lace and embroideries of Versailles had to go, along with so much else, and were preserved only in the dress of servants. France, looking for something new to wear, found what her daughters

needed in the simple forms of Classic antiquity, or at least in something originally suggested by those forms. But it was to England that she turned when she reclothed her sons.

The new clothes had an affinity with those worn by the Puritans of the 17th century and may be said to derive, distantly, from Holland, Spain and perhaps Burgundy. They were predominantly black, relieved by a few touches of spotless white; as the 19th century progressed they became progressively blacker, the last gaieties, such as embroidered waistcoats, being exterminated by the middle of the century. Although Frenchmen had adopted the new style during the anglomaniac period before the Revolution and although after 1815 the dandies of Paris rejoiced in the black simplicities of London, there were protests. All the old charms and graces, the frivolities, the colour and the fantasy that had distinguished the dress of gentlemen when Paris ruled the world of fashion were abolished. The English style was hideous. Nor was it only the French who thought so: the English themselves complained loudly that men's dress in that age was horrible, uncomfortable and ridiculous; societies were created which had as their object the reform of men's dress; but to no avail. Throughout the century and indeed in some degree up to our own day, men's fashions have come from London; for long periods it was the only art form which England was giving to the world.

There never was an art which was so decidedly anti-art. That modern men's clothes were hideous was a first article of faith amongst people of taste. Gents' suiting became the despair of the portrait painter, who concealed it beneath a cloak, a surplice, an academic gown, anything that could appropriately serve as a screen. The statue of the alderman with his trousers, his

ye GORGEOUS YOUNG SWELLS!...

ye ÆSTHETIC YOUNG GENIUSES!...

bulging waistcoat and silk hat, became the very type of philistine art, and it was left for the 'comic' men, the Keenes, the Du Mauriers, a few illustrators and some very determined realists to face the sartorial facts of life.

And yet of course Savile Row represented an aesthetic. The young gentleman who for the first time was able to go abroad in a perfectly fitted, exquisitely discreet, but magnificently expensive version of the fashion of the day, even though he might praise and purchase the productions of Edward Burne-Jones and D. G. Rossetti, was not ill-pleased with his appearance. Once again we find ourselves confronted by a duality of taste.

It is true that the same duality arose in the case of the art of women's fashion, where France, not England, held sway. Fault was certainly found with the crinoline and the bustle, but here the protest came as much from the physician and the moralist as from the artist and was at all events less determined. It was the English art of dress (which incidentally may serve to illustrate several of Pevsner's theses, for it is a conservative art very much dependent on high workmanship and making great use of vertical forms) that best illustrates the division between the artist and the man of fashion.

Pictures from an exhibition

I want now to look at another historical source and I am well aware that in so doing I am going to ask the reader to turn in an unfamiliar direction: the exhibits at the Royal Academy's summer exhibitions of about ninety years ago. Large mixed exhibitions of contemporary work seldom inspire one with aesthetic enthusiasm and the general run of work at the summer exhibitions of Burlington House between the years 1895 and 1900 is not generally admired today. (It is perhaps worth remembering that we often do not know what it is that

we shall admire tomorrow.) But the period has its advantages, the first of which is the abundance of the evidence. By 1895 photographic reproduction had become so developed that it was possible for an enterprising publisher to give us quite a large sample of the work on display in an Academy exhibition. A further advantage is that British art had at this stage attained quite a high degree of unanimity and, although there were some regional groupings such as the Newlyn School, there is very little in the records that I have seen to suggest regional styles or variations; on the contrary, looking at the record as a whole, there is something very like equality of achievement. In addition to this there is the fact that we can equally easily compare the London exhibitions with the pictures of the Paris Salon in order to find out whether we are dealing with a national or an international phenomenon.

We have to remember that the available evidence consists of black-and-white photographs and this is hard upon a nation which has tended to use colour rather than tonality in painting. We have also to remember that the section is not truly representative. All the exhibits had been chosen by a panel of academicians; already there were some young painters who did not care to exhibit at the Academy, while there may have been others who were excluded because they stood for an aesthetic which the hanging committee found unsympathetic. There was also an artistic party which preferred to exhibit at the New English Art Club, although it was as yet hardly large enough or sufficiently influential to form a statistically important element in the English artistic scene. The number of works sent in at this time proves that for a very large majority of painters the Academy was the best, as it was certainly the most lucrative, market-place for their wares.

The contents of the exhibition were very much what one might expect in an academy of arts and in a country with an art history such as England's. The largest category of paintings was landscape. Taking the two years 1895 and 1900, I find 75 landscapes in 1895 and 80 in 1900 (the total of classifiable works in these two years are 213 and 233). The proportion of landscapes, and indeed of all other classifiable pictures, seems to remain fairly constant. Most of the great British landscapists are echoed in these works, but there are a few which seem also to be inspired by the work of Camille Corot. In France, on the other hand, of 145 classifiable works found in the Panorama du Salon for 1900, only three were landscapes and of these two are barely classifiable as such, for they might be better described as nude figures in the open air. The second largest category at the Academy was, and again this might have been anticipated, portraiture: 52 in 1895, 58 in 1900, as against three in the Salon. Scenes of modern life, very largely the life of fishermen, come third (31 and 17). Another kind of genre which today hardly exists was then an important element in both French and English painting: 'historical genre', or perhaps 'costume genre' might be a better term. For, although such pictures did sometimes represent actual historical events, they were more often invented scenes of everyday life, but dressed in the clothes of some previous epoch. The British school favoured the Stuarts, the French favoured the 18th century; the proportion is about the same in both exhibitions: 25 and 35 at Burlington House, 20 at the Salon. The French adventure into two areas which are barely exploited by the English. One is the nude, with or without a historical or mythological pretext, which occurs eight times in 1895 and nine times in 1900 at the Academy; at the Salon there are 54 paintings which can only be classed as nudes and seven which may also be classed as mythology. The other is military scenes; the British give us only two military (or naval) pictures in 1895 and six in 1900, a time when Britain was at war. There are also some marginal cases, for instance the picture of a young lady with her head in her hands sitting in a very large and handsome garden, which is called *In Time of War*. The French, on the other hand, have no fewer than 16 pictures of battle or of military life and two which may be classed as straight anti-British or pro-Boer propaganda. Propaganda is something unthinkable in Burlington House, but at the Salon there was even a moment when M. Debat Ponson had the courage, and it needed courage, to proclaim the innocence of Dreyfus on the walls of the Salon with his painting *Nec mergitur*.

The rough and rapid inquiry that I have made into the general character of the works which found their way into illustrated annuals must not be dignified by the name of research. Nor should the results which are tabulated below be regarded as more than a vague indication of the facts of the case. In passing I would say that they do suggest a form of inquiry which could yield valuable results in hands better equipped than mine.

194

	RA 1895	RA 1900	Salon 1900
History	25	35	20
Landscape	75	80	3
Nudity	8	9	54
Portrait	52	58	3
Genre	31	17	44
Animal	3	14	4
Sacred	6	2	16
Myth	10	6	7
Military	2	6	16
Still life	1	1	1

It should be said that the so-called 'categories' do not represent clear divisions between one kind of painting and another. In some cases, where the painter's intentions have not been clear, the picture has been omitted from the statistics or has been counted twice. *La Tristesse de Pharaon* by M. Lecomte du Nouy obviously has to be classed as a religious picture; but it is a very *fin de siècle* religious picture and unlike most of the sacred images of the Salon it carries no hint of the great masters of the high Renaissance; the number of charming young women who are attempting to raise the pharaoh's spirits and the *sans géne* with which some of them are doing it decided me that the picture must also be classed under 'nudity'. *Whither?* by Mr Byam Shaw, in which a lady and gentleman, dressed in what appear to be medieval clothes, are propelled through an ocean of bubbles and nymphs upon a clearly unseaworthy vessel which at its prow is adorned with an angel holding some kind of gas lamp, beat me absolutely and I left it out.

Rearguard and avant-garde

Even on a very superficial consideration, the evidence that we have just looked at is instructive. Think of the year 1900, the year when all these fetching nudes, feathery trees, folds of satin, puppy dogs, haystacks and high sentiment hung in such vast and formidable a phalanx in the Grand Palais and in Piccadilly. Cézanne was still alive, Picasso was coming to Paris, Courbet and Manet had become positively respectable, Whistler and La Thangue represented revolt north of the Channel. It was a period when in both countries, indeed throughout Europe, there were two quite different worlds of painting – different in intention, in thought and in feeling – and it must at once be admitted that the international affinities are greater than the national differences. Royal Academy art, to put the thing from the avant-garde point of view, stank very much as the Salon stank; but perhaps the Salon, being a bigger healthier body, stank a bit louder. Whatever had happened to English painting (and neither Pevsner nor Fry make this at all clear) had happened pretty well everywhere. This was the painting not of a nation but of the European bourgeoisie at its happiest, most prosperous, most philistine epoch. If the 'rot' set in earlier in England and if the percentage of rot was even higher there than in Europe generally, then that was to be expected; after all, the English invented modern industry, on which the whole social superstructure rested.

When I said, or rather allowed an avant-gardist to say, that the Salon stank louder than the Academy, it may have seemed that I was being unfair to my countrymen. But of course the observation can be taken in more than one way; it may be taken as a compliment to our neighbours, in as much as a stinker wishes presumably to make the biggest possible stink – and this it seems to me the French did. There is a violence in their vulgarity, a strident quality in their compositions, a kind of dreadful craftsmanship and painterly skill that is lacking in the English. English painters cannot manage – they barely attempt – the great 'machines' of the French. In the French religious work there is a kind of mawkish horror which defies description, and in some of their military scenes there is a real emotion of deep chauvinist hatred. This was indeed the age of French Art: France produced some of the very best and most of the very worst pictures in existence.

The French, after all, at the turn of the century still bore in their officially recognized art the marks of a nation which organized the first efficient academy, with the nude as the centrepiece of all teaching, even though as a theoretical 'engine' it had lost its original purpose. A trace of the old ecclesiastical power survived and where previous generations had fulfilled a public need by glorifying the monarchy, that of 1900 glorified the nation in the person of the army and its history. Landscape, portraiture and still-life came low on the academic scale of values, and could be disregarded. The English, on the other hand, found their profit in portraiture and their poetry in the countryside. As for the nude, they found it slightly improper and, although they were a religious nation in 1900, their religion was of a kind to make religious painting suspect to a large section of the faithful. The nearest that most academicians came to their Maker was when they painted the portrait of an archdeacon.

Painting, the younger sister

The word academy may be one of the clues. For all practical purposes, England had no academy until the third quarter of the 18th century. When she did get one, it left the country in a strange position of compromise. In the nature of things, England could not have the kind of institution that resulted from the power of an absolute monarchy; on the other hand, because she had a kind of academy, supported in a more or less platonic way by the Crown but quite independent of Parliament, she did not develop the kind of free market in painting that produced such an abundance of fine work in Holland. But I think the most striking difference between English history and that of most European countries was that painting was a late-comer among the arts. And the reason for that was a historical accident rather than any innate genius or lack of it.

The whole history of the visual arts in England is indeed a strange one. It can hardly be denied that, whether you like them or not, some remarkable activities were undertaken during the Middle Ages. Durham may be considered one of the greatest cathedrals in Christendom; English Romanesque, English Decorated and even Perpendicular represent a formidable achievement; the illuminated texts, the *opus anglicanum* and the alabasters of Nottingham were at all events the work of a country able to live through its eyes and to create remarkable decorations.

Then comes an extraordinary hiatus; an almost complete severance of Britain from the main stream of European art; an ignorance, apparently an indifference, to the grand events of the High Renaissance. The little that England seemed to know of what was going on in Europe came from the Low Countries, so that long after Raphael and Michelangelo, Correggio and the Mannerists had revolutionized the art of painting she behaved as though nothing had happened and, while Titian and his compatriots had given a new meaning to portraiture and landscape, she had nothing more considerable to offer than the charming but minor works of her miniaturists. Rubens was imported, Van Dyck was imported and Lely was so thoroughly imported that we like to think of him as a native; but although William Dobson and later Sir Godfrey Kneller are respectable names and Sir James Thornhill began to bring England back into the main stream of European art there was really for two hundred years and more no English school of painting.

When, with the advent of Hogarth, the English did begin to paint in earnest, they did so under peculiar conditions, or at least under conditions very different from those which prevailed amongst their neighbours. The English language had been made into one of the world's great vehicles for the art of poetry: Spenser, Shakespeare, Milton, Dryden, Pope and, above all perhaps, the translators of the Bible had already spoken, and in speaking given a certain bent, a literary inclination, to their countrymen which left the art of painting a younger sister of the art of writing. How, under the circumstances, could the English avoid being 'poets at all costs', as Fry asked in tones of exasperated despair? And how, with so poetical a cast of mind, was it possible for the English collector not to find a particular delight in the landscapes of Claude, of Poussin and of the Dutch? For these, and for the emotionally strong Venetians, rather than the intellectual, sculptural painters of central and southern Italy, the English have since the 17th century felt a deep affection.

The discipline of words differs from, and is in some ways opposed to, the discipline of the pencil. The poet can leave unsaid a great deal of what the painter must perforce represent. Poetry demands more from the imagination of the reader than painting does from that of the spectator. The more 'poetic' a painting, therefore, the more it will tend to suggest and to evoke rather than to delineate and define; artists of this

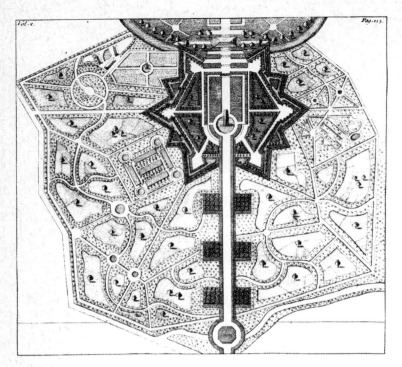

While the rest of Europe still worshipped symmetry and the long vista, landowners in England began to experiment with meandering, picturesque, 'natural' garden design. This early plan for Paston Manor (not used) dates from 1718 and shows both tastes side by side.

persuasion attempt to excite the imagination by deliberately incomplete statement, so that their paint almost has the effect of words. Abstract art is perhaps the logical end of this tendency. At the opposite extreme is the painter fascinated by the world of forms, lines, measurements and proportions, who relies upon exact rather than suggestive statement. This kind of painter is nearer to the architect and the sculptor than to the poet. Venetian painting, if we use this distinction, is 'poetic'; Florentine is 'architectural'.

In his *Discourses*, Reynolds urged his students to follow the strict discipline of Florence, the art of the academies, the art of *disegno*. He himself was too English to obey his own precepts. For the sake of prestige and reputation he attempted the great academic *machines* which depend for their success upon impeccable design; when he obeyed his own true instincts he turned to an art which is much more literary, where likeness, character and associative feeling can have full play, the art of portraiture. Like Garrick torn between Comedy and Tragedy, Reynolds was torn between his hero Michelangelo and his real loves, the Venetians and Rembrandt; he even tried to combine the two and to paint portraits that were also *machines* (in itself a rather English proceeding).

In a society as individualistic as England in the 18th century, the portrait became the dominant art form. It gave plenty of scope for the kind of painterly, evocative, undesigned, pictorial poetry of which

Gainsborough was the grand master. It also produced a whole tribe of lesser men, some of them richly talented, such as Sir Thomas Lawrence, others seeking through charming and suggestive brushwork to achieve a socially acceptable prettiness. But the great outpouring of British pictorial genius was of a more decidedly poetical character than this.

Nature and Romanticism

From quite early in the 18th century Englishmen were looking for a decent but Romantic transition between their great country houses and their countryside. The result was the English Garden, which was to serve as a model for the whole of 19th-century Europe. It was in this field of Romantic landscape that the two greatest English painters were to flourish – Constable, who comes nearest to the purely painterly, purely descriptive and scientific treatment of landscape, and is in consequence very much a painter's painter; and Turner, an immense talent capable of astonishing exactitude and descriptive power who, nevertheless, explodes and annihilates space, painting (as Constable put it) with 'tinted steam', and seeming in his blaze of ravishing colour to abolish the solidity of things altogether. It is not surprising that the most poetical of prosaists, John Ruskin, could see nothing in Constable and found in Turner the greatest genius he could imagine.

It is necessary to remember that this procession of great men is always accompanied by a much longer procession of second- and third-rate artists. By the middle of the last century, the freedom and painterly ease of the great masters had degenerated into a kind of painting which depended entirely upon accent, in which fine brushwork and heavy *chiaroscuro* was used as a cloak to hide weak and indecisive drawing. The process was accelerated by the development of watercolour, a medium which positively encourages misty, vague, poetical half-statements. It was this level of art, and not the masterpieces of Turner and Constable, which confronted a group of young men who were growing to maturity in the 1840s.

To them it also appeared that the slovenly and meretricious practices of so many of their elders were combined with something else, a worldly triviality, a kind of cheap poetry. They called it 'slosh', and they formed a Brotherhood that was to regenerate art and return to a careful, precise, sharply coloured form of painting which, in theory at all events, restored the earnest religious practice of the age before Raphael. There was much else in Pre-Raphaelitism which I have not space to discuss; but one thing should be noted: in Holman Hunt's view this was to be a specifically national school. The first duty of Englishmen was to paint like Englishmen and to turn their backs on all foreigners.

And yet, in a way, Pre-Raphaelitism was a most unEnglish manner. Undoubtedly the young men wanted to be poetical and indeed to be didactic; but the difficulty of being both precise and poetical was very great; to their contemporaries it seemed that they achieved ugliness, and even to themselves it must, I think, have appeared that so rigidly factual a method could not easily be combined with high poetical ideals. Hence perhaps the elaborate and sometimes impenetrable symbolism to which they resorted, hence also the habit of supplying some kind of written programme to explain their meanings. Their many imitators were in a sense wiser; they used the Pre-Raphaelite technique not for poetical or religious purposes but to paint scenes of everyday life. Even so, the method was alien to the English tradition, perhaps to the English nature. The style which I may call 'hard-edge Pre-Raphaelitism' lasted for a decade and most of the masters who attempted to use that technique soon abandoned it. The Pre-Raphaelites themselves were amongst the first to do so, beginning with John Everett Millais; Rossetti had never really enjoyed the hard-edge method; only Hunt continued to the end. The future lay with the softer, more fluent and suggestive art of Rossetti and his disciples and by the end of the century one looks in vain amongst the exhibitors at the Academy for a genuinely Pre-Raphaelite artist. In the end we seem to have returned to the vaguely poetical portrait, the even more vaguely poetical landscape, and at a distance of eighty years it reads like poor verse rather than great poetry.

New directions

To look at this century with any degree of clarity seems to me almost impossible – that is, if we are to attempt anything like a value-judgment on reputations many of which are still in the making. Thus it is only within quite recent years that the great achievements of the Camden Town Group, which ended in 1912, have begun to be realized. But a few words may be said concerning our national orientation.

Already by 1900 there were a number of young artists who had founded an Anglo-French society, which became the New English Art Club. English artists had in fact begun to look to France, not to those French artists who most interest us today, but rather to Corot, to J. F. Millet and to Bastien Lepage, painters who had a great deal to teach about tonality and who seemed to cultivate a comfortably edifying variety of realism. Of Monet they knew a little, but their most important avant-garde painter, Sickert, was the apostle of Degas and was himself, in a discreet way, a literary painter. Not until the 20th century did England really begin to take stock of Impressionism and not until 1910 did Fry show us Post-Impressionism and in so doing shock the public and the artists so deeply that the whole course of British art was diverted. From this time, and until quite recently, British art of the second half of the 19th century was condemned and forgotten. All eyes were fixed on France and through the 1920s and 1930s young artists were eager to know what was happening in Paris.

At the very end of the 1930s a group of young English painters who lived by teaching in a school in London's Euston Road began to perceive that the things that were happening in Paris were not wholly admirable. The triumph of Post-Impressionism had, it seemed, become a social triumph. The public loved the 'amusing' quality of the new idiom. Some of the old giants were still splendidly at work, but others had fallen by the wayside and the younger generation was hardly profound. But it was not until after the Second World War, when the impulse of Euston Road – an effort to create a serious art based upon conscientious draughtsmanship – had begun to be replaced by something more Romantic and decorative, that English artists suddenly realized that they could no longer look to France. France, it seemed, had nothing to offer. In this they may have been wrong (only time can tell) but certainly they no longer look to Paris as they used to. If they look in any direction it is across the Atlantic – it is there that the exciting experiments have been made – but I have a feeling, it is hardly more than that, that English admiration for America is by no means so powerful as the admiration that was once felt for France. Has English painting at last regained the confidence that it lost at the end of the Middle Ages?

Pre-Raphaelitism at its most hard-edged and most poetical: one of Dante Gabriel Rossetti's illustrations to Tennyson's 'Palace of Art'.

10 Language and Literature
The English heritage
of poetry, drama and the novel
KENNETH MUIR

ONE OF THE ADVANTAGES of English as a literary medium is that it consists of a mixture of many different languages. The Anglo-Saxons, from whom the language is basically derived, were not the original inhabitants, and successive invasions by Danes and Normans contributed their quota of words. Borrowing from other languages has continued to the present day. Of course all modern languages absorb words from their neighbours, but English has been insatiable. Basically it is a Germanic language, but half its vocabulary comes from other sources. This means that a writer has an enormous reservoir of words to draw on if he so desires. Over the years words which were once synonymous have developed different shades of meaning. This opens the way to variety, precision and subtlety and, in poetry, to the resonance, ambiguity and untranslatability on which it largely depends.

It should also be noted that in the Elizabethan period there was an enormous enlargement of vocabulary by means of borrowing and coinages from French and Latin. Shakespeare, whose words totalled more than 29,000, coined many of them and used many others which had not previously appeared in print. The great French dramatists of the 17th century were denied this freedom, partly by literary convention, so that Racine had to make do with a vocabulary one-tenth the size of Shakespeare's.

English writers obtain some of their finest effects by using simple words of Anglo-Saxon derivation:

I am a very foolish, fond, old man.

(Shakespeare, *King Lear*)

A violet by a mossy stone
  Half hidden from the eye,
Fair as a star, when only one
  Is shining in the sky.

(Wordsworth, *She Dwelt Among the Untrodden Ways*)

Other writers obtain dignity and sonority by using a high proportion of words of Latin (or French) derivation:

But the iniquity of oblivion blindly scattereth her poppy and deals with the memory of man without distinction to merit of perpetuity. (Sir Thomas Browne, *Urn Burial*)

Best of all, perhaps, are those passages which depend on a juxtaposition of Anglo-Saxon and Romance words:

Absent thee from felicity awhile,
And in this harsh world draw thy breath in pain
To tell my story.

(Shakespeare, *Hamlet*)

When to the sessions of sweet silent thought
I summon up remembrance of things past.

(Shakespeare, *Sonnets*)

During the 18th century it was believed that poetry should be written in a specialized diction, many words being regarded as unpoetical and unsuitable. Dr Johnson complained that Lady Macbeth's famous soliloquy used 'low' words, inappropriate to tragedy:

That my keen *knife* see not the wound it makes
Nor heaven *peep* through the *blanket* of the dark
To cry 'Hold, hold!'

Shakespeare was lucky to be born into the 16th century rather than in the 18th, when propriety and good taste would have been his ruin.

English had another advantage over its main rivals. Although Anglo-Saxon was an inflected language, its inflections have gradually atrophied; and there is no doubt that this has facilitated its use as an international language. Besides being the language of North America and Australasia, as one would expect, it is the second language of much of Asia and Africa.

Before the Norman Conquest there had been a wide variety of alliterative poems: of those which have survived there is one epic, *Beowulf* (*c*. late 7th or early 8th century), the tale of desperate fights against fabulous monsters, numerous poems on Christian topics, a famous short poem, 'The Seafarer', and a splendid celebration of courage in defeat, 'The Battle of Maldon'.

After the Conquest, the language of scholars and of the church was Latin, and the language of the aristocracy was French. Three centuries elapsed before legal proceedings came to be conducted in English, or before we had a king whose mother-tongue it was. It is not therefore surprising that comparatively little good vernacular literature has survived from this period. At last in the 14th century English poetry resurfaced. William Langland's great allegorical poem, describing the corruption, sin, and injustice of society, *Piers Plowman*, is written in a modified form of the old alliterative measure. Another impressive poet, the author of *Sir Gawayne and the Green Knight*, the best of many Arthurian romances, also wrote in alliterative verse, but with rhyming pendants to each stanza. These poets, and the author of the alliterative *Morte Arthure*, are descended from an earlier tradition.

A greater poet, Geoffrey Chaucer, was praised by a contemporary as a 'great translator', although his actual translations from French and Latin are the least interesting part of his work. More important was his blending of the styles and genres of French and Italian poetry with an essentially English strain. Although he took the story of *Troilus and Criseyde* from Boccaccio, and although it embodies the tiresome conventions of courtly love, he turned it into a narrative poem of poignant beauty, and one which contained the germ of the psychological novel. Chaucer's other masterpiece, the *Canterbury Tales*, was left unfinished; but, as John Dryden remarked, 'Here is God's plenty!' Not only are the narrators a superb gallery of contemporary English characters, but the stories they tell are wonderfully varied, from the bawdy of the Miller's to the earnest didacticism of the Parson's, from the humour of the Nun's Priest's to the Pardoner's grim fable.

In the next century Chaucer's finest disciples were the Scots, William Dunbar and Robert Henryson, while in England Thomas Malory's *Morte d'Arthur* (1469/70), the crown and epilogue of medieval romance, was written in prose. One other medieval achievement must be mentioned because no other literature has anything comparable. There were religious plays in several European countries, but only in England do we have the great cycles of mystery plays performed by the guilds in the streets of various cities. Some of the sixty York plays and several of the Chester and Coventry plays are fine: but best of all are the six plays added to the Townley cycle, written by a Yorkshire poet, the best dramatist before the Elizabethans. He possessed imagination, pathos, humour, realism, irony, piety and a sense of character. The Townley plays were performed at Wakefield, possibly by clerics rather than by the guilds. Some of the mystery plays were performed well into the 16th century, and they and the morality plays and interludes which followed ensured an audience for drama when the time came and the first professional theatre was built in London in 1576.

The Elizabethan achievement

By the third decade of the 16th century, if not before, the writing of verse had come to be regarded as a necessary accomplishment of courtiers. Sir Thomas Wyatt's best poems belonged to this tradition (for example, 'They flee from me that sometime did me seek' and 'Once in her grace I know I was'); but he also had the distinction of being the first to introduce the sonnet into England, by translating Petrarch's, and the first to use *terza rima* in his satires and psalms. His poems and those of his friend and disciple, the earl of Surrey, published posthumously in 1557, became a source of inspiration for Elizabethan poets. Yet a generation

'The Shepherd's Calendar' was the first work to spring from the friendship of Edmund Spenser and Sir Philip Sydney. Reviving the form of the pastoral, Spenser uses the month of April (above) to pay homage to Queen Elizabeth.

elapsed between the execution of Surrey and the first great poetry of the Elizabethan age. In the first twenty years of the reign of Elizabeth I (1558–1603), the poets were all small fry. Only Thomas Sackville, in an otherwise dreary collection by various hands entitled *The Mirror for Magistrates*, touched greatness. We may suppose that after the upheavals of the two previous reigns it took some time for the Elizabethan settlement to take root, for consciousness of nationhood to grow under the threat from Spain, and above all for the new grammar schools, founded after the dissolution of the monasteries, to provide a new educated middle class with literary tastes and ambitions. But the right conditions for literature are useless without men of genius; and the friendship of Edmund Spenser and Sir Philip Sidney proved to be as momentous as the later friendship of William Wordsworth and Samuel Taylor Coleridge. They determined to do for English poetry what Pierre de Ronsard and Joachim du Bellay had done for French. This they achieved by using French and Italian models and infusing them with native spirit. Sidney's *Astrophel and Stella* (1591), unlike Ronsard's and Petrarch's sonnet sequences, has a narrative interest. Although *The Faerie Queene*, Spenser's unfinished allegorical poem, exemplifying both public and private virtues, with Queen Elizabeth presented as the true Christian ruler, as the legendary King Arthur had once been, is derived structurally from Italian epic, it is essentially English in spirit; and his 'Epithalamion' is not only the best wedding gift a bride ever received, but so full of joy that it is alien to the Petrarchan tone.

By the example of Sidney and Spenser the general level of poetic craftsmanship was immediately raised, and the poets of the last twenty years of Elizabeth's reign, however unequal in ability, could all write competent and musical verse. There were numerous sonneteers, including Samuel Daniel and Michael Drayton, beautiful narrative poems, including Christopher Marlowe's *Hero and Leander* and Shakespeare's equally lovely *Venus and Adonis* (both of 1593), lyrics by

Sir Walter Raleigh, Thomas Campion and Ben Jonson, to name only a few. It was also the great age of English music and there are scores of fine lyrics scattered through the song-books of the period.

Nor was the literary explosion confined to verse. The prose was equally varied: it ranged from the artificial style of John Lyly and his followers (called 'euphuistic' after Lyly's *Euphues*), Sidney's didactic romance, *Arcadia* (1590), with its cunningly interwoven plots, the wit and invective of Thomas Nashe, the colloquial ease of Robert Greene and Thomas Dekker's documentary accounts of the life of the period, to the majestic cadences of Richard Hooker's *Laws of Ecclesiastical Polity*, Sir Francis Bacon's *Advancement of Learning*, and the more condensed and aphoristic style of his *Essays*. In the next reign there were the superbly dramatic sermons of John Donne. It was no accident that the King James Authorized Version of the Bible (1611), refining on previous versions – Anglican, Catholic, Genevan – should stand with the First Folio of Shakespeare's plays as the twin summits of our literature.

It is not only Shakespeare who makes this period one of the great epochs of world drama. Before the building of the Theatre by James Burbage in 1576 performances had been given in inn yards; ten years later with permanent premises and a stable company, the first great plays began to appear. Marlowe's *Tamburlaine the Great*, in which splendid poetry keeps company with violence and cruelty, was the first. Its success, and that of his *Doctor Faustus*, together with *The Spanish Tragedy* of Thomas Kyd, ensured that blank verse (unrhymed lines with five stresses) would be the medium for all dramatists who wrote for the public stage. From then until the theatres were closed on the outbreak of the Civil War sixty years later, there was an unbroken line of dramatists. These included Ben Jonson with his brilliant satirical comedies, *The Alchemist* and *Volpone* (1606), Thomas Middleton with comedies on the life of London citizens and his great tragedies, *The Changeling* (1622) and *Women Beware Women*, the sombre tragedies of John Webster and Cyril Tourneur, the psychological studies of John Ford, and many others. These dramatists, as well as George Chapman, Dekker, Philip Massinger, Francis Beaumont and John Fletcher, would be more highly regarded, and more often performed, if they were not overshadowed by Shakespeare. T. S. Eliot spoke of their 'impure art'; and it is true that there is not a single flawless play among the hundreds written, and that the dramatists were forced to make continual compromises. Nevertheless we should always remember, as readers often do not, that the plays were written to be performed, and that most of the flaws, since they are not discernible in the theatre, are not flaws at all.

There are few Elizabethan comedies as great as the masterpieces of Molière, but their range is unequalled. One has only to think of the difference between Jonson's *Volpone* and *Twelfth Night*, between Chapman's *The Widow's Tears* and *The Tempest* or between Middleton's *A Chaste Maid in Cheapside* and *A Midsummer Night's Dream*, to appreciate the variety of Elizabethan comedy as a whole. Yet comedy is inevitably a reflection of its own time and it is natural, therefore, that there are more Elizabethan tragedies than comedies in the modern repertory.

Shakespeare's greatness as a dramatist in both genres depends mainly on his poetry – poetry both of conception and of execution; on his ability (as Stendhal put it) to say everything; and on the comprehensiveness of mind which makes him equally supreme in tragedy and comedy. Yet it is significant that his plays are appreciated by audiences throughout the world who have little or no knowledge of English. The quality which survives translation into other languages is his understanding of human nature revealed by his depiction of men and women in action and by his method of characterization, first analysed by Maurice Morgann in 1777, by which we are given 'conflicting impressions' of all his major characters, just as we are of people in real life.

Even if Shakespeare had never written a play, he would still be regarded as a great poet: his sonnets are the finest lyrics of the age, as melodious as Spenser's, as psychologically convincing as the poems of Donne written at about the same time, unequalled in our language as the expression of selfless love – and of lust.

The age of Milton

John Donne, in the last years of the 16th century, was reacting against what he regarded as the artificiality of the Petrarchan conventions as used by his contemporaries. He is much franker on sexual matters than all the Elizabethan sonneteers except Shakespeare. He wrote in a deliberately rugged style to convey a sense of passionate feeling; he used the colloquial language of a witty intellectual. Critics in the 18th century objected to his extravagant conceits; but the fusion of thought and feeling in his best work has earned him and his followers – unhappily called the Metaphysicals – the admiration of modern poets and critics. His later poems are equally witty on religious themes. He influenced other religious poets, such as George Herbert and Henry Vaughan. Another great poet, Andrew Marvell, wrote a dozen poems which combine the wit and subtlety of Donne with an exquisite charm and polish.

The career of John Milton, one of the supreme poets of the world, spans the whole of the 17th century. His early work includes the 'Ode on the Morning of Christ's Nativity', a courtly masque, *Comus* (1634), and the masterly elegy, 'Lycidas'. Then he took part in religious and political controversies, with little time for verse; but the pamphlets he wrote contain passages of unsurpassed eloquence. *Areopagitica* (1644), on the freedom of the press, is the best known, though not obviously superior to three or four others. After a lapse of nearly twenty years, when the Puritan cause for which he had sacrificed his eyesight had been defeated, he resumed his poetical career, *Paradise Lost*, *Paradise Regained* and *Samson Agonistes* being published after the Restoration of the monarchy in 1660. These are partly a kind of inquest on the failure of the English Revolution; and the conclusion of *Paradise Regained* is that the kingdom of heaven can come only by the spread of 'saving doctrine', not by political means. He was right to claim that the theme of the Fall was superior to those of the great epics of the past. He evolved for its expression not merely a structure and imagery that subsumed those of his great predecessors, so that we catch echoes of Homer, Virgil and Dante, but also a new kind of blank verse, based not on the line but on the paragraph, less colloquial than the verse of Shakespeare – appropriately so, since God, Satan, Adam and Eve ought to be allowed a more exalted speech than the characters in a secular play. Naturally enough, Milton was more successful in depicting the fallen angels and Adam and Eve, than God, who 'reasons like a school divine'. But the total effect of the poem is one of sublimity: Milton is not to be blamed that his imitators tried to use his Latinized style for comparatively trivial subjects. *Paradise Lost* is not merely one of the two masterpieces of Puritanism – the other being John Bunyan's *The Pilgrim's Progress*, published in 1678 – it is also the fine flower of Renaissance humanism.

Satire and the beginnings of the novel

In 1660, when the playhouses reopened with a different kind of stage, with scenery, and with actresses replacing men for female roles, Elizabethan plays were altered to suit the taste of the times. The new tragedies were in rhymed verse, with inflated sentiments and unreal characters. Only in comedy did the age make permanent contributions to the nation's repertory. The so-called comedy of manners is at its most sparkling in John Dryden's *Mariage à la Mode*, in Sir George Etherege's *The Man of Mode*, in William Wycherley's *The Country Wife* and in William Congreve's *Love for Love* and *The Way of the World*. In these last two comedies the dialogue is the most polished and wittiest in the language, but varied to suit the different characters; and Millamant of *The Way of the World* is the most fascinating comic heroine since the days of Rosalind and Beatrice.

In the century following the Restoration the dominant poets were Dryden and Alexander Pope. Both of them wrote in the Neoclassical style; both were admirable translators of Classical epics – Virgil and Homer; both were great satirists; and both were concerned with men in society rather than with man in relation to nature. Their favourite form was the closed heroic couplet which Dryden used brilliantly and Pope exquisitely. Their style predominated throughout the century, finely in Samuel Johnson's *The Vanity of Human Wishes* (1749) and in Oliver Goldsmith's *The Deserted Village* (1770).

From the first illustrated edition of Milton's 'Paradise Lost', published in 1688. Satan rises from the burning lake and in the background is seen again, 'high on a Throne of royal state'.

Yet there were many poets who sought for inspiration in nature and in earlier literature. One can mention the medieval imitations of Thomas Chatterton, *The Seasons* of James Thomson, and the odes of William Collins and Thomas Gray, although Gray's famous *Elegy in a Country Churchyard* (1751) is an excellent example of Neoclassicism at its best. Meanwhile Robert Burns was writing the best poetry north of the Border since the 15th century, escaping the gentility of much English verse by writing plainly about the life he knew. It has been suggested that the melancholia of Lady Winchilsea and Gray, the madness of Collins and Christopher Smart, and the suicide of Chatterton may have been caused by the sense of alienation in Romantic poets born too early into the age of reason.

The foremost achievement of English writers in the 18th century was in prose, and especially the virtual creation of the modern novel. Daniel Defoe, in *Robinson Crusoe* and *Moll Flanders*, in which the central characters are also the narrators, created fiction which appeared truer than autobiography. The next in the field was Samuel Richardson, whose novels are all in the form of letters, and whose *Clarissa* is a great tragic masterpiece. Henry Fielding began as a parodist of Richardson's *Pamela*, but soon went beyond parody in *Joseph Andrews*. His masterpiece, *Tom Jones* (1749), with its ingenious plot, its humour and its broad humanity, is a great comic novel. Later in the century Laurence Sterne's *Tristram Shandy*, unique in its style, is concerned with the eccentricities of characters before the birth of the hero: it is a highly sophisticated work of art, while pretending to be artless. At the end of the century Jane Austen wrote the first of her wise and ironic portraits of minor gentry, which are not as exportable as Richardson or Sterne, but which are pre-eminently dear to English readers. The novel thus replaced drama as the dominant literary form. The good plays – George Farquhar's *The Beaux' Stratagem*, Sheridan's *The School for Scandal* and Goldsmith's *She Stoops to Conquer* – carried on the traditions of the comedy of manners, whereas the novelists were breaking new ground.

Prose during this period, although lacking the grandeur of the best 16th- and 17th-century writers, had become a more flexible instrument. This was partly because the pamphleteers of the Puritan revolution wanted to be understood by the common man – Milton's later pamphlets, for example, are written in a more colloquial style than his early ones. The other reason was the determination of the Royal Society, founded in 1662 under the patronage of Charles II, to eliminate 'fulsome metaphors' from the plain prose

Boswell's 'Life of Johnson' attained immediate popularity because of its vivid portrayal of Johnson's personality, especially through his conversations. Boswell, however, had laid himself open to ridicule; this print by Rowlandson shows the two men in Edinburgh.

they advocated. The plainness and lucidity is apparent in Abraham Cowley's essays, in Dryden's prefaces, and in Joseph Addison's papers in *The Spectator*. It is equally apparent in the satirical writings of Jonathan Swift, including the bitter attack on the foibles of humanity in *Gulliver's Travels* (1726) which, by a curious irony, has become in selections a favourite with children. The flexible prose of James Boswell's journals and of his masterly *Life of Johnson*, perhaps the finest of all biographies, and the superb lucidity of the philosophers John Locke and Bishop Berkeley can be understood by everyone and greatly admired by their fellow writers. Johnson, however, in *The Rambler* essays cultivated a more latinate style; so, too, did the most magisterial of historians, Edward Gibbon, in *The Decline and Fall of the Roman Empire*, and Edmund Burke in his *Reflections on the French Revolution*.

The Romantic revolution

The French Revolution, however, and the American Revolution which preceded it, were linked with the age of Romanticism. William Blake wrote on both revolutions. His juvenile volume, *Poetical Sketches* (1783), contained imitations of Collins, Gray and Ossian, besides the earlier poets anthologized in Thomas Percy's *Reliques of Early English Poetry* (1765). Most of the characteristics of the Romantic movement are there to be found – a return to the literature of the past, a return to nature, and the use of the language of ordinary men instead of the poetic diction demanded by Neoclassical theory. The remaining characteristic, political and religious radicalism, is apparent in *Songs of Innocence* (1789), *The Marriage of Heaven and Hell* (1790) and the suppressed and unfinished poem on *The French Revolution*. Blake had few readers in his lifetime, but in the present century he has been hailed as a great religious teacher, and one who refused to separate art and poetry, psychology, politics and religion.

The early work of Wordsworth and Coleridge was conventional enough, but the meeting of the two poets was mutually inspiring, each of them evoking the hidden powers of the other. Both were politically disillusioned and both were dissatisfied with the poetry of the previous century, because it was mainly concerned with the upper classes and because of the artificial diction in which it was couched. Most of the *Lyrical Ballads* (1798) were Wordsworth's, but his best contribution, 'Tintern Abbey', is not a ballad at all, but an expression of his belief that 'nature never did betray the heart that loved her'. The other great poem is Coleridge's *The Rime of the Ancient Mariner*, on the surface an exciting narrative of a haunted voyage into distant seas, but underneath a profound parable of guilt and expiation. In 1800 Wordsworth added some of his finest short poems in the simple diction he advocated. This volume, and one that followed in 1807, contained some of his loveliest work; but by this date he had written all his best poetry, including a version of *The Prelude*, and Coleridge's last masterpiece, 'Dejection', is a kind of epitaph on his short creative period. He became thereafter the greatest of English critics.

The Prelude (written 1795–1805), describing the first twenty-eight years of Wordsworth's life and his preparation for his career as a poet, is magnificent in its account of the influence of nature on his development, and of his enthusiasm for, and his disillusionment with, the French Revolution, from the time when 'Bliss was it in that dawn to be alive' to his nightmares during the reign of terror. 'The mind of man' was the 'main region' of Wordsworth's poem and he was fully justified in claiming that it was both original and important. It is still of absorbing interest as an autobiographical document, as a philosophy of education and as a manifesto on the importance of nature.

Walter Scott began his series of Romantic narrative poems at the time Wordsworth completed *The Prelude*, and he turned to writing the Waverley novels in 1814 when his popularity was overtaken by Byron's. It was a wise decision, for the novels were an exciting blend of history and fiction, which were deservedly popular in Britain and on the Continent.

Lord Byron became famous with the first instalment of *Childe Harold's Pilgrimage* (1812) – an effective travelogue in fluent verse – and notorious when his wife obtained a separation. All his best poems were written after he had been hounded out of the country. These included a greatly improved continuation of *Childe Harold*, several exotic tales, a number of closet dramas, a brilliant satire, *The Vision of Judgement*, a parody of Robert Southey's foolish poem of the same title, and his masterpiece, *Don Juan* (1819–24), a wonderful fusion of his varied talents – descriptive, narrative, lyrical, erotic, satirical – and the only poem which exhibits them all, although his incomparable letters do too.

Byron's fellow exile, Percy Bysshe Shelley, wrote all his best poetry in Italy between 1818 and 1822. He was only twenty-nine when he was drowned, so that the critics who complain of his immaturity are somewhat ungenerous. In fact he matured very rapidly. No doubt he wrote too much – Keats advised him to curb his magnanimity and load every rift with ore; *The Cenci*, a tragedy of tyranny and incest, effective as it is, is too full of Shakespearian echoes; and *Prometheus Unbound*, despite some sublime passages in the first act and at the end of the last, fails as a drama. Dozens of his lyrics were left unrevised and not intended for publication; and some of those he did publish were too declamatory. Yet, when all is said, he is one of the greatest of lyric writers, and his longer poems are extraordinarily varied. He has not always been given credit for qualities quite unlike the 'profuse strains of unpremeditated art' in which he is thought to excel: the colloquial ease of *Julian and Maddalo* (which contains a brilliant portrait of Byron) and of the Letter to Maria Gisborne, and of what is almost the only political poetry which is simple without condescension. What is admitted, even by those who find his beliefs and character repellent, is the new power and profundity, the real maturity, of *The*

Blake's 'Jerusalem' and other so-called 'prophetic' books put forward radical religious views in a highly personal allegorical form that found few readers. This typical page shows his novel technique for engraving and illustrating his own texts.

Triumph of Life, the poem which was cut short by his death.

One of Shelley's finest long poems is *Adonais* (1821), his elegy on Keats, whose best work was crowded into a single year. Keats's early poems had included one splendid sonnet, 'On First Looking into Chapman's Homer', and there are beautiful passages in *Endymion*, together with flaws which the poet was the first to recognize. But his masterpieces were all written in the twelve months beginning in September 1818: the first *Hyperion*, an epic fragment he afterwards criticized as too Miltonic in style; 'The Eve of St Agnes', the most satisfying of his narratives; five of the great odes, beginning with the one addressed to Psyche and ending with 'To Autumn'; 'Lamia'; 'The Fall of Hyperion' – all in their different ways masterly. His letters are singularly interesting, containing some of the best criticism of other poets and revealing a maturity of mind only matched in the best of his poems. It is the letters as much as the poems which have made many readers regard him as temperamentally akin to Shakespeare, especially when it is remembered that he was only twenty-four when he wrote the last of the odes.

Of the six major Romantic poets only Byron was popular. The others were damned by the critics who had been brought up in the Neoclassical tradition, and who were also prejudiced against the poets on political, social, moral and religious grounds. Shelley's poems were printed at his own expense; Wordsworth became reasonably popular only when he had declined into dullness; and Blake's last prophetic book, *Jerusalem* (1804–20), adorned with some of his finest engraved designs, apparently attracted only one purchaser. It would have puzzled any middle-aged reader in 1820 to be told that Thomas Campbell and Samuel Rogers, even Dryden and Pope, would come to be ranked below the poets we have been discussing.

The Victorian age

The Victorians, because they wrote for a public which was beginning to appreciate the Romantics, did not have the same difficulty in attracting readers. Alfred Tennyson, whose first volume appeared less than a decade after the death of Byron, was influenced mainly by Keats. He was a more careful artist, but with less imagination and a less interesting mind. *In Memoriam* (1850), however, on which he worked for some fifteen years, is one of the three great English elegies, and more personal in its grief than either 'Lycidas' or *Adonais*. *Idylls of the King*, Tennyson's attempt to write a kind of Arthuriad, is somewhat disappointing after its splendid first instalment, 'Morte d'Arthur', if only because it victorianized Malory.

Tennyson's main rival, Robert Browning, began as a disciple of Shelley, the 'sun-treader', as he described him; but in his mature work, influenced no doubt by the novel, he specialized in the eccentricities of human behaviour, which he often expressed in dramatic monologues. His actual plays are curiously undramatic, although the multiple perspectives obtained by the use of diverse spokesmen in *The Ring and the Book* (1868–9) – including the murderer, the victim and the pope – showed that he possessed what is perhaps the most important dramatic gift.

Matthew Arnold, the third of this generation of poets, believed that poetry, being essentially a criticism of life, should return to classical standards, Milton being a better model than Shakespeare. Nevertheless, his epic fragments, *Sohrab and Rustum* and *Balder Dead* are less successful than 'The Scholar Gipsy' and 'Thyrsis' (his elegy on his fellow poet, Arthur Hugh Clough). In his later years he wrote little verse, but he became a brilliant critic of literature and society. Although there was a good deal of complacency and

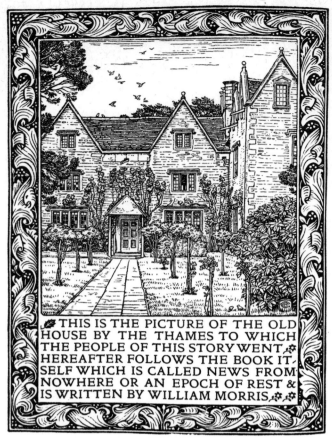

William Morris used his own house of Kelmscott Manor as the setting for his 'News from Nowhere', a Utopian romance set in the 21st century, advocating a return to an idealized medieval world.

hypocrisy in the Victorian period, the Pecksniffs and the Podsnaps were not left uncriticized. Thomas Carlyle, the historian, John Ruskin, the art critic, and William Morris, the poet, assailed in their different ways the illusions of the age. Morris, a founder member of the Pre-Raphaelite Brotherhood, became a master of several arts, the founder of the Kelmscott Press and a writer of verse and prose romances which used the medieval and pagan worlds to show up the evils of modern industrial society. He proclaimed that 'lack of fellowship is death'.

Perhaps the greatest of Victorian poets, although not published until 1918, was Gerard Manley Hopkins, a Jesuit, whose intense appreciation of nature and whose relationship with God were expressed passionately with great metrical and linguistic originality.

Despite the attractiveness of much Victorian poetry, the novel remained the dominant literary form, and one which was enormously popular. There were many good novelists, of whom only a few can be mentioned here, who catered for an enlarged and voracious reading public. Anthony Trollope, a prolific writer and an admirable craftsman, wrote on the behaviour of worldly and unworldly clerics and on political intrigues, and gave a sombre picture of London society in *The Way We Live Now*. Mrs Gaskell had a vein of delicate humour, best displayed in *Cranford*, and she wrote with understanding and compassion on the industrial north. Charlotte Brontë, although making use of melodramatic plots, created heroines, such as Jane Eyre and Lucy Snow, who shared many of her own feelings, and with whom many readers could identify. Her sister Emily, a greater genius, poet as well as novelist, wrote a brilliantly structured novel, *Wuthering Heights*, which exactly fulfils Keats's requirements when he said: 'The excellence of every art is its intensity'. William Thackeray's varied talents are to be seen at their best in *Vanity Fair*, a historical novel set in the Napoleonic period, which enabled him to write more frankly than some Victorians of the world and the flesh. George Eliot, hailed by many critics as the greatest of women writers, and certainly one of the wisest, produced a number of studies of provincial life, novels of 'moral discrimination', of which *Middlemarch* is the most impressive – an account of several families, with all their hopes and disappointments, their ideals and failures.

Finest of all, and the most popular, was the 'inimitable' Charles Dickens, whose creative range was exceeded only by Shakespeare. He had equally at his command humour and pathos, fantasy and realism, satire and tragedy, farce and melodrama. His characters from Pickwick to Wegg, from Micawber to Mrs Gamp, are more real to us than most historical characters and many of our friends; and he provides us with a portrait of the age and a devastating critique of its underlying assumptions. It is no accident that Dostoevsky's early novels were Dickensian.

After Dickens's death in 1870, Thomas Hardy began his series of Wessex novels, in which his country folk are seen 'struggling in vain with ruthless destiny', as *The Mayor of Casterbridge* and *Tess of the D'Urbervilles*. The shocked reception given to *Jude the Obscure* made Hardy give up novel-writing and acquire an equal reputation as a poet.

The 20th-century inheritance

The best novelist of the next generation, Joseph Conrad, a Pole by birth, brought to his writing the lessons he had learnt from the great French novelists and, in *The Secret Agent* (1907) and *Under Western Eyes* (1911), from Dostoevsky. He rivalled the great American novelist, Henry James, in his concern for the novel as an art form. Much of his best work belongs to the early years of the present century, at a time when John Galsworthy was writing *The Forsyte Saga*, Arnold Bennett *The Old Wives' Tale*, and H. G. Wells many of his varied tales and novels.

The writers of the 1920s and 1930s – D. H. Lawrence, E. M. Forster, James Joyce and Virginia Woolf – have attracted more critical attention than Galsworthy or Bennett. Lawrence, whose explicitness on sexual matters made him a controversial figure in his lifetime and since, wrote many fine short stories and novellas. His best full-length novels are the traditional *Sons and Lovers* and the more experimental *The Rainbow*

and *Women in Love*. He had a remarkable power of describing both nature and what Wordsworth called 'unknown modes of being'. Forster used the novel to express his liberal and civilized views on life, *Howards End* and *Passage to India* being accepted classics in his lifetime. Virginia Woolf, like Lawrence and Forster, used poetic symbolism and in her best novels, *To the Lighthouse* and *The Waves*, she relied more on poetic qualities than on the conventions of narrative. Joyce also enlarged the boundaries of the novel. His most impressive work, *Ulysses*, depends very little on the Homeric parallels, ingenious though these are. He describes in great detail a single day in the life of a Dubliner, what he does, what he sees, the thoughts and impressions which pass through his mind. The best example of the 'stream of consciousness' technique is the final meditation of the Penelope of the book, Molly Bloom, uninhibited, unashamed, and poetic in its total effect. Joyce's sheer cleverness, apparent, for example, in his parody of a number of prose styles, overreached itself in his later work, *Finnegans Wake*.

After a century of comparatively insignificant drama, the stage had a remarkable revival in the last years of the 19th century. Oscar Wilde wrote five or six

Oscar Wilde's was an ambivalent genius: on the one hand the exhilerating laughter of 'The Importance of Being Earnest', on the other the fin-de-siècle decadence of 'Salome' which so appealed to Aubrey Beardsley; this drawing dates from 1894.

plays, but his sole masterpiece was the delightfully artificial comedy, *The Importance of Being Earnest* (1895). Another Irishman, and the greatest dramatist since the 17th century, George Bernard Shaw, used his comedies not to criticize aberration from normal behaviour, but to satirize received ideas and institutions, and to propagate his own theories on war, social questions and politics. He possessed an effective polemical style, superbly lucid; and, although it is often said that his characters were mere mouthpieces for his own views, the dramatic interest of his plays usually depends on the clash of ideas embodied in lively characters. Another Irish dramatist, Sean O'Casey, showed in *Juno and the Paycock* (1924) and *The Plough and the Stars* (1926) that it was possible to write poetic plays in prose about Dublin tenement-dwellers in the time of civil war, plays which blend tragedy and wild humour. Samuel Beckett, a disciple of Joyce, had one great success in *Waiting for Godot* (1956), and in this and in the short plays that followed he gave expression to his belief that life was meaningless, in language which is sometimes poignantly beautiful.

Finally we return to the development of poetry during the present century. W. B. Yeats developed from being a charming minor poet and the writer of experimental verse plays, to become the greatest poet of the age in *The Tower* (1927) and *The Winding Stair* (1933).

Wilfred Owen, Isaac Rosenberg and Edward Thomas, three poets who were killed in the First World War, wrote unforgettably of the pity and horror of it, Thomas finding himself as an original nature poet in the last months of his life.

When T. S. Eliot, an American who became a British citizen, began to write, he felt that the Georgians, his immediate predecessors, belonged to an effete tradition and he therefore took as his models the Metaphysicals, Jacobean dramatists and certain modern French poets. His first major work, *The Waste Land* (1922), owed some of its power to Ezra Pound's brilliant cutting. *Four Quartets* (1935–44) is the most satisfying volume of poems since the death of Yeats. Although Eliot wrote a number of verse plays, he never fully exploited the dramatic talent apparent in *Sweeney Agonistes*.

Whereas Eliot became a British citizen, W. H. Auden, of the next generation, left England after the Munich Agreement and became an American citizen. The poetry he wrote in England, because of the rise of fascism, was politically committed; some of the poetry written in America, such as *For the Time Being: A Christmas Oratorio* (1944), was religious; but in both he showed a continuing interest in psychological theories and also a love of the countryside he knew in his youth.

Two other poets may be mentioned: Dylan Thomas and Louis Macneice. The former was extremely popular, partly for his effective showmanship; the latter is still not fully appreciated for his tough honesty and unaffected style.

To attempt to judge living authors would be inappropriate in this brief and very selective survey. We could not be sure that the writers singled out for praise would be those whom future generations would admire. We can only point to the unbroken line of poets during the past four centuries, to Shakespeare, universally recognized as the greatest of dramatists, and to the outstanding contribution of English writers to the creation of the modern novel. There is no reason to doubt that the English-speaking world will continue to produce great literature, even if, as Bishop Berkeley prophesied, its centre will move westward. At the end of the 16th century, when English was spoken by only five million people, Samuel Daniel had prophesied the spread of the language into the New World:

> And who, in time, knows whither we may vent
> The treasure of our tongue, to what strange shores
> This gain of our best glory shall be sent
> T'enrich unknowing nations with our stores?
> What worlds in th'yet unformed Occident
> May come refined with th'accents that are ours?

Since the middle of the 19th century the great writers of the United States have been producing work at least equal to that of their English rivals. But that is another story.

'*Mild surprise of one who, revisiting England after long absence, finds that the dear fellow has not moved.*' The revisitor is Max Beerbohm; the 'dear fellow' is George Bernard Shaw, whose ideas seemed to many besides Beerbohm to be wilfully the opposite of everyone else's.

V
Land and People

ENGLAND was the first country in the world to experience rapid and large-scale industrialization. The crucial years were the last decades of the 18th century and the first decades of the 19th. Other European countries were to take the same path with only a brief time-lag. During the 20th century the rest of the world followed or is following suit. Everywhere the results have been broadly the same: a rise in material standards, a steep increase in population, the growth of large towns, acute discrepancies in the distribution of wealth leading to grave social problems and a vast upheaval in traditional ways of living. When it is over hardly anything is the same as before – the towns, the countryside, the character of the people, all are changed.

In England events followed the pattern that has since become familiar, but the fact that Englishmen were the first to experience them made a serious difference. Nobody foresaw or was prepared for the full effects of industrialization. *Ad hoc* remedies had to be worked out on the spot. The change in labour relations and the proliferation of slums (to give only two examples) entailed a total rethinking of public responsibility, social justice and even the sacred concept of private property. Moreover, England's primacy in industrialization gave the country a lead over the whole of the rest of the world and it became immensely rich. This brought its own advantages, though not to the whole population, but it also brought its problems in the succeeding phase when other nations began to rival and then to surpass England.

In previous sections the emphasis has been upon continuity. In this one it will be upon change. England today (and in this she is not alone) is a compound made up of several thousand years of slowly developing tradition plus two hundred or so of very rapid change. There is only one place where we can catch a glimpse of pre-industrial England, and that is the countryside. In spite of all the transformations and revolutions, there are still villages that consist basically of the buildings that stood in the 18th century or even earlier; still fields that keep their ancient boundaries and hedges, and roads that have followed the same routes since pre-history. Though the English countryside is itself the product of change, the changes have usually been slow and have preserved strong links with the past; but for how much longer can this be said?

And so finally back to the theme which began this book – the English character. How far is it constant and how far fluctuating? How much would an Englishman of Shakespeare's day have in common with an Englishman of today? Perhaps the very search for 'Englishness' is a sign that it is vanishing. Yet most Englishmen still do have a sense of belonging to a people with a definite character. This emerges particularly in times of crisis, and never more strongly than in World War II, the last occasion when all Englishmen felt emotionally bound together in a common cause. One of its manifestations was a turning towards the past, an affirmation of identity with that past. National character may after all be as much a matter of decision as of history.

If there is a birthplace
of the Industrial Revolution, it must surely be Coalbrookdale, a steep wooded valley in the quiet county of Shropshire. Here Abraham Darby found the ideal combination of coal, iron-ore, water-power and river transport, and in 1776 he built the first furnace capable of smelting iron with coke. He was soon able to produce cast iron in quantities far beyond anything that had been produced before. In its early days industry was a rural rather than an urban activity. It was only with the rise of the steam engine, the railways and especially the mechanization of textile manufacture that the great industrial towns began to grow. This painting, by William Williams, of Coalbrookdale in 1777 shows how relatively small was the first impact of industrialization on the landscape, and indeed the site still retains its picturesqueness. (1)

The village through the centuries

Nothing is more evocative of England than its villages. But there is no single type of English village. Regional variations are wide, and every individual example has a history that makes it different from its neighbours.

Ripley, in Yorkshire, with its stocks and market cross, seems rooted in the past. Yet nearly all its buildings date from the 1820s, when the old cottages were rebuilt. (2)

Nidd, a mile to the east, was swept away in the 19th century to make way for a gentleman's park, leaving only the isolated medieval church with Nidd Hall behind it. (3)

Milton Abbas was rebuilt on a new site in the 18th century so that Joseph Damer's mansion (a remodelled abbey) could have a more picturesque setting. More than a hundred houses were demolished. (4)

Lost villages, abandoned for various reasons, have left their traces in the soil. The old streets of Lower Buxton, Bucks. (*right*), can still be clearly recognized, while the rectangular features are plots attached to the dwellings. (5)

The landlord's power meant life or death to the village up to the 19th century. At Averham Park, Notts. (*above*), the deer park on the right has been extended across old open field land which is still identifiable by ridges and furrows. (6)

Church, green and mill-pond: all the traditional elements of the English village are present at Finchingfield, Essex, even if somewhat self-consciously preserved. From a nucleus round the church, it expanded with the local textile industry. (7)

Patterns on the earth

The countryside is a palimpsest on which every generation has written its history. By looking closely at the traces that remain we can reconstruct vanished ways of life. Often invisible on the ground, these ancient patterns are now being revealed by aerial photography and by archaeology.

Stone circles are monuments to Neolithic religion, although their precise function is still a matter of conjecture. Here at Castlerigg, near Keswick, the stones stand amid the ridges and furrows of later ploughing. (8)

Medieval field boundaries show up amid the snow in the Langdale Valley in the Lake District. They represent the 'colonization' of the lower lands by 'inland' and 'intake' enclosures, while the medieval ploughing is outlined by the ridge and furrow. (10)

Harvest, a scene painted in 1857, by J. F. Herring. Note on the left men cutting the grain with sickles and the sheaves which stand on the right. (9)

Beneath the fields of modern farming appear the shapes of the past. *Right*: so-called 'Celtic' field, formed by the creation of banks around an area of cross-ploughing. *Far right*: corduroy patterns of ridge and furrow are cut across by a later road, and a geometric framework of hedgerows is imposed upon the medieval plough-ridges. (11, 12)

England transformed

Between 1800 and 1850 the population of England doubled; between 1850 and 1900 it doubled again. The great majority of the people were concentrated in London and the swollen towns of the Midlands and the north.

What the impact meant in terms of its effect on the appearance of towns can be judged by these two pictures of Leeds in 1745 and 1832. A few landmarks remain. Everything else has been swept away and replaced by huge warehouses and tenements. Problems of health and public order escalated beyond anything that had been known before. (13, 14)

Private charity as it had been practised in the first half of the century could no longer cope with poverty on this scale. No longer could a deserving case (*below*: Poor Law Guardians discuss an application for bread, 1841) be remedied by the generosity of wealthy neighbours; there were too many deserving cases. (15)

Many towns in the north rode to new prosperity on the textile industry. Here was a copybook example of how technical improvement, a free economy and limitless markets could transform society. Steam-power and the new looms forced weaving out of the cottages and into the factories (*above*); output soared, profits soared higher; those with money made more money; those without it could do nothing but sell their labour on terms set by the employers. Around cities like Leeds grew up a warren of crowded, insanitary streets where the workers lived (*left*), while the booming wealth of the business community reflected itself in splendid new town halls (*right*, Leeds again, still black with Victorian soot; it has now been cleaned). Not by chance did Marx and Engels find in England the perfect model of a capitalist state. (16, 17, 18)

Sinews of power

Coal and iron were the trump-cards in the 19th-century power game, as oil has been of the 20th. Britain possesses all three, but whereas in exploiting the first two she was a pioneer, the last has been developed only in the 1970s.

Coal-mining, upon which industry depended, long remained primitive and dangerous. By 1840, when this picture of a Northumberland colliery was painted, steam-winding 'cages' to take the men up and down were only just being introduced. Underground the loads were moved by women and children as well as ponies. (19)

North Sea oil has created its own technology, unlike any that has been seen before. In order to drill the sea bed, huge platforms (*opposite*) have had to be devised, as wonderful and picturesque in our day as coal-mines and iron-mills were in the last century. (21)

Iron developed quickly after the first breakthrough by Darby. James Nasmyth's invention of the steam-hammer made possible the production of even larger components. A painting by Nasmyth himself (*below*) shows it at work. (20)

Money and class

It is said that nothing divides English society more than class, and nothing is harder for the outsider to understand. It is less a question of money than of accent, education, background and friends – things that money can buy, but not immediately.

Class contrasts are now less blatant than they were in 1937, when a photographer took this Eton schoolboy (*right*) watched by three East Enders. But indoors the differences are still acute. *Below*: the National Liberal Club and the Bradford City Band Club. (24, 25, 26)

For the Victorians class entailed attitudes, expectation, even morality. In W. P. Frith's *For Better, for Worse* a poor family waits patiently for some bounty from the wedding. *Below Stairs* by Charles Hunt makes gentle fun of a servants' party about to be surprised by the housekeeper. (22, 23)

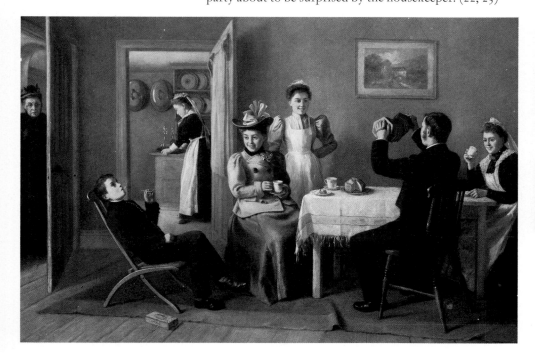

Exclusive and inclusive. A garden party at Buckingham Palace (this one took place in July 1973) is for the select few, and even here a wide distance is preserved between Queen and commoner. Brighton beach is very definitely for the many, a favourite pleasure-resort for Londoners ever since the railways brought it within easy reach. (27, 28)

Travel accelerates

Railways in one sense reflected social divisions, with their first, second and third classes. But in another they helped to erode them, taking the cotton worker to Blackpool as quickly as the queen to Balmoral.

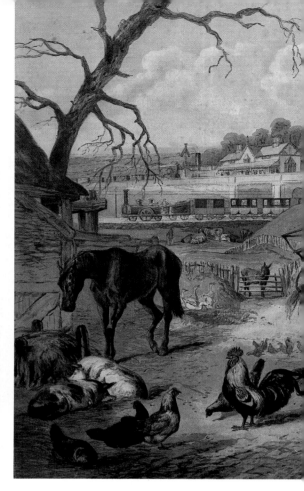

The crowded coaches (overcrowded according to Lami in 1829, *above*) travelled if they were lucky on turnpikes maintained by tolls. But by 1850 (*right*) many coach routes had been put out of business by the railway. (29, 30)

The giant works of railway engineering astonished – and appalled – the Victorians, and it is still difficult to realize that they were built by manual labour alone. *Above*: the deep cutting at Olive Mount, near Liverpool. Greatest of all the engineers was I. K. Brunel, whose Saltash Bridge (*left*) carried the line across the Tamar into Cornwall on two wide spans high enough to allow shipping to pass underneath. Today the road has regained its ascendancy, scouring new grooves across the countryside (*below*) and creating new problems for the environment. (31, 32, 33)

The test of war

If the First World War did a little to break down class barriers, the Second did much more. Common danger and common sacrifice, equal rationing of food and a sense of shared purpose united the nation to an exceptional degree.

The familiar symbols of traditional England took on a new look under wartime conditions. *Left*: an embattled 'Big Ben' surrounded by barbed wire. *Below left*: outside Marlborough House the guardsman has his own air-raid shelter next to the sentry-box. (34, 35)

A soldier says goodbye to his small son. With his gas-mask and label the boy is being evacuated from London to the country. *Below*: the civilian population was mobilized for defence against air attack. (37, 39)

You never know *who's listening*!

CARELESS TALK COSTS LIVES

Comedy survived. Posters like this, urging people not to gossip about security matters, were given wide publicity by the government. (36)

join ARP enrol at any fire station AFS

The Underground stations became air-raid shelters, and some branches were closed to trains altogether. Here (*left*) a concert is organized during the winter of 1940–1. (38)

The country's leaders were able to tap deep wells of patriotic emotion in times of crisis. Churchill's speeches appealed constantly to history and tradition as sources of national pride, and his visits to bombed cities (*left*) invariably raised morale. The charisma of royalty was also used to effect. Here Queen Elizabeth (now the Queen Mother) chats to a girl worker on a farm. (40, 41)

The Home Guard was formed in 1940 to meet the threat of invasion, at first without uniforms and sometimes even weapons. *Right*: life carries on unsubdued by bombs and food shortages. (42, 43)

The posters of the two World Wars make a revealing contrast. In the First the call was based primarily on duty and, by extension, on reproach for those who were shirking. In the Second there was much more appeal to nostalgia, to tradition and the values that were being defended.

'Are YOU in this?' asks Baden-Powell's poster of 1915. The soldier, sailor, nurse, munitions girl, factory worker and even boy scout (Baden-Powell had founded the movement in 1908) are doing their duty . . . but not the idler looking on with his hands in his pockets. (44)

'Your Britain: fight for it now', a poster of 1942. The most potent images of England during and after the two World Wars were drawn from the countryside. They evoked memories of safe, rural, non-industrial England, an unchanged and unchanging homeland. (45)

11 'England's Green and Pleasant Land'
The evolution of the
landscape
RICHARD MUIR

THE LANDSCAPES OF ENGLAND are like clays which have been moulded by many different hands. They display both the characteristics of the natural materials and the preferences of the generations who shaped them. The qualities of Englishness which grace the landscape were acquired over many centuries and were the gift of no single race or culture. There is no one vista or countryside which is England – the country is an assemblage of many contrasting local and provincial cameos. Members of the nation have been inspired and fortified by the magnificent mosaic of regional personalities, but in recent times the qualities of individuality and Englishness in the townscapes and countrysides are yielding to bland, commercialized anonymity. With the progressive sterilization of their setting, the English may lose a vital pillar of the national identity.

England is a very small country, yet it embraces an incomparable array of proud and distinctive geographical regions. Those which variously inspired writers such as Thomas Hardy, D. H. Lawrence or the Brontës were as different as they were English. In outlining the general forces and initiatives which forged the lanes, villages and fieldscapes of the realm, we must not lose sight of the contrasting inherent and acquired personalities of the countrysides.

Based as it is upon the latest insights and discoveries of landscape history, this chapter will include a number of surprises for readers who were weaned on older and outdated versions of the story. The gravest flaw in earlier appraisals was the notion that the main themes only began to emerge in the years following the withdrawal of the Roman legions around AD 410 (now we wonder whether they even did withdraw). The discord between the old and new versions is greatest where it concerns the effects of the centuries of Saxon 'invasion'. To several generations of scholars the Saxons were the one dynamic and creative race and that period the single formative era in the human manipulation of the landscape – a time when the new settlers sallied forth from a myriad of newly created village islands to clear the encircling wildwood and forge the framework of settled agriculture. However, now this period can be seen instead as one of trauma, torpor and decay which is sandwiched between a Roman era when most countrysides were organized, well-peopled and productive, and the final centuries of Saxon rule when vital initiatives in the establishment of new and enduring villages and a more intensive open-field strip farming were taken.

A heavy strand of 'invasionism' ran through the old appraisals. Innovations tended to be attributed to invading races, who imported new ideas and reassessed the resources of their new homeland. Change is a pervasive theme in landscape study – but so too is continuity. Long-established and proven patterns of farming and organization were not lightly discarded and many features of the landscape are much older and more deeply rooted than was once thought, while more change was wrought by evolution than by invasion.

Man did not evolve with the specialized hoof and horn of the herbivore or the fangs and claws of the carnivore. His supreme assets were flexibility and ingenuity, the gifts of a sensitive and adaptable pair of hands and a large brain. Man can survive as a hunter and a gatherer and he can flourish as a farmer; human landscape creation occurred at the first step of the transition from hunting to farming. This step was taken in the latter part of the Mesolithic period or Middle Stone Age, which ended about 4850 BC. It involved the deliberate manipulation of the natural environment and seems at first to have concerned the localized removal of the native wildwood, perhaps to create open hunting ranges or pastures for semi-domesticated red deer or reindeer, or the stripping of trees, such as the elm, of leafy shoots for fodder. The dawn of the New Stone Age was marked by the introduction of grain cultivation from the Continent. This accelerated the removal of the native forest and launched a 'Neolithic Revolution', every bit as important in the evolution of man-made landscape as the Industrial Revolution of the 18th and 19th centuries.

As hunting and gathering came to take second place to a mixed-farming lifestyle based on rearing cattle, sheep and pigs and cultivating primitive cereal strains, so the countrysides of England were able to support a much denser population. As population rose, so too did the demand for new farmlands and for more efficient and permanent methods of farming. By the close of the Neolithic period, the woodlands rather than the clearings formed the islands in most of the English landscape.

Wiltshire, with its long barrows, rows of standing stones and the magnificent stone circles of Avebury and Stonehenge, is one of the few places in England where it is possible to imagine a prehistoric *landscape. A common complaint is that the atmosphere at Stonehenge has been spoiled by tourists, but in 1865 it could evidently be just as crowded when the hare coursers met there.*

The evolution of a landscape

As pioneer farmers exploited new settings, a more detailed awareness of the diversity and variability of the local assets of the countrysides was gained. Some areas were set aside as pastures, others as meadows, ploughlands, woodland reserves and hunting wastes. This exploitation revealed and underlined the different climatic and geological zones which were hitherto only evident as subtle variations in the blanket of natural vegetation. It has often been said that prehistoric farmers shunned the heavily wooded claylands and damper valley bottoms and confined their cultivation to the lighter, more tractable and thinly wooded sandstone ridges, river terrace gravels, glacial sands and chalk downlands. However, field-walking by archaeologists now reveals traces of settlement in almost every type of environment. It seems clear that the more obvious traces of prehistoric occupation survive on the lighter soils because these are the areas shunned by later ploughing which has masked the evidence elsewhere.

The Late Neolithic and Earlier Bronze Age periods have left us an amazing legacy of monuments in the form of massive collective tombs and henges. The chambered tombs, such as the West Kennet, Wayland's Smithy and Belas Knap long barrows, may have rough continental parallels, but no other country can boast such a myriad of stone circles which culminates in the awesome temples of Avebury and Stonehenge. Although certainly not monuments to a unified prehistoric English nation, they are an essentially British development (with Callanish on Lewis and the

Ring of Brodgar in Orkney to rival the drama if not the scale of the English temples).

Even so, the impact of these monuments upon the popular imagination has led to an unbalanced view of the prehistoric world. The proverbial Martian who had only learned of modern England by glimpsing the sports stadia, statuary and churches which are our contemporary ritual monuments would be unable to form a realistic view of modern life and priorities. However, while singularly impressive as works of art and engineering, the tombs and temples do offer broad hints about the bases of prehistoric society. They remind us that at certain times religion and ritual can motivate communities to pinnacles of achievement. They dispel the myths of prehistoric people as primitive savages and suggest societies which could be organized (or exploited) by powerful and effective leaders. Above all, they testify to the unglamorous and repetitive cycles of peasant agriculture – the essence, preoccupation and mainstay of prehistoric life – which had become efficient and productive enough to underwrite ambitious and labour-consuming programmes of monument-making.

We have inherited visions of prehistoric landscapes as being very thinly peopled by tiny communities dwarfed by the forces of their environment. The real picture which gradually begins to emerge deals more in terms of cycles of growth and expansion and of decay or retreat. There were periods when population outstripped the capacities of the farmland and technology and when climatic change caused abandonment at the

226

vulnerable margins of farming. Perhaps too there may have been plagues, comparable to the Black Death of 1348–9, to check the march of progress. In the Earlier Bronze Age the adverse effects of Neolithic soil exhaustion may have been overcome and the countrysides of England may have supported an organized and productive tapestry of land uses. The archaeologist C. C. Taylor has suggested that by the close of the Bronze Age the English landscape was more thickly peopled and more regularly organized than it was almost two thousand years later, when the Domesday survey of 1086 itemized the assets of the Norman realm. Towards the end of the Bronze Age, the adverse effects of climatic change in the direction of cooler, more blustery weather were becoming apparent, and when the Roman invasion of AD 43 terminated the prehistoric era in England, population pressures upon the overused resources of the countryside were evident.

Roman organization, technology and, particularly, Roman imposition of more equable political and economic systems stimulated new waves of settlement and colonization, but in due course the collapse of Roman power signalled a new cycle of retreat and decay. The centuries of the Saxon settlement are still but dimly glimpsed, but the population seems to have fallen while large areas of well-managed countryside surrendered to scrub and woodland. The causes are uncertain, although political turmoil and fragmentation, the collapse of commerce and outbreaks of pestilence may each have played a part.

During the 9th and 10th centuries the recovery of population, perhaps accompanied by new symptoms of overpopulation, stimulated communities to revise their organization of the countryside. If the most important aspect of this reappraisal was the establishment of open-field strip farming, its most enduring epitaph is to be found in the survival of thousands of villages which were founded in these and the two or three centuries which followed.

This succession of colonization, organization and retreat continued throughout the Middle Ages. The optimum climatic conditions which were enjoyed around 1200 lured peasant ploughmen into uplands which may have been untilled since prehistoric times, while a multitude of new assarts rolled back woodlands dating from the Dark Age retreat. However, by about 1300 the landscapes of southern and Midland England were overburdened with swollen villages, the marginal, newly colonized lands were already becoming exhausted, and the early effects of a prolonged deterioration in the climate were being experienced. The Black Death reduced population by at least one third and a succession of later outbreaks ensured that the 13th-century levels were not equalled until after the close of the Middle Ages.

Until the Industrial Revolution changed the economic priorities and bases of English life, most acts of landscape creation were wrought by peasants motivated by the needs to eat and to meet the burdensome dues imposed by their masters. Looming through the landscapes of more recent endeavours are the works of several hundred generations of anonymous, hungry and work-worn peasant families. Quite unintentionally, they created the evolving pageants of rural beauty which modern farming methods are so swiftly destroying.

A pattern of roads

Having glanced at some of the main themes in the landscape story, let us examine some of the facets which compose the English scene. The oldest features of the landscape which are still in active use are lanes and highways. We know that many are prehistoric, although most are frustratingly difficult to date. A few major routeways are ancient and there is little reason to doubt that the majority of winding lanes were first trodden, ridden, carted and thus engraved in the countryside in prehistoric times. Finds of useful Neolithic commodities such as stone axes and pottery tens or hundreds of miles from their sources testify to trading over long distances. While some of these goods may have been gradually dispersed across tribal territories by successive owners, it seems more likely that traders and trade routes were involved.

A few celebrated long-distance routeways like the Ridgeway and the Icknield Way have proven Stone Age pedigrees. In accepting the antiquity of these major highways, we must also imagine networks of feeder roads and local tracks. The great routeways would seldom have existed as single highways, but rather as zones of movement composed of branching and merging trackways. Branches of the Icknield Way are fossilized in the many River Cam villages whose original High Streets led to river-ford crossing points. In the Somerset Levels some of the timber and brushwood roads which have been excavated date from the Neolithic period; and they demonstrate that the need in the Stone Age to get about the countryside was not checked by difficult, marshy terrain.

As the population grew and the frontiers of farming expanded, so the gaps in the road and lane network were filled. The Iron Age network was probably no less dense than that of today, although the routes would hardly ever have been surfaced. Most of England's country lanes, apart from the short, straight enclosure roads of the 18th and 19th centuries, must surely be of Iron Age or earlier vintage, even though most are almost impossible to date without recourse to excavation. The highway and track patterns which the Roman invaders found in England accumulated in a piecemeal and spontaneous manner, but the Roman attitude to transport was quite different. The colonial overlords were probably the first people to form a coherent and overall view of the patchwork of volatile tribal kingdoms that was England. Upon the heterogeneous assemblage of routeways large and small they superimposed an uncompromising network of well-engineered and remarkably finely surveyed highways. Initially they were motivated by military considerations, the need to shuttle legions about the colony with swift efficiency in the pacification of the provinces. In time, with the creation of bustling towns, lucrative mining operations and commercial farming, economic rather than military factors came to the fore, although military roads would still have been needed in the turbulent uplands of the north and west. Most of the major Roman routeways are known, and a good proportion remain as the major arteries of modern England. In a few places, as on Wheeldale Moor in the North Yorkshire Moors, the appearance of a stone-paved and ditch-flanked highway has been preserved. Lesser roads are sometimes marked by surviving ditch-flanked embankments, although hosts of minor Roman lanes would have been ancient when the Romans arrived or undistinguishable from the narrow, twisting holloways of other ages.

Saxon settlers inherited and used the Roman routeways. Dark Age armies ranged widely across the country and their remarkable mobility suggests that much of the Roman network remained usable, if poorly serviced. It was modified in detail by changes in local needs and settlement patterns. Words that survive in place names tell us a little about the Saxon roads and trackways. The *Straets* or streets were important highways and often Roman creations; *Wegs* or ways were of a more localized importance and they often follow parish boundaries; while the *here-paeths* are said to have been used by armies. Of course, many of the routes which carry Saxon names were already ancient when the settlers landed.

However, the maintenance of the Roman system soon degenerated into piecemeal local efforts, and no medieval monarch succeeded in creating or maintaining a national network of roads to compare with the Roman model. The overgrown relics of medieval routeways can be seen at scores of lost village sites – and they often testify to the undistinguished and often downright treacherous communications of the period. Ingenious and thoughtful in many of their local undertakings (moat, millpond and fishpond complexes, for example), in the vital field of road-making the medieval communities paid for the lack of efficient centralized planning and stable government. Often reluctantly and with slipshod workmanship, villagers maintained sections of trackway which were barely adequate for local needs, and long-distance travel often relied upon sections of poorly repaired routeway of a Roman or earlier vintage.

The squalid nature of medieval, and indeed post-medieval, travel is perhaps nowhere better portrayed than at the virtually deserted village of Luddington-in-the-Brook in Northamptonshire, where the puddled channel of the brook itself provided the village with its High Street until shortly before the community petered out in the 19th century. Medieval stone bridges, on the other hand, often built from the bequests of local landowners, display fine masonry and engineering skills. They underline the point that organizational

rather than technological weaknesses were responsible for the poverty of the transport system. The horrendous descriptions of resilient 17th-century travellers like Daniel Defoe and Celia Fiennes show that the problems persisted long after the close of the Middle Ages.

When organized on a parochial basis, road maintenance depended on the grudging and inadequate efforts of peasants who had other, more pressing obligations. The creation of Turnpike Trusts after 1663, but mainly during the 18th century, provided a crucial stepping-stone between the fumbling efforts of the medieval world and the recreation of a genuinely national road system during the second half of the 19th century when dis-turnpiking was completed. In the course of the turnpike era, local and regional trusts were set up to undertake the improvement and maintenance of the more important stretches of highway. The straightening, widening and surfacing costs were (hopefully) recouped from tolls levied on the road users, while the system was rationalized by the closure of lesser duplicating roads which might have appealed to toll-dodgers. Many modern trunk, A- and B-class roads follow turnpiked routes and the numerous surviving 18th-century toll houses remain as attractive roadside epitaphs to the era.

As well as reorganizing the fieldscapes of many English parishes, Parliamentary Enclosure of the period 1750 to 1850 also helped to rationalize local travel. As new field patterns were set out, ancient lanes were widened, straightened or abandoned. Short straight sections of new trackway were often provided to serve farmsteads, but since Enclosure operated on a parish basis, with many years often separating the Enclosure of neighbouring parishes, the new roads were often poorly integrated.

During the turnpike era the new and improved roads faced commercial competition firstly from canals and later, and more seriously, from railways. By the middle of the 20th century a new road-transport crisis had emerged, the existing system being patently incapable of bearing the rising volume of heavy transport vehicles. The creation of a new motorway network which is now approaching completion has eased the problem – at the cost of hundreds of square miles of previously attractive countryside and a legion of archaeological sites. Hundreds of towns and villages remain unserved by much-needed by-passes and suffer the consequences of government preference for words rather than action on important environmental issues. Of course, the great disaster is that for one reason and another the railway system has been prevented from playing its proper and environmentally acceptable role in the movement of freight.

Roads and trackways form important features of the landscape, but their superficial appearances may tell us little about their origins. Enclosure roads of the 18th century often resemble surviving stretches of lesser Roman roads, and sections of paved highway may peep through the undergrowth of a disused lane but be of any vintage from the Roman period to the 18th century. The holloways which can be seen at scores of lost medieval villages could be, and often are, thousands of years older than the villages which they later served. Deeply hollowed lanes of great but uncertain antiquity penetrate the English countryside in a most inviting manner, but as ever more public footpaths are barred or ploughed into oblivion, the English right to view the heritage is rapidly being eroded. Many of these footpaths followed hedgerows and, as the hedgerows are grubbed out in the making of more soulless prairie fields, so the farmers petition to have the old footpaths diverted. Unable to trace the courses of the rights of way, and often intimidated by landowners, ramblers abandon the unequal struggle. And then the farmers can petition to have the right of way abandoned. East Anglia has witnessed far more of these sorry scenarios than are good for the landscape, or for the nation.

Seven villages

The village must lie at the very centre of the expatriate's perception of the English homeland. It is also one of the most misunderstood facets of the landscape. Perceived as age-old and stable, the village is in fact a relative late-comer to the English scene, often ephemeral and generally mobile. Until the Late Saxon period, villages were the exceptions in rural landscapes which were dominated by hamlets and scattered farmsteads. Where prehistoric villages did exist, they tended, like the other settlement forms, to be abandoned after a few decades or a couple of centuries of occupation.

The powerful tendency for settlements to be dispersed and short-lived endured until at least the 8th century, when an event which archaeologists have called 'the Middle Saxon shuffle' occurred: virtually all the existing hamlets and villages seem to have been deserted. Their successors tended to be much more permanent. The causes of the shuffle are unknown, although it has been guessed that they may relate to the traumas of conversion to Christianity, which were perhaps more unsettling than the chroniclers have told. Subsequently, the development of an open-field strip farming system tended not only to provide the basis for greater agricultural production to underwrite rising levels of population, but also to anchor settlements more closely to sites at the hearts of the village-centred complex of ploughstrips, hay meadows, commons and woodlands. We are as yet unable to weave the various strands of evidence together in a coherent theory of village origins, but an early stage in the formation of a landscape of villages may have been the emergence of what one expert has loosely termed a 'linked farm cluster' – a small group of farmsteads occupied by families who had agreed to pool their efforts for the more efficient performance of certain farming tasks.

Meanwhile, in the uplands of the north and west, where the terrain and the climate favoured the pastoral lifestyle, the village remained an anomaly and peasants favoured the more solitary lifestyle of the farmstead or hamlet. Some of the oldest landscapes in England endure in areas such as Cornwall, parts of the Pennines, and in Devon, where Professor W. G. Hoskins has demonstrated the Saxon pedigrees of many dispersed farmstead sites.

The villages which coalesced in the early medieval period were never fossilized and their forms evolved with the passing centuries. No simple classification such as the conventional preoccupation with 'green' and 'linear' villages can summarize the complexity of the English village lay-outs. Some villages were to perish utterly while others survived as shrunken remnants of their former selves. Many have shifted, leaving behind overgrown earthworks of holloways, close boundaries and house platforms. Frequently, neighbouring villages or hamlets with separate foci merged to produce what are known as 'polyfocal' villages. Only a small proportion of villages have remained stable, preserving forms similar to those mapped by pioneer cartographers. Old Byland on the North Yorkshire Moors is such a village – although even this village is a planned replacement for one which the monks moved from the site of the original Byland Abbey.

Throughout this story, the landscape historian is confronted by the two key themes of his calling: continuity and change. Continuity finds expression in the survival, for example, of elements of medieval planning in many village lay-outs. This is so common as to be the norm in many areas of the north of England, such as the Vale of Pickering. Here, a large flock of villages is based on the themes of the long, street-flanking green, the orderly green-side rows of houses and the neat packages of 'tofts', each elongated toft or enclosure serving a particular dwelling. While the dwellings may have been rebuilt a dozen times in their transition from hut-like peasant hovels to attractive cottage homes, the essential planning of the villages has endured. In most northern cases it is hard to believe that the origin of the planning is not to be found in the aftermath of William the Conqueror's brutal Harrying of the North, during the organized rehabilitation of the wasted estates.

Change, though, is a commoner theme. I can demonstrate this by reference to a group of villages strung out along a section of my Nidderdale homeland in Yorkshire. Killinghall, undistinguished in appearance and about three miles from Harrogate, is our first port of call. The present village has a V-shaped form and clings to two roads, the A61 and B6161, which intersect at an angle to provide the V-form. However, Jeffereys's map, published in the 1770s, portrays a very different Killinghall. The village is set well back from the roads mentioned, which appear as mere tracks, while the village farmsteads are clearly set out along the margin of a common. In the years that followed, the Forest of Knaresborough commons were enclosed while the two tracks running across the common became turnpikes. Responding to these important changes, Killinghall migrated from the edge of the now-vanished common to settle beside the bustling new turnpikes. The first edition of the Ordnance Survey 1-inch map shows that in the late 1850s the move was almost complete, and the few buildings persisting at the old village site were known as 'Town Houses', showing that their link with the old 'town' or 'vill' had still to be forgotten.

Just across the river which shares its name is the village of Nidd, now scarcely more than a hamlet of public buildings and charity cottages built around 1900 under the patronage of the family of nearby Nidd Hall. Medieval and more recent documents show that in the Middle Ages and into the 18th century Nidd was a village of medium size, while Jeffereys's map shows that about seventeen dwellings lined the lane which still runs by the church. This village was swept away, probably early in the 19th century when the park surrounding the Hall (which lurks behind the church) was landscaped and enlarged. The hamlet which perpetuates the name of Nidd was developed by later owners who regarded their tenants in a different light, and it was sited outside the park, although the old lane which passes the church is still known as 'Town Street'.

About a mile away and upstream of Nidd is Ripley which, with its cobbled market square, medieval church, cross and stocks and castle, appears to be an exemplary old nucleated village. In many ways it is, but the half-awake visitor will soon notice the handiwork of 19th-century members of the Ingilby family of Ripley Castle. They provided the statue of the boar which figures in the medieval family history – and there are not many English villages which can boast an outlandish copy of a French Hôtel de Ville. In fact, the old village of thatched and cruck-framed, ramshackle cottages was pulled down in the 1820s and the somewhat 'Tudor' gritstone cottages are the prettified replacements. If space permitted, I could invoke the theme of continuity and argue that Ripley may still preserve traces of an alignment along a 'lost' section of Roman road. Change asserts itself when we realize that a lane which wanders unnoticed out of the back of Ripley and is only passable on foot or horseback was, until the 17th century at least, part of the main route from York to Lancaster.

Overlooking Nidderdale, a couple of miles to the west of Ripley, is Clint, today a quite unremarkable row of 20th-century detached houses, salted with an older cottage and farm buildings. They stand on the site of a hitherto unrecorded lost village. Jeffereys's map again serves up the proof, for it shows that the site was deserted by the 1770s. The remains of the medieval village are represented by the fragmented walls of the late medieval hall of the Beckwith family, a cross-base and stocks which are surely miniature copies of those at Ripley and a holloway and earthworks which seem to represent a square-shaped village. The causes of Clint's fall are unknown, but probably not uncommon, and the

decline is poignantly expressed in a carving on the medieval cross-base: 'Palliser the Tailor' made his hoarding of the redundant cross. In due course, 20th-century builders were attracted by the broad valley vistas seen from the lost village site.

Facing Clint across the River Nidd is Hampsthwaite, situated at an intersection of along-valley and cross-valley routes, close to an almost certain Roman bridging point and with a Scandinavian place name. A triangular green lies to the south of the medieval church – one of very few such churches in the Dale – and Hampsthwaite seems to exemplify the nucleated village of popular perception. Centuries of growth and development have masked the originally 'linear' form of the village, which was aligned along a road leading to the river crossing. Later expansion along a road that leads to Killinghall has given the village a roughly T-shaped form; when this road reaches the end of the limb of the T, it takes a sharp dog-leg: this results from the abandonment of the more direct route to Killinghall and the adoption of another more circuitous route.

The most remarkable thing the 18th-century maps tell us about Birstwith, the next village up the Dale, is that it did not then exist. The valley setting of the present village was then deserted, although some small coal mines were being worked (the spoil heaps and older 'bell pits' are now overgrown). On the gritstone plateau overlooking the valley there were close scatters of dwellings, the homes of small farmers who also practised cottage-based textile industries. Many of these homes have vanished while, at the start of the 19th century, a village was formed lower in the valley. The creation of this small settlement of estate and cotton-mill workers was stage-managed by the nouveau riche mill-owners of the Greenwood family from their dominating Neo-Gothic mansion of Swarcliffe Hall. Birstwith is thus an example of the process of 'late nucleation', which developed as villages coalesced at riverside sites in middle Nidderdale where water power was available to drive the new mills. Almost all of these mills have perished and most visitors are unaware of the quite recent industrial origins of so much of the village landscape.

My final example, Darley, lies a couple of miles upstream; it is a polyfocal village and much more complicated than the others that we have visited. Two of its components are represented by separate greens, while on the edge of the village an area known as 'the Holme' appears to be the remains of a third. Here too is preserved a rare survivor of a type of thatched and cruck-framed cottage typical of the vernacular architecture of the area until the 19th century.

Having glanced at all the village forms in a five-mile stretch of Nidderdale we find that none of the examples matches the 'timeless and unchanging' perception of the English village. The originals of two of the villages have been lost through shifting, a voluntary move in the case of Killinghall and a forced removal in the case of Nidd. Clint is a settlement which has been both lost

Part of the Nidderdale area discussed in detail in the text. The earliest of the three maps (right) is that of Jeffereys, published in 1772. Ripley, prominent near the centre, was rebuilt about 50 years after the map was drawn. Nidd, whose church and hall are shown graphically, is to the right, while below Ripley is Killinghall. The site of the modern village of Clint, marked on a map of 1902 (below), was uninhabited in 1772; it is opposite Hampsthwaite, lower left of Ripley, just right of the foot of the 'T'. The next village, Birtswith, again did not exist in the 18th century, though there were small coal-mines nearby. Finally, off the 18th-century map but shown on the one below, comes Darley.

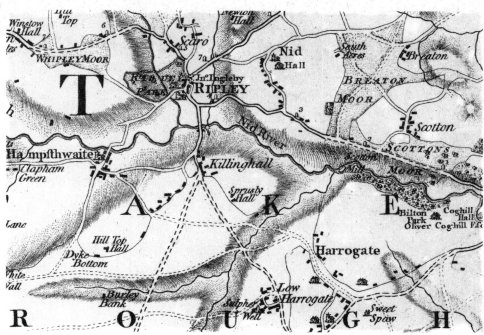

If the first edition of the Ordnance Survey map of the area (1850s) is compared with Jeffereys's map, one can see various changes that have taken place. The village houses of Nidd, strung out along the road to the church, have now disappeared. Killinghall has moved to the right, beside the main road, and where it used to be are only a few farm buildings labelled 'town houses'. It is also interesting to see how Harrogate is growing as a spa town with a new nucleus around its mineral springs. Note too the arrival of the railway, bisecting the landscape from north to south.

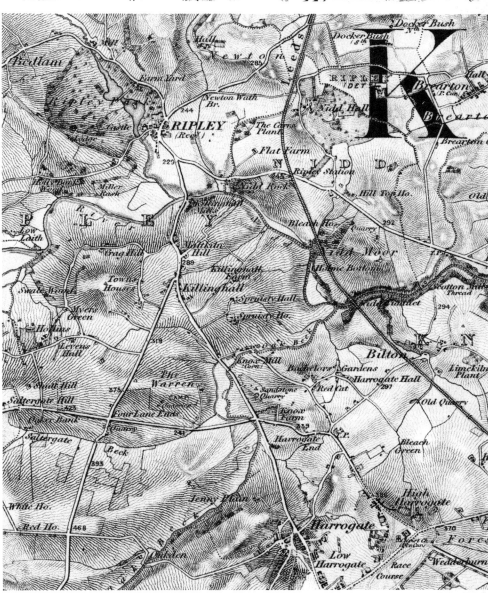

231

and found, while I have not mentioned Whipley, between Clint and Ripley, and Rowden on the outskirts of Hampsthwaite as probable and possible lost villages respectively. Birstwith is a late arrival, Hampsthwaite and Ripley much more complicated than first appearances suggest, while the Darley lay-out is almost impossibly complex.

There is nothing particularly unusual about the villages of Nidderdale; in the relatively few counties where detailed surveys have been made, village shrinking, shifting and complexity are found to be quite normal. Thousands of medieval villages have been abandoned completely. Although yielding nothing to interest treasure-hunters, deserted village sites contain masses of information which could illuminate our understanding of the medieval world, and the paucity of official funding for excavation work is most unfortunate.

The causes of depopulation were varied. In the north of England, the Harrying of the North seems to have wiped the slate of settlement almost bare in some extensive districts, and the numerous planned villages are mostly evidence of organized resettlement in the decades which followed. (In Nidderdale only the small community of now-lost Whipley appears to have survived the Harrying.) The recolonization of the wasted landscapes coincided with the Cistercian monastic penetration of the north and many of the villages next fell victims to the new monasteries, and more particularly to the establishment of monastic granges. On the margins of our Nidderdale study area, Herleshow and Cayton were two of the numerous victims of Fountains Abbey.

As we have seen, the 12th and earlier 13th centuries were periods when the pressures of a swollen population caused villages to be established at the margins of the viable agricultural areas. The deterioration of climate had become marked by the 14th century; a flock of coastal settlements (such as Ravenser and Ravenserrod in the Humber estuary) met violent fates in storms and sea surges, and numerous upland and marginal villages experienced more lingering deaths. They included not only the abodes of communities that were obliged to work the thin, exposed and swiftly exhausted soils of the upland slopes and plateaux, but also villages located on clay vales where the cold soils became waterlogged in the cooler, damper climates. In the Lincolnshire claylands, the excavated lost village of Goltho and perhaps twenty neighbouring settlements may have perished.

During the 14th century the English village must have seemed to be the victim of a deadly conspiracy. In the second decade, scores of northern villages were burned and plundered by Scottish raiders, although almost all, with the possible exception of Leake near Ripon, swiftly recovered. The Black Death was the most fearful event in the nation's history. Even so, remarkably few villages were completely and permanently extinguished. While the Black Death was quite

capable of depopulating a settlement, those afflicted villages which lay on better lands tended to be swiftly repopulated, partly by refugees from the smaller marginal settlements which were surrendering to soil exhaustion and climatic decay. Cublington in Buckinghamshire provides a useful cameo. On its knees in the 14th century, almost certainly from the effects of climatic change on its damp and low-lying site, the village was extinguished by the 'Great Pestilence'. Sixty years later, colonists returned, but wisely chose to build their church and settlement on the higher ground overlooking the crumbling ruins of the original village. In this way the village survived, and in 1970 its community was sufficiently robust to defeat the proposal for a third London airport at Cublington.

The most concerted assault upon village England was still to come. The pestilence had undermined the market for food grains, while the reduction in the peasant labour force encouraged demands for higher wages and kinder terms of service. Meanwhile, the wool market at home and abroad was buoyant and many landowners responded to the changed circumstances by evicting villagers from their estates and replacing them with sheep or cattle. During the Tudor period the removal of villages and creation of sheep runs transformed some areas of eastern England and produced great chains and clusters of deserted parishes in Midland counties like Warwickshire, Oxfordshire and Northamptonshire. Such was the devastation that in the 1480s, the chantry priest John Rous was able to name thirty-eight villages which had perished, all within a dozen miles of Warwick.

The last great assault on the village fold came in the 16th to 19th centuries as the removal of nearby villages accompanied the construction of fashionably isolated mansions in new or extended landscaped parks. At Houghton in Norfolk, Wimpole in Cambridgeshire and Middleton Stoney in Oxfordshire, the characteristic trinity of the majestic hall, the isolated church, marooned in the park at the site of the former village, and the replacement village, sited out of sight beyond the park pale, illustrate the emparking process.

Largely unrecognized by popular writers on the countryside, who prefer to deal in picture-book villages peopled by merry yokels, the lost villages of England serve as reminders that brutality and peasant hardship were basic ingredients in the making of the English landscape.

Fields and farmers

Before the age of the commuter, the village in England had little meaning outside the context of its little empire of ploughlands, pastures and commons – and I have mentioned how the genesis of the village as a common feature of the lowland landscape seems to have been linked to the development of open-field strip farming. Fields, of course, have a much longer pedigree than this. They are the most obvious features of the landscape and therefore tend to be taken for granted –

although a wealth of interest is contained in their forms, patterns and boundaries.

In the course of prehistoric time, the shifting clearings of the first generations of farmers were superseded by expanding networks of permanent fields with their boundaries defined in the landscape by banks, lynchets, ditches and, perhaps, hedgerows. Extensive networks of prehistoric fields emerge in aerial photographs, although the dating of the different forms remains difficult.

'Celtic' fields are small, loosely rectangular packages of land whose shapes seem to have been determined by the light and compromising nature of the pre-Roman ploughs and the need to 'cross-plough' (i.e. plough in two directions) in order to create a tilth. As a result of centuries of cross-ploughing and soil drift, lynchets or banks developed at the margins of these fields. Networks of 'Celtic' fields can be glimpsed in upland areas such as Wharfedale and the Dorset downs where later ploughmen shunned areas that were tilled before the Saxon settlement. Although the landsman will only recognize these field patterns in areas of undisturbed upland plasture, archaeological excavation and air photographs show that, as we would expect, the prehistoric fields blanketed most of lowland England.

Most of the more prominent 'Celtic'-field remains seem to belong to the Late Iron Age and Romano-British period, but fragments of older and different prehistoric divisions can be glimpsed in the long stretches of banked 'ranch boundaries' which sometimes seem to radiate from Wessex hill-forts, and the long walls or 'reaves' which evidence a large-scale partitioning of the Dartmoor landscape. Although much work has still to be done on the dating and identification of ancient field patterns, we must imagine that from at least the beginnings of the Bronze Age, most of England bore a spider's-web tracery of field boundaries.

While various systems of land division into ploughlands, pastures, woodlands and farmstead paddocks and pens existed in the Romano-British period, there is little evidence of the large-scale reorganization of lands into geometrical field patterns as in parts of the continental empire. Variants of a long-established 'infield-outfield' system would have been common in colonial England, with the better plough-lands being kept in good heart and regular production through generous applications of farmyard muck, while parts of the poorer outlying pastures were periodically broken in as outfield ploughland, farmed to swift exhaustion and then rested under a long period of fallow. Rather than importing vital innovations, for several centuries the Saxon immigrants seem to have been content to perpetuate forms of the same system.

In the final centuries of the Saxon ascendancy, a pressure of population on the existing resources of the countryside may again have become apparent. A reappraisal of farming methods and a closer integration of communal efforts allowed a more intensive use of the ploughlands. The greatest value of this was probably to relieve pressure on the indispensable livestock pastures and hay meadows. The corduroy patterns of former plough ridges are common sights in countrysides where grazings cloak areas which were ploughed in the medieval periods – but these recognizable ridges are just the enduring fragments of complete systems of village-based open-field farming which are often misunderstood.

The plough ridges were produced deliberately by a particular method of ploughing in order to assist the drainage of the land. Half a dozen or so parallel ridges combined to form a strip or 'selion' which was often about an acre in area, and was one of a number of strips tenanted by a village peasant and dispersed throughout the various open fields. The strips in turn were grouped together in blocks or 'furlongs' and these were normally the units upon which the simple medieval crop rotations were practised. By tenanting strips scattered throughout a number of furlongs, the peasant had only a small proportion of his strips resting under fallow at any particular time. Probably less important than the furlongs in this scheme of subsistence were the two, three or more vast open fields, each of which embraced a number of adjacent furlongs.

Complementing the ploughlands in the essentially mixed system of lowland farming were the hay meadows, often situated in the damper valley bottoms and providing the fodder which allowed a portion of the village livestock to be supported through the winter, while pasture was available on the extensive commons which lay beyond the open fields, on the fallowing furlongs and in the privately tenanted tofts or closes which often composed the immediate sur-roundings of the village. The commons, wastes, wood pastures and woodlands not only provided invaluable grazing for sheep and cattle and pannage for the swine, but also supplied jealously guarded common rights to constructional timber, fuel, bedding and a multitude of little resources which were essential to peasant subsistence.

Open-field farming was efficient, productive and balanced but it demanded a prodigious degree of peasant co-operation. It was more intricate in its operation than can be easily imagined and required strict supervision by the lord's bailiff and the village reeve. Before the end of the medieval period, the pattern of open fields was interrupted in many places by blocks of hedged closes or more extensive pastures which resulted from the piecemeal enclosure of groups of strips by agreement between the peasant farmers, by the extraction of demesne lands from the tangled patterns of communal farming, and by the conversion of village lands into depopulated sheep runs. Between 1750 and 1850 virtually all the parishes which still sustained open-field systems and commons were repartitioned according to a local Act of Parliamentary Enclosure.

In the lowlands, the simple survey techniques, the

The elm, the most English of trees, has been severely depleted during the last twenty years by the Dutch elm disease. This engraving was made in 1886.

The planting and upkeep of woodland were among the main cares of the 18th-century landowner – a responsibility now usually neglected. In a manual published in 1756 (left), the upper picture shows comparative tree-planting and below 'timber trees raised in rows, with the ground tilled between.'

requirement for the new holdings to be hedged and the preference for fields of a moderate size produced landscapes of rectangular geometry, gridded by hedgerows and punctuated by small game coverts and shelterbelts. In the uplands, Enclosure created a legacy of long straight walls which provide the detail in the sweeping vistas of fell pasture. For all cottagers and most small tenants, Parliamentary Enclosure spelled the death of the remaining vestiges of peasant subsistence, departure to the industrial towns or beyond, or life as a hired farm labourer. Some arbiters of taste have derided the landscapes of Parliamentary Enclosure as uninteresting and monotonous, but in places where the criss-crossing hedgerows are well maintained they are havens for hosts of threatened plants and animals, and generally Enclosure country-side is not lacking in character.

Many very extensive areas witnessed no Parliamentary Enclosure, and the open fields and commons had long surrendered to local enclosures by agreement. Elsewhere, particularly in the west, landscapes which favoured the livestock farmer rather than the plough-man had been divided into hedged closes which might be as old as the Saxon era. Where they survive, these 'early enclosure' landscapes with their sturdy, varied and curving hedgerows provide the most attractive of the English fieldscapes. In other areas still, hedged enclosures of various shapes and sizes lying beyond the margins of the former village open fields may have been the products of medieval assarting, reflecting the piecemeal removal of woodland from areas which

234

became overgrown in the trough of the mysterious population retreats of the Dark Ages. More recent are the valley-bottom traces of post-medieval water meadows where one can sometimes trace the courses of channels used for the flooding of pastures to encourage an early flush of spring grazing. Taken together, these different field patterns of England chart the history of the occupancy of the countryside.

The legacy of woodland

Sharing the countryside with the fields and hedgerows are the threatened remnants of woodland. The advances of the frontiers of prehistoric farming and the ever-present needs for suitable timber for fencing, fuel and hut-building ensured that little natural woodland survived into the Iron Age and that scarcely any pockets of primeval forest remained in England by the start of the Middle Ages. As early as the Neolithic period, it seems that sections of woodland were systematically coppiced to furnish an adequate supply of poles for a multitude of uses. Different systems of woodmanship would have been refined during the prehistoric period. The medieval records reveal carefully managed and highly valued woodlands which were capable of satisfying the intense demands for fuel and constructional materials.

Many woods were divided into different sections yielding specialized types of timber and with each section harvested according to a particular rotation. Standard trees, grown tall and straight and cut in their youth, provided structural timber, while fuel, poles, wattle, tool handles and thatching sways were produced from coppices where the trees were cut back to their boles every five to ten years. Woodland pasture had a more open aspect, with coppice-like timber being harvested from the crowns of pollards, above the reach of browsing cattle. Both pollards and standards were also grown amongst the hedgerows.

The hunting and landscaping enthusiasms of the gentry of the 18th and 19th centuries have left us a legacy of spinneys and shelter-belts, the latter often of poplar or Scots pine, both of which enjoyed periods of fashionability. However, the modern woodland story is one of retreat and decay, the result of the quest for short-term profitability, the falling demand for slow-growing hardwood timber and the consequent collapse of the woodsman's craft. Almost all the coppices and pollards which we see today are out-grown and neglected, while the commercial conifer plantations which darkly blanket the former upland grazings have scant scenic or natural merit. Woodlands which provided variety and contrast in the broader fieldscapes are relentlessly grubbed out, while the onslaughts of Dutch elm disease are threatening the survival of this most English of all trees. The government now provides 85 per cent grant aid for woodland clearance and a recent survey shows that only one farmer in a hundred has even a basic understanding of woodland management. As with so many facets of the countryside, the present situation is depressing and the future ominous.

Accident and artifice

This minimal survey of the legacy of roads and trackways, villages and lost villages is attempted at the expense of introducing some more widely understood facets of the rural scene – the churches, industrial relics, castles and dwellings. None of these topics can be summarized in the space of a few lines, and so we pass them by – while noting that the use of the local stone or timber building materials in the making of homes and churches adds enormously to the visual personalities of the different regions.

I have said that there is no one English landscape, but many. The lovely countrysides were produced quite accidentally as by-products of the peasants' and farmers' needs to prosper or survive. When wealthy Englishmen of the post-medieval centuries manufactured landscapes to surround their rural mansions, they often turned to Italian inspirations. The contrived scenery which they created had none of the relaxed and accidental charm of the true English countryside. Some distinctive national processes have helped to heighten the unique qualities of the English scene – notably Parliamentary Enclosure, which banished the vistas of peasant farming that in part endure upon the Continent. A few features of the detail in the English scene seem to derive from national quirks and preferences, such as the fairly general lack of interest in round apses in the earlier medieval churches, and the full-blooded enthusiasm for the Perpendicular, which scarcely died in the provinces even during the height of the classical vogue.

In general, however, the landscapes of England were created accidentally in the interactions between man and the land which supported him. Where human endeavours harmonized with their natural geographical setting, good scenery was the result. The many cycles of change which I have introduced produced landscapes of majestic and uncontrived beauty. Throughout the country these fine old landscapes have yielded to or are threatened by the visual sterility of modern farming practices.

The English are famed for the length of the national fuse. Slow to act and reluctant to take purposeful or decisive action when the interests of the national community are threatened, the English may lose their scenic heritage before they respond to the vandalism of the grubbed-out hedgerows, the featureless factory fields, the ploughed-up public footpaths and the fertilizer-polluted rivers. The countrysides which inspired and fortified the nation are under sentence. The desert which is much of Cambridgeshire, northern Suffolk and Bedfordshire today foreshadows the Yorkshire, Warwickshire and Northamptonshire of tomorrow and the Worcestershire and Herefordshire of our children.

The poets, painters and country-lovers of the next generation will find little stimulation or reward in the black carpets of conifers and prairie ploughlands with which curious national and EEC policies afflict the nation. To the very hilt, we are subsidizing the wastelands which are the successors of the rich green tapestry of hedgerow, pasture and woodland. We will be judged by the landscape legacy which we pass on to those who follow. They may only be able to learn about the England that was from old photographs and paintings – and they will neither understand nor forgive. Lost countrysides cannot be recreated and the only real hope for the future of our landscape lies in the fact that when the English are eventually stirred into purposeful action, the nation is relentless in the pursuit of its goals. Appeasement in conservation has failed and a new crusade is needed.

Steam-threshing in the 1850s, one of the early applications of mechanized power to agriculture. Improved versions of these machines were operated until relatively recently although now the combine harvester rules the battered croplands.

12 A Nation of Shopkeepers
Commerce, town life and the Industrial Revolution
SYDNEY CHECKLAND

THE FORCES that altered the face of England from the later 18th century were basically economic. They took two forms, namely the extension of world commerce and finance, and the creation and adoption of a new range of technologies. In both respects England, for reasons deep rooted in her past and in that of Europe, took the lead. The twin forces of trade and technology carried English society away from its traditional life of the countryside, based on the village, the tenant farmstead and the great house; in its place they brought intensive urbanization, with the mass of Englishmen, women and children depending on industrial employment for their livelihood. From the cities and from industry came also the new basic tenor of their lives, revolutionizing their family relations, their working conditions, their recreation, their welfare, their hopes and fears, their hostilities and affinities, their allegiances, their self-views and their belief systems. The English and the Scots were the first peoples to undergo this bewildering complex of changes, passing through it in the space of little more than two generations.

Because they were the first in a sequence which almost all human societies were to experience or to aspire to they became for a time the dominant world nation, at least over those parts of the globe that could be penetrated by sea and by trade. They acquired an empire that in its extent, diversity and splendour seems now to be almost a dream. Within England the unique and unrepeatable conditions under which the labour force necessary for industrialization was brought together and subjected to a new form of discipline, profoundly affected the attitudes of labouring men and women to society, their own place in it, the claims they might make upon it and the forms of industrial and political organization they should adopt in order to assert such claims. Just as empire, long after it had vanished, was to have continuing effects on England's attitudes and performance, so too the conditions under which she industrialized were to reach forward in time in the form of sustaining myths affecting the attitudes of workers and employers long after the conditions out of which they came had passed away.

Beliefs concerning wider reality were also deeply affected by the experience of industrialization, not only beliefs concerning the structure of society and the place of the individual and the family within it, but also about the natural world and, largely as a consequence, about God and man and the relations between them. Indeed, just as England took the lead in trade and industry, so too, it was especially in England that human speculation entered upon its modern phase. This meant that not only was understanding of the natural world greatly extended but also, largely in consequence of this, the existence of a supervising and caring God was seriously called in question: the fearful possibility was posed that perhaps man was alone in a universe that was indifferent to him and that with God dismissed, human life had entered upon a phase in which it was impelled by forces man had released but could not control. And yet the English continued to believe in one or other of the forms of the Christian faith, subscribing as they had always done to religion as combining mystery and morality.

All of this was the product of Western man's inquisitiveness and acquisitiveness as these attributes began to converge with a new force in the England of the later 18th century. This outcome was nobody's intention. It was brought about by the cumulative effect of a great number of individuals and groups of individuals acting as inventors and innovators, driven by their compulsions for self-expression and material gain, operating within a context which in England, by the cumulative accidents of history, made it possible.

The conditions necessary for England to lead the world in irreversible change, based upon an increase and extension of productivity, can certainly be listed. But they continue to defy satisfactory synthesis. England had achieved cultural and political unity generations earlier, with property well protected at least since 1688 against both private theft and state expropriation; the rule of law, although not free of class bias, was closer to natural justice than in most countries. England had long been successful in overseas trade, and by the later 18th century London was taking from Amsterdam the role of the world's leading money market. There was a vigorous middle class, with a strong individualist tradition, willing to accept commercial and industrial risks. Agriculture was undergoing a revolution based upon enclosure, producing larger and more efficient farms, able to take advantage of new systems of cultivation and animal husbandry. The population had been rising from about the mid-century, providing an expanding labour force. Mechanical ingenuity thrived both among artisans such as the millwrights and among middle- and upper-class men who were incited by the great burst of Western

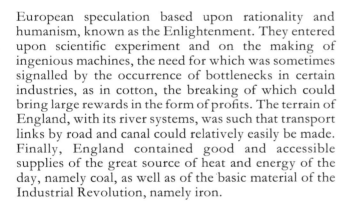

The industrial slavery of women and children: in 1842 (above) baskets of coal were still dragged along the mine tunnels on runners, with children, able to stand upright, pushing from behind. Children were also used in the spinning mills (right) where they could creep underneath the 'mules', which drew out and twisted the threads.

European speculation based upon rationality and humanism, known as the Enlightenment. They entered upon scientific experiment and on the making of ingenious machines, the need for which was sometimes signalled by the occurrence of bottlenecks in certain industries, as in cotton, the breaking of which could bring large rewards in the form of profits. The terrain of England, with its river systems, was such that transport links by road and canal could relatively easily be made. Finally, England contained good and accessible supplies of the great source of heat and energy of the day, namely coal, as well as of the basic material of the Industrial Revolution, namely iron.

The three phases of change

Before we can consider the effects on the lives of the English of the eager exploitation by men of business of the opportunities thus presented, it is necessary to consider the general nature and phasing of their impact. Three formative periods can be identified.

There was the Industrial Revolution (roughly 1780 to 1830), some fifty years in which appeared the factory system in cotton and woollen manufactures (the dazzling epitome of the new modes of production), together with feats of engineering, road and canal building, accompanied by dramatic increases in output in coal, iron, metal wares, weaponry, ships and food production. There had been almost continuous war from 1793 to 1815 with Revolutionary and Napoleonic France, during which the British state as purchaser became a major source of economic stimulus and distortion.

Secondly, with the late 1830s began the Victorian age, reaching its peak in the 1870s or 1880s. This was

the time of British world supremacy, reflected in the *Pax Britannica*, sustained and enforced by the Royal Navy, but resting ultimately on the great lead in productivity Britain had gained, based on industrialized production. But even at this peak of confidence and assertion there were misgivings. What was the new materialism and the new science (especially that of Darwin) doing to the fabric of belief, of society, of the family? What of the inequalities of wealth and income, becoming yet more gross as productivity increased? What of the great social defaults in the form of bad housing and the physical deterioration of the poorer classes?

Thirdly, in the 1870s and 1880s Britain entered upon her phase of economic maturity, a condition in which dependence upon industrial production and exports, together with the urban way of life, was far advanced. Foreign rivalry in output and in trade was asserting itself as the British lead was first narrowed and then lost. Agriculture, having been prosperous for a generation or more, was confronted with a flood of cheap cereals from the great plains of North America, carried to Britain by railway and steamship. The industrialized labour force had found an organized identity both industrially through the trade unions and politically through the franchise. As real incomes failed to grow significantly in the new century there were great waves of unrest. It was in this situation that the Liberal government elected in 1906 embarked upon a programme of welfare provision including old age pensions (1908) and unemployment insurance (1911). Meanwhile France as the hereditary enemy had yielded place to Germany, newly unified in 1870 under Prussian leadership: this meant that the demands of the army,

237

By the *1880s* England's competitors, in Europe, America and
Japan, were outstripping her, producing in England poverty and
unemployment and even displacing British goods on the home market.
Pressures grew for some form of economic protection.

alternation between prosperity and depression. This
overall pulsing of the system meant that the men of
business were brought under discipline by the
possibility of credit curtailment and bankruptcy in the
down-swing and crisis: they naturally sought to ease
their position by exerting downward pressure on wages
and by the discharge of workers. On the labour side the
unions resisted such pressures in depression, and
pressed for a larger share in times of prosperity. It was
preoccupation with this cycle that tended to dominate
the minds of both employers and workers, rather than
the trends inherent in the longer term.

The business dynamic

The men of business, seizing upon the opportunities
provided by trade and technology, remade the face of
England. It was they who inspired the phrases 'a nation
of shopkeepers' (filched by a contemptuous Napoleon
from Adam Smith's *Wealth of Nations*), and 'the
workshop of the world'. The greater shopkeepers were
the merchants and financiers, standing in a long
tradition going back to medieval times. The masters of
the workshops and factories were a new breed of men
who organized industry. In important ways their
outlook and value systems were different from those of
the merchant princes. The latter had long ago learned
that the way to status and power was to acquire land,
and that the way to acceptance was by judicious
marriages into impecunious noble families. This was
reinforced by adopting the landed ethos, together with
the Church of England and the élitist education of the
public schools and Oxford and Cambridge universities.

The new industrialists, on the other hand, were a
brasher lot altogether. In Manchester, Birmingham and
elsewhere they believed in their own set of values, often
Nonconformist in religion and hostile to landed
privileges and pretensions. In a sense they were the core
of Liberal England, whereas the grander merchants and
the monied men gravitated, generation by generation,
toward the Conservatives. Of course there were traders
on the smaller end of the scale, especially the
'shopkeepers' in the narrow sense: their sympathies
approximated more to those of the industrialists. These
lesser traders, together with the clerks, constituted the
petty bourgeoisie.

It was mainly among the industrialists and the petty
bourgeoisie that evangelicalism thrived, although it
also had a strong working-class base through Methodism, the Baptists and other Nonconformist sects. It was
a religious dynamic going back through the 18th
century, which stressed the need for an active
proselytizing and a spreading of the good news of God,
together with a responsibility for doing good works in
earthly life for the benefit of the less fortunate members
of society. Evangelicalism evades definitive analysis,
but it was real enough. The desire to do good took a
compelling hold on a section of the English middle
classes: among the Quakers and Unitarians and other
Protestant sects there arose business families eager to

and especially the navy, added pressure to the budget.
Within the United Kingdom itself there was threat of
civil war, with Protestants and Catholics arming against
each other in Ireland.

The English, when overtaken by world war in
August 1914, were in many ways a deeply divided
people. And yet they were not polarized. There was still
a real sense of identity, as their near-unanimity in
embracing the war demonstrated. Parliamentary
democracy was still the pride of the English people:
only a very few ardent anarchists and syndicalists
wished to see it destroyed. The very complexity of the
groups that composed the English people in their phase
of industrial maturity was a prophylactic against simple
polarization. It was reinforced by the continuous
tendency of successive governments to make political,
industrial and welfare concessions to relieve the
pressure points. Governments followed the responsive
rather than the innovative mode. Although there was
great debate over each such capitulation, governments
could make them down to 1914, secure in the belief that
they were still a fair way from the limits of concession.
There was, by now, lurking in the background and
haunting this conciliatory pragmatism, the question:
how far could governments go in impairing the market
system and its basis, private property, before it would
break down, making it necessary to find a new set of
foundations upon which to rest the economy and
society?

Within the general phasing of these three periods
there was the trade cycle: the roughly decennial

improve the condition of England as with William Wilberforce, the Booths, the Rowntrees, the Cadburys and the Chamberlains. Evangelicalism converged from the 1860s with the rise of social science, thus combining attempts at economic and social theory with systematic gathering of data. Even when evangelicalism entered into its phase of secularization in the later 19th century, as with Sidney and Beatrice Webb and the Fabian Society, the redemptive urge, although now cut free of the soul and its needs, continued to be powerful in English life.

In the age of industrial maturity from the 1880s there were increasing signs that the ethos of the landed men was penetrating deep into the entrepreneurial class, especially where success and wealth were extended over several generations. There was a tendency to buy estates, to take up the pursuits of the countryside, to lose interest in business and to decline to put money at risk in adopting new ventures and in modifying old ones. A large part of English ownership and management, having attained status and comfort, thus lost the urge to pursue wealth and self-expression through industry and trade. Some, especially in the older heavy industries, had become potentates, whose self-view led to irresponsiveness and a failure to see the future of their industry as a whole. As against this, however, a new set of businessmen, with the old energies and eagerness, was coming into being to exploit the second great cluster of inventions then coming on stream, especially in chemicals, electricity and the application of the new internal combustion engine.

Commerce: its achievements and its creed

The economic achievements of the men of commerce and the industrialists were of course interrelated. The ability of merchants to penetrate foreign markets (thus acquiring the means to pay for imports of food and raw materials) depended in large measure on industrial performance, namely the ability of manufacturers to supply a range of goods which would sell abroad at prevailing price levels. It is true that as the Empire expanded certain markets for British goods extended, especially in India and Africa: indeed Britain's trading surplus with India was an important means whereby she could meet her deficits with other countries. On the whole, however, the ability to sell abroad depended in large measure on industrial efficiency and the provision of merchanting services such as finance and insurance. This was particularly the case with engineering products and shipbuilding, especially when other countries such as Germany and the United States began to rival England.

The export achievement was indeed remarkable. By 1914 Britain had accumulated between £3,500 and £4,000 millions of assets abroad, the fruit of her commercial and industrial success. The interest and dividends on this world-wide nest-egg further strengthened the British balance of payments. Because

Britain had adopted free trade from the 1830s, culminating in the 1850s, with no interference with capital movements, her large international earnings were continuously recycled, thus sustaining and powering the world trading system.

This was greatly to Britain's benefit. But so favourable was the world trading opportunity that her men of business, uninhibited by government, committed her more and more to supplying its needs. It seemed right that success should be followed up: the few voices warning of the precariousness thus being generated were unheaded. Never, indeed, has any market-based economy stood back from the opportunity to sell. So it was that Britain was committed by her business men to a range of world markets, to a structure of production and to a regional distribution of population appropriate to her brief period of ascendancy, but which could become immense liabilities when her world trading dominance faded.

The liberal economic creed represented the philosophy of a nation of shopkeepers and workshop masters in their age of ascendancy. It had four major components. These were free trade, an automatic monetary system based upon the gold standard, the balanced budget and a refusal by the state to operate on the distribution of incomes by regulating wages. These were the four pillars of the Gladstonian economy: all four were still firmly in place when war came in 1914. Only one of them had been brought under serious threat: Joseph Chamberlain in 1906 urged a return to the tariff as the basis for a programme of governmental economic management, but his campaign suffered heavy electoral defeat.

Although the four great liberal pillars stood intact until the First World War, there were three senses in which the liberal philosophy was being outflanked. The provision of welfare was widening as one area of social dereliction after another became apparent. Secondly, as welfare and warfare competed for resources, the tax system and the principles on which it rested came under question: the progressive principle was adopted with respect to the inheritance tax in 1894 and in 1906 as affecting the income tax. Thirdly, successive governments were making concessions to labour, on both the industrial and political fronts. At all three levels the business men had to find a response. Because of the differences in the situation of the various groups, there was a wide divergence. Broadly speaking, by the later 19th century those in the older lines of production, for example, cotton, certain branches of engineering and shipbuilding, had difficulty in meeting the demands made upon them by their labour, for the threat to their share of world markets meant that they stood for minimal welfare expenditure and consequent taxation. The generation of new-style industrialists, in chemicals, glass, tobacco, soap, oil, automobiles, and large-scale retail trade, with a more secure home market, were much more self-confident.

Men and machines

Meanwhile, in consequence of the actions of the business men, new modes of work and new modes of life were asserting themselves.

It was the factories and mines which epitomized the new industrialized conditions. Men, women and children were gathered together in great numbers to provide the human skills and muscle necessary to serve the machines, the engines and the handling gear. Even though the factory system depended upon getting a higher output per unit of labour input than ever before, using improved equipment and organization, it was highly labour intensive, concentrating human effort in productive units of unprecedented size. Factories under these conditions had to be highly structured both in plan and in operation: the humans they ingested became integrated with the machines and with the clock. This was a relationship which all too readily lent itself to debasement through prolonged hours, speeding up of machinery, bad ventilation, exposure to accident, disease and deformity, together with vacuity of mind and the disruption of home life through the employment of women.

The mines provided an even more fearsome potential for human degradation. To be sure, there were no machines to set their relentless tempo, because of the inevitably manual nature of the task of coal getting; the new technology took the form of improved lifting and haulage gear together with ventilation and lighting. But there were the ever-present dangers of roof falls, explosion and flooding, suffocation and lung disease, hazards that were often increased with improved production methods. To these must be added the unstable nature of the markets for coal, making

Back yard of a London slum, 1878. The old Georgian terrace is given over to multiple occupation and a gas-works invades the garden.

employment and wage levels precarious and aggravating conflicts between owners and miners.

In the workshops, especially in engineering, a different atmosphere could prevail. Here mass production of textiles or fuel was not the requirement – instead each job had at least a degree of uniqueness, carried out by skilled men. The same was true of the shipyards, where master craftsmen enjoyed respect and a reasonable income. The workshops provided the machines for mass production in the factories, together with the steam engine and machine tools – machines for making machines. The men on whose skill they depended organized themselves from 1824 onward in craft unions, regulating entry, demarcating jobs and bargaining over wages, thus ensuring themselves a share in the benefits of higher productivity.

On the wider scene most of the English were still engaged in the 1850s and later in occupations prevalent before the Industrial Revolution – making boots and shoes, clothing and hats, saddlery, metal products of great diversity, barrels, paints and carts and coaches, as well as putting up houses, churches and public buildings, running shops and warehouses. This vast miscellany of tasks did not attract the attention focused upon the factory system and the mines, for they, like engineering, did not generate the same abuses and labour struggles. They contained various proportions of skilled and unskilled labour.

By the 1830s two great sets of issues stood between the workers and their employers, namely the conditions of work and the level of wages. The abuses of the factories and mines were dramatically brought to public attention by a series of royal commissions inquiring into hours and intensity of work, the treatment and schooling of children, ventilation and space, dangerous machinery and indeed all aspects of working conditions. Terrible examples of human abuse were brought to light.

The state had no experience in regulating such matters. But by the Factory Act of 1833 and the Mines Act of 1844 it was committed to regulation and inspection, extended by a continuing series of statutes. Each had to be fought through in its own time and under its own conditions. The initial Bill typically was weakened, with major provisions being deleted in the face of the opposition of most factory and mine owners. But each moved forward the frontier of control, bit by bit. In its early stages this was largely a middle-class achievement, brought about by the pressure of philanthropists, with allies from the landed class. Owners in general complained that such regulation would raise costs and thus slow economic growth. They were also deeply resentful that the state should intervene in their activities, intruding into the relationship between them and their workers. But some began to learn that the rudiments of good management lay in a work force made efficient and co-operative by better conditions.

By the later 19th century philanthropic zeal as the

force behind regulation was replaced by the workers' own pressure through their unions. Also regulation was extended far beyond the factories and mines, for example by the Factory and Workshops Act of 1867. But a basic problem remained, namely how far should the state go, in each of the various lines of production, in imposing improved conditions?

The other great issue between workers and employers was the level of wages. Here too the state could not avoid adjudication. But having abandoned all participation in wage fixing in 1813, governments declined to be drawn back into the wages arena. Instead they operated indirectly on this crucial matter by setting the rules of the contest between capital and labour, doing so through trade union law. Down to 1824 unions were completely illegal: in that year this general disability was removed, but a further Act of 1825 introduced a host of ambiguities. There followed a struggle that still goes on, to define the limits of trade union powers against recalcitrant workers as to picketing and the closed shop, and as to the liability of the unions for losses caused by their strikes.

Highlights of this complex struggle stand out. There were the two Acts of 1871 which made the legality and legal status of the unions secure. The Act of 1875 cleared the unions of the danger of being charged with strikes being conspiracies against the public (provided the dispute was a specific one with a given group of employers); it also permitted picketing for the purpose of providing information. The Trades Disputes Act of 1906 was crucial: henceforth the unions under no circumstances were to be held responsible for torts, that is for civil wrongs for which damages could be claimed: the losses caused by strikes, from 1906 onward, were to be borne by the employers, third parties or the community.

So it was that the state stayed outside of wage determination, a posture approved by politicians, trade unionists and capitalists alike. The result was that the battle of strikes and lockouts, particularly bitter in coal, engineering and the docks, went on without state intervention, except insofar as police and the military were occasionally used, as in the coal-mining village of Tonypandy in 1910 to restore order.

The outcome in terms of wage levels was a highly complex one. The skilled men, of course, did best, especially when after 1850 they adopted the 'New Model' principle of going for carefully defined objectives. Indeed they gained fairly continuously from the 1830s to 1914 in terms of real wages, although the improvements enjoyed were slight after 1900. The unskilled (their ranks increased by the immigrant Irish) made few gains before the mid-century: thereafter, in general their real incomes improved to a degree, but they were always subject to the cyclical instability of the economy and to the longer-running difficulties of industrial maturity from the later 19th century.

Behind all this lay the haunting fear of unemployment and the workhouse. In the 1880s the semi- and

Throughout the 19th century private charity and public organization battled with the problems of urban poverty. Here soup-tickets are given out in 1886.

unskilled men began to form their own 'industrial' unions. At the same time there was a return to ideology in this newly expanding part of the trade union world, including various forms of socialism, communism, anarchism and syndicalism, providing the rationale for a small but dedicated minority of disrupters. The frightening outburst of industrial unrest from 1911 to 1913 was made possible by these developments. But the craft unions continued to be cautious about revolutionary or even radical proposals.

Social classes: the widening gulf

No less important than wages and the conditions of work were the new conditions of living in the industrial cities. Here, as in the factories and mines, there was serious deterioration before action could be undertaken to ease it. In all of the fast-growing industrial towns of the north, and in London, there developed dense slums, where overcrowded houses and lack of water and sanitation spread disease and debility. Inevitably it was those who were the least skilled who accumulated in such places. They had not even such communal support as had been present in the English and Irish countryside. The supply of housing accommodation, in spite of the pressure upon it, did not increase, except by subdivision – there was no incentive to build on the scale required because people would not have been able to afford to pay for the improved conditions. Drunkenness was widely prevalent, a means of escape which merely made the realities more difficult to deal

Before the coming of the railways a network of canals had linked the country's rivers, making it possible to transport heavy goods wherever they were needed.

with. The family, so often capable of sustaining men, women and children in adversity, too often broke down. Once demoralization had overtaken the family or the individual a self-confirming fate asserted itself. Some sought escape through crime, but most became what the middle classes called the residuum and what Marx called the lumpenproletariat. They were a challenge to the consciences of the middle classes, as well as being a threat to the civil peace and even, perhaps, to political stability.

These factors interacted to cause fearful scenes of suffering and degradation of the kind depicted by Dickens and others. They have their parallel today in the cities of the Third World as they experience the relentless impact of industrialization.

But not all of the working class lived in slums. The more skilled men could rent or acquire their modest villas and achieve standards of comfort and security on which the future of their children could be built. Such men could base their personalities on the dignity of their craftsmanship, their wives could embellish their modest homes, their children could have some hope of wider horizons through education. The family as a whole could enjoy a degree of leisure, holidays and changes of scene made possible by cheap excursion trains.

To all of this the longer-term budgeting involved in improving the family's housing was crucial: this could be helped by saving through the saving banks and the Friendly Societies, sustained very often by the mother's determination to keep her family 'respectable', with a code of cleanliness and behaviour which distinguished it as sharply as possible from that of the slum dweller.

Close to the artisan, both as neighbours and in ethos were the growing army of the petty bourgeoisie, the clerks and the small shopkeepers.

Between the respectable working class and the slum dwellers there was, of course, a large middle ground where respectability and fecklessness mingled as individuals and their families struggled with their fate. The areas of the cities where this occurred tended to be middle ground in the spatial as in the social sense.

The prosperous middle classes were, of course, a further urban component. Before Victoria they often lived within the cities, but increasingly from the 1830s they removed themselves from the urban deterioration which their enterprises had created. They progressed typically westward, clear of the smoke, effluvia, noise, drunkenness and crime. They built more and more impressive houses on their westward march, until a good many had passed beyond the urban perimeter to become quasi-country gentlemen. Social abdication and the urban morphology that reflected it inevitably meant that the class pattern in one sense became more stark. But in another way the very segregation of classes, with wealth and poverty largely invisible to one another, reduced the levels of social envy and social conscience. There was, too, an effect on civic government: continuous physical withdrawal from the city by the prosperous meant, with some notable exceptions, that civic government often passed to the hands of business men of the second or third order. On the other hand, the middle-class men who ruled the cities had no compunction about enforcing a rigorous system of law and order. At a more general level it can be argued that had the upper middle class remained committed to the life of the cities where its wealth was generated it would have been much more concerned with the need to counter social deterioration and to enter upon a planned approach to the shape and nature of urban life, perhaps calling to its aid the central government.

The social and spatial configuration of the English cities reflected the prevailing pattern of industrial and political power. Not until this had shifted in favour of the working classes, and not until a degree of consensus had developed among the working classes themselves, was it possible, from the later 19th century onward, to substitute a controlled surveillance of English civic life for the market principles that had dominated most of Victoria's reign.

But the potential for such control must not be overestimated. There were long-term forces at work inherent in the trend of technology that were scarcely detected, let alone brought under control. One of the most potent of these had to do with transport, that great remaker of patterns of population and occupation. The railway revolutionized the long haul; the short haul, by horsepowered carts, remained unchanged throughout the 19th century. A combination of greatly cheapened long-distance carriage and of dear (and getting dearer) short hauls, lay behind the agglomerative process that brought into being cities of the new scale of size and concentration, tying the majority of the labour force close to their jobs, and determining the fundamental shape and nature of urban life.

The fight against poverty

The conditions of urban living, like those of working, could not evolve in a wholly autonomous manner. Inevitably, as the worst aspects of deterioration manifested themselves they induced societal and political responses. These took place at both the central and local governmental levels. Initiatives from above (the Parliament at Westminster) and from below (local government) converged to produce a programme of amelioration that was both complex and typically in arrears of needs, involving a transfer of resources from the rest of society to the social casualties.

The only legally required social provision when the Industrial Revolution overtook England was the Poor Law, governed by statutes reaching back to Tudor times, under which each parish, with its guardians and overseers, was to provide not only for the 'impotent' (namely the aged, the orphans, the incapable and the lunatic), but also, under certain conditions, for the able-bodied unemployed.

Over the centuries the Poor Law went through cycles of rigour and relief, in one phase being tightened and in the next being eased, depending on prevailing conditions, ideas and political configurations. The later 18th and early 19th centuries were a time of easing, as represented in general by the Speenhamland System (of 1795) under which the poor, suffering wartime conditions, were relieved in a manner which by the standards of the day were generous, with an easing of the tests of eligibility. But by the 1830s opinion had veered round to the idea that the Poor Law should be greatly stiffened: this was done under the Poor Law Act of 1834. Relief to the able-bodied was now only to be given within the workhouse, and it was to be governed by the principle of 'less eligibility', under which the best-treated recipient of poor relief was to be less well off than the lowest-paid worker, thus opening up a 'deterrent gap' that was intended to stop the award of relief from damaging the incentive to work. In addition the regime of the workhouses was to be tightened up, including segregation of the sexes and the breaking up of families and the performing of labouring tasks. The principles of 1834 were to be the basic official central government doctrine right through to 1914, although with some easing modifications.

These principles were indeed harsh, intended by their largely middle-class promotors to purge society of the threat of a debauched labour force. But the attempt to avoid one kind of social decay could produce another, namely a debased system of workhouses destructive of the dignity of both masters and inmates, in which the inhumanity of the one and the dejection and disintegration of character of the other could cause a cumulative mutal debasement. Scandalous reports

from time to time reached the public; Dickens and others attacked the workhouses. The hatred and resentment of the workhouses among the labouring classes combined with a determination, as the authors of the Act had intended, to avoid them at all costs.

But there was a third working-class response. It was resistance. Many of the guardians and overseers, especially in the industrial-urban north, soon realized that any attempt to enforce the Poor Law in its full rigour would not only be iniquitous, given the fluctuating nature of employment, but would also be dangerous, with the prospect of rioting. Accordingly, the award of poor relief outside of the workhouse was common, together with other easements. The Poor Law commissioners in London tried to insist on the 'principles', but the local implementors often went their own way, producing an enormous variety of provision over the country. In the later 1860s the commissioners made an attempt to restore rigour and uniformity. But in the 1890s the Local Government Board, which had taken over responsibility for the Poor Law in 1871, introduced a greater humanity into the system, providing a range of 'comforts'. Between 1905 and 1909 a royal commission sat on the Poor Law, instructed to ascertain the real position and to advise the government on what should be done. The Majority Report, although it made useful structural proposals, was infused with the old fear that too gentle a handling of the poor would destroy their moral fibre; the Minority Report saw poverty as a misfortune rather than a moral failure, giving its victims a moral entitlement to a reasonable standard of living. The government of the day, confronted by these antithetical views, did nothing. The workhouse continued to be a dominant social reality, the threatening and resented background of a large part of working-class life.

In the new century, however, there were two radical innovations. In 1908 the reforming Liberal government, under the influence of Lloyd George, lifted one important category of social need outside the Poor Law, namely the aged. Old age pensions, modest to be sure, but paid as of right, were introduced in that year. The aged were thus made an explicit and largely unconditional charge on the nation. But the able-bodied unemployed were too big a responsibility for even Lloyd George to impose wholly upon the state. Instead, the Unemployment Insurance Act of 1911 adopted a combination of the insurance principle, and that of shared participation: workers would subscribe voluntarily to an insurance fund, thus giving them unemployment benefit as of right; their employers would also contribute, as would the state. Down to 1914 it seemed as though this tripartite formula was the answer to unemployment, with the fund in comfortable credit.

What, however, of the conditions prevalent in the cities in which, from 1851 onward, the majority of the English were to live? Two related considerations forced themselves upon the attention of governments and city councils, namely those of health and efficiency. Health made its impact first. The slums, very serious by 1830, posed the health problem in its most pressing form, with high death rates and the danger of infection for the population as a whole, including the middle classes.

The core of the problem was the disposal of wastes, both human and industrial. The human, being the more pressing, was dealt with first. This involved the establishment of systems of sanitation, based on cart haulage and increasingly on sewers. The latter required water in great quantity. So it was that city governments had to turn to massive schemes of infrastructural provision, borrowing in the money market and making the debt a charge on the rates. The provision of water supply and sanitation is indeed a great constructional saga, the drama of which is hidden beneath the streets. The reform of local government under the Act of 1835 helped to make this possible. Industrial wastes, of vast bulk, were a different matter. Enormous heaps of slag and other wastes accumulated in city and country, casually left by the firms concerned, becoming permanent features of the industrial landscape. Only the wastes from the more noxious chimneys were brought under measure of control, beginning with the first Alkali Act of 1863.

The efficiency of the labour force of course depended in large measure upon its health; the realization was dawning by the 1840s that sickness was a leading cause of pauperization of the family. Edwin Chadwick's *General Report on the Sanitary Condition of the Labouring Population of Great Britain* of 1842 was the precursor of the Public Health Act of 1848. It set up a General Board of Health in London: this was to encourage local authorities to establish Boards of Health and to appoint Medical Officers of Health, and to undertake water and sanitation schemes. In 1854 the Board of Health was greatly weakened, largely through local government hostility, and in 1858 it ceased. But in the same year the Medical Department of the Privy Council was founded. Its head, John Simon, a man of both tact and drive, promoted a whole range of legislation, affecting sanitation, epidemics, burials, food defilement and adulteration, and venereal diseases. Public Health Acts of 1872 and 1875 extended and codified the health provisions.

The efficiency argument received a great stimulus from the Second South African War (1899–1902). It was found that two out of every five intending recruits to the army were below the standard set. An Interdepartmental Committee on Physical Deterioration in 1904 confirmed that there was indeed ground for alarm and need for action. It was a serious matter that two-fifths of the imperial race should be unfit. But the science of nutrition had scarcely begun. Even more important, it soon became clear that physical standards depended upon diet and housing, and that these two matters depended upon income, which in turn led to fundamental questions concerning the division of the

national product between classes and within the working class. In consequence, diet (apart from the beginning of school meals in 1906), together with housing, were left to the operation of the market.

There was, however, one aspect of efficiency on which the state could act without being drawn into an unlimited and irreversible involvement in the economy and the social structure. This was education. Elementary provision first became the subject of serious national report in 1861; the recommendations of the Newcastle Commission were the basis of the Revised Education Code of 1862. The Department of Education now assumed a central role. Government grants were made subject to tests of cost-effectiveness, based on the examination system, and supervised by inspectors: thus the examination system entered the lives of English children and, indeed, their parents.

But the basic difficulty was one of coverage: the Church of England had its system of schools, as did the various Nonconformist denominations. The rivalry between the two was bitter, but it did serve to generate zeal. The government could coerce neither faction. Accordingly, when in the great Education Act of 1870 it sought to make elementary education universal, it could only do so by accepting the presence of the two rival systems and filling the gaps. It did the latter by establishing its own set of schools under School Boards throughout the country. Elementary schooling was made compulsory in 1880 and from 1891 it was made free. So was laid the basis for general elementary literacy in England.

The Education Act of 1902 wound up the School Boards, passing elementary education directly to the local authorities, and making it a charge on the rates. Each local authority was to set up an education committee. The formerly 'voluntary' schools were to continue to be under their managers who would, as in the past, control religious education within them, but would in all other aspects of education carry out the directions of the Local Education Committee. The religious education stipulation brought bitter resentment and passive resistance from the Nonconformists who objected that their rates should support the pernicious doctrines of the Church of England. The Act also improved the provision for secondary education by bringing the smaller, older grammar schools within the education committee's control and financing them, and by encouraging the foundation of new grammar schools. But the Act failed to respond to the challenge of improving scientific and technical education.

Class and politics

As the forces of change released by the Industrial Revolution worked themselves out in the many ways that have been considered, the great questions of power and consent were continuously present. Broadly speaking, the pattern of power passed through three phases: from dominance by the land-based aristocracy

The need for universal elementary education was admitted, but the existence of rival church schools for some time stood in the way of a state system. In July 1870, the year of the Education Act, 'Punch' published this cartoon, with Mr Punch protesting to a policeman (John Bull): 'Yes, it's all very well to say, Go to school! How are they to go to school with these people quarrelling in the doorway? Why don't you make them move on?'

and gentry of England, to the commercial and industrial middle classes, to be challenged in their turn by the emergence of labour. This progression represented, of course, a pattern of continuously widening participation in power. It may be that the process of industrialization makes this inevitable, because of the need for consent, made more pressing by the vulnerability of a system resting upon an ever-sophisticating technology to disruptive action by organized groups. The British state thus found itself making more and more concessions to labour power, each being used as the springboard to the next. Similarly with the electoral franchise: the Great Reform Bill of 1832 admitted the middle classes to participation in the state; that of 1867 did the same for the urban male skilled worker and that of 1884 widened the franchise yet further, bringing in the agricultural labourer. With each such extension the appeal made to the electorate by the political parties had to become wider; the result was a continuously expanding bidding for votes. Political and industrial concessions interacted: a widening of the franchise in favour of labour meant that further industrial concessions would follow.

It is, of course, argued by some that the entire system was one of exploitation of the worker by the ruling class or classes. It is certainly true that elements of real power resided in the landed and industrial interests, that these were often exploitative, and that in the short and medium term at least the wielders of power had available means of obfuscation, persuasion and social control that could fortify their position. But these were never unlimited and they were always subject to the long-term forces of erosion.

However the demanding and making of concessions clearly cannot go on indefinitely. Eventually the power positions are reversed, with the former suppliant dominant. The English by 1914 were still a considerable distance from this. The Liberal government in power when war came had been seeking a balance of class that would represent some kind of equilibrium between the surviving elements of landed and especially industrial and financial power, and the aspirations of labour as organized politically and industrially. Lloyd George's Liberalism was prepared to depart a long way from that of Gladstone, especially in the direction of welfare expenditure and away from minimal government, but it was still Gladstonian in honouring the four great canons of economic policy that had been built into the Liberal creed when British industrialists enjoyed world leadership. On the Labour side the feeling by 1914 was that there were so many concessions still to be sought that a positive and specified programme was not yet a pressing matter.

The distortions and aggravations of war

The First World War brought a suspension of debate, and of the traditional liberal values, although not altogether of internal stresses. The state became the organizer of the economy and of the labour force, largely under the Ministry of Munitions, and the controller of civil liberties under the Defence of the Realm Act. Because governmental spending outran tax income and state borrowing ability, as it had done in the war against Napoleon, and with the gold standard suspended, prices rose steeply and the national debt greatly increased. Some industries, especially shipbuilding and heavy engineering, together with cotton, were stimulated by wartime need and post-war shortage at the very time they should, in the longer perspective, have been contracting in favour of newer lines of production. Markets were lost to competitors, especially in the Far East. Labour, although it had

245

largely accepted the government's priorities during the war, had become much better organized and more powerful, able to state its claims more effectively, and to press for them. The Labour Party in 1918 adopted a new constitution; Clause IV pledged the party to the nationalization of the means of production, distribution and exchange. In the same year the vote was extended to all males over 21, and to females over 30; in 1928 women were enfranchised on the same basis as men. By and large the English people had accepted the necessity to fight Germany. They did so on the basis of the need to stop a continental aggressor with a strong militaristic and imperialistic drive, together with the challenge to respond to Germany's violation of the neutrality of Belgium as guaranteed by England. Once hostilities had fully developed there seemed no escape until the war was won – the men at the front had to be supplied and those who had been killed could not be betrayed.

Thus it was that the vast tragedy of the First World War weakened the place of England in the world, distorted her economy at a time when adjustment was essential, destroyed much of her overseas wealth and lost her important markets. Moreover it left her with an unprecedented inflation, and with the confrontational psychology in industrial relations developed in the 19th century as strong as ever. Germany had been defeated, but England had been irreparably weakened.

The years between the wars

How was England to respond to her new situation? Her politicians and people did so almost instinctively: they chose to try to return to what now seemed to be the halcyon days of late Victorian and Edwardian times. The wartime controls were hastily abandoned. Deflation was imposed in order to make it possible to return to the gold standard at the pre-war parity in 1925. This was done in the hope that London would resume its place as the money market of the world. Freedom of trade was resumed. The demand by the miners that the inefficient coal industry be nationalized was fobbed off. Capacity in shipbuilding and cotton was further extended. Nostalgia rather than analysis ruled in both government and business.

The collapse of the post-war boom in 1921 partly revealed the precariousness of England's position. But it was the General Strike of 1926 that showed the stresses that had developed. It lasted only nine days, although the coal miners stayed out for eight months. The trade unions gained nothing, except perhaps an addition to their legend; indeed Stanley Baldwin's Conservative Trade Union Act of 1927 was a serious set-back for them. Although the unions largely abandoned overt militancy between 1926 and 1939, they continued to gain in strength as a new pattern of very large unions emerged, led by Ernest Bevin and his Transport and General Workers Union.

The world crisis that had begun with the collapse of the Wall Street stock market in October 1929 forced the British government into new lines of policy. The gold standard and free trade, two great pillars of Gladstonian economics, were abandoned in 1931: it was *force majeure* that brought the new perspective. The government reverted to the mercantilism that Adam Smith had so soundly condemned in his *Wealth of Nations* over a century and a half earlier. A tariff was adopted and was vigorously manipulated, there was an attempt to revive the Empire as a system of trading preference reminiscent of the Navigation Acts, and the government supported industry in an effort to cartelize international markets.

The tariff, together with a system of bilateral treaties, achieved some limited successes, but Britain in this connection must bear her share of blame for the rise of a protective system which strangled world trade as a whole. The rehabilitation of the Empire as a trading entity, tried at the Commonwealth Conference in Ottawa in 1932, had no real success. Attempts to organize markets in the Pacific with the Japanese, and in Europe with Germany, failed. The new freedom to use the monetary mechanism to generate demand (now that the gold standard had been abandoned) was not exploited: much to the annoyance of John Maynard Keynes the pound sterling was not manipulated, nor were budgetary deficits adopted to stimulate demand at home. The governmental response to world conditions after 1931 was thus to seek a larger share of world trade by various forms of protectionism and market manipulation, a course very dangerous for a country so dependent on international trade.

From 1931 unemployment, already chronic for ten years, became very much worse as world trade and aggregate demand remorselessly contracted. Unemployment insurance and various other devices provided protection against the worst deprivation, but there was much wastage of human potential and much loss of human dignity. The means adopted by the government to stimulate trade could do little to ease this vast burden of unemployment. The programme of subsidized housing provided some relief, as well as improving living conditions, but it was not enough. There were programmes for the restructuring of sectors of English industry, as in shipbuilding, coal, steel and cotton; although something was achieved, the real need was for a recovery of markets. Only with the coming of rearmament in the later 1930s was the situation eased.

Yet for all this England was still the possessor of a great empire, and was numbered among the great powers. Her people were still proud of their nation, and perhaps in particular of their parliamentary system. Although the older industries were in serious difficulty, newer ones were rapidly developing, involving automobiles, chemicals and electricity in their many manifestations (including artificial fibres and the wireless) and retail trade. Indeed by 1938 it was not the state of the economy and society that was worrying, but the fear that the country was about to be overtaken by another and even more terrible war.

Stop-go and 'stagflation'

The Second World War was indeed a fearful affair. It required that Britain strain every sinew to produce the means, first to stand alone against Hitler's Germany, and then to take a full part in the great campaign of European liberation. Once more her heavy industry was stimulated against her longer-term interests, her foreign reserves were used up, her price levels and debt raised. Labour, too, continued to gain in stature, as mobilized by Ernest Bevin. Although labour in general, as in 1914 to 1918, accepted the justice and indeed the unavoidability of the war, it rejected the political philosophy of Conservatism, and the leadership of Winston Churchill, bringing in the Labour government of Clement Attlee in 1945. The Trade Union Act of 1927 was at once repealed. Meanwhile, both politicians and bureaucrats had accepted Keynesian ideas that the state should accept responsibility for the stability of the economy, to be brought about by monetary and fiscal means, together with William Beveridge's ideas about welfare (enshrined in the Beveridge Report of 1942), based on the idea of a basic level of provision below which no one should fall.

In the peace, however, these two commitments meant that governments found it very difficult to maintain a stable path. There was a succession of stop-go policies: when the economy became too active, causing balance of payments difficulties and a threat to sterling, it was necessary to cut expenditure and contract the credit supply; the reverse was necessary when aggregate demand was insufficient. At the same time public expenditure rose continuously. The growth of the public sector thus caused was further extended by the Labour Party's programme of nationalization, starting in 1946: coal, steel, the railways, airways, gas, electricity, atomic energy, all were taken over and placed under boards. Because of Conservative objections to public ownership, some industries were in and out of nationalization, as with steel and road haulage.

On the whole, however, in spite of the distortions of war, the difficulties of keeping the economy stable, and the struggle over public ownership, the general trend was upward. England, although not performing so dramatically as West Germany or Japan, did well.

Although the philosophy of the trade unions was still confrontational, this did not do serious damage while the world economy and Britain's trading position within it were satisfactory. All manner of social provisions was made, including the National Health Service; the educational system, including the universities, was much extended. There were regional policies aimed at spreading prosperity and employment so that not too much of it was pre-empted by London and the south-east and the West Midlands. Much of the housing stock was renewed and a national system of motorways built. The exploitation of North Sea oil opened an unexpected new and highly prosperous range of industries. England half-way through the 1970s was doing well. But there was hidden danger. She and much of the world, no longer constrained by the gold standard and the balanced budget, had been generating a long-term inflationary trend.

Then came the oil shock of the mid-1970s. The oil-producing countries entered upon a concerted policy of levying on the developed countries at an altogether higher and ever rising level. Simultaneously, world economic activity, for the first time seriously since the war, faltered. The hidden tensions began to emerge as stagnation and inflation formed a pair which economic theory had treated as impossible. The trade union movement, historically in opposition to employers, now adopted a position of open confrontation, as government and the public and private sectors sought to reduce costs. Expectations had so long been geared to rising real wages that the new reality of contraction could not be accepted.

The Conservative government elected in 1979 sought to meet these challenges by a massive reduction in spending aimed at reducing its deficit and its borrowing requirement, by this means contracting the money supply. This was done in the expectation that inflation could be controlled and even reversed, thus creating conditions of international competitiveness that would stabilize the economy and permit it to resume growth. Economic and social policy was thus based, for the first time in English history, on a theoretical construct, one derived ultimately from the quantity theory of money.

'*It's a great opportunity brothers, we could go on strike for parity with Volkswagen, Fiat, Renault ...*': *a cartoon from 'Punch' satirizes the propensity of British workers to find any excuse to go on strike – in this case, Britain's entry into Europe, where workers are apparently better off, is seen as providing such an opportunity.*

13 The English: Custom and Character
How the nation sees itself
ASA BRIGGS

◆

'BEFORE you can rectify the disorders of a state,' wrote Voltaire, 'you must examine the character of a people.' Examining the character of the English has been a favourite occupation for foreigners, not least for Frenchmen, England's closest neighbours. One of the travellers of the 19th century, Alexis de Tocqueville, was sufficiently different from many of his fellow-countrymen to make the striking claim that so many of his 'thoughts and feelings' were shared by the English that England had become 'a second native land of the mind' for him. Like many Englishmen, however, he was puzzled by much that he observed. 'I cannot completely understand', he noted, for example, 'how the spirit of association and the spirit of exclusion came to be so highly developed in the same people, and often to be so intimately combined. . . . What better example of association than the union of individuals who form the club? What is more exclusive than the corporate personality it represents? . . . The same applies to almost all civil and political associations.' It certainly applied, in De Tocqueville's view, to what was usually regarded as the most basic of all English institutions – the family. 'See how families divide up when the birds are able to leave the nest.'

For many foreigners and for some Englishmen, such puzzles have pointed to what seemed to be contradictions, contradictions not only of a pluralist society, with a network of voluntary associations, but of a society in depth, where the present could not – and cannot – be explained adequately in terms only of the recent past. In consequence, there has been much talk of 'cant' and 'hypocrisy', at its height when British power was also at its height in the 19th century. It was then, too, that the notion of *perfide Albion* was widely publicized. Even as far as the clubs and associations were concerned, there seemed to be oddities, if not contradictions. The *Royal* Society for the Protection of Cruelty to Animals (1824) preceded the *National* Society for the Prevention of Cruelty to Children (1889). Inside a London club the Czech writer Karel Čapek observed in 1925 that a man from the Continent gives himself an air of importance by talking, an Englishman by holding his tongue. He also began one of the last chapters in his *Letters from England* with the remark: 'In England I should like to be a cow or a baby.'

Čapek's letters are only one example of a genre which includes books such as Misson's *Memoirs and Observa-*

tions in his Travels over England (1719) and Taine's *Notes on England* (1872). By the last quarter of the 18th century, the view – or views, for there was no unanimity of perception – across the Atlantic was as significant as the view – or views – across the Channel. One particularly percipient American observer, the novelist Henry James, studying England from near and from afar, noted how the 'tone of things' was heavier in England than in the United States: 'Manners and modes are more absolute and positive; they seem to swarm and to thicken the atmosphere about you. Morally and physically it is a denser air than ours.' By contrast, James's father was unconvinced that the English were worth much effort, let alone much subtlety. Having read Ralph Waldo Emerson's influential *English Traits*, which appeared in 1856, he felt that the distinguished Bostonian had been too appreciative: 'The manners – the life – he was investigating haven't the depth either for good or evil he attributes to them. . . . They [the English] are an intensely vulgar race, high and low; and their qualities, good or evil, date not from any divine or diabolic depths whatever, but from the most obvious and superficial causes. They are the abject slaves of routine, and no afflatus from above or below ever comes, apparently, to ruffle the surface of their self-complacent quietude. They are not worth studying.'

There is a second relevant genre, the very existence of which disproved the reflections of James (Senior) – anatomies of England by Englishmen themselves, few of which have been expressive of 'self-complacent quietude'. Anthony Sampson's *Anatomy of Britain* (1962), not surprisingly, was more concerned with the malaise and deeper problems of a declining industrial Britain than with its successes and aspirations but, long before Britain was industrialized, Dr John Brown's *An Estimate of the Manners and Principles of the Times* (1752) revealed the same stance – and went through even more editions. 'Honour' was being converted into 'vanity', Brown complained, and Britain was passing through an 'important and alarming crisis' from which it might not recover.

There is a third relevant genre – tours of exploration from London into the provinces which supplement and to some extent qualify the anatomies. The fascination of John Leland's *Itinerary* (1546) has been vividly appraised by A. L. Rowse in his account of 'the Elizabethan discovery of England'; and for later centuries Daniel Defoe's *A Tour through England and Wales* (1724), William Cobbett's *Rural Rides* (1830) and J. B. Priestley's *English Journey* (1934) are equally indispensable. Such books still appear regularly, the latest of them Richard West's *An English Journey* (1981). It cannot be said that any of the authors of these superior travel books are unruffled, or the kind of people who hold their tongues. West is as sure as Cobbett was that an 'old England' is disappearing – visually as well as socially – and that a worse England is taking its place.

Three fundamental points that are made in all such books are: first, that despite the geographical smallness of England there is immense variety; second, that there are regional as well as local differences, not only that between north and south, but one equally old between east and west; and third, that – while finding cultural expression – these diversities are influenced by landscape, by weather and, not least, by the distribution of natural resources, including not only coal and iron, which became important to the economy even before the Industrial Revolution, but wood and stone and water.

The weather has often been picked out as the most important influence of all; even Francis Bacon noted that the English usually talk first about the weather. For centuries, indeed, the ups and downs of English prices – and incomes – were affected by the weather more than by any other factor. In the 18th century even the merits of the British Constitution could be directly related to the weather, which was this time treated as a beneficent influence:

> Thy Seasons moderate as thy Laws appear,
> Thy Constitution wholesome as the year.

There seemed to be an equally direct relationship between the weather and early industrial growth. The Lancashire cotton industry pushed ahead, it was claimed, because Lancashire had a damp climate: thereby even Manchester's raininess was transformed from a nuisance into a social benefit. It was rain, too, according to Dorothy Wordsworth, that helped to make the Lake District what it was, a district in itself of infinite variety. For George Santayana in the 20th century what governed the individual Englishman was 'his inner atmosphere, the weather in his soul'.

Yet the travel writers were even more concerned with outer appearances than with inner atmospheres, with the sense both of variety and of change, something that comes out particularly strongly in Defoe. 'Wherever we come, and which way soever we look,' he wrote in his *Tour*, 'we see something new, something significant. ... The fate of things gives a new face to things, produces changes in low life, and innumerable incidents; plants and supplants families, raises and sinks towns, removes manufactures and trades; great towns decay and small towns rise.'

In the 19th century, the railway was recognized as bringing in a completely new tempo of life, changing

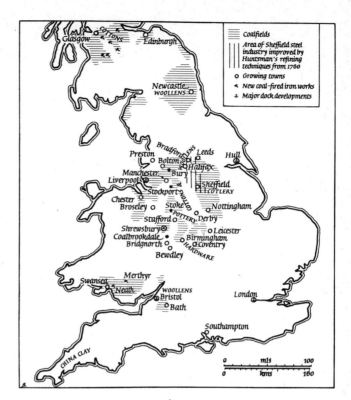

British resources and industrial strength in 1815. Benjamin Huntsman in the mid-18th century had discovered a method of making cast steel that was almost as revolutionary as Abraham Darby's technique in iron.

economic and social relationships and in the process introducing a new sense of punctuality and of 'haste'. 'Now we are whirled about, and hooted around, and rung up as if we are parcels, booking clerks, or office boys', wrote the positivist Frederic Harrison in his Victorian memoirs. The motor car was still to come, first as a luxury, then, at least for those who could afford it, almost as a necessity. Whereas the steam engine had begun by revolutionizing work and had only later gone on to transform locomotion, the internal combustion engine from the start gave a new sense of power (and property) to individuals and their families. Englishmen never took it up quite like the Americans in their country of huge distances, but after 1945 all official forecasts of its British appeal were underestimates. Thus, in 1945 the Ministry of Transport predicted a 75 per cent increase in the numbers of motor vehicles by 1965: the numbers had, in fact, doubled by 1950. Not surprisingly in the age of the motorway – the first was built as early as 1958 – it was frequently suggested, as in the Beeching Report on the railways of 1963, that the greater part of the railway system was uneconomic.

The paradoxes of progress

The railways had been a symbol of change, with some Englishmen welcoming them enthusiastically and others attacking – or fearing – them. Englishmen have seldom been in doubt about their identity, but they have frequently, perhaps consequentially, been profoundly suspicious of large-scale change. The Tudor critique of agrarian change preceded the 18th- and 19th-century critique of industrial change, the latter the biggest industrial change the world had ever seen. In the early 18th century Defoe had been willing to welcome change, but in the early 19th century Cobbett was angered by it. And whereas Defoe propounded a philosophy of life which proclaimed industry as a virtue before the rise of large-scale industry as a sector of the economy, Cobbett defended old and threatened values. Defoe looked forwards to a golden age; Cobbett, for all his political radicalism, backwards. During the 19th century, it was the kind of philosophy propounded by Defoe which seemed to have won the day. Yet in the 20th century, change associated with the shift towards a 'post-industrial society' has been as strongly criticized and resisted as the shift towards an industrial society. New technology, which made possible both the Industrial Revolution and post-industrial society, has always generated as much fear as hope: it did so even when England's economic power was internationally recognized, and it has done so even when it has been undermined. There has been an intellectual as well as a proletarian strand in such criticism and resistance, often associated with the belief that the 'heart of England' is in the countryside.

There may have been general changes, of course, in both attitudes and in values. Thus, whatever Defoe might have written earlier on the subject, it has been claimed that there was a completely different approach to work in the late 18th and early 19th centuries when compared with the late 20th. Compare, for example, with most contemporary comment in the 1980s, a comment of Bulwer Lytton on this subject in *England and the English* (1833): 'I think that I need take no pains to prove the next characteristic of the English people ... viz., their wonderful Spirit of Industry.' This, Lytton added, 'has been the saving principle of the nation, counteracting the errors of our laws, and the imperfections of our constitution'. Charles Dickens, who did so much to establish the sense of an English national character, was more guarded when, in his novel of industrialism, *Hard Times* (1854), he described the English not as the most hard-working but as the most hard-worked people in the world.

Simple propositions about attitudes towards work – or leisure – require complex analysis, both economic and psychological. Explaining comparative productivity in Britain and the United States in 1948, when many of Britain's ills were attributed to the fatigues of the Second World War, L. Rostas found it necessary to pay attention not only to technology, trade unions and management but to social barriers and to social objectives outside the workplace: 'It is not that the objective factors (better layout, longer runs, planning of work etc.) cause the [American] operative to work fast, but rather that those factors enable the [American] operatives to fulfil their one clear object, namely to earn as much as they can.'

The absence of this 'one clear object' in England was apparent even in the early Industrial Revolution. Money was never the only measuring rod. Nor was the ideal of the money-maker ever the only ideal. Traditional codes – and customs – survived.

Rank, degree and deference

Taine described England as haunted, in contrast with France, by the ghosts of the feudal spirit: 'The lord provides for the needs of his dependant, and the dependant is proud of his lord.' Defoe had been haunted by none of these ghosts even in the early 18th century, yet that century saw a consolidation of the great landed estate as well as an expansion of industry: and during the middle years of the 19th century, when Taine was writing, the great landed estate was still an economy and a society in itself. Despite fears expressed during the successful fight to repeal the Corn Laws (1846), the position of the aristocracy and gentry remained exceptionally strong – so strong that Richard Cobden, chief repealer, strengthened, though in vain, his attack on feudalism after 1850. Already in the 1830s De Tocqueville had noted that while 'the French wish not to have superiors, the English wish to have inferiors. The Frenchman constantly raises his eyes above him with anxiety. The Englishman lowers his beneath him with satisfaction. On both sides there is pride, but it is understood in a different way.' Even after the fall of land prices and rents in the late 19th century and the great inrush of foreign corn and frozen meats, the sense of superiority associated with land did not completely wither away.

It is not only deference which has often been singled out as an English trait. Another related feature has received equal attention – the Englishman's natural sense of order. As recently as 1955, Geoffrey Gorer in his book *Exploring English Character*, describes the English people as 'among the most peaceful, gentle, courteous and orderly populations that the civilized world has ever seen'. 'Football crowds', he went on by way of illustration, 'are as orderly as church meetings.' Even if the general proposition is still held to stand, the same illustration could not be chosen today. Yet here we return to diversities of attitudes as well as of appearances. The generalization had not always stood before 1955, as Gorer recognized. The English did not enjoy their 1955 reputation in the Middle Ages, in the Tudor period or in the 17th or 18th centuries. There was little evidence of a natural sense of order in the London riots of 1736, 1768 and 1780 which gave London the reputation of being more turbulent than Paris. It seemed, indeed, to Horace Walpole in 1780, that half of London would quickly be 'reduced to ashes'. Populist Protestantism and anti-popery were battle cries then, as they were to be later. For some Englishmen, indeed, the national identity was a Protestant identity and they sought to trace it back, when they were arguing and not marching or burning, to a time long before the Protestant martyrs, to John Wycliffe and the Lollards.

The 1768 riots, however, were accompanied by different cries – those of 'Wilkes and Liberty' – providing a necessary reminder that it is misleading to focus exclusively on English 'deference' and to ignore alternative strains in English society. The age of Wycliffe was also the age of the Peasants' Revolt (1381), and if the Reformation in England produced an Erastian church, proclaiming a philosophy of order, it also produced an energetic and deliberately Nonconformist Puritan movement. The struggles of the 17th century, culminating in the Civil War and the brief Puritan Commonwealth, eventually saw the defeat of the Puritans as the controlling force of the country. Yet the conception of independence was not lost. The chapel as well as the club could unite sociability and exclusiveness, and quite different traditions of independence and community could be nurtured there from the tradition of order transmitted through the parish church. Of course, in 1768 John Wilkes was no Puritan, and the cries of liberty then had little to do with that particular tradition. Yet it was the acceptance or rejection of that tradition which did much to determine attitudes both to the American and French Revolutions. There was always a 'for' and an 'against' in England, just as apparent in 19th- and 20th-century attitudes to empire as in 18th-century attitudes to revolution.

In fiction, authority and independence are well-related in Herman Melville's *Billy Budd* (published in 1924) which looks back to the wars with Revolutionary France, when there was ample evidence both of national pride in fighting the French and of fear of mutiny, of naval officers maintaining authority and of English sailors demanding their 'rights' as 'freeborn Englishmen'. War could succeed in unifying traditions. Thus, in *Poems Dedicated to National Independence and Liberty*, William Wordsworth, who had begun by sympathizing profoundly with the French Revolution, was quick to see that Napoleon could threaten English freedom as Englishmen saw it:

> We must be free or die, who speak the tongue
> That Shakespeare spake; the faith and morals hold
> Which Milton held ...

When the Napoleonic struggles were pushed back into memory, Englishmen divided again and reverted to seeing things in 17th-century terms. 'We are Cavaliers and Roundheads before we are Liberals and Conservatives', wrote the historian W. H. Lecky.

By then, of course, there were complaints, from Matthew Arnold among others, that Puritanism was stifling the English spirit rather than freeing it. There were also new forces at work in society which could inspire equally mixed reactions – notably Evangelicalism. Following John Wesley's death the Evangelicals found a home both inside and outside the Church of England, influencing thereby both church and chapel; and they had a restraining influence on customs and habits. In its origins Evangelicalism was a religion of the heart, a 'vital' individual religion not only of outward observance but of personal salvation. But before long its impact on public 'causes', such as anti-slavery, was as powerful as its impact on individual conscience. Moreover, it influenced attitudes in all sections of the population, from 'high' to 'low'. It was not content to retreat into exclusivity: it had a message for all, and it was prepared to use public authority to enforce it. If Gorer was right in his belief that there was a big change in Englishmen's attitudes to 'order' in the mid-Victorian years, part of the explanation may lie here; and within this frame the particular strength of Methodism, which set out to appeal to the 'low' as well as the 'high', was that it could generate change from within: in particular, it could convert the 'wicked' into the 'respectable'.

Gorer did not trace concern for 'respectability' back into the 18th century, though it is obvious enough in, for instance, Defoe. In the 19th century it largely accounts for the abolition both of cruel sports (some of which survived and flourished) and of still existing medieval or Tudor fairs and festivals. Bartholomew Fair, for example, so brilliantly satirized by Ben Jonson in the 17th century, languished in the 19th under official pressure and died out by 1854. Two years later, the police forces were reformed by legislation – another event not noted by Gorer, but raising the question of how much the change in attitudes he identified depended on improved police control.

The identification of the 1850s as a key decade in change was, therefore, as Gorer made clear, a hunch rather than a result of research. Yet he was surely right to focus on what he called 'public life' in his chronology. 'So far as novels and memoirs can be taken as evidence,' he begins, 'the English people don't seem to have changed their character very much, and I don't think that anybody would argue that the characters in Fielding or Smollett, Jane Austen or Dickens, could possibly belong to any other nation.' As far as public life was concerned, however, 'there does seem to have been this remarkable change from the Roaring Boys to the Boys' Brigade, from John Bull to John Citizen.'

Landmarks of change

It is notoriously difficult to locate precisely in time shifts in attitudes and values: and Gorer's middle years of the 19th century, quieter though they were in domestic history than the preceding and later years of the century – not to speak of the period since 1955 – are also associated with one of the most strident displays of English nationalism during the Crimean War. If crime rates were falling – and the statistics are controversial – there was still no shortage of vicarious violence. Nor did John Bull ever completely change into John Citizen: indeed, it required the Education Act of 1870 and the new Board Schools to help form John Citizen and two world wars in the 20th century to bring about any changeover, and since the 1960s the changeover has been far more difficult to perceive.

What seems likely is that the mid-19th-century changes, which point both backwards and forwards in time, make a new kind of national and individual character necessary. Industry had to become a matter of habit and routine, not a new explosive force: it depended for its performance on punctuality, regularity and discipline. Self-help had to be extolled, along with the gospel of work and the belief in thrift. Competition had to be preached as well as – or even more than – practised. Much of this was new. In the 18th century, work was irregular and often undisciplined, particularly before the move from the home to the factory. Even the Bank of England was closed for forty-seven weekdays in the year in 1761. Birth and marriage determined life chances more than self-help, and debt, held up as an aristocratic trait, was often preferred to thrift. Combination was a characteristic of early industry – far more than competition.

In order that the change might take place smoothly, it was obviously more desirable to develop new attitudes, and the character traits that went with them, by implanting them from within rather than by imposing them from without. The policeman and the judge were to be necessary agents in the process, and respect and deference were to be accorded to them, but in the first resort at least the actual transformation of

'Invasion indeed! That's a game two can play at!' 'Punch'
perpetuates the image of an indignant and belligerent John Bull, who
here is responding to the threat of French invasion in 1859.

character was in the hands of other agencies – schools, particularly Sunday Schools (an invention of the 1780s), voluntary bodies, many of them guided by religious (notably Evangelical) conviction, and publicists, most of whom had 'risen in society' themselves.

The application of 'the spirit of association' to philanthropy and to social reform, far more significant during this period than the role of the state, pre-dated and post-dated the period itself. Meanwhile the state inspected and regulated, but it did not drive, and if only for this reason – diversity of traditions was another – there was bound to be more than one version of what John Citizen should be like.

Yet there was increasing suspicion among social critics, always plentiful in the Victorian age, that the degree of conformity being demanded was too great, and in the same year as Samuel Smiles's *Self-Help* (1859), John Stuart Mill published his famous essay *On Liberty* in which he complained of the 'increasing inclination to extend unduly the powers of society over the individual'. His final proposition overlaps with that of Voltaire, with which this chapter began, for he concluded that 'the worth of a state, in the long run, is the worth of the individuals composing it'. With particular reference to England, he was more concerned about the pressures of society than the controls of the state, for in England, he believed, 'from the particular circumstances of our political history, the yoke of opinion is perhaps heavier, that of law ... lighter than in most other countries of Europe'. It was not that individual Englishmen were losing their freedom to the state: they were rather losing their individuality to the society and the culture.

The same point has been made about mid-Victorian society and culture by a 20th-century historian, interested in what he called the 'equipoise' of the system. After examining the influences brought to bear on the mid-Victorian Englishman, W. L. Burn concluded that social disciplines were more potent than legal restraints in their influence on behaviour, if only because in some spheres they were more rigorously enforced: 'A town council might well refuse to institute a prosecution against a manufacturer, whose operations constituted a nuisance, but the trustees of a grammar school were unlikely to be equally tolerant of an usher who lived openly in adultery or publicly proclaimed himself an atheist.'

It is interesting to note how sex and religion are combined in this passage about the strength of conviction in 19th-century England, although 'indifference' apparently increased as the century went by. As far as sex was concerned, there were blatant double standards. Indeed, the main charge of hypocrisy levelled then and since against the Victorians may well centre on this point. The mid-Victorian years, different in their tone not only from the Regency period but from all previous periods of English history, were years when prostitution thrived and when men and women were expected to have different codes of morality. The

'The British Character: Exaltation of Freedom': an English cartoonist, 'Pont', gently mocks the London businessman on his way to work. His lifestyle, demeanour and dress make him instantly recognizable. Despite his freedom, envied by foreigners, to think and act as he pleases, the Englishman imposes numerous codes and regulations upon himself.

womanly woman was placed on a pedestal; the manly man was recognized to have frailties, though when they were found out they were usually not condoned. Social restraints were powerful from the court downwards. This, too, had certainly not always been the case, for in the 16th and 17th centuries foreign visitors had noted 'the freedom of women, tending to boldness': earlier still, England had been considered by a Venetian ambassador to be a country given up to kissing, dancing, singing and junketing.

Victorian hypocrisy was often associated with the Puritan inheritance, but sometimes more recent writers have ventured on more general and more dubious propositions. 'The English are not a sexual nation,' wrote Somerset Maugham in 1932, 'and you cannot easily persuade them that a man will sacrifice anything important for love.' By the end of the decade, notwithstanding, Queen Victoria's great-grandson, Edward VIII, was said to have done just that, and by the 1960s 'swinging' London had established a reputation, however unjustified, for 'permissiveness' which left Paris (and New York) in the shade. Some of the sharpest criticism of this permissiveness and its alleged social consequences came, indeed, from across the Atlantic. At that time, it seemed as if everything Arnold had written about English conformity (or Puritanism) was obsolete. English eccentricity had often been noted and frequently admired. Yet that was an individual matter. What now seemed to be happening was a transformation in the behaviour of whole social groups. Moreover, the law was being modified to bring it into less open conflict with what were now claimed to be socially acceptable norms.

Leisure, literature and history

Vicissitudes of mores, described by some observers as trends or cycles, point to the difficulties of generalizing consistently about national character. Unlike many historians, Gorer had no doubt that national character existed, provided that it was identified in terms of clusters and traits formed and brought together consciously or unconsciously in early life. Yet he, too, believed that it could and did change, and that different people might interpret it in different ways. One of the interpreters, the distinguished American historian Henry Commager, in an essay written to commemorate the centenary of Emerson's *English Traits*, did not even believe that there had been a break. 'National character', he wrote in 1948, 'is everywhere wonderfully tenacious, but nowhere is it more tenacious than with the English, who have, after all, something of a patent on tenacity. This is the first and most obvious of English traits – the stability and permanence of the English character. Come hell or high water, the Englishman remains imperturbably English. He is, it would seem, less affected by the currents and cross-currents of history than people of any other nation; he is less affected, too, by passing fashions, whether of literature or of dress or of food.'

A year earlier, George Orwell, who had hesitated before using the term 'national character' in his fascinating book *The English People*, written in 1947 (long before there was evidence of 20th-century English 'permissiveness' and when the country was still under the shadow of the Second World War), came to a somewhat similar conclusion. Like Gorer, however, he turned to literature as much as to historical experience when he drew his conclusions – for example, that 'a profound, almost unconscious patriotism and an inability to think logically are the abiding features of the English character, traceable in English literature from Shakespeare downwards.'

He might have made as much of sport as of literature, for this has figured prominently in both the self-identification and the evolution of character. The English, either as participants or as spectators, had a passion for sports which long preceded the development of professional football and the growth of the football crowd: Blaine's *Encyclopaedia of Rural Sports*, published in 1840, went through many editions. Of all rural sports, hunting was the most deeply rooted in rural society; horse-racing, 'the sport of kings', brought aristocracy and crowds together, sometimes in unlikely alliances; so, too, did boxing; and the fact that there was betting on both brought townsfolk in as well, if often at a distance. Yet it was cricket and football that began in the 19th century and continued in the 20th to capture the national imagination.

Cricket was thought of as more than a game: with its complicated rules, only Englishmen and foreigners speaking the English language (plus exiles and their descendants) could understand it, and in the 20th century it could appeal, in Test Matches with Australia in particular, to the deepest national instincts. When during the 1890s the aesthetes were replaced by the athletes, *Punch* could write:

Then here's for cricket in this year of grace,
Fair-play all round, straight hitting and straight dealing,
In letters, morals, art and commonplace,
Reversion unto type in deed and feeling.

Soccer never quite suggested this, but in the 20th century it became *the* national game, with a quite different and more democratic folklore. Amateurs could hold their own in cricket – and in tennis – for far longer than they did in football. As early as the 1880s, prestigious amateur football teams were being beaten by tough professionals from the industrial north and Midlands. A contributor to a famous late 19th-century 'Badminton' series on sports doubted whether football had 'the steady vitality of cricket'. If not, it did have something else – the capacity to inspire loyalty and to feed rivalry both inside the country and outside.

'Team' sports were held to bring out individual qualities among the players, while demanding 'discipline', and their organization was usually carried out in 'clubs'. For these reasons alone – and leaving out other characteristic British sports, like rugby – the history of sport is not merely a *part* of English social history: it reflects the whole of it, from village to city. Emigration carried it across the seas; competition took it to Europe and to most other continents; and at home it has percolated through society, via schools on the one hand and radio and television on the other. It figures in literature, also, with memorable hunting scenes in 18th-century novels like *Tom Jones*, and football and rugby

scenes in many 20th-century novels like *This Sporting Life*, and indeed in films like *Chariots of Fire*.

The relationship between literature and social history is complex, yet one aspect of it is of practical significance. 'Men are apt to acquire peculiarities that are continually ascribed to them', wrote the American author Washington Irving in his *Sketch Book*, published in 1820. 'The common orders of the English seem wonderfully captivated with the *beau ideal* which they have formed of John Bull, and endeavour to act up to the broad caricature that is perpetually held before their eyes.' It was a caricature which changed during the 19th century, when John Bull finally grew up into *paterfamilias* and, through the pages of *Punch* (1841), captivated the middle classes (through identification) even more than the 'common orders'. Even John Citizen during the Second World War and just after it encouraged others to be like him. So, too, did the swingers of the 1960s though their models were singers and there was deference, even reverence, for them rather than identification with them. The star took the place of the lord, with the sports star just as popular as the star of stage or screen.

During the middle years of the 19th century, chosen by Gorer for what he considered to be a period of crucial change, one particular English novelist, Charles Dickens, did more perhaps than any other writer to establish national stereotypes, almost justifying by himself a later suggestion of Aldous Huxley that nations are to a large extent invented by novelists and poets. Indeed, as early as 1850 a reviewer said of Dickens that he was 'so thoroughly English that he is now part and parcel of that mighty aggregate of national fame which we feel bound to defend on all points against attack'. Dickens is far more complex than such remarks suggest, for he never offered verbal photographs of places or people: the world he created was his and not everyone's. Nonetheless, if we consider him along with a number of other mid-Victorian novelists who memorably described their age – Anthony Trollope, for example, who was called 'a special correspondent for posterity' while he was still alive – we can learn much about customs: old customs which were disappearing, but could be caught for a time on the printed page, and new customs in the making.

Dickens himself knew how transitional and formative his own time was: 'The world would not take another Pickwick from me now', he believed as early as 1849. He was also deeply concerned about the increasingly routinized world of work which was the foundation of all else in society. 'It surely cannot be allowed', he had stated in a speech of 1844, 'that those who labour day and night, surrounded by machinery, shall be permitted to degenerate into machines themselves; but on the contrary that they should assert their common origin in that Creator, from whose wondrous hands they come.' The word 'hands' is an emotive one; its use by factory employers to describe

The 'noble art of self-defence' – boxing – was a sport that brought all classes together. At one time it was as aristocratic as fencing. In the 1820s Mr Jackson of Bond Street, London (right) taught both. But the custom of offering prize money, as well as that of betting on the result, tended to degrade it into a rather brutalized profession.

their 'labour force' shocked both Dickens and John Ruskin. But while Ruskin could be surprisingly chauvinistic, no foreign observer ever drew a more plausible picture of English national prejudice than Dickens did in *Our Mutual Friend* (1865) through his culture-bound but immortal Mr Podsnap.

If literature has been a major influence in the delineation of national character, historians have also contributed a formidable share. While they have usually been sceptical of literary and psychological exposition, they have made much of the alliance between the Englishman and his history. This, they have claimed, has enabled 'tradition' and 'progress' to be reconciled. In addition, they have argued, the alliance has saved England not only from revolution but from the tyranny of abstract ideas, and if the price to be paid has been 'the inability to think logically', the price has not been heavy. The English have avoided the uprooting of things which have been organic to the development of society, culture and the constitution. and have given new meaning to old forms within new contexts. They have been able in consequence to skip the ages. Thus, when the social historian J. R. Green looked back from the 19th to the 18th century, he was reassured to find that 'all the features of English life, in fact, all its characteristic features are already there. We see mills grinding along the burns, the hammer rings in the village smithy, the thegn's hall rises out of its demesne.' It is through the accumulation of detail, including detail of landscape as much as of document, that the historians have traced continuities and attempted to explain difference and change.

At least from the time of Edmund Burke onwards, historians of different political persuasions have shared 'Whig' perceptions, sometimes tracing back dominant themes to the continuing sense of an island inheritance, sometimes to the first 'mixing of the peoples', and sometimes – this was true long before Burke – to the special dispensation of Providence.

Old and new were thereby interrelated as well as juxtaposed or contrasted. In the process, what is specifically English was isolated in the details of landscapes as much as in the language of documents, with the ordering of different layers of history accounting for present conjunctions. 'Our liberty', wrote Dickens's contemporary T. B. Macaulay, 'is neither Greek nor Roman; but essentially English. It has a character of its own – a character which has taken a tinge from the sentiments of the chivalrous ages, and which accords with the peculiarities of our manners and our insular situation. It has a language, too, of its own, and a language singularly idiosyncratic, full of meaning to ourselves, scarcely intelligible to strangers.' In this century, Herbert Butterfield, who did more than any other historian to draw attention to Whig perceptions of continuity and change, and to their limitations, himself praised the 'Whiggism' inherent in the processes of change. 'Under the Whig system', he wrote in his *The Englishman and his History* (1944), 'reforms have been overdue on many occasions; yet by the passage of time they have been able to come by a more easy and natural route and with less accompaniment of counter-evil; and we have at least been spared that common nemesis of revolutions – the generation of irreconcilable hatreds within the State. And while conflict can be mitigated in this way, the world has had a chance to grow in reasonableness.'

There have been signs in recent years of an increasing challenge to such interpretations of history, reflecting social and cultural as well as economic and political changes of the kind that have made Gorer's 1955 exploration of English character seem out of date; and in such circumstances Voltaire's dictum has in effect been modified to read: 'Before you can rectify the character of a state, you must examine the disorders of a people.' Some recent historians have taken the fact (which so interested De Tocqueville) that the English have not experienced a revolution of the French type to be a failure, not a success, while 'the spirit of exclusion and of association' extolled by him has been felt by others to be a source of economic weakness when it has shown itself in the form of contemporary trade-unionism: so, too, has the process whereby trade unionists have in various ways been 'taken outside the law'. More recently still, the English have been accused by American historians of failing adequately to adapt themselves to industrialism, in spite, or perhaps because, of the fact that they experienced – and generated – the first Industrial Revolution.

Yet as the shapes of history have changed, our own preoccupation with it has been maintained. New generations of social historians may reject the Whig assumptions of earlier historians, but they look for continuities themselves – no longer in the higher echelons of society but now in the history of the 'common people'. As they rewrite English history as 'history from below', they may be just as concerned with traditions of revolt as with traditions of authority. They may be just as anxious to conserve the symbols of the past as other historians. Moreover, their preference for social history – as distinct from other kinds of history, particularly the diplomatic and the military – has strong 19th-century roots. The great constitutional historian Bishop Stubbs set out to write a history 'which reads the exploits and characters of men by a different light from that shed by the false glamour of arms, and interprets positions and facts in words that are voiceless to those who have only listened to the trumpet of fame'. It was Stubbs who, like many of his contemporaries, insisted that custom had been more potent than law in early English history, 'custom modified infinitesimally every day'.

In the 20th century the last of the explicitly Whig historians, G. M. Trevelyan, Macaulay's nephew, wrote a best-selling *Social History of England* (1941), which ended not with a panegyric of progress, but with a lament for what was lost. 'The modern Englishman', he concluded, 'is fed and clothed better than his ancestor, but his spiritual side, in all that connects him with the beauty of the world, is utterly starved as no people have been starved in the history of the world.' In such circumstances – and they were wartime circumstances, with England in danger – Trevelyan placed his hope less in poetry than in history: and never was the alliance between the Englishman and his history more forcefully demonstrated than in the huge sales of Trevelyan's book.

Spiritual and material comfort

To what extent was the modern Englishman fed and clothed better than his ancestor, and how fair was it to describe him as spiritually starved? The second question is more easily dealt with than the first. In 1941, when Trevelyan's *Social History* appeared, print, among many other things, was rationed, and the first edition of his book had to appear in the United States. Yet in the middle of a protracted and perilous war, there was more emphasis on the 'things of the spirit' than there had been during the 1930s. Travel might be restricted –

except for people serving in the Forces – but there was no shortage of entertainment, diversionary or uplifting. One new 20th-century invention, broadcasting, had been developed in Britain since 1922 with a high sense of cultural mission (too high for many listeners); while another late 19th-century invention, the cinema, was at the height of its popularity. Adult education, which had a long tradition in England going back before compulsory and institutionalized school education to the struggle of individuals 'to acquire knowledge under difficulties', was booming. There was talk of a musical renaissance comparable to that in Tudor England, and there were war artists, among them Henry Moore, England's greatest sculptor, recording impressions of wars as they had never been recorded in England before.

It is true, of course, that at the deepest level the power of religion was less strong than it had been in previous wars – the historian of religion David Edwards has called ours 'the secular century' – yet at least some Englishmen felt that they were wielding 'the sword of the spirit' and the churches and chapels were often fuller than they had been in peacetime. There was certainly ample rhetoric of the spirit in such speeches as that by General Smuts in 1942 when he claimed that glory had not departed from the land – 'that inward glory, that splendour of spirit, which has shone over this land from the soul of its people, and which has been a beacon light to the oppressed and downtrodden peoples in this new martyrdom of man'. Harold Nicolson quoted these words at the end of an anthology, *England*, published in 1944.

This, too, was one of a genre. Both world wars, different though they were in their scale, their modes of warfare and their consequences, have nurtured anthologies. Perhaps the first to be published in the Second World War was *The English Vision* (1939), edited by Herbert Read, which took one of its texts from D. H. Lawrence, a more unexpected contributor than Smuts. 'I really think', Lawrence had written in a letter of 1922, 'that the most living clue of life in us Englishmen is England, and the great mistake we make is in not uniting together in the strength of this real living clue – religious in the most vital sense – uniting together in England and so carrying the vital spark through.'

'Uniting together' in wartime was easier in the Second World War than it was in the First, when there had been obvious divisions between the brass-hats and the politicians, 'Blighty' and the trenches, the privileged and the deprived. It was also easier than it had been during the 1930s or in the turbulent years between 1910 and 1914. During the Second World War, however, it was not merely a matter of propaganda. A fair system of rationing, including both food and clothing, meant that people from different sections of the country were treated alike, while a number of proposals for post-war changes in a wide range of services, including social security and education, offered new hope for the post-war future. Paradoxically, Englishmen were better fed when Trevelyan's book appeared – and when England was blockaded – than they had been during the 1930s. Indeed they were better fed than they were to be in the years of austerity immediately following the war, when there was a serious shortage of fats, and when bread, unrationed during the war, was put on ration. Even in 1947, however, rations provided more nutrients than average pre-war diets, the worst features of which had been exposed by John Boyd Orr in his influential study, *Food, Health and Income* (1936). What was missing was choice, something that had always been denied to the majority of Englishmen, and that was given full play only in a period of unprecedented 'affluence' after 1955.

To see in perspective either spiritual or material comfort it is necessary to consider far longer periods than the 20th century, when many of the relevant statistics – and in both cases they are limited and patchy over the centuries – have been collected. In the first case (the spiritual), it is necessary to relate secularization to the rise of science, technology and industry, and in the second case (the material) to make a detailed study of prices, incomes, family budgets, diets and associated social indicators.

It is difficult in each case, however, to generalize about the Middle Ages, where the base lines begin. Medieval religion was authoritative and pervasive, but there was a wide gulf between precept and practice. Medieval standards of living always involved sharp contrasts, linked at every point to contrasts in ranks, places, seasons and years. There was an attempt, however, to impose order even in relation to material things – to suppress usury, to enforce sumptuary codes of clothing, to regulate the prices of basic necessities. The prices of bread and ale were fixed, for example, by nationally set assizes, the former lasting, though in a weakened form, until the early 19th century, the latter disappearing in the 17th. We can trace the long-term changes in the same way as we can trace, though not easily date, the process whereby large numbers of Englishmen effectively ceased to be 'religious' and all religious bodies (with the Church of England retaining its special place) gradually reduced to the status of denominations or sects. However, we must note at the same time that we have not yet disposed of the concerns issuing as recently as the early 1970s in 'prices and incomes policies', despite recent revivals of late 18th- and early 19th-century market philosophies. Nor have we ceased to inherit 'values, dispositions and orientations', as Bryan Wilson has called them, from 'the religious past. The completely secularized society has not yet existed.'

We can follow the quest for material comfort from castle to house, cottage to bungalow, terrace to suburb, noting such landmarks as the shift to more elegant furniture in the 18th century, a wider range of domestic service in the 19th century – when the family was idealized – and the expansion of the durable consumer goods industries in the 20th, changing everyday life in the home more than it has ever been changed before. The English have been described as a nation of shopkeepers: more pertinent, perhaps, in relation to such sequences is that they have been a nation of customers. A parallel sequence is that which leads from the country store to the supermarket. At every point in the process, however, different social groupings have perforce behaved in different ways. 'The food of the poor' has been different from 'the food of the rich', the former more English, the latter influenced by fashion, including foreign fashion. Prices have limited choice more than rationing has: thus, in 1767 Jonas Hanway – who had noted how certain articles of consumption, particularly tea, which had previously been luxuries, were 'descending to the Plebaean order' – observed also how 'from the high price of meat, it has not lately been within their reach. As to milk, they have hardly sufficient for their use.' Thus, in the early 20th century, Rowntree was demonstrating that in York, as English a city as any city could be, fifteen per cent of the population were bound to live in poverty even if every penny was spent on bare essentials with the strictest economy: 'They must never go into the country unless they walk. They must never purchase a halfpenny newspaper or spend a penny to buy a ticket for a popular concert. They must write no letters to absent children, for they cannot afford to pay the postage. They must never contribute anything to their church or chapel. . . . They cannot save, nor can they join sick club or Trade Union, because they cannot pay the necessary subscriptions. The children must have no pocket money for dolls, marbles or sweets. The father must smoke no tobacco and must drink no beer. The mother must never buy any pretty clothes for herself or her children.' Rowntree came from a Quaker family outside the English establishment, and he was being deliberately unsentimental when collecting statistical evidence and presenting social results in this manner. More than thirty years later, when he was still collecting evidence, the surveys of Boyd Orr concerning food and of Richard Titmuss and others concerning health, showed just how diverse the fortunes (and life styles) of different Englishmen could be.

All attempts to 'unite together' have been in danger of foundering on the rocks of the English system of social stratification, which changed in the early 19th century from a system based on rank, order and degree to a system based on class. The system has often been commented upon by Englishmen and foreigners though, according to Priestley who has condemned it, 'only a foreigner who has spent years in this country could begin to understand what divides one accepted class from another'. In the 19th century it was often emphasized that it was an open system, quite unlike a caste system. In the 20th century it has often been said that it is giving way to a more complex and more nuanced system of status. Yet in both centuries pleas for 'one nation' suggested that there are at least two. The system is frequently accused of holding back economic growth, as much by limiting aspirations as by diversifying standards of living and life styles. At this point psychology is as relevant as economics. As Priestley once more has insisted, it is wrong to think that the system is imposed from the top: it gains its strength from what happens below. 'I can imagine twenty assorted English in a lifeboat beginning to observe, after the first few hours, their necessary class distinctions. I saw it happen among working women bombed out during the war, when almost immediately they sorted themselves out in terms of microscopic class differences invisible to me. But then it is women ... who have the sharper eye for these distinctions.' It is therefore not strange that social stratification has always been a more carefully studied field in England than any other branch of sociology and that observation and statistical compilation have been given more attention than theory.

This was one of the points made – significantly in the broadcast Reith lecturers – by G. M. Carstairs, and subsequently published in book form in 1963 under the title *This Island Now*. This series of lectures, which provided a not too distant but nonetheless necessarily distanced vantage point from our own time, was sufficiently controversial to provoke popular attack, particularly, and perhaps characteristically, on those sections dealing with the more open attitudes towards sexual behaviour which Carstairs discovered among the younger generation. But it is not necessary to accept all his conclusions to acknowledge the value of his work to historians.

The title of the lectures, drawn from W. H. Auden's 'Look, Stranger, at this Island Now', catches many echoes. The first chapter pleads for a more systematic study of national character, recognizing the existence of sub-cultures, each with a way of life and a system of values which influence the behaviour of its members. In our single island there are sub-cultures based not on privilege but on deprivation. There are also groups under threat, like the middle-middle-class, who 'can no longer identify each other by their clothes or their accents; and their favourite holiday resorts have been invaded'. The second and third chapters deal, as Gorer might have done, with early years and adolescence and, although they touch on continuity and change, favourite themes of historians, they rely on evidence which historians do not always use. The fourth chapter on the changing role of women deserves historical underpinning: it concentrates rightly, given the preoccupations of 1962, on earlier marriage, smaller families and increased expectation of life for women. The fifth, which has a title derived not from sociology but from literature – a poem by T. S. Eliot – is for this reason alone in keeping with a tradition: it is in keeping with a different, if allied tradition, in that it is as much concerned with 20th-century losses as with 20th-century gains. The last chapter, on the changing British character (and Carstairs was writing as a professor at Edinburgh University on the British rather than the English), is not surprisingly both the most dated and the most controversial today. The character has continued to change. The 1960s was an exciting decade with few moorings. But if Carstairs were writing about the present, he might well pick out other points. It is not likely, however, that he would abandon the comparative dimension, which is a necessary element in all studies of different inheritances and different responses.

Lytton prefaced his *England and the English* with the quotation from Voltaire with which this chapter began. A 20th-century Frenchman, Pierre Maillaud, exiled to England during the Second World War, advised Frenchmen in his book *The English Way* (1945) that while Englishmen had a different view of the State not only from Germans but from Frenchmen, there was one English tenet that should be generally acceptable – 'The State must not be stronger than the society which it represents and must not turn that society into a regulated machine.' There has never been anything mechanistic about English social history.

'*The man who lit his cigar before the Royal Toast*': *a joke that plays on the English concern with unwritten codes of behaviour. It is, however, not only the man who has broken the rules who is being satirized by the cartoonist; he is also laughing at the class of people who would be scandalized by such a blunder.*

Select Bibliography

1 Who are the English?

Barlow, Frank *The English Church, 1000–1066, 1066–1154* London 1963; New York 1979.
The Feudal Kingdom of England, 1042–1216 (3rd ed.) London 1972.
Hunter-Blair, Peter *Introduction to Anglo-Saxon England* (2nd ed.) Cambridge 1977.
Roman Britain and Early England Edinburgh 1963
Brooke, C. N. L. *From Alfred to Henry III: a history of England 871–1272* Edinburgh 1961.
Davis, R. H. C. *The Normans and Their Myth* London and New York 1976.
Finberg, H. P. R. *The Formation of England, 550–1042* London 1974.
Loyn, H. R. *Anglo-Saxon England and the Norman Conquest* London 1962.
Mayr-Harting, H. *The Coming of Christianity to Anglo-Saxon England* London 1972.
Le Patourel, John *The Norman Empire* Oxford 1976.
Richmond, I. A. *Roman Britain* Harmondsworth 1955.
Sawyer, R. H. *From Roman Britain to Norman England* London 1978.
Stenton, Doris Mary *English Society in the Early Middle Ages* (2nd ed.) Harmondsworth 1952.
Whitelock, Dorothy *The Beginnings of English Society* (2nd ed.) Harmondsworth 1952.

2 The Medieval Centuries

Beresford, M. W. and J. K. St Joseph *Medieval England: an aerial survey* Cambridge 1958.
Bolton, J. L. *The Medieval English Economy 1150–1500* London 1980.
Bridbury, A. R. *Economic Growth: England in the later Middle Ages* London 1962.
Carus-Wilson, E. M. *Medieval Merchant Venturers* London 1954.
Cottle, B. *The Triumph of English 1350–1400* London 1969.
Davies, C. S. L. *Peace, Print and Protestantism* London 1977.
Dickens, A. G. *The English Reformation* London 1964.
Elton, G. R. *The Tudor Revolution in Government* Cambridge 1953.
Gillingham, J. *The Wars of the Roses* London 1981.
Hilton, R. H. *Bondmen Made Free* London 1973.
Holmes, George A. *The Later Middle Ages 1272–1485* Edinburgh 1962.
Keen, M. H. *England in the Later Middle Ages* London 1973.
Knowles, David *The Religious Orders in England* Vols 1–3 Cambridge 1948–59.
Macfarlane, Alan *The Origins of English Individualism: the family, property and social transition* Oxford 1978.
McFarlane, K. B. *John Wycliffe and the Beginnings of English Non-conformity* London 1952.
The Nobility of Later Medieval England Oxford 1973.
Williams, P. *The Tudor Regime* Oxford 1979.

3 Ruling Dynasties and the Great Families

Dewhurst, Jack *Royal Confinements* London 1980.
G. E. C[ockayne] *The Complete Peerage* Vols I–XII London 1910–59.
Goodwin, A. (ed.) *The European Nobility in the Eighteenth Century* London 1953.
Levine, M. *Tudor Dynastic Problems 1460–1571* London and New York 1973.
McFarlane, K. B. *The Nobility of Later Medieval England* Oxford 1973.
Nicolas, Sir Harris *The Historic Peerage of England* (rev. ed. W. Courthope) London 1857 (most convenient for quick reference, if somewhat out of date).
Oxford History of England Oxford 1936–65.
Pinches, J. H. and R. V. *The Royal Heraldry of England* London 1974 (useful also for royal pedigrees).
Powell, Enoch and Keith Wallis *The House of Lords in the Middle Ages* London 1968.
Turberville, A. S. *House of Lords in the Eighteenth Century* Oxford 1927.
Wagner, Sir Anthony *English Genealogy* (2nd ed.) Oxford 1972.

4 'Mother of Parliaments'

Bagehot, W. *The English Constitution* London 1867.
Butt, Ronald *The Power of Parliament* London 1967.
Cormack, Patrick *Westminster Palace and Parliament* London 1981.
Dicey, A. V. *The Law of the Constitution* London 1885.
Gilmour, Ian *The Body Politic* London 1969.
Hailsham, Lord *The Dilemma of Democracy* London 1978.
Jennings, W. I. (Sir Ivor) *Parliament* Cambridge 1938.
Keir, D. L. *Constitutional History of Modern Britain* London 1938.
Maitland, F. W. *The Constitutional History of England* Cambridge 1908.
May, T. E. *Treatise on the Law, Privileges, Proceedings and Usage of Parliament* (1st ed.) London 1844 (constantly revised).
Powell, Enoch and Keith Wallis *The House of Lords in the Middle Ages* London 1968.
Rhodes James, R. *An Introduction to the House of Commons* London 1961.

5 The Unity of the Kingdom

Bagwell, Richard *Ireland under the Tudors* London 1885–90.
Ireland under the Stuarts London 1909–16.
Barrow, G. W. S. *The Kingdom of the Scots* London 1973.
Beckett, J. E. C. *The Making of Modern Ireland 1603–1923* (new ed.) London 1979.
Burleigh, J. H. S. *Church History of Scotland* London 1960.
Clarke, A. *The Old English in Ireland 1625–42* London 1966.
Edinburgh History of Scotland Vol. 1 'Scotland: the making of the kingdom' (A. A. M. Duncan) Edinburgh and New York 1971; Vol. 2 'Scotland: the later Middle Ages' (Ranald Nicholas) Edinburgh and New York 1974.
Falls, Cyril *Elizabeth's Irish Wars* London 1950.
Kee, Robert *Ireland: a history* London 1980.
MacDonagh, Oliver *Ireland: the Union and its aftermath* Englewood Cliffs 1968; rev. ed. London 1977.
Mackinnon, James *The Union of England and Scotland* London 1896.
Mansergh, Nicholas *The Irish Question 1840–1921* (new ed.) London 1965.
Morris, J. E. *Welsh Wars of Edward I* New York and London 1901.
Nowlan, Kevin *The Politics of Repeal: a study in the relations between Great Britain and Ireland 1841–50* London and Toronto 1965.
Orpen, G. H. *Ireland under the Normans 1169–1333* (4 vols) Oxford 1911–20.
Pakenham, Thomas *The Year of Liberty: the story of the Great Irish Rebellion of 1798* London 1969.
Quinn, D. B. *The Elizabethans and the Irish* Ithaca, NY, 1966.
Rees, W. *South Wales and the March 1284–1415* New York and London 1924.
Salzmann, L. F. *Edward I* London 1968.
Stones, E. L. G. and Grant G. Simpson (eds) *Edward I and the throne of Scotland 1290–1296* (an edition of the record sources for the Great Cause) Oxford 1978.
Williams, T. D. (ed.) *The Irish Struggle (1916–26)* London and Toronto 1966.

6 Exploration and the First British Empire

Allen, H. C. *Great Britain and the United States, 1783–1952* London 1954.
Becker, Carl *The Declaration of Independence* New York 1922.
Black, J. B. *The Reign of Elizabeth, 1558–1603* Oxford 1936.
Boorstin, D. J. *The Americans: the colonial experience* New York 1958; Harmondsworth 1965.
Brebner, J. B. *North Atlantic Triangle* Yale 1945.
Davies, Godfrey *The Early Stuarts 1603–1660* Oxford 1937.
Mackesy, Piers *The War for America, 1775–1783* London 1964.
McNeill, W. H. *America, Britain and Russia: their cooperation and conflict, 1941–1946* London 1953.
Miller, J. C. *Origins of the American Revolution* Boston 1943; London 1945.
Morgan, E. S. *The Birth of the Republic* Chicago 1956.
Morison, S. E. *The European Discovery of America: northern voyages* New York 1971.
Nicholas, H. G. *Britain and the United States* London 1963.
Notestein, Wallace *The English People on the Eve of Colonisation* New York and London 1954.
Wright, Esmond *Fabric of Freedom, 1763–1800* New York 1961; London 1965.

7 The Rise and Fall of the Second British Empire

The history of the Empire and Commonwealth is studied in the greatest detail in a number of collective works: *The Cambridge History of the British Empire* Cambridge, 1929–59; *The Cambridge History of Africa* Cambridge 1976–; *The Oxford History of South Africa* Oxford 1969–71; *The Oxford History of East Africa* 1963–76. Each of these are in several volumes, with publication spread over many years. For the period since the First World War much may be found in the series *The Survey of (British) Commonwealth Affairs* published for the Royal Institute of International Affairs. The authors were successively W. K. Hancock, N. Mansergh and J. D. B. Miller. Works by individual authors include the following:
Beckett, J. E. C. *The Making of Modern Ireland 1603–1923* (new ed.) London 1979.
Beloff, M. *Imperial Sunset* Vol. 1 'Britain's Liberal Empire' London 1969.
Calder, Angus *Revolutionary Empire* London 1981.
Carrington, C. E. *The British Overseas* Cambridge 1950.
Creighton, Donald *Dominion of the North* (new ed.) London 1958.
Harlow, V. T. *The Founding of the Second British Empire* (2 vols) London 1952, 1964.

Heussler, R. *Yesterday's Rulers: the making of the British Colonial Service* London 1963.
Hutchins, F. G. *The Illusion of Permanence – British Imperialism in India* Princeton 1967.
Kennedy, P. M. *The Rise and Fall of British Sea Power* London 1976.
Lyons, F. S. L. *Ireland Since the Famine* London 1971.
Mansergh, N. *The Commonwealth Experience* London 1969.
Monroe, E. *Britain's Moment in the Middle East* London 1963.
Morris, James *Pax Britannica* London 1968.
Heaven's Command London 1973.
Farewell the Trumpets London 1978.
Robinson, R. J. Gallagher and A. Denny *Africa and the Victorians* London 1961.
Spear, P. *Penguin History of India* Vol. 2 (rev. ed.) Harmondsworth 1978.
Wasserstein, B. *The British in Palestine* London 1978.
Wint, Guy *The British in Asia* London 1954.
Woodcock, George *The British in the Far East* London 1969.
Woodruff, Philip *Men Who Ruled India* (2 vols) London 1954.

8 Religion in the Life of the Nation

Bede *A History of the English Church and People* (Penguin ed.) Harmondsworth 1955.
Bossy, John *The English Catholic Community, 1570–1850* London 1973.
Brooke, Z. N. *The English Church and the Papacy from the Conquest to the Reign of King John* Cambridge 1931.
Chadwick, Owen *The Victorian Church* London 1966.
Collinson, P. *The Elizabethan Puritan Movement* London 1967.
Deansley, Margaret *The Pre-Conquest Church in England* (2nd ed.) London 1963.
Hyamson, A. M. *A History of the Jews in England* (2nd ed.) London 1928.
Kitson Clark, G. *Churchmen and the Condition of England, 1832–1885* London 1973.
Knowles, David *The Religious Orders in England* Vols 1–3 Cambridge 1948–59.
Moorman, J. R. H. *A History of the Church in England* London 1953.
Norman, E. R. *Church and Society in England, 1770–1970* Oxford 1976.
Parker, T. M. *The English Reformation to 1558* (2nd ed.) London 1966.
Rearden, B. M. G. *From Coleridge to Gore. A century of religious thought in Britain* London 1971.
Rupp, E. G. *Studies in the Making of the English Protestant Tradition* Cambridge 1947.
Thompson, D. M. *Nonconformity in the Nineteenth Century* London 1972.
Trevor-Roper, H. R. *Archbishop Laud* (new ed.) London 1962.
Woodforde, James *The Diary of a Country Parson, 1758–1802* London 1949.

9 Art and Popular Taste

Croft-Murray, Edward *Decorative Painting in England, 1537–1837* London 1962.
Frey, Dagobert *Englisches Wesen in der Bildenden Kunst* Vienna 1942.
Fry, Roger *Reflections on British Painting* London 1934.
Gaunt, William *A Concise History of English Painting* London and New York 1964.
Grant, Col. *Chronological History of the Old English Landscape Painters* (2 vols) n.d.
Hunt, W. Holman *Pre-Raphaelitism and the Pre-Raphaelite Brotherhood* London 1905.
Oxford History of English Art Oxford 1949–.
Pevsner, Nikolaus *The Englishness of English Art* London 1956.
Redgrave, R. and S. *A Century of Painters of the English School* (rev. ed.) London 1947.

Rothenstein, Sir John *Modern English Painters* (2 vols) London 1952–6.
Strong, Roy *The Renaissance Garden in England* London and New York 1979.
Watkin, David *English Architecture: a concise history* London and New York 1979.
Waterhouse, Ellis *Painting in Britain 1530–1790* Harmondsworth 1953.
Whitley, W. T. *Artists and their Friends in England, 1700–1799* (2 vols) London and Boston, Mass., 1928.
Wilenski, R. H. *English Painting* (4th and rev. ed.) London 1964.

10 Language and Literature

There are numerous anthologies of English literature, such as *The Oxford Book of English Verse* Oxford 1974; *The Oxford Book of Sixteenth Century Verse* Oxford 1950 (and so on for each century up to the present one); *Elizabethan Lyrics* (ed. Norman Ault) London (4th ed.) 1960. Critical and historical works include the following:
Allen, Walter *The English Novel* London 1954.
Cecil, David *Early Victorian Novelists* London 1934.
Daiches, David *A Critical History of English Literature* London 1960.
Evans, B. Ifor *English Poetry in the Later Nineteenth Century* London 1933.
Ford, Boris (ed.) *A Guide to English Literature* Harmondsworth 1954–73.
Hough, Graham *The Romantic Poets* London 1953.
Ker, W. P. *English Literature: medieval* London 1911.
Kettle, A. C. *An Introduction to the English Novel* London 1951, 1953.
Leavis, F. R. *The Great Tradition* London 1948.
Legouis E. *A Short History of English Literature* Oxford 1934.
Muir, Kenneth and S. Schoenbaum (eds) *A New Companion to Shakespeare Studies* London 1971.
Nicoll, Allardyce *British Drama* London 1925.
Oxford History of English Literature Oxford 1945–.
Potter, Simeon *Our Language* Harmondsworth 1950.
Tillotson, Kathleen *Novels of the Eighteen-forties* Oxford 1954.
Watt, Ian *The Rise of the Novel* Harmondsworth 1963.
Wedgwood, C. V. *Seventeenth-Century English Literature* London 1950.

11 'England's Green and Pleasant Land'

Beresford, M. W. *The Lost Villages of England* London 1954.
and J. G. Hurst *Deserted Medieval Villages* London 1971.
and J. K. St Joseph *Medieval England, an Aerial Survey* (2nd ed.) Cambridge 1979.
Hoskins, W. G. *The Making of the English Landscape* London 1955.
One Man's England London 1973.
English Landscapes London 1973.
Muir, Richard *The English Village* London and New York 1980.
The Shell Guide to Reading the Landscape London 1981.
Lost Villages London 1982.
Rackham, Oliver *Trees and Woodland in the British Landscape* London 1976.
Rowley, Trevor *Villages in the Landscape* London 1978.
Shoard, Marion *The Theft of the Countryside* London 1980.
Taylor, Christopher G. *Fields in the English Landscape* London 1976.
Roads and Tracks of Britain London 1979.
Wood, Eric S. *Collins Field Guide to Archaeology in Britain* (2nd ed.) London 1979.

12 A Nation of Shopkeepers

Briggs, Asa (ed.) *Chartist Studies* London 1962.
Chadwick, E. *Report on the Sanitary Conditions of the Labouring Population, 1842* (new ed.) M. Flinn, ed., 1965.
Fraser, Derek *The Evolution of the British Welfare State* London 1973.
Harrison, Brian *Drink and the Victorians* London 1971.
Hewitt, M. *Wives and Mothers in Victorian Industry* London 1958.
Hunt, E. H. *British Labour History, 1815–1914* London 1981.
Hurst, J. S. *Elementary Schooling and the Working Classes, 1860–1918* London 1979.
Milward, A. S. *The Effect of the Two World Wars on Britain* London 1970.
Mitchell, B. R. and P. Deane *Abstract of British Historical Statistics* Cambridge 1962.
Musson, A. E. *The Growth of British Industry* London 1978.
Pelling, H. *A History of British Trade Unionism* London 1963.
Perkin, H. J. *The Origins of Modern English Society, 1780–1880* London 1969.
Rose, G. *The Struggle for Penal Reform* London 1961.
Sayers, R. S. *A History of Economic Change in England, 1880–1939* London 1967.
Smith, F. B. *The People's Health 1830–1910* London 1979.
Thompson, E. P. *The Making of the English Working Class* London 1963.
Wohl, Anthony S. *The Eternal Slum: Housing and Social Policy in Victorian London* London 1977.
Winch, Donald *Economics and Policy. A Historical Survey* London 1969.

13 The English: Custom and Character

Brown, John *An Estimate of the Manners and Principles of the Times* (2 vols) London 1752.
Butterfield, Herbert *The Englishman and his History* Cambridge 1944.
Carstairs, G. M. *This Island Now* London 1963.
Cobbett, William *Rural Rides* (Penguin ed.) Harmondsworth 1981.
Cole, G. D. H. *The Condition of Britain* London 1937.
The Post-War Condition of Britain London 1956.
De Tocqueville, Alexis *L'Ancien Régime et la Révolution* Paris 1850 (many English eds).
Defoe, Daniel *A Tour through England and Wales* (orig. pub. 1724) London, Toronto and New York 1928.
Emerson, Ralph Waldo *English Traits* London 1856; Boston, Mass., 1857.
Gorer, Geoffrey *Exploring English Character* London 1955.
Halsay, A. H. (ed.) *Trends in British Society since 1900* London 1972.
Lytton, Bulwer *England and the English* London and New York 1833.
Macfarlane, Alan *The Origins of English Individualism: the family, property and social transition* Oxford 1978.
Maillaud, Pierre *The English Way* London 1945.
Misson, Henri *Memoirs and Observations in his Travels over England* London 1719.
Orwell, George *The English People* London 1947.
Priestley, J. B. *English Journey* London 1934.
Read, Herbert (ed.) *The English Vision* London 1933.
Sampson, Anthony *Anatomy of Britain* London 1962.
Taine, H. A. *Notes on England* Paris and London 1872.
West, Richard *An English Journey* London 1981.

Sources of illustrations

Index

Page numbers in *italics* refer to illustrations